THE AMERICAN NUMISMATIC SOCIETY

MUSEUM NOTES
XI

THE AMERICAN NUMISMATIC SOCIETY
NEW YORK
1964

ALL RIGHTS RESERVED BY
THE AMERICAN NUMISMATIC SOCIETY

PRINTED IN GERMANY AT J. J. AUGUSTIN, GLÜCKSTADT

CONTENTS

ANCIENT

R. Ross Holloway. Damarete's Lion   1

Irwin L. Merker. Notes on the Abdalonymos and the Dated Alexander Coinage of Sidon and Ake   13

O. H. Dodson and W. P. Wallace. The Kozani Hoard of 1955   21

Alfred R. Bellinger. Philippi in Macedonia   29

Otto Mørkholm. Seleucid Coins from Cilicia ca. 220–150 B.C.   53

Otto Mørkholm. The Accession of Antiochus IV of Syria   63

Margaret Thompson. A Hoard from Thessaly   77

John Kroll. The Late Hellenistic Tetrobols of Kos   81

Margaret Thompson. Ptolemy Philometor and Athens   119

Lydia H. Lenaghan. Hercules-Melqart on a Coin of Faustus Sulla   131

C. H. V. Sutherland. An Unpublished Coin in the Name of Tetricus II   151

Howard L. Adelson and George L. Kustas. A Sixth Century Hoard of Minimi from the Western Peloponnese   159

MEDIAEVAL AND MODERN

Alfred R. Bellinger. Three More Hoards of Byzantine Copper Coins   207

Joan M. Fagerlie. A Miliaresion of Romanus III and a Nomisma of Michael IV   227

Anthony Cutler. The Stavraton: Evidence for an Elusive Byzantine Type   237

Herbert J. Erlanger. A Hoard of Leeuwendaalders from Aintab   245

H. Enno van Gelder. A Provisional List of Dutch Lion-Dollars   261

CONTENTS

ORIENTAL

George C. Miles. A Portrait of the Buyid Prince Rukn al-Dawlah — 283

Paul Balog and Jacques Yvon. Deux Trésors de Monnaies d'or des Croisés — 295

Paul Bedoukian. Gold Forgeries of Tigranes the Great of Armenia — 303

George C. Miles. A Mamlūk Hoard of Ḥamāh — 307

H. F. Bowker. The William Ewart Gladstone Medalet — 311

Werner Burger. Manchu Inscriptions on Chinese Cash Coins — 313

UNITED STATES OF AMERICA

Eric P. Newman. The James II 1/24th Real for the American Plantations — 319

METHODS

Paul Bedoukian. Aluminum Foil Impressions for Numismatic Studies — 333

DAMARETE'S LION

(See Plates I–II)

I. THE SEAL OF THE EMMENIDS

When the Duke de Luynes identified the early dekadrachm of Syracuse (PLATE I, 1) as the Damareteion of ancient tradition, he established a numismatic landmark of great importance.[1] Not only is the date of the Damareteion fixed to 480 B.C., but the historical circumstances of its issue are known in some detail. In recent years Willy Schwabacher has contributed a lucid summary of scholarship on this subject, and Heinrich Chantraine has explored the political significance of the series.[2] But the relation of Damarete to the coin nicknamed for her remains far from clear.

Two Greek encyclopedias compiled under the Roman Empire, those of Pollux and Hesychios, refer to the Damareteion.[3] The historian Diodoros, who wrote in the first century B.C., gives fuller information, appended to his account of the successful Carthaginian embassy sent to Gelon, tyrant of Syracuse, after the destruction of the Carthaginian army at Himera in 480 B.C. οἱ δὲ Καρχηδόνιοι παραδόξως τῆς σωτηρίας τετευχότες ταῦτά τε δώσειν προσεδέξαντο καὶ στέφανον χρυσοῦν τῇ γυναικὶ τοῦ Γέλωνος Δαμαρέτῃ προσωμολόγησαν. αὕτη γὰρ ὑπ' αὐτῶν ἀξιωθεῖσα συνήργησε πλεῖστον εἰς τὴν σύνθεσιν τῆς εἰρήνης, καὶ στεφανωθεῖσα ὑπ' αὐτῶν ἑκατὸν ταλάντοις χρυσίου, νόμισμα ἐξέκοψε τὸ κληθὲν ἀπ' ἐκείνης Δαμαρέτειον· τοῦτο δ'εἶχε μὲν Ἀττικὰς δραχμὰς δέκα, ἐκλήθη δὲ παρὰ τοῖς Σικελιώταις ἀπὸ τοῦ σταθμοῦ πεντηκοντάλιτρον.

> Having thus saved themselves unexpectedly, the Carthaginians undertook to carry out Gelon's terms, and more than that, they promised to give a gold crown to Damarete,

[1] H. Duc de Luynes, "Du Démarétion," *Annali dell'Istituto di corrispondenza archeologica* 2 (1830), 81 ff.
[2] W. Schwabacher, *Das Demareteion* (*Opus Nobile* 7, Bremen, 1958); H. Chantraine, "Syrakus und Leontinoi," *JfNGG* 8 (1957), 7–19.
[3] Pollux, *Onomasticon*, 9:85; Hesychios, *Lexicon, ad verb.*

Gelon's wife, who, at their request, had been of the greatest assistance in the conclusion of the peace. Rewarded with a crown of one hundred talents gold, she caused a coin to be struck which was called after her the Damareteion. The coin weighed ten Attic drachms, and among the Sicilians it passed as a fifty litra piece on account of its weight.

11:26:3

The historical core of Diodoros' story is this: after Himera the Syracusans struck a dekadrachm which became known as the Damareteion. To this he adds an explanation: the coinage was made possible by the Carthaginian gift of a gold crown to Damarete in recognition of her good offices during the negotiation of the peace treaty. The tradition preserved in Pollux is that Damarete collected the jewelry of the women of Syracuse to aid Gelon's war effort. Hesychios says that the contribution of her own jewelry provided for the coinage.

These tales and Diodoros' story of the gold crown all smack of the uninformed conjectures of the man in the street. The striking of the dekadrachm denomination as well as the addition of a laurel wreath to the reverse head of Artemis-Arethousa marks the Damareteion and its associated tetradrachms and fractions as a victory coinage.[4] This accords perfectly with the historical core of Diodoros' account, but the historical circumstances alone do not explain the origin of the Damareteion nickname.

Chantraine has added immeasurably to our understanding of the Damareteion by examining it in connection with the contemporary coinage of Leontinoi.[5] In the late 480's Leontinoi and Syracuse accounted for the vast majority, if not all, of the coins issued in Gelon's empire except, of course, at Gela. The subjection of Naxos by Gelon's predecessor Hippokrates about 492 resulted in the suppression of the coinage of the oldest Greek colony in the island. Kamarina and Catane do not seem to have struck coins before the middle of the fifth century. At the moment of the Carthaginian invasion, moreover, Syracuse and Leontinoi were cooperating closely in the issue of their coins. A reverse

---

[4] Cf. R. R. Holloway, "The Crown of Naxos," *ANSMN* 9 (1962), 1–8.
[5] Op.cit., to which the reader is referred for the pertinent ancient sources and modern discussions.

with the Syracusan Artemis-Arethousa head type was cut with the legend ΛΕΟΝΤΙΝΟΝ (PLATE I, 2). The chariot obverse employed with this die shares with the Damareteion group obverses the symbol of a lion added in the exergue. The same obverse type with the lion in the exergue is also found in conjunction with two Leontinoi Apollo head reverses (PLATE I, 3, 4). At Leontinoi the symbol seems particularly significant since another running lion appears below the Apollo head of these two reverses. The reverse lion accompanying the Apollo head is surely the *parasemon* of the city, the canting badge also employed as a full type in the Leontinoi coinage. But why two lions? Surely the lion of the obverse exergue must have the same meaning as its double at Syracuse.

Head's idea that the lion of the Damareteion might have symbolized defeated Africa no longer seems satisfactory.[6] Evans saw the lion as the symbol of Pythian Apollo, whom Gelon honored, among other gods, after Himera.[7] At Syracuse, however, Gelon's principal victory monument was the new temple of Athene,[8] and Evans' interpretation does not clarify Damarete's relation to the coin which came to be called by her name.

In emphasizing the political importance of the lion symbol which connects Syracuse and Leontinoi, Chantraine raises the question of its relation to the governing tyrannies of the two cities.[9] The Syracusan tyrant Gelon, son of Deinomenes, began his career as an officer of Hippokrates of Gela in the 490's. After serving as Hippokrates' lieutenant during the reduction of all of eastern Sicily save Syracuse, Gelon succeeded him in 487 and two years later added Syracuse to his domains. Gelon's brother Hieron remained as governor of Gela, and both married daughters of Theron, the new tyrant of Akragas. Consequently, Gelon's wife Damarete held a dynastic link between the Deinomenids of Syracuse and the Emmenids of Akragas.

[6] B. V. Head, "On the Chronological Sequence of the Coins of Syracuse," *NC* (1874), p. 10.
[7] A. J. Evans, "Syracusan 'Medallions' and their Engravers," *NC* (1891), pp. 325–334.
[8] Cf. B. Pace, *Arte e Civiltà della Sicilia Antica* 2 (Milan *et alibi*, 1938), p. 230 ff.
[9] Op.cit., to which the reader is again referred for the pertinent sources and discussions.

A case can be made for believing that in 480 Leontinoi was ruled by a henchman of Gelon's, Ainesidamos, son of Pataikos.[10] Apparently rule through lieutenants, either members of the tyrant's family or of his inner circle, was the only system of governing dependent cities which occurred to these Sicilian dynasts. Gela was ruled by Gelon's own brother. Kamarina was held by Glaukos of Karystos. At Zankle, Hippokrates had installed an Ionian refugee named Skythes, whose son was also to serve Gelon. One of Gelon's companions in Hippokrates' service was Ainesidamos, son of Pataikos. They remained on good terms during the period of unrest which brought Gelon to power at Gela. At some unspecified time Leontinoi did have a tyrant named Ainesidamos, and Gelon would almost certainly have used a henchman to rule the city he had taken over with Hippokrates' other domains. Plausible historical conjecture identifies Ainesidamos, son of Pataikos, as the tyrant of Leontinoi and places his rule under Gelon. Remarkably enough, Ainesidamos was also the name of the father of Theron of Akragas, the grandfather of Damarete. Thus two questions hang about Ainesidamos, son of Pataikos. Can it be proved that he was tyrant of Leontinoi? And was he an Emmenid? The lion symbol in the exergue of the Damareteion is a clue.

In the Second Olympian Ode, composed in honor of Theron of Akragas in 476, Pindar gives the genealogy of the Emmenid family.[11] It was traced back to Thersandros, the son of Argeia and Polyneikes, thus making the Emmenids a branch of the Labdacid family of Bronze Age Thebes. The marriage of Polyneikes and Argeia is part of the story of the civil wars which followed the death of Oidipous when Polyneikes was ousted from the city by his brother Eteokles and sought aid at the court of Adrastos. The tale of his arrival in Argos is told by the mythographer Apollodoros as follows:

ἐβασίλευε δὲ Ἄργους Ἄδραστος ὁ Ταλαοῦ· καὶ τοῖς τούτου βασιλείοις νύκτωρ προσπελάζει, καὶ συνάπτει μάχην Τυδεῖ τῷ Οἰνέως φεύγουτι Καλυδῶνα. γενομένης δὲ ἐξαίφνης βοῆς ἐπιφανεὶς Ἄδραστος διέλυσεν αὐτούς, καὶ μάντεώς τινος ὑπομνησθεὶς λέγοντος αὐτῷ κάπρῳ καὶ

[10] Cf. particularly T. J. Dunbabin, *The Western Greeks* (Oxford, 1948), 383–384 and the stemma, p. 484, and the doubts expressed by R. van Compernolle, *Étude de chronologie et d'historiographie siciliotes* (Brussels and Rome, 1960), 372–374.
[11] Ll. 39–85.

λέοντι συζεῦξαι τὰς θυγατέρας, ἀμφοτέρους εἵλετο νυμφίους· εἶχον γὰρ ἐπὶ τῶν ἀσπίδων ὁ μὲν κάπρου προτομὴν ὁ δὲ λέοντος.

> The king of Argos was Adrastos the son of Talos. Coming up to his palace at night, Polyneikes got into a fight with Tydeus the son of Oineus, himself in exile from Kalydon. The hue and cry went up all at once; Adrastos appeared on the scene and separated them. Recalling that a certain prophet had said he would yoke his daughters to a wild boar and a lion, he took them as sons-in-law. For Tydeus bore the protome of a wild boar as his shield device, and Polyneikes the protome of a lion.
> 3:6:1

The text of the oracle is preserved in a fragment of Mnaseas, the Greek geographer of the third century B.C. Κουράων δὲ γάμους ζεῦξον κάπρῳ ἠδὲ λέοντι,/οὕς κεν ἴδης προθύροισι τεοῦ δόμου ἐξ ἱεροῖο/ἁμοῦ στείχοντας, μηδὲ φρεσὶ σῆσι πλανηθῆς.

> Yoke the weddings of your daughters to a boar and a lion whom you see from your holy house coming together at its porch and do not be afraid in your heart.
> from Schol. Eurip. *Phoinissai* 409
> (FHG 3: p. 157, no. 48)

The oracle was current in the fifth century and was known to Euripides.[12] Apollodoros' account shows how it was rationalized in antiquity. The lion was the badge of Polyneikes.[13] By inheritance it would be the badge of his descendants, the Emmenids.

In 480 B.C. the seal of the Emmenids appears on the coinage of Leontinoi and Syracuse. Damarete, the queen of Syracuse, was an Emmenid, and we may also identify the governor of Leontinoi as another Emmenid, Ainesidamos the son of Pataikos. The Emmenid lion on the coins of Syracuse and Leontinoi is a subtle compliment paid by the tyrant of Syracuse to his father-in-law, the tyrant of Akragas, and to the Emmenid clan. Together they had defeated Carthage, and through the heraldic symbol of the Emmenids, Gelon acknowledged the dynastic and military alliance which had made victory possible.

---

[12] *Phoinissai*, ll. 408ff., *Hiketides*, ll. 132ff.
[13] Polyneikes wearing a lion's skin: Statius, *Theb.* 1:482–492, Schol. A. Hom. *Iliad* 4:376, Schol. Eurip. *Phoin.* 409 and 421; his shield bearing a lion-headed sphinx: Schol. Eurip. *Phoin.* 409.

Among the denominations of the Syracusan victory coinage struck on this occasion the dekadrachm was impressive and unusual. No Sicilian had ever seen a silver coin of this size before. To give the new pentakontalitra a nickname was inevitable, and it became known as the Damareteion not for any reason invented by popular tradition but because the lion was the badge of the Emmenids and was recognized as the device of Damarete's family.

II. THE DAMARETEION MASTER AT LEONTINOI

Erik Boehringer held that the master of the Damareteion reverse no. 266 in his catalogue was also the artist employed by Gelon's successor Hieron to cut dies for the tetradrachm which commemorated the refounding of Catane under the name Aitna in 476 B.C. (PLATE I, 5).[14] This attribution has met with favor from Bernard Ashmole, but it has also encountered serious criticism.[15]

The greatest difference between the two heads is to be found in the rendering of the eye. If the Aitna obverse is to be attributed to the Damareteion master, we must suppose that in the space of four years he had taken up and mastered the representation of the profile eye. A less obvious but no less telling difference in the style of the two heads is the structure of the neck and the treatment of the lower line of the bust. The Damareteion master represents the sterno-mastoid muscle of the neck as a straight line. In the Aitna obverse the sterno-mastoid line is a curve sweeping in a broad arc from beneath the ear to the front of the neck. In finishing off the line of the bust the Damareteion master makes a clean cut across the neck. The head of the Aitna satyr, on the other hand, is cut off in a curved line which drops from the back of the neck to meet the arc of the sterno-mastoid muscle under the chin.

Seltman and Schwabacher have pointed to the resemblance of the

---

[14] *Die Münzen von Syrakus* (Berlin, 1929), 41.
[15] "Late Archaic and Early Classical Greek Sculpture in Sicily and South Italy," *Proceedings of the British Academy* 20 (1934), pp. 110–111. Criticism has been voiced by G. E. Rizzo, "Qualche osservazione sull'arte delle monete di Siracusa," *Boll. d'Arte* 31 (1938), pp. 385–86, W. Schwabacher, "Zu den Münzen von Katana," *RM* 48 (1933), 121–126, and C. T. Seltman, *Greek Coins*[2] (London, 1955), 133.

satyr head of the Aitna coin to the Dionysos head of the Naxos tetradrachm apparently struck to commemorate the return of the exiled citizen body in 461 (PLATE I, 6).[16] The rendering of the neck muscles and the curving line of the lower edge of the bust are the same in both dies. I would take these mannerisms, together with the minute etching of the beard, to be the diagnostic traits pointing to the common authorship of the two dies.

The Aitna tetradrachm in Brussels is unique, and all the recorded specimens of the Naxian tetradrachm come from a single pair of dies.[17] This circumstance would suggest that on both occasions the Aitna master was commissioned to cut one set of dies for a special issue. At first glance the reverses hardly seem the work of the same hand or even of the same quarter century. The satyr of the Naxos coin is drawn with remarkable command of the principles of foreshortening and with a knowledge of anatomy equal to the most advanced contemporary sculpture. By comparison the Zeus of the Aitna tetradrachm is a stiff archaic figure. The radiating pattern of his robe and the combination of profile and frontal renderings belong to the world of late sixth-century vase painting. An instructive parallel is provided by the seated Zeus and Athene which decorate a red-figure kylix by Oltos now in the Tarquinia museum and dated about 510 B.C. (PLATE II, 7).[18] Yet the numismatic arguments in favor of the common authorship of these dies are so strong that we may venture an explanation of the difference of style.

Zeus Aitnaios was not a god invented for Hieron's new city; he was the ancient deity of the towering volcano of Aitna.[19] For this reason the prototype of the Aitna master's die could have been a painting of the late sixth century. A painting it must have been, not a statue, for sculptural prototypes were easily brought abreast of contemporary

---

[16] Loc.cit., footnote 15, and accepted by H. A. Cahn, *Die Münzen der sizilischen Stadt Naxos"* (Basel, 1944), 49, note 18.

[17] Ibid., to no. 45.

[18] J. D. Beazley, *Attic Red-Figure Vase Painters* (Oxford, 1942), p. 38, no. 50, most recently illustrated by P. E. Arias and M. Hirmer, *Tausend Jahre Griechische Vasenkunst* (Munich, 1960), p. 63, pl. 100–104.

[19] A. B. Cook, *Zeus*, vol. 2, pt. 2 (Cambridge, 1925) 908–909, finds no evidence of the cult of Zeus Aitnaios before Hieron's new foundation of Catane as Aitna. The cult may not be an extremely early one, but there is no reason to consider it an invention of Hieron's.

styles, witness the coinages of Kaulonia and Poseidonia in the fifth century. In his reproduction, the Aitna master betrays himself in only one detail. A true son of the age of Myron and Pythagoras of Rhegion, he could not resist indicating the muscles of the right shoulder and forearm of the Zeus with anatomical precision. Otherwise, he has faithfully transferred an archaic painting to his coin die. The case of the Naxian satyr is different. This figure was not the reproduction of a painting of the preceding generation. It was the Aitna master's own creation, and in it he was free to take full advantage of the newest discoveries of perspective foreshortening.

The acceptance of the Aitna and Naxos reverses as the work of the same master brings into question the authorship of the dies of a third coin, a tetradrachm of Catane in the British Museum, which was thought to have begun the coinage struck at that city after the return of her exiles and the recovery of her original name in 461 (PLATE II, 8). Seltman and Schwabacher compare the drapery style and the articulation of anatomical detail in the Catane piece with the reverses of the Aitna and Naxos coins.[20] But the comparison is more that of one fine coin with another than of characteristic mannerisms which identify the style of an individual artist. As a stylistic argument it is not convincing. Moreover, the tetradrachm in the British Museum is probably not the first striking of the new Catane issues. The first coin of the series appears to be the tetradrachm from the Ognina Hoard which has a unique reverse type, Nike flying right, and is die linked to the subsequent running Nike pieces (PLATE II, 9).[21] This circumstance also sets the Catane tetradrachm in the British Museum apart from the work of the Aitna master, which, as we know it, consisted of specially commissioned dies for inaugural issues.

Unlike the Aitna master, the Damareteion master appears as one of the craftsmen, albeit the chief artist, of the Syracusan mint in 480. His activity has been studied in detail by Boehringer and includes a tetradrachm which follows the Damareteion series as well as the majority of the dies for the victory coinage itself (PLATE II, 10).[22]

[20] Loc.cit., footnote 15.
[21] G. E. Rizzo, *Monete greche della Sicilia* (Rome, 1946), p. 102, nos. 1 and 2.
[22] Op.cit., pp. 36–41. The tetradrachm reverse which follows the Damareteion series is no. 275. The relation of the Damareteion master to the obverse dies

The Damareteion master did not take part in the creation of the important Sicilian commemorative issues of the 470's and 460's. Nevertheless, the search for his work outside Syracuse need not be a fruitless undertaking.

As we have seen, 480 was a year of close cooperation between the mints of Syracuse and Leontinoi. Rizzo's collection of Leontinoi material shows the two obverse dies in the Apollo head tetradrachm series which uses the Emmenid lion as a reverse symbol.[23] In one, the head of Apollo is represented in a gross and unrefined style (PLATE I, 3). The other, however, is a die by a finer hand (PLATE I, 4). When placed beside the dies of the Damareteion master it exhibits the same mannerisms of style. The thin ridged eyebrow, the eye, marked by a chevron-like upper lid, are the same. Like the Aitna master, the Damareteion master included or omitted detailed treatment of the eyeball depending on the emphasis desired. The nose of both heads is composed of a thin ridge along the top with a deep hollow below and an accentuated nostril, above which there is a secondary swelling. Also alike are the puffy lips, slightly separated in the Damareteion head, set in a cheek which rises to give a slight indication of the cheekbone, the chin, and the slanting straight line of the sterno-mastoid muscle. We may compare the treatment of the lower edge of the bust, the linear, yet not minute handling of the hair, and finally, the form of the skull. In view of the close ties in the production of the coinages of Leontinoi and Syracuse in 480, so close as to suggest the work of a single mint, it is hardly surprising to find a Leontinoi die made by the Damareteion master.

The style of the Damareteion master appears suddenly at Syracuse, dominates the coinage of 480, and disappears. One looks in vain for some trace of his hand in Gelon's abundant war coinage (485–480) or in the issues of the preceding regime. After a single tetradrachm following the Damareteion series his hand is not seen again. His use of the frontal eye at a time when artists of less talent, such as his colleague in the Leontinoi Apollo head group (PLATE I, 3), had learned

---

used with his reverses cannot be clarified. Stylistic comparison is useless. The obv. die used with the Artemis-Arethousa rev. at Leontinoi is signed ЯА, A. J. Evans, *NC* (1894), p. 207, no. 1, pl. 7:7.
[23] Op.cit., footnote 20, p. 134, nos. 14 and 15.

the profile rendering gives his work an old-fashioned quality[24]. He was a man of mature years, if not already old, when he cut his dies at Syracuse, and one is even led to question whether he was a Syracusan by birth. Numbers of Geloans and Kamarinians as well as citizens of Megara Hyblaia and Likodeia Euboia had been brought to Syracuse by Gelon in the years after 485. Was the Damareteion master one of these? The sudden appearance of his style in a dominant role at the mint of Syracuse lends support to such a speculation. The sudden disappearance of his work after the execution of his masterpiece at the moment when he had embarked on the cutting of dies for the standard tetradrachm series suggests a further inference. His years in Syracuse were few, and by the end of 479 he was dead.

R. ROSS HOLLOWAY

[24] Close inspection of the Brussels tetradrachm by the Damareteion master (Plate II, 10) in a magnified slide shows that the upper and lower lids are drawn frontally with an opening at the lacrimal gland and that the eyeball is frontal: ⌔. This is the treatment given the eye in the Damareteion dies. In fact the eye of the head of the Brussels tetradrachm is almost an exact duplicate of the eye of the head of the Boston Damareteion reverse. The Damareteion master's Leontinoi tetradrachm (Plate I, 4) has the same frontal lids, but the eyeball is not indicated.

Illustrations:

1. London, British Museum. Boehringer, *Die Münzen von Syrakus*, no. 376, *BMCat. Sicily*, Syracuse no. 63. Photo, ANS.

2. Paris, Bibliothèque Nationale. J. Babelon, *De Luynes Cat.*, no. 990. Photo, Bibliothèque Nationale.

3. London, British Museum. *BMCat. Sicily*, Leontinoi no. 10. Photo, ANS, after G. E. Rizzo, *Monete Greche della Sicilia*, pls. 22 and 24.

4. New York, American Numismatic Society. Photo, ANS.

5. Brussels, Bibliothèque Nationale. P. Naster, *De Hirsch Cat.*, no. 269. Photo, Bibliothèque Nationale.

6. New York, American Numismatic Society. Photo, ANS.

7. Tarquinia, Museo Nazionale. Detail of exterior of Attic red-figure kylix by Oltos. Photo after Arias-Hirmer, *Tausend Jahre Griechische Vasenkunst*, pl. 102.

8. London, British Museum. *BMCat. Sicily*, Catane no. 2. Photo, ANS, after G. E. Rizzo, *Monete Greche della Sicilia*, pl. 9.

9. Syracuse, Museo Nazionale, inv. 54492, from the Ognina Hoard, S. P. Noe, *A Bibliography of Greek Coin Hoards*[2], no. 749. Photo, Museo Nazionale.

10. Brussels, Bibliothèque Nationale. Boehringer, *Die Münzen von Syrakus*, no. 387. Photo, Bibliothèque Nationale.

Thanks are gratefully expressed to Mlle Jacqueline Lallemand (Brussels), Mr. G. K. Jenkins (London), M. Jacques Yvon (Paris), and Sig:ra Mariateresa Currò (Syracuse), for their courtesy in assisting in the collection of photographs.

NOTES ON ABDALONYMOS AND THE DATED ALEXANDER COINAGE OF SIDON AND AKE

In 1916 E. T. Newell published a study of the coinage of Sidon and Ake, and this has formed the basis for all subsequent investigation of these two mints.[1] Newell claimed that the gold staters and silver tetradrachms struck at Sidon and lettered consecutively were issued between 333/2 and 306/5. At first the mint initials and the numbering were in Phoenician letters, i.e., coins marked *aleph* and *beth* indicating years 1 and 2, with a *tsadik* indicating Sidon. Later the mint mark is indicated by the Greek letters Σ or ΣΙ, with *zayin*, *cheth*, *teth* and *yodh* for the years 7, 8, 9 and 10 of the era. Later the Greek alphabet is used for the numbering, beginning with Κ, which stands for the tenth year, indicating that the changeover came in that year, and continuing (Λ is missing) to Ω which stands for 24. After Ω the die cutters began at the beginning of the alphabet again, but they added ͱ or Μ to differentiate these coins from the earlier ones. In this series the coins are dated from Α to Δ, 1 to 4 (25 to 28). Thus we can identify coins struck in Sidon in the years 1, 2, 7–10, 12–28 of some era. Newell has shown that the earliest of these coins were struck in Alexander's lifetime, because the coins marked Ν, Ξ, Ο and Π (years 13–16) were struck in the name of Philip III who died in 317. The era established by Newell for these coins was inaugurated by the battle of Issos in the fall of 333.

The basis of the present article is a Sidon issue with Ptolemaic types which is of the utmost significance for the chronology of the Alexander coinage.[2] On the obverse in a circle of dots is a head of

---

[1] *The Dated Alexander Coinage of Sidon and Ake*, Yale Oriental Series— Researches, Vol. II (New Haven, 1916).
[2] E. T. Newell, *The Coinages of Demetrius Poliorcetes* (London, 1927), p. 40, n. 52; A. B. Brett, "The Aphlaston, Symbol of Naval Victory or Supremacy on Greek and Roman Coins," *Trans. Int. Num. Cong.* (London, 1938), p. 26 and pl. IV, 7; M. Dunand, *Fouilles de Byblos* (Paris, 1939), pp. 410f., no. 6371, pl. XC; G. Kleiner, "Alexanders Reichsmünzen," *Abh. Berlin, Phil.-hist. Kl.* (1947), nr. 5, p. 51, n. 46; A. B. Brett, "Athena ΑΛΚΙΔΗΜΟΣ of Pella,"

Alexander r. with ram's horns and wearing an elephant's scalp. On the reverse in a circle of dots is Athena Alkidemos r. with spear and shield, to l. upwards ΑΛΕΞΑΝΔΡΟΥ, in field l. ΣΙ, in field r. X and eagle perched on thunderbolt. The ΣΙ clearly indicates the mint of Sidon. The X shows that it was struck in the 22nd year of an era used at Sidon, most probably the same era as on the Alexanders of Sidon. Ptolemy controlled Phoenicia from 320 to 315,[3] for a short time in the year 312,[4] and after 287.[5] If this issue was struck in 315 or before, some of the coins with Philip III's name struck in the years 13 to 16 would have been struck before Alexander's death, a patent impossibility. Ptolemy assumed the diadem in 306, and consequently satrapal types after this date are quite improbable—the Philip coins also militate against so late a date. The only possible solution to the problem is to date the coin in 312, equate X with 22, and thus accept Newell's chronology which begins the Alexander coinage of Sidon in the year 333/2 and ends it in 306/5.

As far as I know there are only two coins with Alexander types from Sidon of the year 312/1. One of these was known to Newell and is illustrated in his work (pl. IV, 16). The other was in the hoard found in the excavations at Byblos.[6] Bellinger has shown that the OX in the

---

ANSMN, IV (1950), p. 60, pl. XI, 6; A. R. Bellinger, "An Alexander Hoard from Byblos," *Berytus*, X (1952–53), p. 47, pl. VI; Brooks Emmons, "The Overstruck Coinage of Ptolemy I," *ANSMN*, VI (1954), p. 75.

[3] On Alexander's death Syria had been assigned to Laomedon of Mytilene (Diod. XVIII, 3, 1), and in the division at Triparadeisos Laomedon was confirmed in his office (Diod. XVIII, 39, 6). In 320 Ptolemy seized Phoenicia and Koile Syria (Diod. XVIII, 43); Appian, *Syriaka*, 52; Marmor Parium, *FGrH* 239 B 12). Diodoros places this seizure in the archon year 320/19, while the Marmor Parium places it in 319/8. In 318/7 Eumenes led an army into Phoenicia, but was almost immediately forced out (Diod. XVIII, 63, 6 and 73, 2). Ptolemy held the territory until 315 when it was taken by Antigonos Monophthalmos (Diod. XIX, 58, 1–4).

[4] In the spring of 312 Ptolemy defeated Demetrios, the son of Antigonos, near Gaza, and all of Phoenicia and Koile Syria lay open to the Ptolemaic army. Ptolemy won over Sidon (Diod. XIX, 86, 1), but when Antigonos appeared on the scene, Ptolemy prudently retired to Egypt (Diod. XIX, 93). It seems quite certain that Ptolemy held the city for only several months (cf. Plut., *Demetr.*, 5–6 and Paus. I, 6, 5).

[5] E. T. Newell, *Tyrus Rediviva* (New York, 1922), pp. 21–23; W. W. Tarn, *Antigonos Gonatas* (Oxford, 1913), pp. 104ff., esp. p. 105, n. 33.

[6] A. R. Bellinger, *Berytus*, X (1952–53), p. 42, no. 53 (Maurice Dunand, *Fouilles de Byblos*, p. 410, no. 6339, and pl. LXXXVII).

field l. is an error for X and the fact that the two coins share the same obverse die confirms it. He also states that the error is probably a sign of the disorder in the mint attendant on the Ptolemaic evacuation of the city. There are also only two coins with Ptolemaic types and the letter X. One, in the possession of E. T. Newell and now in the trays of the American Numismatic Society, came from the Abu Hommos hoard. The other was in the Byblos hoard.[7] These two coins share the same obverse die, but the reverse dies are different.

In 1947 G. Kleiner attempted to prove that Alexander's own coinage (the Herakles and seated Zeus silver and Athena and Nike gold) was first issued after the fall of Tyre in 332/1. Obviously this theory flounders if the coins of Sidon dated in the year 1 belong in 333/2 (Newell, no. 8, pl. I, 10–12).[8] Kleiner, therefore, tried to date the first year of this coinage to 332/1. The able reviewers of Kleiner's work,[9] although they generally reject Kleiner's basic premises, do not condemn explicitly his redating of the Sidonian coinage. But his redating must be condemned on the basis of the Ptolemaic coins with Σl and X. We have, therefore, another proof of the untenability of Kleiner's main thesis that the Alexander coinage was first struck after the capture of Tyre.

The dated coinage of Ake is a different matter.[10] Newell has shown that the coins of Ake are numbered from 20 to 39 and from 8 to 11. The obverse die of coins marked 39 was used for a coin marked 8, leading to the conclusion that the lower series immediately follows the higher one. The paucity of coins marked 8 leads one to assume that 39 and 8 represent the coinage of one year during which the dating system was changed.[11] The 8 should represent the eighth year of a

---

[7] A. R. Bellinger, *Berytus*, X (1952–53), p. 47, no. 140 (Maurice Dunand, *Fouilles de Byblos*, pp. 410f., no. 6371, and pl. XC).

[8] Newell described the coin in *Demetrius Poliorcetes*, p. 40, n. 52. Kleiner knew of this passage, p. 51, n. 46, but misinterpreted Newell's note by taking Newell's X to mean ten rather than *chi* = 22.

[9] There are three reviews that discuss Kleiner's work in detail, *CR*, LXIV (1950), pp. 66f. (Seltman); *AJA*, LVI (1952), pp. 227f. (Wallace); *JHS*, LXIX (1949), p. 121 (Jenkins). Recently G. K. Jenkins, "An Early Ptolemaic Hoard from Phacous," *ANSMN*, IX (1960), pp. 27f., and Brigitte Kuschel, "Die neuen Münzbilder des Ptolemaios Soter," *J.f.N.u.G.*, XI (1961), pp. 9–16, have recognized the significance of the coin and rejected Kleiner's date.

[10] See Newell, *The Dated Coinage of Sidon and Ake*, pp. 39–63.

[11] Ibid., pp. 62f.

new era to which the Ake mint conformed. Perhaps it is an era reflecting Antigonid control of the city. Newell placed the year 20 in 326 and continued the series down to 304. Kleiner, after a note of Regling, tries to show, on the basis of the hoard evidence, that Ake's dates are one year earlier than Newell suspected, and that Sidon 6 is equated with Ake 20.[12] We know a number of sizable hoards of Alexander coins with the dated coins of both Sidon and Ake. The logical assumption is that the last dated coins of these two mints in each hoard ought to be contemporary.

In the Saida hoards (Noe, nos. 881, 882, 884) the last Sidonian coin is from the year K (10) = 324/3, while the latest Ake coin is marked 24.[13] The equation gives the result, Sidon's K (10) = Ake's 24 = 324/3 B.C. In the Demanhur hoard (Noe, no. 324) the last Sidon coin is dated O (15) = 319/8, while the last Ake coin is from the year 29.[14] Therefore, Sidon 15 = Ake 29 = 319/8. A similar situation is to be seen in the Byblos hoard (Noe, no. 175).[15] Here the last coin of Sidon is dated Ω (24) = 310/09, while the last coin of Ake is dated 38. Sidon 24 = Ake 38 = 310/09. In the Aleppo hoard (Noe, no. 29) the last coins of Sidon were dated ^M_B (26) = 308/7, and the last coins of Ake were 39 of the old era and 9 of the new.[16] Sidon 26 = Ake 9 = 308/7. Using these equations, and the equation Sidon X (22) = 312/11, we arrive at the following table, from which it would seem that these two mints stopped striking Alexander coins at the same time in 306/5 B.C.[17] Newell gave two possible explanations for the phenomenon. He thought that the mints of Sidon and Ake might have stopped striking because of the economic dislocation attendant

---

[12] Kleiner, op.cit., p. 50, n. 41.
[13] Newell, *Sidon and Ake*, p. 57; K. Regling, "Zur Münzprägung der Brettier," *Festschrift C. F. Lehmann-Haupt* (1921), p. 83, n. 2.
[14] Newell, *NNM*, 19, pp. 55f. Ibid., pp. 134ff., we have a reference to Ake 29 corresponding to the year 319/8, and several references to Ake 20 corresponding to 327/6. A glance will show that one or the other must be wrong. From the context it seems that the first correlation was probably a lapsus calami or a typographical error, although it is possible that Newell realized the difficulty of his dating of the Ake coins in the Demanhur hoard without thinking it through for the rest of the Ake coins.
[15] A. R. Bellinger, *Berytus*, X (1952–53), p. 47.
[16] *Sidon and Ake*, p. 58.
[17] For the reasons see *Sidon and Ake* pp. 37f.; also Kleiner, p. 52, n. 46.

DATED ALEXANDER COINAGE

Year	Sidon		Ake ($1 = 347/6$)	
333/2	⚵	(1)		
332/1	Ϭ	(2)		
331/0		(3)		
330/29		(4)		
329/8		(5)		
328/7		(6)	=	(20)
327/6	N	(7)	| =	(21)
326/5	⋎	(8)	|| =	(22)
325/4	Θ	(9)	||| =	(23)
324/3	ꝀK	(10)	|||| =	(24)
323/2		(11)	||||| =	(25)
322/1	M	(12)	|||||| =	(26)
321/0	N	(13) ⎫	||||||| =	(27)
320/19	Ξ	(14) ⎬ Philip III	|||||||| =	(28)
319/8	O	(15) ⎨	||||||||| =	(29)
318/7	Π	(16) ⎭	≡	(30)
317/6	P	(17)	| ≡	(31)
316/5	Σ	(18)	|| ≡	(32)	[1]
315/4	T	(19)	||| ≡	(33)	[2]
314/3	Y	(20)	|||| ≡	(34)	[3]
313/2	Φ	(21)	||||| ≡	(35)	[4]
312/1	X	(22)	|||||| ≡	(36)	[5]
311/0	Ψ	(23)	||||||| ≡	(37)	[6]
310/09	Ω	(24)	|||||||| ≡	(38)	[7]
309/8	MA	(25)	||||||||| ≡	(39)	|||||| (8)
308/7	MB	(26)	||||||||	(9)
307/6	MΓ	(27)	−	(10)
306/5	MΔ	(28)	| −	(11)

upon the siege of Rhodes in 305/4, connected with the renewed importance of the city of Tyre.[18] Alternately he suggested, and this seems to me much more probable, a connection with the inauguration of a series of Tyrian Alexanders. Antigonos Monophthalmos began the striking of Alexander coinage at Tyre about the year 306, perhaps in connection with his Egyptian expedition of that year. He then closed down the mints at Sidon and Ake and transferred their function to the mint at Tyre.

What conclusions can be drawn from this table about the eras used by these two mints? The first era of Ake began in the year 347/6, and was used on the coins from 328/7 to 309/8. Since we have no sources for the internal history of Ake in this period, we can only point out that 347/6 is about the end of the great revolt of the satraps. Newell has suggested that this era is that of the reign of the local kinglet[19] about whom we know nothing. Thus, he would come to the throne toward the end of the great Phoenician revolt and would die in his thirty-ninth year of office. At this point, Newell suggests, a new era connected with Antigonos was introduced. Kleiner suggests, because the same thing did not happen at Sidon, that the kinglet revolted and was replaced by Antigonos.[20] Aside from the coins we have no knowledge of the internal history of Ake in this period, but it is surprising that Diodoros did not mention such an event if it really did happen.

In Sidon the situation is somewhat different. Here the coins are numbered consecutively from 1 to 28, and we know something of the internal history of Sidon in this period. But what era is in use at Sidon? It can be either an era of Alexander the Great; either the battle of Issos or of Alexander's taking of the city of Sidon, or it can be an era of the local king, Abdalonymos. If it is the latter, this means that Abdalonymos held on as ruler of Sidon through thick and thin until at least 306/5. The Ptolemaic coins from Sidon in 312/11 mili-

---

[18] H. Seyrig, "Sur une prétendue ère tyrienne," *Syria*, XXXIV (1957), pp. 93–98, has shown that Tyre quickly recovered her prosperity after her destruction by Alexander and struck coins between 331 and 306. This would tend to discount the importance of the economic reasons for the end of the dated Alexanders of Sidon and Ake.
[19] *Sidon and Ake*, p. 59.
[20] Op.cit., p. 28.

tate against this, for they would indicate that Abdalonymos was more than expert at switching sides, and for this reason it does seem that the era in use at Sidon is an era of Alexander.

When Alexander appeared in Phoenicia after his victory at Issos in 333 he was welcomed by the local populations, and as he proceeded south he received the surrender of a number of cities including Sidon. Actually the Sidonians, who had revolted against the Persians in 351/0 and were virtually annihilated by them, summoned Alexander to free them from the Persian yoke. Strato, the King of Sidon who was compromised by his friendship with the Persian King, was expelled and Abdalonymos replaced him as King of Sidon. All our sources stress the fact that Abdalonymos was a descendant of the old royal family, and his accession to the throne would please both Alexander, who wanted to secure Sidon and remove an ally of the Persian King, and the Sidonians, who probably hated the ruler imposed on them by the Persians. After this Abdalonymos disappears from our sources.[21]

Despite this lack of evidence, or rather because of it, scholars have constructed ingenious theories about Abdalonymos. One theory holds that Abdalonymos was able to maintain himself until 312/11 when Antigonos removed him from his position after the Antigonids regained the city because of his basic loyalty to Ptolemy.[22] Another assumes that the era appearing on the coins of Sidon is not an era of Alexander, but of Abdalonymos, and that he ruled at least until his twenty-eighth year. According to this theory Abdalonymos stands for *Reichseinheit*, i.e., he was a partisan of Antigonos.[23]

Until new evidence turns up we shall not be able to say anything further about Abdalonymos. We can, however, outline the history of Sidon in this period.[24] On Alexander's death the city along with the

---

[21] Arrian, *Anabasis*, II, xv, 6; Diod. XVI, 41–45; Arrian does not mention this incident at all. Justin, XI, 10, 7–9 and Curtius, IV, 1, 16–26 call him Abdalonymus and place this at Sidon. Diodorus, XVII, 46–47 calls him Ballonymus and places it at Tyre. Plut., *De Alex. Fort.*, II, 8 gives him the usual name, but puts it at Paphos.
[22] G. Moser, *Untersuchungen über die Politik Ptolemaios I in Griechenland (323–285 a. Chr. n.)* (Diss. Leipzig, 1914), pp. 113–116.
[23] Kleiner, op.cit., pp. 25, 28.
[24] See above and notes 4, 5, 6, 7.

rest of Phoenicia passed under the control of Laomedon of Mytilene until 320. From 320 to 315 the city was in the hands of Ptolemy. In 315 Antigonos entered Phoenicia and summoned the kings of the Phoenician cities to meet him. The King of Sidon was probably among them. Antigonos established a shipyard at Sidon and he or his son Demetrios held the city until 287 B.C. with the exception of a short period in 312, when Ptolemy defeated Demetrios in the battle of Gaza and won over Sidon. A short time later the city was abandoned to Antigonos. In 302, shortly before the battle of Ipsos, Ptolemy besieged Sidon, but did not take the city.[25] Any one of these shifts in power i.e., 323, 320, 315, or 312 could have brought Abdalonymos' reign to an end, if he were still alive.

IRWIN L. MERKER

[25] Diod. XX, 113, 1–2.

THE KOZANI HOARD OF 1955
(See Plates III–VI)

The small hoard of 27 coins which is the subject of this paper was stated by the dealer from whom it was secured to have been found near Kozani in southern Macedonia in 1955. Number 28, the much worn Aesillas tetradrachm, was specifically stated by the dealer to have been found along with the others; it cannot, obviously, have been buried with them originally. No details of the circumstances of the find were available. The hoard is on exhibition in The Money Museum at the National Bank of Detroit, Detroit. The coins in the hoard are as follows:

Chalkis drachms (5)

>   Obv.: Head of nymph r.
>   Rev.: Eagle tearing snake. ΧΑΛ. Symbol.

1. Symbol: ⊐ below eagle. 3.30 gms. ↙ Much worn.
   There is no doubt about the symbol, although it is illegible on this specimen, for the obverse die is the same as that of CH 301 in the possession of W. P. Wallace, on which the symbol is clear. Obverse dies do not seem to have been carried over from one symbol group to another among these Chalkis drachms.

2. Symbol: ⊞ above wing. 3.27 gms. ↑c Much worn.
   The coin probably, but not certainly, belongs to this symbol group. By ↑c is meant that the axis of the head has been taken, as we would do it, through the top of the head and the center of the neck. In some series it is taken through the brow and the nape of the neck: ↑n, in others through the crown and the front of the neck: ↑f.

3. Symbol: ⊞ above wing. 3.30 gms. ↑c Much worn.

4. Symbol: ⊞ above wing. 3.43 gms. ↑c Worn.

5. Symbol: caduceus to r. 3.63 gms. ↑n Very slightly worn.

Athenian tetradrachms (8)

>   Obv.: Head of Athena r.
>   Rev.: Owl r., olive branch and crescent behind, ΑΘΕ in front.

6. 16.81 gms. ← Much worn.

7. 16.79 gms. ← Worn.

8. 16.69 gms. ↙ Worn.

9. 16.82 gms. ← Somewhat worn.

10. 16.87 gms. ↙ Somewhat worn.

11. 17.00 gms. ↙ Somewhat worn.

12. 16.79 gms. ↙ Slightly worn.

13. 17.06 gms. ← Slightly worn.

Ptolemaic tetradrachms (14)

Obv.: Head of Ptolemy I r.
Rev.: Eagle standing l. on thunderbolt. ΠΤΟΛΕΜΑΙΟΥ ΒΑΣΙΛΕΩΣ (ΠΤΟΛΕΜΑΙΟΥ ΣΩΤΗΡΟΣ on 26 and 27). Letters and monograms.

14. Ptolemy I. 13.80 gms. ↑f ⚹ |AP Much worn.
    I. N. Svoronos, Τὰ Νομίσματα τοῦ Κράτους τῶν Πτολεμαίων no. 246, pl. viii, 26.
    10 or 12 punches on obv. and 2 on rev.

15. Ptolemy I. 13.76 gms. ↗ ⚹ |AP Worn.
    Sv. no. 246, pl. viii, 26.
    About 4 punches on obv. and about 8 on rev. Probably an overstrike.

16. Ptolemy I. 13.80 gms. ↗ ⚹ |AP Worn.
    Sv. no. 246, pl. viii, 26.
    2 punches on obv. and at least 3 on rev. Perhaps an overstrike.

17. Ptolemy I. 13.85 gms. ↑f P A Worn.
    Sv. no. 247, pl. ix, 1.
    3 or 4 punches on obv. and 3 or 4 on rev.

18. Ptolemy I. 13.60 gms. ↑cf P ⱸ Worn.
    Sv. no. 250, pl. ix, 4.
    About 5 punches on obv. and 1 or 2 on rev. An overstrike.

19. Ptolemy I. 13.89 gms. ↑cf P Ⲙ Slightly worn.
    Sv. no. 252, pl. ix, 8.
    No punches.

KOZANI HOARD OF 1955

20. Ptolemy I. 13.80 gms. ↑f P ΑP Somewhat worn.
    Sv. no. 255, pl. ix, 11.
    About 7 punches on obv. and 3 or 4 on rev. A very small sickle-shaped punch is impressed twice on the obv.—by the nose and by the chin.

21. Ptolemy I. 13.69 gms. ↑cf P ΑP Somewhat worn.
    Sv. no. 255, pl. ix, 11.
    5 or 6 punches on obv. and perhaps 1 on rev. Probably an overstrike.

22. Ptolemy II. Tyre. 13.80 gms. ↑cf H club Worn.
    Sv. no. 637 (279 B.C.), pl. xix, 9.
    2 round punches on obv. and 2 punches on rev. Probably an overstrike.

23. Ptolemy II. 14.12 gms. ↑cf ΣT ΑΡ Slightly worn.
    Sv. no. 368 (285–271 B.C.), pl. viii, 27.
    1 oval punch near mouth and perhaps 1 or 2 on rev. An overstrike.

24. Ptolemy II. Tyre. 14.13 gms. ↑f ⚤ club Somewhat worn.
    Sv. no. 644 (267 B.C.), pl. xix, 14.
    1 or 2 punches on obv. and 1 or 2 on rev. An overstrike.

25. Ptolemy II. Tyre. 14.11 gms. ↑c ⚤ club Somewhat worn.
    Sv. no. 644 (267 B.C.), pl. xix, 14.
    An annulet before mouth and at least 2 punches on rev. Probably an overstrike.

26. Ptolemy II. 14.01 gms. ↑c T ΜΕ Λ (= Year 30) ☉ Somewhat worn.
    Legend—ΠΤΟΛΕΜΑΙΟΥ ΣΩΤΗΡΟΣ.
    Sv. no. 770 (256 B.C.), pl. xxv, 7.
    1 or 2 punches on each of obv. and rev. Probably an overstrike.

27. Ptolemy II. 14.17 gms. ↑c T ΜΕ ΛΒ (= Year 32) ☉ Very slightly worn. Legend—ΠΤΟΛΕΜΑΙΟΥ ΣΩΤΗΡΟΣ.
    Sv. no. 775 (254 B.C.), pl. xxv, 11. No punches.

Aesillas tetradrachm (1)

Obv.: Head of Alexander r. ΜΑΚΕΔΟΝΩΝ. Ϙ
Rev.: Club between money-chest and quaestor's chair. AESILLAS Q.

28. 13.87 gms. ↑c Very much worn. 92–88 B.C.
    This coin is clearly an intrusion in the hoard, for it is both much later and more worn than any of the other coins.

At least half of the Ptolemaic tetradrachms in this hoard seem to be overstrikes,[1] and all but two of them (nos. 19 and 27) have received small punches on both obverse and reverse. The shapes of the punches are sometimes hard to distinguish, but many of them are simple and obvious:

> A plain round punch is common—see nos. 14, 15, and 22 (where the punches are so deep that they show through on the other side).
>
> An oval punch occurs—see nos. 22 rev. and 23 obv. The trace of a central spine perhaps suggests that it is intended to represent a Macedonian shield.
>
> A small deep square punch occurs once—on the eagle in no. 24.
>
> A triangular punch occurs on no. 25, between the eagle and the club.
>
> A crescent-shaped punch is the most common of all; sometimes, as on the reverse of no. 20, it seems to have been imprinted several times. Care is needed in distinguishing these punches, for traces of the undertype in restruck coins sometimes look like a crescent punch.
>
> Two more complicated punches with clear devices are the *leaf* on the cheek of no. 24, and the *cross* on the rev. of no. 16.

As none of the other coins in the hoard was punched it seems safe to assume that the Ptolemaic tetradrachms received their punches before they reached Greece. These punches are presumably the marks of private bankers, but it is not clear for what reason or reasons they were impressed.

The Greek hoards containing Ptolemaic coins have been studied by Mme Irene Varoucha-Christodoulopoulou in an important article[2] in which she shows that most of them were buried in the Peloponnesos or in Euboia. She also shows that Ptolemaic coins found in Greece were mostly struck by the first two Ptolemies. Our hoard extends to

---

[1] In "The Overstruck Coinage of Ptolemy I," *ANSMN* VI (1954), 69–84, Brooks Emmons deals with an earlier series of tetradrachms of Ptolemy I ("Type D" *Obv.*: Alexander in elephant skin headdress, *Rev.*: Athena Alkidemos) all of which seem to have been overstruck on preceding issues of heavier weight which, she suggests, were called in for the purpose. The Ptolemy I tetradrachms in our hoard belong to still later issues with further reduced weights; about half of them seem to be overstruck. Of the six tetradrachms of Ptolemy II in our hoard all but the last appear to be overstrikes.

[2] Πτολεμαϊκὰ νομίσματα στὴν κυρίως Ἑλλάδα by Εἰρ. Βαρούχα-Χριστοδουλοπούλου, pp. 668–679 in Ἐπιτύμβιον Χρ. Τσουντᾶ Athens, 1941.

southern Macedonia the area in which we have evidence that this money circulated. The largest of these hoards is the Eretria hoard of 1937 which is also discussed in *The Euboian League and its Coinage* (*NNM* 134, New York, 1956, 41–49) where ca. 235 B.C. is suggested as its burial date. Several of the issues which appear in our hoard (e.g., nos. 19, 20, 21, 22, 23, 26) appear also in it, and show on the whole very similar wear. Attention may also be called to the recent discoveries of Ptolemaic coins—mostly issues of Ptolemy II—in Attica.[3]

The tetradrachms of Ptolemy II in our hoard provide a reasonably good date for its burial. The two latest of them carry regnal dates—30 and 32—which place them respectively in 256 and 254 B.C. The second of these coins shows very little wear, but the first gives the impression of having circulated for a considerable number of years. The three coins minted at Tyre show a good deal of wear; the earliest of them (number 22) carries the regnal date H = 7 and so was minted in 279 B.C., the other two are dated ca. 267 by Svoronos. The burial of the hoard must clearly be put after the middle of the century, but not very long after, and near the date of the Eretria hoard of 1937; it is perhaps reasonable to guess ca. 240–230 B.C.

This burial date is consistent enough with the worn condition of the first four of the Chalkis drachms, which are usually dated in the late fourth century.[4] Of these drachms, number 1 belongs to the "trident l." group; it is hard to say whether the single specimen is more or less worn than nos. 2, 3 and 4, which belong to the "冂 above wing"

---

[3] See "Koroni: A Ptolemaic Camp on the East Coast of Attica," by E. Vanderpool, J. R. McCredie and A. Steinberg, in *Hesperia* 31 (1962), 26–61, and "Συμβολὴ εἰς τὸν Χρεμωνίδειον Πόλεμον 266/5–263/2 π. Χ." by Εἰρ. βαρούχα-Χριστοδουλοπούλου, Ἀρχ. Ἐφ. 1953–4 (In memory of G. P. Oikonomos), Part III (Athens, 1961), 321–349.

[4] B. V. Head, in *Historia Numorum*[2] (Oxford, 1911), dates these Chalkis drachms "369–336 B.C.," but this is clearly rather too early, and E. T. Newell remarks in *Alexander Hoards* IV, *Olympia*, *NNM* 39 (New York, 1929), 17, that "the accepted dating of these pieces in the last half of the fourth century is probably correct." That they in fact run down into the third century is suggested in *The Euboian League and its Coinage* by W. P. Wallace (*NNM* 134, New York, 1956), 32, n. 68. The only attempt so far to arrange the different symbol groups chronologically—a very rough attempt, for which the evidence was not presented—is to be found in "Impurities in Euboean Monetary Silver," by E. J. Allin and W. P. Wallace in *ANSMN* VI (1954), 37, n. 5, and pl. ix.

group. These three coins show the poor style which earns the group the designation "barbarous" in the *British Museum Catalogue of Central Greece*.[5] Number 5, which belongs to the "caduceus" group, is as little worn as any coin in the hoard; it should, accordingly, be dated close to 250 B.C. This conclusion, confirming that the caduceus group belongs in the third century (as has already been suggested—see note 4 above), and indeed towards the middle of it, would be of some importance if the appearance of the coin did not, unfortunately, raise the question whether it too, like number 28, may not be an intrusion. Its shinier and cleaner surface certainly distinguishes it from all of the other coins of the hoard, and one cannot feel confident that it was originally buried with them.[6] Under the circumstances its value as evidence is slight.

The Athenian coins in the hoard differ a good deal among themselves in the amount of circulation they have seen: the first three are considerably worn, the last two much less so. The owls on these two least worn specimens are represented in a curious manner which makes them appear to be wearing skirts. While there is nothing exactly similar among the numerous specimens illustrated by Svoronos in *Les monnaies d'Athènes*, still numbers 2, 3 and 4 on his plate 23 (illustrating the latest period before the New Style) are fairly close.[7] The olive branch behind these owls has leaves which are pointed, and smaller than is usual. Again, there are no exact parallels in Svoronos, but similarly small olive leaves seem to occur only on this same plate: numbers 4 and 11, and numbers 20–24 among the final group of tetradrachms with symbols. These parallels suggest that our two least worn tetradrachms should be put near the end of the Old Style series, not long before the owls with symbols which seem to have been the immediate precursors of the New Style. Four drachms of this issue with symbols appeared in "fresh and uncirculated" condition in the

---

[5] *BMC Central Greece*, p. 111. This group is much more numerous than any of the other groups of Chalkis drachms, so that its poor style is probably the result of pressing poor workmen into service when a large issue was suddenly required and competent die cutters were not available (see *NC*, 1962, 25, n. 2).
[6] We are greatly indebted to Professor Hansjorg Bloesch, of Winterthur, and to Miss Margaret Thompson, for examining and discussing this coin. They felt that it is possible, but perhaps improbable, that it formed part of the original burial.
[7] Cf. also drachms 14–16 on this plate.

Corinth hoard of 1938, which was buried about 215 B.C.,[8] and so should be dated no earlier than about 220 B.C. These two latest Athenian tetradrachms of our hoard will thus be earlier than the beginning (perhaps ca. 229 B.C.?) of the issue with symbols—perhaps considerably earlier, for there may have been a gap between the last regular Old Style issues and the group with symbols.[9]

Miss Margaret Thompson has pointed out an interesting difference in the form of the decoration of Athena's helmet, between that characteristic of most (if not all) of the fourth century issues, and that which is found on the gold issue of 295/4 B.C.[10] The decorative tendril changes from form 1 to form 2 (see the diagram below). She also pointed out to us a third form, contemporary with or slightly later than form 2,[11] and the distinctive, rather sprawling, tendril of the issue with symbols. The four forms may be represented as follows:

The difference between forms 2 and 3 may be clearly seen by comparing PLATE III, 6 with PLATE III, 9. The sequence suggested seems to be borne out by a consideration of the hoards illustrated by Svoronos on his plates 26–32. In his first hoard, from Egypt, illustrated on plate 26, the coins with form 1 decoration (numbers 1–19) are more worn than those with form 2 decoration (numbers 22–31);

---

[8] Numbers 138–141, illustrated on pl. II, in "The Corinth Hoard of 1938" by Sydney P. Noe, *ANSMN* X (1962), 9–14.

[9] Such a gap is perhaps suggested by the fact that none of the 72 Athenian tetradrachms in the large 1938 hoard from Thessaly at the American Numismatic Society (unpublished) is in very fresh condition; indeed all show some and most show very considerable wear. This hoard has not yet been fully studied, but the existence in it of tetradrachms of Antigonos Gonatas in mint condition suggests a *terminus arte quem* of ca. 235 B.C., and I. L. Merker, in *ANSMN* IX (1960), 42, proposes a burial date "during the decade of the 240's, shortly after c. 250." The Athenian tetradrachms in the Eretria hoard of 1937 were similarly worn; see note 14.

[10] See "A Hoard of Athenian Fractions," *ANSMN* VII (1957), p. 6.

[11] In the Thessaly hoard mentioned above (note 9) all 72 specimens seem to belong (about 20 are hard to be sure about as the back of the helmet is often more or less off flan) either to type 2 (34 or 35 of them) or to type 3 (17 or 18 of them), and there seems not much difference in the degree of wear of the two groups, although the specimens with type 3 helmets seem to be slightly less worn. Most of the coins which Svoronos puts latest (his plate 23) show type 3 helmets, and the long curling tendrils of the series with symbols (also illustrated on plate 23) are an obvious development from type 3.

types 3 and 4 do not occur. In Svoronos' Hoard VI, from Kiouleler in Thessaly,[12] illustrated on his plate 31, all issues seem to be of types 2 or 3, those with type 2 (for instance, nos. 2, 12, 24 and 38) being perhaps slightly more worn than those with type 3 (such as nos. 4, 17, 20, 31 and 32). In his hoard III, from Sophiko,[13] illustrated on his plate 28, most of the pieces seem to have type 3 decoration, but some specimens, like numbers 31 and 34, have type 2, and these seem perhaps rather more worn than the others.

In our hoard the three most worn Athenian tetradrachms apparently show type 2 helmet decoration (not visible in number 7) while the last five probably have type 3 (in number 9 the shape of the tendril is clear, in number 10 it is certain although somewhat obscured by die-breaks, in numbers 11, 12, and 13 it is uncertain but probable).[14] Since type 2 was already established at the beginning of the century, and type 3 had suffered further elaboration by the time of the issues with symbols (which perhaps begins about 229 B.C.), it seems reasonable to date our Athenian tetradrachms over a fairly long period in the first half of the third century.

In short, this small hoard was probably buried about 240–230 B.C. It supports Mme Varoucha's observation that most of the Ptolemaic coins found in Greece were struck by the first two Ptolemies, and extends the area from which these have been reported. It provides doubtful evidence (since coin no. 5 may be an intrusion) that the Chalkis drachms with the caduceus symbol were struck towards the middle of the third century, and good, though not extensive evidence for the arrangement of the third century tetradrachms of Athens.

O. H. DODSON AND W. P. WALLACE

[12] E. T. Newell, in *Western Seleucid Mints, ANS Numismatic Studies* 4, New York, 1941, p. 42, n. 20, suggests a burial date for this hoard of 279 B.C.

[13] Newell, loc.cit., p. 187, refers to "the Sophiko Hoard, which was probably buried during the lifetime of Seleucus II ..." The dates of Seleukos II are 246–226 B.C.

[14] Many of the 31 Athenian tetradrachms of the Eretria hoard of 1937 were badly corroded and have not been cleaned. However, examination of photographs of about twenty of them seems to show that the "owls" of this hoard were closely comparable to those under discussion here—the helmets show either type 2 or type 3 decoration, all show definite wear, and those with type 3 seem slightly less worn than those with type 2, although the difference is not striking.

PHILIPPI IN MACEDONIA

(See Plates VI–XI)

GOLD AND SILVER

The acquisition by the American Numismatic Society of two coins of Philippi, a gold stater and a drachm, as a gift from Mr. Berry (*SNG The Burton Y. Berry Collection*, New York, 1961: 45 and 46) gives occasion for a general study of the gold and silver of that mint, since its organization, though simple, has never been discussed.

On Philippi we have some explicit ancient testimony. Diodorus reports (XVI.3.7) that in 360–59 the people of Thasos settled a place called Krenides. In 357 they appealed to Philip for protection against the Thracians (Stephanus of Byzantium, s.v. Φίλιπποι), and when he had defeated them he put new settlers in the town, renamed it for himself and developed the neighboring gold mines until they produced an income of over 1,000 talents.[1] There are no coins with the name Krenides, but gold and bronze is known of "The Mainland Thasians" which without question comes from that settlement.[2]

"Krenides"
360–356 B.C.
Gold Stater

1. Head of young Heracles r. in lion's skin headdress. His neck ends in a curved line with no sign of the lion's paws. Except just before and behind the ear, the hair is entirely covered by the lion's head,

---

[1] Diodorus XVI.8.6; Strabo VII.34.42; Beloch III.1, pp. 230–232. As to the ambiguous evidence on the early name and fortunes of the place, which does not concern us here, cf. G. F. Hill, *Historical Greek Coins*, p. 79, n. 1 and H. L. Jones, *Strabo*, Loeb Edition, Vol. III, pp. 358f., n. 4.

[2] Stanley Casson, *Macedonia, Thrace and Illyria*, Oxford, 1926, p. 70, says "There seems no special reason to assume, with Head, that they were struck at Philippi." The special reason is the identity of style. George Le Rider, "Trésor de Monnaies trouvé à Thasos," *BCH*, 1956, pp. 1–19, suggests that they were struck at Thasos (pp. 10f.) but again the identity of style with the first issues of Philippi seems to me conclusive.

whose open mouth shows a single prominent tooth above and below. The mane is shown by stiffly curved lines. *Rev.*: ΘΑ ΣΙΟΝ to l. upward. ΗΠ ΕΙΡΟ to r. upward. Tripod with three handles, the middle leg a double line; from the two handles at the sides fillets ending in three bunches. Above, laurel branch, butt to l. In field lower l. cantharus. PLATE VI, 1

8.55 gm. Paris. Gaebler, *Die Antiken Münzen von Makedonia und Paionia*, Zweite Abt., p. 100,1.

2. Similar head.
   Rev.: ΘΑΣΙΟΝ above. ΗΠΕΙΡΟ beneath. Club, behind which is a strung bow. PLATE VI, 2

   11 mm. Gaebler, op.cit., p. 101, no. 2; 11 mm. 1.27 gm. *ANS-Newell; 12 mm. 1.37 gm. ANS-Newell; 11 mm. 1.10 gm. *SNG Copenhagen* no. 290, *BCH*, 1936, p. 173.

Philippi
(Of the same style as "Krenides")
Gold Staters

1. Head of young Heracles r. in lion's skin headdress. The neck ends in a curved line. Except just before and behind the ear, the hair is covered entirely by lion's head, whose open mouth shows a single prominent tooth above and below. The mane is formed by a line of close strokes curving around the mouth with two lines behind it of slightly curved, very narrow V's.
   Rev.: ΦΙΛΙΠΠΩΝ to l. upward. Tripod with three handles, the middle leg a double line; from the two handles at the sides fillets ending in three bunches. Above, laurel branch, butt to l. In field upper r. Phrygian cap. PLATE VI, 3

   8.62 gm. B. V. Head, *A Guide to the Principal Coins of the Greeks*, London, 1959, p. 38, 16.

2. Same.
   Rev.: Similar but in field r. caduceus. PLATE VI, 4

   8.60 gm. *De Luynes*, no. 1571; 8.59 gm. *Königliche Museum zu Berlin Beschreibung der antiken Münzen*, p. 117,1.

The resemblance of both types to the gold with ΘΑΣΙΟΝ ΗΠΕΙΡΟ makes it certain that these followed immediately and are, therefore, the first issue of Philippi.

PHILIPPI IN MACEDONIA

Silver Tetradrachms

3. Head of young Heracles r. like that on the gold staters.
   Rev.: ΦΙΛΙΠΠΩΝ to l. upward. Tripod like that on the gold staters. In field r. long handled axe. PLATE VI, 5
   13.24 gm. Gaebler, op.cit., p. 101,4; 13.25 gm. *Hirsch Sale* 1910, no. 146; 12.86 gm. *De Luynes* no. 1572; 13.2 gm. *Beschreibung* p. 118,7; 13.23 gm. Lucien de Hirsch Coll. Brussels, no. 985.

4. Same.
   Rev.: Similar but in field r. dolphin downward. PLATE VI, 6
   13.4 gm. *Rhousopoulos* no. 943; 13.0 gm. *De Luynes* no. 1573; 13.23 gm. SNG Copenhagen no. 292.

Drachms

5. Similar head of young Heracles.
   Rev.: ΦΙΛΙΠΠΩΝ to l. upward. Similar tripod. In field l. long handled axe. PLATE VI, 7
   3.18 gm. *De Luynes* no. 1574; 3.28 gm. *ANS-Berry.

6. Same.
   Rev.: Similar but in field r. dolphin downward.
   3.24 gm. (holed). Gaebler, op.cit., p. 101; Imhoof-Blumer, *Monnaies grecques*, 90.109; 3.11 gm. *Ratto Sale*, 1927, no. 509; 3.10 gm. *Hirsch Sale* 25, 1909 (Philipsen), no. 414; 3.12 gm. *Beschreibung*, p. 118,9.

7. Same.
   Rev.: Similar but in field r. race torch.
   3.11 gm. *SNG Lockett* no. 1364 = *Pozzi Coll.* Geneva 1921, no. 812.

8. Same.
   Rev.: Similar but in field r., strung bow.
   PLATE VI, 8
   3.05 gm. *ANS-Newell; 3.10 gm. *BMC*, p. 96, no. 4; 3.24 gm. *SNG Copenhagen* no. 293.

Hemidrachms

9. Similar head of young Heracles r.
   Rev.: ΦΙΛΙΠΠΩΝ to l. curving upward. In field r. long handled axe.
   1.65 gm. *Hirsch* 33, 1913, no. 625; 1.61 gm. *Naville* XV, 1930, no. 462; 1.52 gm. ANS-Newell; 1.77 gm. *Beschreibung*, p. 118,12.

10. Same.
   Rev.: Similar but in field r. dolphin downward.
   PLATE VI, 9
   1.58 gm. *Pozzi Coll.* no. 814; 1.54 gm. Rhousopoulos no. 944; 1.5 gm. *Adolph Hess Nachf.* 1936, no. 643; 1.48 gm. *Naville* XIII, 1928, no. 449; 1.49 gm. *ANS-Newell; 1.46 gm. ANS-Newell (Pierced); 1.33 gm. *Weber*, no. 1992; 1.61 gm. *SNG Lockett*, no. 1365; 1.54 gm. Ashmolean ex Milne (Pierced).

11. Same.
   Rev.: Similar but in field r. strung bow.   PLATE VI, 10
   1.60 gm. *De Luynes* no. 1575; 1.59 gm. *Pozzi Coll.* no. 813; 1.55 gm. *Weber 1908 Hirsch* 21, no. 1134; *Burel, Feuardent* 1913, no. 143; 1.55 gm. *ANS-Newell; 1.38 gm. ANS-Newell (Pierced); 1.55 gm. *Beschreibung*, p. 118,10; 1.52 gm. Ibid., no. 11; 1.54 gm. *BMC* p. 97,5.

12. Same.
   Rev.: Similar but in field r. grain of wheat.   PLATE VII, 11
   1.63 gm. Gaebler, op.cit., p. 101,6; 1.52 gm. *Sir Hermann Weber Coll, Spink* 1922, no. 1991; 1.49 gm. *Bement Sale I Naville* VI, 1923, no. 677; *Collignon Feuardent* 1919, no. 186; 1.55 gm. *ANS-Newell; 1.5 gm. *Beschreibung*, p. 118,13; 1.56 gm., 1.52 gm. *BMC*, p. 97, 6f.; 1.63 gm. *SNG Copenhagen*, no. 294.

13. Same.
   Rev.: Similar but in field r. ear of wheat.
   1.5 gm. *Schlesinger* 13, *Hermitage* 1935, no. 605.
   1. grain of wheat.

14. Same.
   Rev.: ΦΙΛΙΓ to r. downward, ΓΩΝ to l. downward. In field lower l. grain of wheat.
   1.6 gm. *Hirsch* 12, 1904, no. 97; 1.58 gm. *Ratto Sale* 1927, no. 510; 1.91 gm. ANS.

Philippi
(Second style)
Gold Staters

15. Head of young Heracles r. in lion's skin headdress, the paws wrapped around the neck. The mane is formed by two rows of wavy lines. The wide-open jaws show no conspicuous teeth and allow Heracles' hair to be seen from forehead to ear. His features are more rounded and less severe.

PHILIPPI IN MACEDONIA 33

Rev.: ΦΙΛΙΓΓΩΝ to l. upward. Tripod with three handles, the legs ending in lion's feet. No laurel above. In field r. horse's head r.

PLATE VII, 12

8.59 gm., P. Lambros, *Sur six Médallions d'Or inédites de Philippi*, Corfu, 1855; two other specimens, ibid.; *BMC*, p. 96, no. 2; 8.59 gm. *Pozzi Coll*, no. 811; 8.58 gm. *Rhousopoulos*, no. 942; 8.58 gm. *Bement Sale* I no. 675; 8.6 gm. *Beschreibung*, p. 117,3; 8.58 gm. *SNG Copenhagen* no. 291; 8.48 gm. *Lucien de Hirsch Coll. Brussels*, no. 984.

16. Same.
    Rev.: Similar but in field r. horse's head l.
    8.605 gm. Lambros, loc.cit.; 8.58 gm. *Egger* 40, *Prowe* 1912, no. 527; 8.55 gm. *Hirsch* 1906, no. 214; 8.57 gm. *Hamburger* 98, 1933, no. 494; 8.59 gm. *Beschreibung*, p. 117,2.

17. Same.
    Rev.: Similar but in field r. lion's head r.
    8.615 gm. Lambros, loc.cit.; 8.58 gm. *Sotheby* 1904, no. 47; same reverse die, *Collignon Feuardent*; 8.52 *De Nanteuil Coll.* 1925, no. 751 = *Weber*, no. 1988 = *Bement*, no. 124; 8.62 gm. BM ex Seltman.

18. Same.
    Rev.: Similar but in field r. stag's head r.
    8.62 gm. Lambros, loc. cit.; two other specimens ibid.; *BMC*, p. 96, no. 3; 8.6 gm. *Hess Vogel Coll.*, 1929, no. 208; 8.59 gm. *Naville* XVII, 1934, no. 340; 8.57 gm. *Boston MFA Warren Coll.*, no. 593; *Montague* II, *Sotheby*, 1897, no. 107; *Bunbury, Sotheby* 1896, no. 679; ibid., no. 680; *R. and F. Durufle*, 1910, no. 316; 8.57 gm. *Beschreibung*, p. 117,4.

19. Same.
    Rev.: Similar but in field r. stag's head l. PLATE VII, 13
    8.63 gm. Lambros, loc.cit.; 8.62 gm. *Jameson* I, no. 960; 8.59 gm. *Weber*, no. 1989; 8.58 gm. *Hirsch* 35 *Philipsen*, no. 413; 8.58 gm. *ANS-Berry; 8.57 gm. *Hirsch* 21 *Weber*, no. 1131; *Late Collector, Sotheby*, 1900, no. 196.

20. Same.
    Rev.: Similar but in field r. bunch of grapes.
    8.655 gm. Lambros, loc.cit.; 8.59 gm. *De Luynes*, no. 1570; 8.62 gm. *Sotheby*, 1921, no. 225; 8.58 gm. *Beschreibung*, p. 117,5; 8.57 gm. Ibid., p. 118,6.

Silver tetradrachms

21. Head of young Heracles r. like that on the gold staters.
    Rev.: ΦΙΛΙΓΓΩΝ to r. downward. Tripod with three handles, the middle leg a double line; from the two handles at the sides fillets

ending in three bunches. Above, laurel branch, butt l. In field l. club, handle down. In ex. HPA.

14.27 gm. *Weber, Hirsch* 21, no. 1132 = *Sir Hermann Weber, Spink* 1922, no. 1990; 14.20 gm. *Schlesinger* 13 *Hermitage*, 1935; 14.27 gm. *BM NC* 1920, p. 107; 13.95 gm. *Beschreibung*, p. 118,8 (no mention of HPA).

22. Same.
    Rev.: Similar but in field l. ear of wheat. No inscription in ex.

PLATE VII, 14

14.07 gm. ANS-Newell (*Bement* I, no. 676).

Something must be said of the weights. The gold is simple. The weights cluster about 8.58 gm.; the single piece of Krenides of 8.55 gm. obviously belongs to the same standard, the Attic, which had already been issued by the Chalcidic League, whose gold seems to have influenced that of Philip.[3] The silver, however, is surprising. The early tetradrachms average 13.17 gm., and even applying Hill's formula of the frequency norm plus 1 per cent raises it only to 13.37 gm. As usual, the fractional issues are somewhat below standard: the drachms average 3.15 gm., the hemidrachms 1.55. But we have enough data to give a consistent picture and that obviously has nothing to do with Olynthus, whose tetradrachms show a standard of 14.50 gm.[4] Nor has it anything to do with the misnamed "Persic" standard of Philip's predecessors or the standard of Philip himself. It is, however, clearly related to the standard inaccurately called "Paeonian" on which the abundant coinage of Damastion was based, and to that phase of it which extended down to 360, for in the immediately succeeding period the weight of Damastion coins drops sharply, perhaps a devaluation intended to hold their market against interference from other mints.[5] Damastion was very obviously much affected by the Chalcidic League, but it would seem that Philippi

---

[3] For the Chalcidic gold, D. M. Robinson and P. A. Clement, *Excavations at Olynthus*, Part IX, Baltimore, 1938; Group L, 392–383 (p. 44); Group S, 364–361 (p. 68); Group T, 361–358 (p. 71); Group W, 352–350 (p. 83).

On Philip's use of the Chalcidic standard, Percy Gardner, *A History of Ancient Coinage*, p. 423, "Philip seems to have taken the standard alike of his gold and silver coins from Olynthus." On his borrowing the obverse type from Olynthus, A. B. West, "The Early Diplomacy of Philip II of Macedon Illustrated by His Coins," *NC*, 1923, pp. 174f.

[4] *Olynthus* IX, pp. 208f.

[5] J. M. F. May, *The Coinage of Damastion*, Oxford, 1939, pp. 12f., p. 83, n. 1.

proposed to compete for influence in the Paeonian region, and she may be considered one element in the circumstances that finally put an end to Damastion's coinage.[6]

Philippi did not, however, persist in her original plan, for the tetradrachms of the Second Style are heavier, and though the four weights that we have are not full, they must be regarded as belonging with the tetradrachms of Philip which continued the standard of the League. An attractive hypothesis is that this change came at the time of the conquest of Olynthus in 348 and the ending of the League's coinage. Philippi, either independently or under Philip's direction, may have been prepared to supply the place of that important silver, and the short duration of the Second Style will then have resulted from Philip's decision to make his own greatly increased output of tetradrachms do that work.[7]

Did the gold cease at the same time? Apparently not. A feature of all the First Style coins is the laurel branch over the tripod, and this the Second Style silver retains, but the gold does not. The inference is that the silver is an intermediate step between the two classes, a product of the very first use of the Second Style. The symbols on its two varieties: club and ear of wheat, do not occur on the gold, but the First Style gold and silver also have different symbols. Probably the Second Style gold was coined as soon, or nearly as soon as the silver, but not sooner because it has no laurel. There are six varieties of the gold, or four if we make the probable assumption that the horse's head r. and l. and the stag's head r. and l. each belong to a single emission. If the gold was coined annually it continued for four

---

[6] May, op.cit., pp. 162f.

[7] An ambiguous statement of Newell's must be cleared up. In *Royal Greek Portrait Coins*, p. 10, he says, "We may be sure that these two cities (Pella and Amphipolis) were throughout his reign the principal centers of coining. In addition, a series of gold staters, silver tetradrachms, drachms and hemidrachms, as well as copper coins, all with autonomous types and inscriptions—were coined at Philippi." On this and the following page he then describes the early tetradrachm having the bearded rider with the kausia, after which come the words, "About 358 B.C. Philip secured Crenides and renamed the little mining town Philippi. He at once commenced to strike here the gold and silver coins mentioned above." By this he certainly meant the autonomous gold and silver of Philippi, but the juxtaposition has deceived the editors of *SNG Copenhagen* into assigning, on Newell's authority, the bearded horseman tetradrachms to Philippi, an attribution which the autonomous silver makes impossible.

years after the introduction of the Second Style. But it is not certain that it was coined annually. In the case of the Chalcidic League, the four issues of gold came 392–383, 364–361, 361–358, 352–350, and while we need not assume a duration of 30 to 40 years for Philippi (which would extend through the reign of Alexander) there is nothing impossible in the assumption of a dozen years (which would extend through that of Philip).

This is opposed to the orthodox view. The authorities all agree that the right of coining gold and silver was taken from Philippi and that thereafter the town was used as a mint for Philip's own coins. The basis for this is Müller's identification of three staters and a diobol (Nos. 86–89) with a tripod as symbol as from the mint of Philippi. With these go a stater, a tetradrachm and a drachm of Alexander (Nos. 145–147). But an article of von Sallet in 1882 (*ZfN* 9, pp. 138–189) discusses the sharing of an obverse die by Müller's No. 88 and a stater with the symbol of his No. 233, with the conclusion that they were issued by a mint other than Philippi. The implications seem to have been overlooked by later writers, but confirmation comes from the Demanhur Hoard where Müller's tetradrachm No. 146 is assigned to Amphipolis (*Demanhur* 1458). The fact is that the royal mint of Philippi is a myth. There is no evidence that Philip's gold or silver—or Alexander's—were ever struck there.

To sum up the dating of the autonomous types: the upper limit of the First Style is 356 when the town got its new name. Of the First Style there are two varieties of gold, two of tetradrachms, four of drachms, five of hemidrachms. We may consider a total of six issues certain, for all the symbols of the larger silver are repeated on the hemidrachms, except the race torch. Either in the year of that issue there were no hemidrachms or there is one with a race torch not known to me; in either case six issues of silver are accounted for, which means six years. Assuming the earliest beginning, assuming that silver was struck every year, and assuming that we know all the varieties, the First Style would have continued from 356–351. There is nothing in the latter year which seems likely to have occasioned the change in style, the heavier standard for tetradrachms and the abandonment of drachms and hemidrachms but, as already suggested, the taking of Olynthus in 348 and the end of Chalcidic League coinage would provide just such an occasion. It is not worth while to spin theories accounting for the extra year or two; we may confidently date the First Style 356–349 B.C. The Second Style silver, then, will have been struck ca. 348, 347 and the gold 348–345 at the very least. The phenomenon of the longer continuation of autonomous gold than of autonomous silver is certainly unexpected, but that is what the evidence shows.[8]

THE DRAMA HOARD

In Newell's trays is a bronze hoard said to have been found at Drama in Macedonia (Noe 338) composed of coins of the city of Philippi, of Philip II and of Alexander III. Drama is 10 miles northwest of the site of Philippi, 25 miles northwest of that of Amphipolis. Recently the American Numismatic Society acquired another larger lot of nearly exactly parallel composition though the condition of the coins was not as good: there is more corrosion and there are more illegible specimens. But it had been in the possession of the dealer from whom it was purchased for many years and it seems evident that it is the residue from which the better pieces had been picked out for Newell's hoard. There is no evidence of any further body of material;

[8] When did Philip's own gold begin? It is the general assumption that it was in 356 at the beginning of his reign. To this West objects (op.cit., pp. 176f.). His first point is very well taken. Plutarch, *Alexander* 3.5, speaks of the simultaneous announcement of the victory of Philip's horse at Olympia and of the birth of Alexander, i.e., 356. In *Alexander* 4.5 he records the fact that Philip used his victorious Olympic chariot as a type for his coins. It is sometimes assumed that the horse and the chariot were victorious at the same time, but West rightly urges that such a double Olympic triumph would certainly have been reported, whereas Plutarch mentions only the horse in 356. If that is not the year for the chariot then presumably it is 352, 348 or 344. The first has nothing particular to recommend it; 348 would make his gold a continuation of that of the League; in 344 came the reorganization of Thessaly when the towns were deprived of their independence. West suggests that Philippi's right of coinage may have ended at the same time and that would, of course, explain very neatly the cessation of our Second Style gold. This point is made with all due reservations and only because there is so much unsettled about Philip's coinage. The use of Plutarch's remark for dating purposes is dangerous; it is likely enough that the tale is only an attempt to explain the type. It is worth recalling, however, that in the early years of his reign Philip was by no means well provided with gold. There is a story which goes back to Duris of Samos that he owned one gold cup weighing 50 drachmae which he took to bed with him and kept under his pillow (Athenaeus IV. 155 c, d).

that is always a possibility but in any case the number we now have is quite enough to justify analysis. In the catalogue I have listed the two lots separately under *1* and *2*, *1* being Newell's Drama Hoard. Coins illustrated on the plates are denoted by an asterisk preceding the entry number.

Philippi

The civic coins fall into four groups.

Group I

Head of young Heracles in lion's skin headdress.
Rev.: ΦΙΛΙΠΠΩΝ to r. downward. Tripod. Above, laurel branch.
    a. No paws around neck. Small tripod with fillets from side handles.
    b. Paws around neck. Small tripod without fillets.
    c. Paws around neck. Large tripod without fillets.

Group II

Similar head.
Rev.: Similar but without laurel branch.

Group III

Similar head.
Rev.: ΦΙΛΙΠΠΩΝ to l. upward. Same type.

Group IV

Similar head.
Rev.: ΦΙΛΙΠΠΩΝ to r. downward. Same type.
The coins are as follows.

			1	2
Group I a				
*1. Head r.	*Rev.*: to l. ivy leaf		4	4
2. Head l.	Same			4
3. Head r.	to l. grapes		1	1
Group I b				
*4. Head r.	to l. grapes		1	3

Group I c

*5. Head l.	to l. ☉	3	2
6. Head l.	to l. ⊕		2

Group II

7. Head r.	to l. upright club and grain of wheat	4	7
*8. Head l.	Same	8	3
*9. Head l.	to l. race torch	7	4
*10. Head l.	to l. M and ear of grain	3	7
*11. Head l.	to l. bow in case	6	14
*12. Head l.	to l. cantharus	1	

Group III

*13. Head l.	to r. cantharus	4	4
*14. Head r.	to r. grapes		1
*15. Head r.	to r. IΠ and amphora	1	
16. Head l.	no symbol	1	

Group IV

*17. Head r.	no symbol	18	45
	Uncertain Group I		1
	Uncertain Group III		3
		62	105

This is not an exhaustive list of varieties. From the easily accessible *BMC*, Gaebler and *SNG Copenhagen* I get the following supplements.

Group I

Fraction. Head r. Gaebler, pl. XX, 9. To r. crescent. *SNG* 302, 303. Symbol obscure. 1.40 gm., 1.05 gm.

Group II

Head r. To l. ᛖ over ear of grain. *BMC* 11.
Head l. To l. wreath. *BMC* 19.

Head l. To l. cista. *BMC* 21; *SNG* 298.
Head r. To l. K over ear of grain; to r. H. *BMC* 10.

Group III

Head r. To r. ear of grain *BMC* 9.
Head l. To r. grapes over IΠ *BMC* 12.

The criterion of style is not so easy to apply to the bronze as to the silver and gold since the cutting is less fine, and only Group I a is to be connected with assurance with the First Style, 356–349. But since Nos. 3 and 4 both have the symbol grapes it is reasonable to suppose that Group I b is a continuation of I a and that the two together provide issues datable in the time of the First Style which might be adequate for 8 years. The Second Style silver, however, has been dated to the years 348, 347 and it is obviously impossible to squeeze all the rest of the bronze into so short a time. If we assume that Nos. 5 and 6 are varieties of the same issue; likewise Nos. 7 and 8; No. 10, *BMC* 9, 10, and 11; Nos. 12 and 13; No. 15 and *BMC* 12; Nos. 16 and 17, there are 11 issues (neglecting others that my casual search has not encountered). At the rate of the earliest bronze, 1 in 2 years, that would give us a span of 22 years and would bring us down to 327 B.C. when Alexander was on the point of invading India. If we suppose an issue every year the coinage of this civic money will still continue to 335, that is through the reign of Philip and for a year after his death. We have already seen the likelihood that the gold coinage lasted through his lifetime. We are now forced to the conclusion that the bronze extended into the reign of Alexander. The condition of these fine fourth century pieces is so nearly uniform as to give us no indication of their order of issue.

Philip II

Head of Apollo

Rev.: ΦΙΛΙΠΠΟΥ Horseman

No symbol   1   2

*18. Head r. Horseman r. wearing kausia   2   1

PHILIPPI IN MACEDONIA

		Symbol only	1	2
19. Head r.	Horseman r. wearing taenia as always hereafter.			
		barley grain	1	4
*20. Head r.	Horseman r. bucranium		3	7
21. Head l.	Horseman r. same			3
*22. Head r.	Horseman r. serpent		1	4
*23. Head r.	Horseman r. spearhead		11	6
24. Head r.	Horseman l. same			2
25. Head l.	Horseman r. spearhead downward			1
*26. Head r.	Horseman r. prow		1	2
*27. Head r.	Horseman r. helmet facing		2	1
*28. Head r.	Horseman r. star		5	4
*39. Head r.	Horseman r. crescent		1	
*30. Head r.	Horseman r. forepart of bull		2	
21. Head r.	Horseman r. dolphin		1	2
*32. Head r.	Horseman r. ivy leaf		1	2
*33. Head r.	Horseman r. club		1	1
34. Head r.	Horseman r. trident		2	2
*35. Head r.	Horseman l. same		1	
*36. Head l.	Horseman l. ✸ (this common symbol is impossible to identify. It has been suggested that it is an insect, an ill-made prow or a degenerate thunderbolt. None of the possibilities is likely)		7	11
37. Head l.	Horseman r. head of goat		1	2
*38. Head r.	Horseman r. same		3	
*39. Head r.	Horseman r. kausia		4	11
40. Head l.	Horseman r. kausia (?)		1	
41. Head l.	Horseman r. thunderbolt lateral			6
42. Head l.	Horseman r. thunderbolt vertical		4	16
*43. Head r.	Horseman r. thunderbolt lateral		3	7
44. Head r.	Horseman r. thunderbolt vertical		1	4
45. Head r.	Horseman r. fly			1
46. Head r.	Horseman r. grapes			1
47. Head r.	Horseman r. cantherus			1

		1	2
With letter or monogram			
48. Head r. Horseman r. A/		4	6
*49. Head r. Horseman r. A/ B		3	4
*50. Head r. Horseman r. A/ club		1	1
*51. Head r. Horseman r. A/ bow		1	1
52. Head r. Horseman r. A/ trident		2	
*53. Head r. Horseman r. Ᵽ trident		4	1
54. Head r. Horseman r. Ᵽ			3
55. Head r. Horseman r. N			3
*56. Head r. Horseman r. NI		1	4
57. Head r. Horseman r. N trident		1	4
*58. Head r. Horseman l. N		4	2
59. Head r. Horseman r. E		2	17
60. Head r. Horseman r. Ǝ		4	2
61. Head l. Horseman r. Ɛ			2
62. Head r. Horseman r. A		3	7
*63. Head r. Horseman r. Λ		6	4
64. Head r. Horseman r. Ḁ		2	
65. Head r. Horseman r. Γ		9	16
66. Head r. Horseman r. Γ dolphin			1
67. Head r. Horseman l. Γ			1
68. Head l. Horseman r. thunderbolt in Γ			1
69. Head r. Horseman r. ΔI		2	2
*70. Head r. Horseman r. ⲎP		1	4
71. Head r. Horseman r. ⲎH			2
*72. Head r. Horseman r. I		1	3
*73. Head r. Horseman r. ⊙		4	3
74. Head r. Horseman r. ♀			4
*75. Head r. Horseman r. ⊙P		4	3
76. Head r. Horseman r. A♀			1
*77. Head r. Horseman r. Æ		1	1
78. Head r. Horseman r. ΛA			1
79. Head r. Horseman r. ΛY			1
80. Head r. Horseman r. Δ ?		1	
*81. Head r. (A on *obv.*) Horseman r. E		4	7
82. Head l. (A on *obv.*) Horseman r. E		2	1

		1	2
83. Head r. (A on *obv.*) Horseman r. A		6	1
*84. Head r. (A on *obv.*) Horseman r. Γ		1	
Head r. (A on *obv.*) Horseman r. uncertain symbol		1	1
		135	217

Doubles

		1	2
*85. Head r.	Horseman r. E thunderbolt 8.932 gm.	1	
*86. Head r.	Horseman r. Ǝ 7.660 gm.	1	
*87. Head r.	Horseman r. A 8.027 gm.	1	
Head r.	Horseman r. uncertain symbol		3
		3	3

There are two indications of the order of striking of Philip's coins. No. 18 shows the horseman wearing a kausia, the broad-brimmed Macedonian hat. There is also silver on which the horseman wears a kausia; he is bearded, but the scale of the bronze is too small to show whether our horseman is intended to be bearded or not. That silver is generally put first[9] and presumably the associated bronze should be also. Then, a specimen of No. 83 is struck over a coin like No. 51: a portion of the bow shows beneath the later striking. Except for the instance noted, the contemporary silver issues seem to give no help with the arrangement. It is immediately apparent how badly we need a systematic study of Philip's coinage when we begin to face the question of the time it took to produce all these varieties. The neatest arrangement would be to have an issue each year with its distinctive magistrate's mark, but clearly this will not do without some adjustment, for we should have more years than there were in Philip's reign, 359–336. There are 31 varieties with no symbol or with symbol only, which is more than enough to take care of his maximum of 24 years, assuming that we have all the varieties. The number of varieties may be reduced to 24 by making the probable combination of the same symbol with different positions of the head or horseman. But, in addition, disregarding the uncertain symbols, our list shows 36 entries with letter or monogram. This can and should be reduced by com-

---

[9] West, *NC*, 1923, pp. 174f.

bining various forms of the same letter and issues whose only difference is the position of head or horseman; it is also reasonable to combine N and NI, ☉, ႃ and ☉P and, more doubtfully perhaps, the varieties having A on the obverse with the others bearing the same reverse letter. Another means of reduction is to combine Nos. 48–52 and assume that N is the magistrate for the year. This raises the interesting question whether his subordinates: B, club, bow, trident served for part of a year each or worked simultaneously in different places (with N working sometimes alone without subordinate). Similarly Nos. 55–58 may be assumed to be the product of N working sometimes alone, sometimes with a subordinate: trident. But this is as far as consolidation can go and we are left with 14 issues with letter or monogram which is still too many. Consideration of the problem must be postponed until we have listed the coins of Alexander.

Alexander III

Head of young Heracles r. in lion's skin headdress.
Rev.: ΑΛΕ ΞΑΝΔΡΟΥ between club and bow-in-case.

		1	2
88.	Club below, handle l. no symbol	2	4
*89.	Club below, handle l. one handled cup below	4	
*90.	Club below, handle l. ear of grain below		1
*91.	Club above, off flan dolphin below		2

With letter

		1	2
*92.	Club above, handle l. E below	10	11
*93.	Club above, handle l. ΔI below	1	
94.	Club above, handle l. I below		1
95.	Club above, handle l. K below		1
96.	Club below, handle l. Λ below	1	
97.	Club below, handle l. ΜΡ below		1
98.	Club below, handle l. A below		1
	Club below, handle l. uncertain symbol	1	
	Club above, handle l. no visible symbol		3

PHILIPPI IN MACEDONIA

Same type.
Rev.: Club and quiver instead of bow-in-case.   *1*   2

99. Club above, handle l. no symbol	3	11
100. Club below, handle l. no symbol		5
*101. Club below, handle l. upright caduceus above	2	
102. Club above, handle l. lateral caduceus above, star below		1
*103. Club below, handle l. thunderbolt above	4	3

With letter

104. Club above, handle l. thunderbolt above, Δ below	9	8
105. Club above, handle l. thunderbolt above, ∇ below	1	
*106. Club below, handle r. Δ above, thunderbolt below		1
*107. Same but *head l.* on *obv.*		1
*108. Club below, handle r. Δ above, ear of grain below	1	
*109. Club below, handle r. ∇ above, ear of grain below	1	
*110. Club below, handle r. Δ above, trident below	1	2
111. Club above, handle r. trident above, Δ below (?)		1
112. Club below, handle r. Δ above, star below	3	1
*113. Club below, handle l. ∇ above, grapes below, stem l.	1	6
*114. Club below, handle r. Δ above, grapes below, stem r.	1	1
*115. Club below, handle r. ∇ above, grapes below, stem at top	1	
*116. Club below, handle r. Δ above, ivy leaf below		1
*117. Club below, handle l. Δ above	1	
*118. Club above, handle l. Δ above	1	2
119. Club above, handle l. Δ below		1
*120. Club above, handle l. A above	1	1
121. Club below, handle l. A below		2
*122. Club above, handle l. Π above	5	13
123. Club below, handle r. Π below		1
*124. Club below, handle r. Γ below	1	
125. Club below, handle r. Γ (?)	1	
*126. Club above, handle l. ⋉ above		1
127. Club above, handle l. ⋈ (?) below		1
128. Club above, handle r. ⊙ in field l., l below		1

		1	2
*129. Club above, handle l. Λ above		2	2
*130. Club above, handle l. ⊁E above		24	31
*131. Club below, handle r. ME below		1	1
*132. Club above, handle l. ⋊ above		1	
*133. Club above, handle l. K above		1	1
*134. Club below, handle r. K below		2	1
*135. Club below, handle r. ΛA below		1	
*136. Club below, handle l. Φ below			1
137. Club below, handle r. Φ below			4
*138. Club below, handle r. ΦI below		2	2
139. Club below, handle r. IN below			1
Club below, handle l. uncertain symbol			3
Club off flan	symbol off flan	1	
		92	137

Similar head of Heracles
Rev.: BA between quiver above and club below, handle r. Serpent below.

*140. *SNG Copenhagen, Macedonia*, pl. 27, 1026–1028. "C. 320 B.C."   1

Similar types. Uncertain symbol.

141.   1

Head of Apollo r.
Rev.: AΛE ΞANΔP Horseman l., thunderbolt below.

*142. Ibid., pl. 27, 1030. "Amphipoli c. 310–300"   1

Similar head of Heracles
Rev.: ΣA above AΛE ΞANΔPOY between club, handle r., above and strung bow surrounding bow case. Below, P.

*143. Ibid., pl. 27, 1049. "Cyprus, Salamis, c. 332–320 B.C."   1

Similar head of Heracles.
Rev.: BAΣIΛEΩΣ between bow-in-case above and club below, handle l.
Race torch below. Countermarked lion's head r.

*144. Ibid., pl. 29, 1117. "Anonymous bronze after c. 311   1
B.C."
Head of Nymph r.
Rev.: Tripod, to l. and r. KY and Il. Cantharus lower l., monogram lower r.

*145. *BMC, Mysia*, p. 37, no. 137. "Cyzicus"   1

Total   292   462

    On the standard type the difference between the bow-in-case and the quiver is not always recognized but it is quite obvious that we have to do here with separate series. No symbol is common to both classes and only one letter: Λ which appears below with the bow-in-case and above with the quiver. Is the difference in place of striking or in time? There are difficulties either way. To assume that there is a difference in time is to suppose that one class used first symbol alone and then letter, and that the second reverted to symbol alone before beginning its longer output of letters. The difference is of a kind generally associated with difference of mint, but I cannot separate them on stylistic grounds and both classes share letters with coins of Philip which do not seem possible to divide. Perhaps under Alexander there were two workshops in the town at the beginning but the bow-in-case soon ceased.

    To return to the problem of Philip's too numerous strikings. I had thought of the hypothesis of simultaneous issues of different varieties not apparently connected, which would reduce the number of years when bronze was struck by an amount impossible to calculate. But Miss Thompson suggests a more plausible theory. It will be noticed that the majority of Philip's issues (if we accept the consolidated list) have neither letter nor monogram, whereas only 5 of Alexander's have symbols alone. Two of these are dolphin and thunderbolt which also occur as symbols under Philip. The list will show that some of the letters also are common to both kings: E, Ɛ, A, Γ, ΔI, I, ⊙, ΛA. While this is not a long list it is not negligible. The theory suggested is that Philip's own issues used symbols alone, and that those bearing his name with letters or monograms are posthumous, struck parallel with Alexander's types. The posthumous striking of gold and silver with Philip's types is well established, and this would only extend the principle to the small change. To be sure, Philip's posthumous tetradrachms were on a different standard from Alexander's and so may have served an economic purpose, but that was not true of the gold which would be, like this, a concession to sentiment and custom. The problem of getting all the issues into the years available would then be settled. Nos. 18–47 of Philip would be those of his lifetime while Nos. 48–80 would very well fit into that of Alexander.

As may be seen from the list, which has been organized with this possibility in mind, Alexander's coins can be arranged in the same way: first the issues with symbols only (the dolphin and thunderbolt being shared with Philip); then a large output of Δ and his subordinates: thunderbolt, ear of grain, trident, star, grapes and ivy leaf, which would be parallel to Philip's group (probably of a different year) under Ν, with Ρ and Ν showing the latest examples of letter and symbol combined. Thereafter would come Alexander's letters and monograms: 12 varieties after Δ. The presence of Nos. 140–144, which are probably posthumous, assures us that these bronzes lasted through Alexander's reign—and perhaps for some years thereafter. There would therefore be ample time to take care of the Philip and Alexander coins we know without resorting to the possibility of simultaneous issues not apparently related. That might later be forced on us by the discovery of a large number of varieties not in the Drama Hoard, but with our present information, it seems most likely that posthumous bronze of Philip continued to be struck with a regularity and in a quantity matching Alexander's own issues, the two series sometimes being entrusted to one official, but more generally to different ones.

Where were our royal coins struck? Newell seems to have begun the arrangement of this hoard—to which he never gave more than passing attention—on the assumption that the coins came from Amphipolis, and then to have been assailed by doubts. Almost all of Alexander's coins with Δ were labelled "Amphipolis" but thereafter there is no indication, except that Nos. 50 and 94 are marked "Mint"? For there is a difficulty that he himself had made it impossible to overlook. The letters and symbols on these bronzes do not agree with the symbols on the silver. It is true that the tetradrachms show thunderbolt, grapes and ear of grain, but it is clear that on the bronze it is Δ that is the important differential, and Δ does not appear on the silver. This in itself would be no necessary bar to considering Amphipolis as the probable mint, for Newell had already recognized that the systems of symbols on bronze and silver might be quite independent of each other.[10] But, as it happens, there are bronzes with different types whose symbols do agree with those of the silver of Amphipolis, and which he assigned to that city. In his *Reattribution*, pp. 12 f., he dealt with the fractions of the tetradrachms, five denominations of silver and two of bronze, whose reverses show one or two eagles on a thunderbolt, or a thunderbolt alone, which had been regarded as the first issue of the reign. He showed that, instead, they were connected by symbols with the sequence of tetradrachms (then attributed to Pella, but subsequently corrected to Amphipolis) which was the central part of his study. The bronzes then known to him bore the symbols wreath (cf. tetradrachm type VIII), ivy leaf (cf. tetradrachm type X) and crescent (cf. tetradrachm type XXIX). There is a bronze at Yale with a bunch of grapes as symbol (cf. tetradrachm type XI); there are also some with no symbol which apparently he did not then know, but he said of fractional silver with no symbol, "these, I think, we may reasonably attribute to the opening years of the tetradrachm series" (i.e., types I–VI). If this be allowed, the minor silver and bronze combined show 15 correspondences with the tetradrachms, types I–XXXIV, of Series A. This is a reasonable proportion, since the fractions are clearly not struck with the regularity of the tetradrachms. But this carries us only down to 327 according to Newell's later calculation. What is the bronze of Amphipolis for the rest of the reign and the interregnum? There are two candidates: bronze of the same types of Heracles head and eagle on thunderbolt, one having Λ and one A in place of symbol. They can hardly be separated from the others in place of minting, but they do not have the same reason for being attributed to Amphipolis: Λ and A do not appear on the tetradrachms of that city (except for the late ones with Λ and a race torch). It is not impossible that the bronze,

[10] *Demetrius*, p. 120. "It is probable that the less valuable metal was coined either in a special *officina* of the mint and under the supervision of an entirely different set of magistrates or, as is very likely, the coining of bronze pieces was farmed out to private individuals. Such a practice may have been more prevalent in ancient times than we suspect or have the means of determining."

originally entrusted to the same officials who issued the tetradrachms, was later given over, as Newell suggests, to a separate officina or to private individuals. But it compromises the neatness of the original argument for Amphipolis.

Now the dilemma is obvious. If the Alexanders of the Drama Hoard belong to Amphipolis, as Newell's earlier labels assert, what are we to do with the other type? Are we to suppose that the two alternated, or that the eagles belong only to the earlier years, the bows and clubs to the later? In either case, why are the eagles not represented in the hoard? Style and condition give no indication of a break between our Philips and our Alexanders, and it can hardly be seriously suggested that some discriminating individual, ancient or modern, weeded out all the eagles from preference. A further complication is the fact that the weights of the two types are different. While the bow and club coins weigh over 6.00 gm., the eagles weigh about 4.00 gm. Should the second be regarded as a fraction of the first? That might explain their non-appearance in the hoard, but it would not get rid of the difficulty of having fractions (in two denominations: Newell's Bronze II, *Reattribution*, pp. 12 f.) whose symbols paralleled the silver while those of the larger denomination did not. Nor does the appearance of the two types suggest that they belong together.

Apparently we must relegate one group to some other mint. In favor of Amphipolis for the royal coins of the Drama Hoard is the general probability that this mint of the first importance would provide the largest amount of money in all metals; against it is the problem of the two types: the equally difficult alternatives of combining them or of displacing to another site the home of that type definitely connected with Amphipolis by symbols. In favor of Philippi is the homogeneous appearance of the royal and civic coins in the hoard. If there were no critical decision involved it would certainly be agreed that they all came from the same mint. Against Philippi is the fact that we should be forced to accept unexpected consequences. It would mean that the city of Philippi, which was not the capital,[11] was

[11] Is it not possible that Philip originally intended it to replace the old capital of Pella, as Pella had earlier replaced the still older capital of Aegae? This is the first instance known to us of the naming of a town after its human founder—a practice to become so familiar under Alexander—and it may be that the special circumstances of its origin entitled it to special treatment thereafter.

allowed to strike its own types and simultaneously those of the king.[12] What would be the purpose of this double function? Was the right of coining bronze so early recognized to be a source of revenue, as it came to be later, and was Philippi being allowed in this way her share in the king's profit? This question cannot be avoided by assigning the royal bronze to Amphipolis. Why was the striking of civic bronze permitted to continue at Philippi into the period of the kings when it did nowhere else?[13]

And the issuance of the king's bronze would not be merely a minor function. Philippi would appear to have been the main source of royal Macedonian bronze. Neither the eagles nor any other group can compete in size with the types of Philip and Alexander represented in the Drama Hoard, and unless same means can be found hereafter to distribute those types among several mints, we must believe that the bulk of the small change designed for Macedonia was the product of one city. No one would have supposed *a priori* that the city was Philippi.

There is nothing to be gained by pressing a solution for which the evidence is not sufficient. It can only be said that a new possibility has arisen as to the location of the main Macedonian mint for bronze. However, other considerations may be useful in the future study of the Alexander coinage. It is well to know that regal and civic issues could be simultaneous in the same district, whether or not in the same city. It is clear that bronze may have a set of symbols quite independent of silver and gold. This is not always true,[14] but attention to the eagle series shows that there may be both correspondence and lack of correspondence within the same group, so that we must be on our guard against preconceptions and too great reliance on analogy. It is well to

---

[12] Amphipolis is the only other place for which such a combination can possibly be suggested. It is taken for granted that the autonomous issues ceased when Amphipolis became a royal mint (e.g., Gaebler, pp. 32f.) and the three denominations of bronze are consequently dated before 357. But that is probable rather than proven. No other town presents even a doubtful case.

[13] An old theory needs to be repeatedly denied since it is repeatedly asserted: that bronze coins had no value outside the city of their origin. The evidence of hoards and excavations combine to refute it. To the possessor of the Drama Hoard the bronzes of Philippi 10 miles away were certainly as worth keeping as those of the kings.

[14] E.g., *Tarsos*, pp. 38–40.

know that a bronze issue may be so large as to employ a senior official with subordinates, and well to be aware of the possibility that Philip's small currency in Macedonia persisted through the reign of his successor.

These are cautionary matters which may make the study of Alexander's bronze safer, but are not likely to make it easier. There is no need to point out how inconclusive this investigation has been, but I do not believe that it requires apology. It was not undertaken in the expectation of finding easy answers, but in the conviction that no answers at all were possible until the questions had been asked. We need a great deal more information before we can have much confidence in our conclusions, but where there are so many problems unsolved one must begin somewhere and it is to be hoped that this will be received, as it is intended, as a beginning only, which may lead to more profitable studies in the future.

ALFRED R. BELLINGER

SELEUCID COINS FROM CILICIA CA. 220–150 B.C.

(See PLATES XII–XIII)

I. THE MINT OF TARSUS

It has long been considered an enigma that practically no Seleucid silver coinage from the period ca. 220–150 B.C. can be attributed to the district of Cilicia. It is particularly surprising that we have apparently no silver coins from the great and important city of Tarsus, renamed Antiochia on the Cydnus in the third century B.C.,[1] between the first years of Antiochus III and the reign of Alexander Balas (150–145), when a peculiar local type, the hero Sandan standing on a horned animal, was first introduced on the royal silver.[2]

Since the publication of E. T. Newell's masterly studies on the *Eastern* and *Western Seleucid Mints* we have at our disposal a complete record of the Seleucid coinage down to and including Antiochus III. Perhaps a careful investigation of the coinages of Antiochus III may help us to solve the "Cilician riddle." Let us first consider the iconography of Antiochus III as exemplified by the continuous coin series from the prolific mint at the western capital, Antioch on the Orontes. Antiochus III ascended the Seleucid throne at the age of 18 in 223. His first coin series (ca. 223–213) shows a very young and smooth face, untouched by the toils of governing the extensive empire.[3] The second series (ca. 213–208) shows a transitional portrait, the smooth youthfulness giving way to a more mature expression.[4] The hair at the side of the head recedes, leaving a bald patch at the temple below the diadem. With the third series yet another portrait appears. Here the king looks still older, his face is lean, sometimes nearly emaciated, the bald forehead and the long pointed

---

[1] Cf. *RE* Zweite Reihe IV, s.v. Tarsos, col. 2418f.
[2] Cf. D. H. Cox in Goldman, *Tarsus* I, 52. Imhoof-Blumer, *Monnaies grecques*, 433, no. 96.
[3] *WSM* nos. 1044–1053, pl. xxvi, 11–18; xxvii, 1–7.
[4] *WSM* nos. 1067–1074, pl. xxviii, 1–11.

nose are the most prominent features.⁵ With several variations and a greater or lesser degree of idealization, this type is carried on to the end of the reign. We have thus two easily distinguishable portraits, the first and the third here mentioned, joined by a small group of transitional style. According to Newell's chronological scheme the intermediate group dates between 213 and 209/8.⁶

The same general stylistic development of the royal portrait can be traced at other mints as well. It goes without saying that the evolution did not run absolutely parallel at all places. Sometimes the "transitional" style comprises only very few obverses while at other mints it appears on a substantial quantity of dies. The same stylistic features might make their appearance at different mints at different times.⁷ However, Newell was certainly right in his main conclusions on the portraiture of Antiochus III.

Only at one mint does Newell's arrangement seem to me to contradict his own general principles. At Tyre we find the line of stylistic development rather confused.⁸ For the sake of brevity and clarity I give a list of the tetradrachms attributed to Tyre arranged according to my view of the evolution of the portrait style:

WSM nos. 1251–52   pl. XLV 1–2
      1253   pl. XLV 3
      1268   pl. XLVI 3–4
      1261–64, 1266–67   pl. XLV 12–15, 18; pl. XLVI 1–2
      1260   pl. XLV 11
      1255   pl. XLV 5–6
      1270   pl. XLVI 6

This arrangement, as compared with Newell's classification, calls for a few comments. Let us first look at the dating of *WSM* nos. 1253 and 1268. As to the first coin Newell describes the portrait as "still somewhat youthful." In my opinion this is a clear understatement. The portrait is very youthful indeed, and closely related in style to the preceding coins, *WSM* nos. 1251–52, as well as to the first series

---

⁵ *WSM* nos. 1088 ff., pl. xxix, 8 ff. The first coin of Series III is especially characteristic, the following coins being more idealized. Cf. *WSM*, 150.
⁶ *WSM*, 143.
⁷ *WSM*, 396.
⁸ *WSM*, 200–208.

from Antioch. It is, consequently, most surprising that Newell dates this obverse die to the period ca. 201–197, when all parallels point to a date 15–20 years earlier. Much the same applies to *WSM* no. 1268, only here the incongruity is made more striking by the dating which is to the last period of Antiochus III's reign, 197–187. On the other hand, Newell's dating of *WSM* no. 1255, ca. 201–197, is quite consistent with the parallel material from other mints, but the place in the Tyrian sequence is questionable. To place this coin, clearly showing the late portrait, before *WSM* no. 1268 with the youthful head comes close to destroying all argumentation from the position of portrait style.

All the difficulties inherent in Newell's classification derive from a single fact. Except for a very short period, 219–217, where Newell places *WSM* nos. 1251–52, Antiochus III was only able to strike coins in Tyre after his final acquisition of Coelesyria in 201–200, while the silver coins attributed to Tyre would fit much better as the output of a mint working for Antiochus III continually throughout his reign. Of course one can object that the development of portrait style at Tyre might possibly differ from that of other mints. Even if one accepts some modifications of Newell's arrangement, the attribution to Tyre might be saved in this way. In principle this attitude is justified, but in this particular case it will not do. From the bronze issues certainly struck at Tyre after 201 (*WSM* nos. 1256–59 and 1272–1280), many of which are dated according to the Seleucid Era, we know that at Tyre at this period a "late" portrait of Antiochus with bald forehead, long pointed nose, and hollow cheeks, was used. The conspicuous discrepancy between the portraits such as *WSM* pl. XLVI, 3–4 (silver dated by Newell ca. 197–187), and *WSM* pl. XLVI, 8–10 (bronze issues of 197/6, 196/5 and 194/3), cannot be explained away. We can hardly assume that the silver coins of a certain mint lagged behind the less important bronze issues of the same place stylistically.

Let us now examine Newell's reasons for attributing this silver to Tyre. In his first work on the subject[9] he adduces, as far as I can see, four arguments:

---

[9] *NNM* 10 (1921). Newell's later works on this series (*NNM* 73 [1936] and *WSM*, 200–208) seem to present no new arguments for the attribution.

1. It is "difficult to believe," nay "in fact, impossible," that the important commercial town of Tyre should have stopped issuing silver coins between 201 and 150, when the well known series with "eagle" reverse of Phoenician weight was introduced by Alexander Balas.[10]

It is always difficult to argue for or against probabilities. In this connection I should like to point out that the equally important commercial and maritime centers of Sidon and Berytus did not, as far as I know, produce any silver coins during this period,[11] the only certain issues of Seleucid silver from a Phoenician city before Alexander Balas being the coins of Seleucus IV, Antiochus IV, and Antiochus V from Ace-Ptolemais.[12]

2. Newell finds a close connection between the Tyrian bronze coins and some of the tetradrachms, pointing to the similarity between the portraits and in the style of the die-cutting.[13]

Stylistic similarity is a rather vague and subjective criterion. In my opinion the parallels adduced by Newell are not conclusive, all the portraits being of the same "late" type. This gives them a certain similarity, which need not imply a common place of origin.

3. On some of the tetradrachms and drachms (*WSM* nos. 1260, 1263, 1266–68, 1271) a club appears as symbol—"the customary attribute of Tyrian Heracles and the usual symbol of the mint of Tyre."[14]

Here we arrive at Newell's best argument for the attribution to Tyre, and I have a strong suspicion that this club-symbol was the point of departure for his theory. As the club is also found on most of the related issues of Antiochus III's successors down to Demetrius I, Newell was undoubtedly right in concluding that this symbol was the mint mark of the city where the coins were issued, not a magistrate's personal badge. Equally certain is the fact that the club as the attribute of Heracles-Melqart was one of the most important

---

[10] *NNM* 10 (1921), 2–3.
[11] We have no statistics on the relative importance of the Phoenician cities during the first half of the second century. During the latter half, Tyre certainly acquires a dominant position, but until 150, Sidon and Berytus were at least equally important. It is my impression that during this period Sidon has the best claim to be regarded as the *prima inter pares* of the Phoenician communities.
[12] See, most recently, Mørkholm, *Studies in the Coinage of Antiochus IV* (1963), 44 ff.
[13] *NNM* 10 (1921), 7.
[14] *NNM* 10 (1921), 16.

numismatic types and symbols used at Tyre.[15] However, two points may be made in this connection. On the Tyrian issues of Ptolemy V, struck immediately before the Seleucid conquest, as well as on the Tyrian coins of Alexander Balas the club symbol is never used alone but always surmounted by the monogram of Tyre.[16] Here the reference is explicit, but the use of a club alone has not the same significance. As a coin type or symbol the club may be found nearly anywhere in the Greek world, as there are any number of cities where the cult of Heracles was prominent.

4. The tetradrachms of Demetrius I from our series "closely resemble in style and technique" the succeeding Phoenician tetradrachms of Alexander Balas.[17]

Again a subjective argument from style, which is not conclusive. To stress a more tangible aspect of numismatics, it is worth pointing out that there is absolutely no connection between these two issues as regards moneyers' monograms, which one might expect if they derived from the same mint.

No one of Newell's arguments for attributing our silver to Tyre is decisive, and the development of the portrait of Antiochus III tells strongly against it, indicating, as already stated, a mint under Seleucid control throughout the reign. On the other hand, Newell was undoubtedly right in ascribing the coins "to a mint whose location could not have been at any very great distance from Antioch, that is to say, as far away as Asia Minor or Babylonia. We must, therefore, look nearer home—perhaps in Cilicia, Syria, or along the Phoenician coast."[18] Having accepted the western origin of the coin series, we must now find a mint which was in the possession of Antiochus III throughout his reign (thus ruling out Phoenicia) and where the cult of Heracles took a prominent place. Both conditions are best satisfied by Tarsus, whose local hero, Sandan, was identified

---

[15] Cf. *BMC Phoenicia*, pl. xxix, 18–19; pl. xxx; pl. xxxi, 9 and 14; pl. xxxii, 1 and 4. Cf. also the bronze coin *WSM*, pl. xlvi, 14.

[16] Svoronos, Τὰ νομίσματα τοῦ κράτους τῶν Πτολεμαίων, nos. 1297–98, pl. xlii, 23. *NNM* 34 (1927), 15–17.

[17] *NNM* 10 (1921), 38.

[18] *NNM* 10 (1921), 6. After the peace of Apamea, 188, a mint in Asia Minor outside Cilicia is, of course, excluded.

by the Greeks with Heracles.[19] On a Tarsian bronze issue of this period the club of the hero is actually used as the obverse type.[20] Consequently, in my opinion, Tarsus has the best claim as the mint of the silver series here under discussion. However, a difficulty is created by the existence of *WSM* nos. 1328–29, two early coins of Antiochus III, the only silver of this reign which has up to the present day been attributed to Tarsus. In my opinion these coins belong elsewhere, and quite provisionally I venture to suggest an attribution to Laodicea ad mare.

Thus the existence of a continuous issue of silver coins from Tarsus down to the reign of Demetrius I has been established.[21] In passing, I should like to point out that under Seleucus IV more coins were issued here than appears from the material listed by Newell. An issue with the symbol *Nike* ascribed by him to Antioch[22] shows so close a resemblance to some of the Tarsus coins, that it must originate in the same mint (PLATE XII, 1–3, 5).

II. THE MINT OF SOLI

The attribution to Tarsus of the silver formerly ascribed to Tyre has consequences for another Seleucid series. As *WSM* nos. 1282 to 1287 Newell has listed a small and compact group of tetradrachms, which show a marked stylistic affinity with his "Tyrian" silver.[23] Before we proceed to discuss this issue it will be necessary to list the coins struck by Antiochus III's successors at the same mint. They are all in silver. The die-position is ↑↑ with small variations.

---

[19] Cf. *RE* Zweite Reihe I, s.v. Sandon.

[20] See D. H. Cox in Goldman, *Tarsus* I, 49.

[21] A drachm of Antiochus IV with the symbol club was actually found during the excavations in Tarsus. Cf. D. H. Cox in Goldman, *Tarsus* I, 46. Of course, the find spot of a single coin is not very revealing for its place of origin.

[22] *SMA*, 14, no. 33. Of this issue the following specimens are known to me: a) New York, ANS; 16.97 gm. (PLATE XII, 2). b) Paris, *Rois de Syrie* no. 472; 17.10 gm. c) Athens, 16.75 gm. d) Vienna, 17.0 gm. (PLATE XII, 5). e) Glasgow, *Hunter Coll.* III, 38, no. 2; 17.14 gm. f) Paris, from the excavations at Susa. g) Cambridge, *General Coll.*; 17.08 gm. h) Beirut, American University Coll. no. 2487. Specimens a–c were struck from one obverse die, d–g from another.

[23] *WSM* no. 1281 may belong to the same mint. The bird symbol in the l. field is by Newell taken to be the dove of Ascalon, but it might well be an owl.

SELEUCID COINS FROM CILICIA

Seleucus IV

187–175 B.C.

1. *Obv.*: Diademed head of the king r.; fillet border.
   Rev.: Apollo seated l. on omphalos, holding in r. hand arrow, l. hand resting on bow; ΒΑΣΙΛΕΩΣ ΣΕΛΕΥΚΟΥ; in l. field *head of Athena* l.; in exergue ⋈ and ΣΑ. Tetradrachm.
   a. 17.03   Glasgow, *Hunter Coll.* III, 38, no. 9, pl. lxvi, 3. PLATE XII, 6.

2. Same types and inscription as preceding. *Rev.*: in l. field ΔΙ above *owl*; in r. field ΟΝ. Drachms.
   a. 4.07   New York, ANS. Chisel cut. PLATE XII, 4.
   b. 4.12   Berlin. *Rev.*: Letters and symbol in l. field off flan.

Antiochus IV

175–164 B.C.

1. *Obv.*: Diademed head of the king r.; fillet border.
   Rev.: Apollo seated l. on omphalos, holding in r. hand arrow, l. hand resting on bow; ΒΑΣΙΛΕΩΣ ΑΝΤΙΟΧΟΥ; in l. field ^N_O above *head of Athena*; in r. field ΣΑ. Tetradrachms.
   a.   Paris, from the Susa excavations.[24] PLATE XII, 7.
   b. 17.15   Turin, *Fabretti*, no. 4628.[25]

2. Same types and inscription as preceding. *Rev.*: in l. field ⋈ above *owl perched on bunch of grapes*; in r. field ⋔. Tetradrachm.
   a. 16.85   Paris, *Rois de Syrie*, no. 517. PLATE XIII, 1.

3. Same types and inscription as no. 1. *Rev.*: in l. field ⋔ above *owl*; in r. field ΣΑ. Tetradrachms.[26]
   a. 17.00   London, *BMC Seleucid Kings*, 111, no. 4a. PLATE XIII, 3.
   b. 16.96   Paris, new acquisition ex *SNG* III (Lockett Coll.), no. 3123 ex Naville Sale VII, 1924 (Bement Coll.), no. 1680.
   c. 17.05   Turin, *Fabretti*, no. 4631.

---

[24] I am much indebted to M. le Rider of the Bibliothèque Nationale for sending me a plaster cast of this important coin and allowing me to publish it.
[25] Nos. 1a–b are from the same pair of dies. I owe my best thanks for photographs of the coins in Turin to Dr. Anna Serena Fava.
[26] Nos. 3a–c are from the same dies and share the obverse die with no. 2a.

Demetrius I

162–150 B.C.

1. *Obv.*: Diademed head of the king r.; laurel wreath.
    Rev.: Tyche seated l. holding in r. hand short staff, in l. hand cornucopiae; ΒΑΣΙΛΕΩΣ ΔΗΜΗΤΡΙΟΥ; in l. field ⋈ above *owl*; in r. field ⊢Ε. Tetradrachms.[27]
    a. 16.74   *Coll. Jameson* III, no. 2349. PLATE XIII, 4.
    b. 16.69   Hess/Leu Auction Sale, April 16, 1964, no. 239.

Demetrius II

First reign, 146–138 B.C.

1. *Obv.*: Diademed head of the king r.; fillet border.
    Rev.: Apollo seated l. on omphalos, holding in r. hand arrow, l. hand resting on bow; [Β]ΑΣΙΛΕΩΣ [Δ]ΗΜΗΤΡΙΟΥ [ΦΙ]ΛΑΔΕΛΦΟΥ [ΝΙ]ΚΑΤΟΡΟΣ; in l. field *owl*; in exergue AR. Drachm.
    a. 4.02   New York, ANS. PLATE XIII, 5.

As already stated, the general similarity in style and fabric of *WSM* nos. 1282–87 with the silver thought to be Tyrian was pointed out by Newell, and consequently he attributed the coins to an uncertain mint in southern Coelesyria, mentioning Sidon, Ace-Ptolemais, and Damascus as possibilities.[28] A survey of the whole series listed here confirms the accuracy of Newell's stylistic observation. Furthermore, some moneyers' monograms and initials such as ΣΑ, ⋈, ⋈ are common to both series, revealing most probably the same persons working at two mints within the same area. With the removal of the "Tyrian" silver to Tarsus in Cilicia we must look for the mint of our coins in the same province. Besides stylistic similarity and the reappearance of various monograms, there is another feature which marks the coins under discussion as a coherent series issued by one mint: the symbols *head of Athena* and *owl*. As they appear from the time of Antiochus III until the first reign of Demetrius II, we can

---

[27] Nos. 1a–b are from the same dies.
[28] *WSM*, 211.

assume with confidence that they must stand for the city in the same way as the club on the preceding series. Thus we have to look for a mint in Cilicia, where Athena and her owl were prominent. Unfortunately we are left with several possibilities. Mallus, or its harbour Magarsus, could boast of the famous cult of Athena Magarsis.[29] At Seleucia ad Calycadnum Athena was the dominant coin type during the Hellenistic period[30] and the same applies to Soli, where the owl also occurs on some bronzes.[31] However, a curious detail may strengthen Soli's claims to be the mint of our series. While Athenas and owls occur frequently on coins from all parts of the Greek world, the symbol *owl perched on bunch of grapes* is, as far as I know, of the greatest rarity. But during the fifth and fourth centuries B.C., the stock reverse type of the silver coins from Soli was a bunch of grapes. A fourth century issue, a specimen of which is illustrated (PLATE XIII, 6), even shows the owl as a symbol standing in the field beside the bunch of grapes.[32] As the obverse of this coin shows the head of Athena, we have here combined the same three elements which appear as symbols on the Seleucid coins. This can hardly be due to pure coincidence.

The attribution to Soli of the silver coins here described seems to me by far the most probable. However, the city was only acquired by Antiochus III in 197 during his general attack on the Ptolemaic possessions along the southern coast of Asia Minor.[33] In keeping with the date is the fact that no coins of this mint show the early portrait of Antiochus III. A further confirmation of the Cilician origin of the coins may be found in the following consideration. I have pointed out that the peculiar symbol *owl perched on bunch of grapes* (Antiochus IV, no. 2) is also found together with the monogram ₳ on a tetradrachm struck by Ariarathes IV of Cappadocia (PLATE XIII, 2); I explained this as an indication of a political alliance between Syria and Cap-

---

[29] See Lacroix, *Les reproductions de statues sur les monnaies grecques*, 130f. During the first half of the second century Magarsus, under the name Antioch on the Pyramus, was apparently more important than Mallus.
[30] Cf. *SNG Cop.*, 33, nos. 196ff.
[31] Cf. *BMC Lycaonia, Isauria and Cilicia*, pl. xxvi, nos. 11-13 and 15; pl. xxvii, 2.
[32] Cf. *BMC Lycaonia, Isauria and Cilicia*, pl. xxvi, 4-7; *SNG Cop.*, 33, nos. 235-36.
[33] Livy XXXIII, 20, 4; Hieronymus, *Comm. in Daniel* 11, 15-16 (= Jacoby, *Fragmente der griechischen Historiker* II C, no. 260, p. 1224, F 46).

padocia during the reign of Antiochus IV.[34] At the time of this discovery I thought that Antiochus IV had supplied his neighbour with personnel for the establishment of a mint in Cappadocia, even if it seemed rather odd that he should have chosen to send people from a mint in distant Coelesyria to Cappadocia. If, as I now believe, the symbol *owl perched on bunch of grapes* is a mint-mark of Soli, we must assume that the mint of that city was placed at the disposal of Ariarathes IV, who struck his coin there. In any case, Cilicia was the Syrian province bordering Cappadocia, so that the relation between the coins of Antiochus IV and Ariarathes IV makes better sense if we assume that the Seleucid coins originated in this province.

OTTO MØRKHOLM

[34] Mørkholm, "Some Cappadocian Problems," *NC* 1962, 409f.

THE ACCESSION OF ANTIOCHOS IV OF SYRIA

A Numismatic Comment*

(See PLATES XIV–XVI)

During the last decade several papers have been devoted to an analysis of the events leading up to and immediately following the accession of Antiochos IV to the Seleucid throne. A most valuable Babylonian cuneiform king list published in 1954 has stimulated research on the chronology of these events[1] and at the same time offered some new evidence on the other intricate question related to the accession, namely the identity of the boy Antiochos, whose portrait appears on a series of silver coins struck at the mint of Antioch about this time.[2] Prior to 1953 the *communis opinio* was that a son of Seleukos IV was represented,[3] but in that year A. Aymard in a penetrating study of the problem arrived at the conclusion that the boy

---

* This paper is an enlarged version of a lecture delivered at the ANS summer seminar 1962. For valuable help and guidance through the intricacies of the English language I am much indebted to Joan Fagerlie and Margaret Thompson.

The following abbreviations are used: ANS, American Numismatic Society Collection; *BMC, Catalogue of the Greek Coins in the British Museum*; *CAH, Cambridge Ancient History*; Fabretti, *Regio museo di Torino ordinato e descritto da A. Fabretti, F. Rossi e R. V. Lanzone* ..., vol. III, *Monete greche*, Turin, 1883; *Hunter Coll.*, Macdonald, *Catalogue of the Greek Coins in the Hunterian Collection*, Glasgow 1899–1905; *JIAN, Journal international d'archéologie numismatique*, Athènes; *NNM*, Numismatic Notes and Monographs edited by the American Numismatic Society; *OGIS*, Dittenberger, *Orientis Graecae Inscriptiones Selectae*, Leipzig 1903–05; *REA, Revue des études anciennes*, Paris; *RFIC, Rivista di filologia e d'istruzione classica*, Turin; *Rois de Syrie*, E. Babelon, *Catalogue des monnaies grecques de la Bibliotheque Nationale, Les Rois de Syrie*, Paris 1890; S. E., Seleucid era; SMA, E. T. Newell, "The Seleucid Mint of Antioch," *American Journal of Numismatics*, 1917/1918.

[1] A. J. Sachs & D. J. Wiseman, "A Babylonian King List of the Hellenistic Period," *Iraq* XVI, 1954, 202–211. Cf. J. Schaumberger, "Die neue Seleukidenliste BM 35603 und die makkabäische Chronologie," *Biblica* XXXVI, 1955, 423–435; A. Aymard, "Du nouveau sur la chronologie des Séleucides," *REA* LVII, 1955, 102–112; E. Manni, "A proposita di una nuova lista babilonese di re ellenistici," *RFIC* XXXIV, 1956, 273–278.

[2] The time and place of minting of these coins were definitely established by Newell in *SMA* 19–21.

[3] Cf. E. Bevan, *CAH* VIII, 713–14 and Newell, *NNM* 73, 1936, 11–12.

was a son of Antiochos IV appointed co-ruler by the father shortly after his accession.[4] The clinching evidence was thought to be afforded by a Babylonian tablet dated August 14, 173 B.C. under "Antiochos and Antiochos his son kings." The king list mentioned above seems to support Aymard's thesis in the most explicit way by giving the exact dates of the co-regency of father and son.

To take up the problem anew may seem unprofitable or even unnecessary. However, I am convinced that an important body of material bearing on the question has not yet been properly evaluated. The coins are frequently mentioned and used for illustration but in my opinion their value goes further than that. Only by collecting all available specimens and arranging them into a series on the basis of a study of the dies from which the coins were struck, can the historian hope to extract all the information offered by the numismatic material towards a solution of the problem in question. Accordingly a *corpus*, comprising the silver coins of the boy king Antiochos from the mint of Antioch together with the first series of silver issued at the same mint by Antiochos IV, is here published.[5]

THE BOY KING ANTIOCHOS[6]

Obv.: Diademed head of young boy r.; fillet border.

Rev.: Apollo seated l. on omphalos, holding in r. hand arrow, l. hand resting on bow; to r. and l. downwards ΒΑΣΙΛΕΩΣ ΑΝΤΙΟΧΟΥ; in outer l. field tripod; in exergue monogram or letter.

---

[4] A. Aymard, "Autour de l'avènement d'Antiochos IV," *Historia* II, 1953/54, 49–73. Aymard's identification is accepted by G. le Rider, Congresso internazionale di numismatica 1961, *Relazioni* I, 78. On the other hand M. Zambelli, "L'ascesa al trono di Antioco IV Epifane di Siria," *RFIC* XXXVIII, 1960, 363–389, reverts to the view of Bevan. This paper only came to my knowledge recently and even if I agree with Zambelli on the question of the boy's identity, on many points I cannot subscribe to his arguments.

[5] The boy king also struck tetradrachms at Tyre (cf. *NNM* 73, 1936, no. 28a) and Susa (Paris, *Rois de Syrie* no. 332), but these few specimens are of no special importance for our purpose. Nor do the bronze coins of Antioch offer any help. The series: veiled female bust r./elephant's head l.,ΒΑΣΙΛΕΩΣ ΑΝΤΙΟΧΟΥ (*SMA* 21) may have been issued by both kings.

[6] In the list of coins the dies have been numbered, A 1, A 2, etc. denoting the obverse (anvil) dies, P 1, P 2, etc. the reverse (punch) dies of the tetradrachms. The same system, but with small letters, is used for the few drachms. The

ANTIOCHOS IV OF SYRIA

1. Tetradrachms. *Rev.*: in exergue ₽.

A 1–P 1	16.97	London, *BMC* (Seleucid Kings) 24, no. 2.
A 1–P 2	17.00	Oxford, Ashmolean Museum (PLATE XIV, 1).
A 1–P 2	16.91	Glasgow, *Hunter Coll.* III, 53, no. 2.
	17.21	Turin, *Fabretti* no. 4582.[7]

2. Tetradrachms. *Rev.*: in exergue ԺP.

A 1–P 3	17.08	London, *BMC* (Seleucid Kings) 24, no. 1 (PLATE XIV, 2).
A 1–P 4	17.05	Paris, *Rois de Syrie* no. 329.
A 2–P 5	16.79	Munich. (PLATE XIV, 3).
A 2–P 5	17.11	Glasgow, *Hunter Coll.* III, 53, no. 1, pl. lxvii, 1.
A 2–P 6	17.08	New York, ANS ex Hirsch Sale XXV, 1909 (Philipsen Coll.) no. 2901. *SMA* pl. iii, 45.

3. Tetradrachms. *Rev.*: in exergue Δ.

A 1–P 7	16.60	Oxford, Ashmolean Museum (PLATE XIV, 4).
A 1–P 8	17.22	Paris, *Rois de Syrie* no. 325.
A 1–P 9	17.01	The Hague, Six Foundation.
A 2–P 10	15.72	New York, ANS (oxydized and cleaned). *SMA* pl. iii, 52.
	16.93	Turin, *Fabretti* no. 4581.

4. Tetradrachms. *Rev.*: in exergue B.

A 2–P 11	17.03	London, *BMC* (Seleucid Kings) 24, no. 3, pl. viii, 1. *SMA* pl. iii, 51.
A 2–P 11	17.05	Paris, *Rois de Syrie* no. 330, pl. viii, 17.
A 2–P 12	17.00	Glasgow, *Hunter Coll.* III, 53, no. 3 (PLATE XIV, 5).

5. Tetradrachms. *Rev.*: in exergue ₳K.

A 2–P 13	17.10	Budapest.
A 2–P 13	17.2	Leningrad, Hermitage Museum. *JIAN* 13, 1911, 152, no. 382.
A 2–P 14	17.17	Berlin, Imhoof-Blumer (PLATE XIV, 6).

6. Tetradrachms. *Rev.*: in exergue ϙ.

A 2–P 15	16.3	Leningrad, Hermitage Museum. *JIAN* 13, 1911, 153, no. 383 (oxydized).

second column gives the weights in grammes. The die position has not been indicated. It is generally ↑↑ with very few and insignificant deviations of the type ↑↖ or ↑↗. Most of the specimens come from well-known public collections. The sales catalogues are listed by dealers, the name of the owner, when known, appearing in parentheses. For their permission to publish coins in their charge and for their kindness in providing me with casts or photos I am indebted to the curators of the various collections.

[7] The coins in the Turin collection being for the time inaccessible, I have not been able to indicate their dies.

A 2–P 15	17.01	Coll. Jameson, *Monnaies grecques antiques*, Vol. I (Paris, 1913) no. 1683 ex Sotheby Sale 1908 (O'Hagan Coll.) no. 652. *SMA* pl. iii, 46.
A 2–P 15	17.09	Weber Coll. vol. III, part II (London, 1929) no. 7896 ex Sotheby Sale 1884 (Whittall Coll.) no. 1422.
A 2–P 16	16.85	Paris, *Rois de Syrie* no. 328. Pellerin, *Mélanges de Médailles* I, 135, pl. iii, 17, (from Latakia hoard, *NNM* 78, 1937, no. 603).
A 2–P 17	17.18	P & P Santamaria Sale, October, 1949, no. 82 (17.27 gr.) ex Schlessinger Sale, February, 1935, no. 1451. *JIAN* 13, 1911, 153, no. 384 (PLATE XIV, 7).

7. Drachms. *Rev.*: in exergue ⚹.

a 1–p 1	3.95	New York, ANS. (PLATE XV, 1).
a 2–p 2	3.67	Paris, new acquisition (PLATE XV, 2).

8. Tetradrachm. *Rev.*: in exergue ⚹.

A 2–P 18	17.09	Naville Sale X, 1925, no. 945 ex Sotheby Sale 1896 (Montagu Coll.) no. 700 (PLATE XV, 3).

9. Tetradrachm. *Rev.*: in exergue ⚹.

A 3–P 19	16.50	Paris, *Rois de Syrie* no. 327 (PLATE XV, 4).

10. Tetradrachms. *Rev.*: in exergue ΓP.

A 3–P 20	16.69	Paris, *Rois de Syrie* no. 326 (the weight given there, 17.70 gr., is a mistake).
A 3–P 20	17.18	Berlin (PLATE XV, 5).

On the following tetradrachms the monogram or letter in the exergue is off flan:

A 1–P 21	17.10	Paris, *Rois de Syrie* no. 331. Coll. de Luynes no. 3296, pl. cxx (PLATE XV, 6).
A 3–P 22	17.08	Brussels, Coll. de Hirsch no. 1672.
A 3–P 22	16.99	Ward Coll., *Greek Coins and their Parent Cities* (London, 1902) no. 782 ex Sotheby Sale 1896 (Bunbury Coll. II) no. 465.
A 3–P 22	16.62	A. E. Cahn Sale, November, 1933, no. 406 ex Glendining Sale, March, 1931, no. 1150 ex Helbing Sale, November, 1928, no. 4061 ex Naville Sale X, 1925, no. 1049 (PLATE XV, 7).

ANTIOCHOS IV

Obv.: Diademed head of the King r.; fillet border.

Rev.: Apollo seated l. on omphalos, holding in r. hand arrow, l. hand resting on bow; to r. and l. downwards ΒΑΣΙΛΕΩΣ ΑΝΤΙΟΧΟΥ; in l. and r. fields one or two symbols; in exergue monogram.

ANTIOCHOS IV OF SYRIA

1. Tetradrachms. *Rev.*: in l. field tripod, in r. lyre, in exergue ΓΡ.

    | A 1–P 1 | 17.05 | Paris, *Rois de Syrie* no. 516 (PLATE XV, 8). |
    | A 1–P 1 | 17.11 | New York, ANS. |
    | | 16.91 | Turin, *Fabretti* no. 4630. |

2. Tetradrachms. *Rev.*: in l. field tripod, in r. lyre, in exergue ⚹.

    | A 2–P 2 | 16.82 | Berlin. |
    | A 2–P 3 | 16.93 | London, *BMC* (Seleucid Kings) 34, no. 3. |
    | A 2–P 3 | 16.97 | The Hague, Six Foundation (PLATE XVI, 1). |
    | A 2–P 4 | 17.01 | Milan, former Brera Coll. no. 3160. |
    | A 2–P 4 | 16.70 | Naville Sale X, 1925, no. 1024 ex Naville Sale V, 1923, no. 2798. |
    | A 3–P 5 | 17.05 | The Hague, inv. no. 7041 (PLATE XVI, 2). |
    | A 3–P 5 | 17.02 | London, *BMC* (Seleucid Kings) 34, no. 4, pl. xi, 2. *SMA* pl. iii, 44. |

3. Tetradrachms. *Rev.*: in r. field lyre, in exergue ⚹. In l. field erasure of tripod.

    | A 3–P 6 | 17.00 | The Hague, inv. no. 7043 (PLATE XVI, 3). |
    | A 3–P 6 | 17.06 | Glasgow, *Hunter Coll.* III, 41, no. 3, pl. lxvi, 8. |
    | A 3–P 6 | 16.70 | Vinchon Sale, May, 1959, no. 587 (chisel cut). |
    | | 15.41 | Turin, *Fabretti* no. 4627. |

4. Drachm. *Rev.*: in r. field lyre, in exergue ⚹.

    | a 1–p 1 | 3.91 | Paris, *Revue Num.* 1959–60, 13, no. 16, pl. ii ex Coll. Chandon de Briailles (PLATE XVI, 4). |

5. Tetradrachms. *Rev.*: in l. field lyre, in exergue ⚹.

    | A 3–P 7 | 17.1 | The Hague, inv. no. 7044 (PLATE XVI, 5). |
    | A 3–P 7 | 17.10 | Cambridge, Fitzwilliam Museum, General Coll. |
    | A 3–P 7 | 16.90 | Copenhagen, *Sylloge Nummorum Graecorum* 35, no. 183. |
    | A 3–P 8 | 17.00 | Paris, *Rois de Syrie* no. 515. |
    | A 3–P 8 | 16.96 | Berlin. |
    | A 3–P 9 | 16.98 | New York, ANS ex Naville Sale X, 1925, no. 1023. |
    | A 3–P 9 | 17.15 | Paris, *Rois de Syrie* no. 514, pl. xii, 1. *Coll. de Luynes* no. 3309, pl. cxx. *SMA* pl. iii, 42. |
    | A 3–P 10 | 16.91 | London, British Museum ex Sotheby Sale, 1896 (Bunbury Coll. II) no. 488. |
    | A 3–P 11 | 17.04 | Glasgow, *Hunter Coll.* III, 41, no. 2. |
    | A 3–P 12 | | Münzen und Medaillen A.G., Fixed Price List 226, Sept.-Oct., 1962, no. 10. |
    | A 4–P 13 | 17.13 | Berlin (PLATE XVI, 6). |
    | | 17.2 | *JIAN* 13, 1911, 150, no. 329. |

A discussion of the chronology of the two coin series listed above may profitably start with the first series of Antiochos IV. The beginning of this coinage must undoubtedly coincide with the king's accession to the Syrian throne late in the year 175 B.C. But for how long were these coins struck? The acknowledged authority on the Seleucid coinages, E. T. Newell, gives the dates 176/5 to 170/69 B.C.[8] However, a comparison with the two later series of Antiochene tetradrachms of the same king shows this to be highly improbable. The material at my disposal, including the coins from practically all important coin cabinets as well as the illustrated sales catalogues within my reach, comprises the following number of tetradrachms:[9]

    Series I   23 specimens struck from 4 obverse dies
    Series II   89 specimens struck from 17 obverse dies
    Series III 136 specimens struck from 36 obverse dies

Even assuming that the first, rather uneventful, years of Antiochos IV might have demanded a lesser output of coins than the period after 170 B.C., which saw the war with Egypt and the Maccabean revolt in Judaea, it does not seem possible that only four obverse dies should have been used at Antioch for nearly half the reign, five years out of eleven.[10] On the basis of the numbers recorded above I should suggest the dates 175–173 for Series I, 173–169 for Series II, and 169–164 for Series III. This distribution of the coins takes into account the probable increase in the coinage of the later years of the reign. The introduction of the title Νικηφόρος on Series III will then be connected with the first campaign of Antiochos IV in Egypt in 169 B.C., certainly

[8] *SMA* 17 ff.
[9] The list only comprises the specimens the dies of which are known to me. Series II (*SMA* 22 ff.) consists of the tetradrachms with seated Zeus as the reverse type and the inscription ΒΑΣΙΛΕΩΣ ΑΝΤΙΟΧΟΥ ΘΕΟΥ ΕΠΙΦΑΝΟΥΣ. On the coins of the third series (*SMA* 28 ff.) the royal title is amplified by adding ΝΙΚΗΦΟΡΟΥ. The obverse dies are counted separately for each series in spite of the fact that one die is carried over from Series I to II and another one from Series II to III. Thus the total of obverse dies used by Antiochos IV at Antioch amounts to 55. See Mørkholm, "Studies in the Coinage of Antiochus IV of Syria," *Hist. Filos. Medd. Dan. Vid. Selsk.* 40, no. 3 (Copenhagen, 1963), 11 ff. and 24 ff.
[10] This implies that our record of obverse dies used in Series I is virtually complete. In fact this assumption seems to be valid, when the ratio of known specimens to obverse dies is 6:1 or above. See M. Thompson, *The New Style Silver Coinage of Athens*, 1961, 711. It now happens that three tetradrachms of Series II were struck with the obverse die A 4, which was carried over from Series I (PLATE XVI, 7), bringing the total of coins certainly struck from the first four obverse dies to 26 or more than 6 coins per obverse die. In any event the numbers given in the text show that our record is more complete for the first series than for the two succeeding, which is a further argument for rejecting Newell's dates.

an event apt to produce this amplification of the royal title. The date 173 B.C. for the transition from Series I to II is rather arbitrary, of course, but the coinage of the first series seems to have been produced over a period of some length. Especially instructive is the use of the obverse die A 3 with three different reverse types (nos. 2, 3, and 5 in the list above), the one of which (no. 3) was made by the difficult process of erasing a symbol on an already finished die. The natural conclusion to be drawn from the material at hand is that for some time A 3 was the only obverse die in use at the mint of Antioch,[11] the output being reduced to a small fraction of its normal volume.

Turning now to the coins of the boy king Antiochos the problem is whether these coins were issued simultaneously with the first series of Antiochos IV, as assumed by Newell in *SMA* on the basis of a rather small body of material, or before that series, i.e., filling a gap between the coinages of Seleukos IV and Antiochos IV. The coins themselves definitely suggest the latter possibility. How else are we to explain the occurrence on this series of eight different moneyer's monograms,[12] only two of which are found on the first series of Antiochos IV? Why should six moneyers have restricted their activity to the coins of the boy king if both series were struck at the same time? Furthermore there is nothing comparable to the changing use of symbols on the reverses of the first series of Antiochos IV. We are here dealing with a homogenous group of coins, which may very well have been minted during a very short period. A few months will suffice.[13] The conclusion imposed by the coin material, when studied

[11] This die may very well have been used for a year or more. The life span of an obverse die obviously depends on the production rate of the mint. According to M. Thompson, *The New Style Silver Coinage of Athens*, 1961, 721, the obverse dies at Athens in the second century B.C. lasted from one to five months. However, the dated Alexander coinage from the small mints at Sidon and Ake in the late fourth century B.C. shows the same obverse dies used with reverses dated to three or even four successive years. Cf. E. T. Newell, *The Dated Alexander Coinage of Sidon and Ake*, 1916, 19f. (obverse dies XXXII and XXXIII) and 45ff. (obverse dies XX and XXIV). See also G. F. Hill, *BMC* (Phoenicia) Introduction p. xxxiii for an obverse die of Arados used during four years.
[12] ᴁ and ᴁ are taken to represent the same moneyer.
[13] For comparison see the posthumous coinage of Antiochos IV at Antioch in the year 146/45 B.C. (*NC* 1960, 25–30). This issue which can have covered only a few months comprises 39 silver coins (tetradrachms and drachms) struck from 12 obverse dies and signed by 11 moneyers.

without any preconceived ideas, is that the issue of the boy king did in fact precede the first issue of Antiochos IV, even if we cannot rule out the possibility of a partial overlapping of the two series.

To get a clear notion of the historical background for the coin series we must now direct our attention towards the evidence available from other sources. Of prime importance is the Babylonian cuneiform king list mentioned above. The following translation of its paragraphs relating to Seleukos IV and Antiochos IV is reproduced from the first edition:[14]

Rev. vv. 8–9

"The same year (125 S.E.), Se(leukos IV) his son sat on the throne. He ruled 12 years. Year 137 (S.E.), month VI, day 10, Se(leukos) the king died ..."

Rev. vv. 10–15

"The same month (VI, 137 S.E.) An(tiochos) his son sat on the throne. He reigned 11 years. The same [year] (137 S.E.), month VIII, An(tiochos) and An(tiochos) his son (ruled) as kings. [Year 1]42 (S.E.), month V, at the command of An(tiochos IV) the king, An(tiochos) the (co)-regent, his son, was put to death. [Year 14]3 (S.E.), An(tiochos ruled as) king (alone). [Year 148 S.E., month] IX it was heard that king An(tiochos) [died ...]"

Substituting Julian dates[15] for the Babylonian of the tablet it appears that Seleukos IV died on September 3, 175 B.C. In the same Babylonian month, i.e., before September 22 his son (sic) Antiochos IV ascended the throne. A few months later, between October 23 and November 20, 175 B.C., Antiochos appointed his son also named Antiochos, co-ruler of the Seleucid kingdom. The two kings ruled

---

[14] Cf. *Iraq* XVI, 1954, 208. On p. 204 the editors give the following comment on their translation: "Brackets [ ] enclose whatever is completely broken away in the text, and parentheses () contain anything which, strictly speaking, is not in the original text but may be needed occasionally to make the translation intelligible."

[15] The dates here given are taken from Parker & Dubberstein, *Babylonian Chronology 626 B.C.–A.D. 75*, 1956, 23. They differ slightly from the dates of Sachs and Wiseman. The speculations of E. Manni, *RFIC* 1956, 273–278, on the possible use in the king list of a modified Babylonian calendar, the year beginning in autumn instead of spring and the Babylonian names of the months being transposed according to this, are quite unfounded. Cf. Zambelli, *RFIC* 1960, 363, note 2.

together for nearly five years, until Antiochos the father during the Babylonian month July 31 to August 28, 170 B.C. had his son killed.

Despite its short and factual style the evidence of the tablet cannot be accepted without question. In the first place the compiler of this list has made a blunder in calling the Antiochos of v. 10 the son of Seleukos IV. The following sentence, mentioning his 11 years of reign, shows beyond doubt that Antiochos IV, the brother of Seleukos IV, was meant. The next difficulty arises from the chronology of the events. From Appian we happen to know that Antiochos, while he was staying at Athens, received the news of the murder of his brother by his prime minister Heliodoros. With the help of King Eumenes of Pergamon and his brother Attalos he was able to drive Heliodoros from Syria and ascend the Seleucid throne.[16] The rôle played by the Pergamene princes in this affair is further elucidated by an Athenian decree found in Pergamon praising Eumenes and his brothers for their ready assistance to Antiochos, the friend of the Athenian people. The inscription tells us, that the Pergamenians escorted Antiochos to the Syrian border, provided him with money and an army, and gave him the diadem and the other royal insignia.[17] It seems quite impossible that this whole chain of events, the news of Seleukos' death travelling to Athens, Antiochos' journey from Athens to somewhere in the Pergamene kingdom, his consultation with Eumenes, the assembling of troops etc., and the advance to Syria, can have taken place in the 19 days intervening, according to the maximal interpretation of the king list, between the death of Seleukos and the accession of his brother.[18] Common sense suggests that Antiochos IV can, at the

[16] Appian, *Syr.* VIII, 45.
[17] *OGIS* 248, vv. 15–18:

Μέχρι τῶν ὁρίων τῆς ἰδίας βασιλείας συμπρο-
ελθόντες καὶ χρήμασι χορηγήσαντες καὶ
δυνάμεις παρασκευάσαντες καὶ τῶι διαδήματι
μετὰ τῆς ἄλλης κατασκευῆς κοσμήσαντες (sc. the Pergamene princes)

The Athenian origin of the decree has been established by M. Holleaux, "Un prétendu décret d'Antioche sur l'Oronte," *Études d'épigraphie et d'histoire grecques* II, 1938, 127–147 (reprinted from *Revue des études grecques* XIII, 1900, 258–280).

[18] On the travelling speed in antiquity see Louis E. Lord, "The Date of Julius Caesar's Departure from Alexandria," *Journal of Roman Studies* XXXVIII, 1938, 19–40. Even if we accept the suggestion of Zambelli, *RFIC* 1960, 373, that Antiochos IV dated his accession from the day when he received the royal

earliest, have arrived in Syria about the time which the king list gives for the nomination of his son as co-regent, October–November 175 B.C. A confirmation of this dating can be found in a bronze coin of Tyre, struck with the portrait and name of Seleukos IV in the year 138 S.E.,[19] which according to the Macedonian calendar used in the western part of the Seleucid empire ran from October, 175 to October, 174 B.C. While it is quite feasible that this coin might have been struck in a period of turmoil after the death of Seleukos, its minting is hardly possible once Antiochos IV was in power. However, the inaccuracy of the Babylonian king list, written about 140 B.C., can be easily explained. Antiochos IV was naturally eager to suppress the memory of Heliodoros and the irregular circumstances of his own accession, and this was done most effectively by reckoning the beginning of his reign from the moment of his brother's death, thus simply forgetting about the unpleasant interval of a few months between the two reigns. The same pious fiction caused the author of Maccabees I to date the beginning of Antiochos IV's reign to 137 S.E. = October, 176 to October, 175 B.C.[20]

So far two facts have been ascertained. In the first place the coins of the boy king were issued, at least in part, before the coins of Antiochos IV, that is to say before the latter's arrival in Syria. Secondly a *vacuum* of a few months existed between the death of Seleukos IV and the accession of his brother Antiochos IV, a period of sufficient length for the striking of these coins. If this be granted, the question of the identity of the boy on the coins is also settled. Only a son of Seleukos IV could have issued coins before the arrival of Antiochos IV at Antioch. According to the portrait he was about five

---

diadem from Eumenes of Pergamon before entering Syria, the 19 days seem hardly sufficient. In any case, what is essential to my argument is the date of Antiochos IV's arrival at Antioch, the mint of the coins issued by the boy king. Zambelli, ibid., 386f. accepting the date of the king list for the accession of Antiochos IV, goes on to use the extraordinary speed in the movements of the Syrian prince and the Pergamenians as an argument that they were really privy to the murder of Seleukos IV. Of this as well as the supposed Roman sanction of the plan we have not a single shred of evidence.

[19] Cf. E. T. Newell, *NNM* 10, 1921, 19, no. 27. I have inspected the coin, which is now in the ANS. Newell's reading of the date is beyond doubt.

[20] Cf. Macc. I, 1, 10. On the question of the two different Seleucid eras used in Macc. I, see J. C. Dancy, *I Maccabees: A Commentary*, 1954, 48–51 and Schaumberger, *Biblica* 1955, 423–435.

years of age. Presumably he was put on the throne by Heliodoros to conceal the minister's usurpation of power. In fact we have in our literary sources a few scattered references to this boy. A fragment of John of Antioch says that Antiochos IV had a son of Seleukos IV killed but shifting the blame of the murder to some other people (presumably his helpers) he put those to death also. The same incident is mentioned by Diodoros. Here Antiochos IV is not referred to explicitly, but the actual murderer of the young prince is named Andronikos. This Andronikos has generally, and I think rightly, been identified with the homonymous person who according to the Jewish tradition was put to death by Antiochos IV about 171/70 B.C. for the murder of the former Jewish High Priest Onias III, then living in exile near Antioch.[21] It is unlikely that two high Seleucid court officials, both named Andronikos, should have been executed on a charge of murder during the first half of Antiochos IV's reign. From these references it seems certain that Seleukos IV at his death left a son in Syria. The coins show that he was named Antiochos, and the portrait indicates that he was a younger brother of the later Demetrios I, who was at that time a hostage in Rome.[22]

It now remains to explain the Babylonian sources mentioning a son of Antiochos IV as co-regent from 175 to 170 B.C.[23] The first thing which leaps to the eye is the strange parallelism in the destinies of the two boys, the nephew of Antiochos IV known from the coins and the Greek historical tradition, and his son known only from the Babylonian tablets. Both of them occupied the Seleucid throne as minors, and

---

[21] Cf. John of Antioch, *Fragmenta Historicorum Graecorum* (ed. C. Müller) IV, 558, fr. 58; Diod. Sic. XXX, 7, 2; Macc. II, 4, 34–38.

[22] It has been thought unlikely that Seleukos IV would send his elder son as a hostage to Rome, but if the Romans demanded a Seleucid prince in exchange for Antiochos (IV), who had been kept as hostage since 189 B.C., Seleukos would have had no choice. Certainly the Romans would not have accepted the younger son, a 4–5 year old child in 176 B.C. As to the name Demetrios, it is surprising that the elder son and heir to the throne got a name without precedent in the Seleucid dynasty. (Cf. Aymard, *Historia* II, 1953, 57). However, we cannot but accept the fact, strange as it is.

[23] Besides the king list we have a Babylonian tablet dated August 14, 173 B.C. under "Antiochos and Antiochos his son kings." Cf. A. T. Clay, *Babylonian Records in the Library of J. Pierpont Morgan* II, 1913, 86, no. 38. See Aymard, *Historia* II, 1953, 59, for other cuneiform documents mentioning the co-regency without giving the relationship between the two kings.

both of them lost their lives at the instigaton of Antiochos IV, even at approximately the same time if we accept the identification of the Andronikos of Macc. II with the one mentioned by Diodoros. This striking coincidence has not failed to arouse some curiosity and various explanations have been offered. Aymard thought that the Babylonian scribe of the king list confused the murder of the nephew with the natural death of the son and co-regent, stressing the inherent improbability that Antiochos IV could have murdered his own son without scandalizing his contemporaries and evoking some comment on his atrocity in the Greek historical tradition which is generally not too friendly to him.[24] The last writer to discuss the problem, M. Zambelli, also finds the answer in a supposed error of the scribe. According to his view the king list here, as at other places, gives a wrong filiation by calling the co-regent Antiochos the son of Antiochos IV instead of nephew.[25] This attempt at an explanation is extremely weak, because Zambelli has to assume that exactly the same mistake was made quite independently by the scribe of the tablet dated August 14, 173 B.C. A telling point against both explanations is the fact that they can fit the evidence of the king list into their respective conceptions of the political situation only by assuming grave errors on the part of the Babylonian scribe.

The only solution to this crucial problem, so far as I can see, consists in assuming that the nephew and son mentioned in the various branches of the historical tradition, was in fact one and the same person, a son of Seleukos IV proclaimed king by Heliodoros after his father's death and later, at the accession of Antiochos IV, adopted by his uncle. The theory of an adoption is the only one which can reconcile the divergent elements of the tradition.[26] It must be borne in mind that we have no reason to reject one part of the evidence in favour of the other. The Greek historical tradition is practically contemporary, going ultimately back to Polybios, and the Babylonian appears in a contemporary cuneiform tablet. Both traditions apparently are of equal value.

[24] Cf. Aymard, *REA* 1955, 110–112.
[25] Cf. Zambelli, *RFIC* 1960, 371.
[26] If we have no other cases of adoptions within the Seleucid dynasty, this is simply because sons and heirs were always present.

If the son of Seleukos IV was adopted by Antiochos IV, who definitely intended to be the ruler of Syria,[27] this most likely was a result of some kind of compromise between various political factions in Syria. We have some rather vague indication that Antiochos IV was not received with equal enthusiasm in all quarters.[28] From Polybios we know that a certain Apollonios, a high official of Seleukos IV, retired to the city of Miletos. The words of Polybios imply that he did so at the accession of Antiochos IV, but this was clearly not the case as he can be identified with the Apollonios mentioned in Macc. II, first as governor of the province of Koile Syria and Phoenicia under Seleukos IV and later as the trusted ambassador of Antiochos IV to the Ptolemaic court during the first years of his reign.[29] Presumably the same Apollonios headed an embassy to Rome in 173 B.C., where his position at the Seleucid court and his influence with the king were acknowledged by a handsome gift.[30] His service under Seleukos IV and Antiochos IV, his subsequent retirement to Miletos at some unknown date, and the later connection between his sons and Demetrios, the surviving son of Seleukos IV and in the eyes of some people the legitimate heir to the Syrian throne, combine to suggest that during the first years of Antiochos IV's reign this Apollonios belonged to a faction loyal to the young co-regent. This would also give a reasonable ex-

[27] In Appian's account of the accession (*Syr.* VIII, 45) and the Athenian decree *OGIS* 248 the boy king is not mentioned at all. There is no evidence that Antiochos IV ever thought of himself as a guardian, preserving the rights of his nephew until he came of age (so Bikerman, *Institutions des Séleucides*, 1938, 19). On the contrary he wanted to rule in his own right. The existence of the boy, already proclaimed king before the arrival of Antiochos IV in Syria, necessitated the adoption and the acceptance of the boy as co-regent as the only workable solution for the moment.

[28] Cf. Hieronymus, *Comm. in Dan.* 11, 21 ff. (Jacoby, *Fragmente der griechischen Historiker* II, B, no. 260 [Porphyrios of Tyre] fr. 49), who speaks of an Egyptianizing faction. Josephus, *Ant. Jud.* XII, 236 tells the story of the Jew Hyrkanos, who killed himself at the accession of Antiochos IV from fear of the new king.

[29] Cf. Polyb. XXXI, 13, 2–3 and Macc. II, 4, 4 & 21–22. The identification rests on the fact that Macc. II records the name of Apollonios' father Menestheus, while among the three sons of the Polybian Apollonios we meet another Menestheus. This is quite in accordance with the normal Greek usage of naming a son after his grandfather.

[30] Cf. Livy XLII, 6, 6. This identification is, of course, not certain, but probable in view of the other known data of Apollonios' career.

planation of the murder of the boy. As the rallying-point of a political faction, he was, in spite of his extreme youth, a potential menace to Antiochos IV. If my date of 173 B.C. for the introduction of the second series of tetradrachms at Antioch is correct, this year saw a definite step in the direction of exalting Antiochos IV at the cost of his co-regent. Of course the boy had always been a *collega minor*,[31] but now Antiochos IV effectively separated himself from the rest of mankind by indroducing his devine title Θεὸς 'Επιφανής on his coinage. During the same year, most probably, a son of his own flesh, the later Antiochos V, was born to Antiochos IV.[32] It is easy to see how these events might have strained the relations between uncle and nephew and their respective followers. After all Antiochos IV was a very ambitious man, well aware of his own capability and imbued with the most exalted ideas of his position. Once his rule in Syria was consolidated, he would certainly be most impatient of any real or imaginary check on his political power. Exactly how the situation developed in the years following 173 B.C. we do not know, but in 170 B.C. it became critical. On the eve of the war with Egypt the tension within the Seleucid dynasty resulted in the murder of the young co-regent, the nephew of Antiochos IV and his son by adoption. This ill-fated boy has left very few traces in history, the most important being perhaps his coins, which show what is undoubtedly the best and most natural child portrait of the Hellenistic Age.[33]

OTTO MØRKHOLM

[31] On this conception see Bikerman, *Institutions des Séleucides*, p. 22f.

[32] We have two traditions on the birth date of Antiochos V. According to Appian, *Syr.* 46 and 66 he was nine years old at the death of Antiochos IV in 164 B.C., while Porphyrios (Jacoby, *Fragments der griechischen Historiker* II, B, no. 260, fr. 32,13) puts his birth twelve years before the same event, i.e., a full year before the accession of Antiochos IV to the Syrian throne. But in my opinion Antiochos IV could hardly have contracted a suitable marriage, while he was still held as hostage in Rome. Accordingly the date of Appian seems to me the most probable.

[33] After the conclusion of my manuscript a most interesting coin has turned up: a gold octodrachm showing on the obverse the jugate heads of the boy king and a female, who from the age can only be his mother. The reverse with the monogram ⋈ corresponds exactly to the silver coins listed above as no. 2. This coin confirms my argument and proves that the coins of the boy king were issued before the appearance of Antiochos IV in Syria. The implications for the rôle of Heliodoros and the Queen, Laodike, in the plot against Seleukos IV can only be dealt with after the publication of the new coin.

A HOARD FROM THESSALY

(See Plates XVII–XVIII)

In the spring of 1962 a small lot of hoard coins, tetradrachms of Perseus and of Athens in good to excellent condition, was offered on the Paris market. The Athenian pieces without exception belonged to the early New Style series with monograms and abbreviated names. Four specimens of each coinage were purchased by the dealer but five had been sold before word of the find reached me. The remaining tetradrachms, two of Athens and one of Perseus, are reproduced on Plate XVII, 1–3.[1]

Subsequent investigation has provided additional data on the hoard and although it has now been dispersed beyond hope of precise reconstitution, its general composition seems well established and definitely worth recording. Over 100 coins were in the original deposit which was unearthed in Thessaly, probably at or near Tricca, in 1961 or 1962.[2] In addition to the tetradrachms which went up to Northern Europe, a substantial number of pieces from the hoard came on the Greek market in 1962. Perseus coins in excellent to FDC state appeared in Athens (Plate XVII, 4); thirty other examples of the same issues in equally fine condition were seen at Tricca and with them uncleaned New Style tetradrachms, all of the first series (196–169 B.C.).[3] The hoard was also said to have contained two tetradrachms of Philip V with shield obverse and some tetradrachms of Thasos, all early strikings of good style.

Only six coins can be identified with certainty as coming from the hoard:

[1] This hoard, under the heading *Greece 1961*, was mentioned briefly in "Athens Again" (*NC* 1962, 318f.) but at the time my earlier article went to press I had information only on the Paris coins and had not yet received casts of them.
  For the record as it appears here, I am indebted to Georges Le Rider, Peter R. Franke, Christof Boehringer, and several European dealers.
[2] The earlier date is the more likely in that part of the hoard was already in Paris early in 1962.
[3] A tetradrachm of 170/69 (Thompson, *The New Style Silver Coinage of Athens*, no. 304) is specifically cited as the latest of the Athenian pieces.

Perseus
>2 heavy tetradrachms of 173–171 B.C. (*ZfN* 1928, 23, no. 15) from the same pair of dies.
>>Münzen und Medaillen XXV, 444, gr. 16.75.
>>Commerce Athens ↑. PLATE XVII, 4.
>
>1 light tetradrachm of 170–168 (*ZfN* 1928, 26, no. 23).
>>Commerce Paris, gr. 15.43 ↑. PLATE XVII, 3.

Athens
>1 tetradrachm of 179/8 (Thompson 127 with new reverse).
>>Münz. u. Med. List 222, 12.
>
>1 tetradrachm of 176/5 (T. 171 with new reverse).
>>Commerce Paris, gr. 17.01 ↑. PLATE XVII, 1.
>
>1 tetradrachm of 171/0 (T. 271 with new reverse).
>>Commerce Paris, gr. 16.88 ↑. PLATE XVII, 2.

There are other pieces which may be linked tentatively with this Thessalian deposit. According to one report three separate finds of Perseus tetradrachms were made during 1961–1962: the hoard under present discussion, another from Tricca, and still another from an unspecified location. The coins represented as coming from the three deposits were all in very good to FDC condition. Prima facie, this is suspicious, especially in view of the fact that Perseus tetradrachms are not often found in a hoard context.[4] It is possible, of course, that three new lots of almost uncirculated Perseus coins turned up at approximately the same time, two of them at least with a Tricca association, but it seems more likely that we have again the familiar pattern of a single hoard dispersed through different channels. If this is so, four tetradrachms described as belonging to the Tricca hoard (PLATE XVII, 5–7 and Kress Catalogue 123, 116) should be included in our Thessalian find.

Well-preserved examples of the early New Style series are also uncommon in a hoard context. Thirteen such coins covering the years between 193/2 and 171/0, all in good or very good condition, were offered to the Athens Cabinet in 1961 or 1962 (*BCH* 1962, 422, no. 9).

[4] Noe (*NNM* 78) lists only five deposits and although others have undoubtedly been discovered since 1937, the total can scarcely be very high.

One wonders if they did not come from the same source as the New Style tetradrachms seen in Paris and Tricca.

Regardless of the uncertainties involved in identifying individual hoard coins, the basic composition and chronological termini of the deposit are well defined:

Tetradrachms of Philip V	186–179
Tetradrachms of Thasos	early 2nd century
Tetradrachms of Athens	196–169
Tetradrachms of Perseus	178–168

A single report links the Thasos and Philip tetradrachms with the Athens and Perseus material but the source is reliable and there is no reason to doubt the association. Head (*HN*, 265 f.) assigns the spread-flan coinage of Thasos to the period after ca. 146 B.C., connecting its inception with the closing of the Macedonian mints in 148, and this date has been generally accepted. There is, however, considerable stylistic variation in the series as a whole. Without question the crude and degenerate specimens which comprise the bulk of the coinage are the characteristic output of a mint operating in the late second and early first centuries, but there are also coins of superior workmanship and execution. The ΔI issue in particular, with its carefully-modelled types and neat inscriptions struck on large flans with hammered edges, should on grounds of style alone be placed in the first half of the second century.[5] Heretofore there has been no precise hoard evidence to challenge the traditional dating for the spread-flan coinage of Thasos. Now the presence of early tetradrachms in a hoard which

---

[5] A coin from the ANS Collection (PLATE XVIII, A) illustrates the excellent workmanship of this issue. Another example is to be found in List 220 of Münzen und Medaillen where the piece is dated ca. 180 B.C.

The hammering of the flan, clearly visible on both coins, is characteristic of Thasian tetradrachms of good style. This peculiar technique seems to have been especially prevalent in the Euxine region, in Thrace and in Northwestern Anatolia, appearing on regnal issues of the late third and early second centuries and on a variety of civic strikings which must antedate 155 B.C. on the evidence of the Babylon hoard (*ZfN* 1928, 92 ff.). Unfortunately it cannot be considered a firm chronological criterion since hammered edges do occur at a later date, commonly on the money of the Bithynian kings and sporadically elsewhere, but the technique is basically a phenomenon of the first half of the second century.

cannot have been buried much later than 168 B.C. makes it apparent that the chronology of the series must be revised. It can no longer be maintained that Thasos, after regaining independence in 196, waited fifty years before re-opening her mint. Some autonomous silver was produced in the period between Cynoscephalae and Pydna.

Several sources attest the association of Perseus and early New Style tetradrachms in this Thessalian hoard. Estimates of wear for individual specimens range from good to FDC, and these reports on condition are confirmed by the six pieces specifically identified as hoard coins. The three Perseus tetradrachms are dated by Mamroth to 173–171 and 170–168 B.C. None has had much use. The Athenian tetradrachms of 179/8 and 176/5 have circulated but are still very well preserved, while the later striking of 171/0 is in even better condition.[6] The evidence of wear for these six hoard coins is in complete accord with the recorded chronologies of the two series; the Athenian and Macedonian issues are clearly contemporary.

The obvious historical occasion for the interment of a substantial number of well-preserved tetradrachms of 178–168 B.C. is the Third Macedonian War. During that struggle Thessaly was repeatedly invaded by the Roman and Macedonian forces and the situation of Tricca, at the eastern end of the important Metsovon pass, was particularly vulnerable. The burial of our hoard may plausibly be connected with the campaigns leading up to Pydna or with Paullus' punitive expedition into Epirus shortly after the defeat of Perseus.

MARGARET THOMPSON

[6] The Nike tetradrachm was struck from a badly worn obverse die which has produced a weak impression marred by breaks and flaws. All three coins, curiously enough, have been maltreated. On the trident piece (Münz. u. Med. List 222) the lower wing of the owl has been gouged, while on the thyrsos and Nike tetradrachms (PLATE XVII, 1–2) metal has been shaved from the bodies of the two amphoras and there are unmistakable indications of scraping on the plumage of the owls. Except for this surface damage, however, the details of the Nike reverse are very sharp.

THE LATE HELLENISTIC TETROBOLS OF KOS
(See Plates XVIII–XXIV)

In 1960 the American Numismatic Society was bequeathed, as part of the collection of the late David M. Robinson, a hoard of 70 Koan coins all belonging to the series described as "drachms of reduced weight or tetrobols" and customarily dated to the period 166–88 B.C. The Robinson hoard, together with an unpublished hoard of 27 of these coins, purchased jointly by the Ashmolean and British Museums in 1935 (Noe 276), has practically doubled the number of extant coins of this type and has made a reasonably complete study of the entire coinage possible.[1] In addition to the new hoard material, photographs or casts of 118 pieces have been gathered from publications and from a number of unpublished museum collections, bringing the total number of coins examined in this study to 215. Probably no other Koan series survives in such quantity.

These coins bear on the obverse the profile head of Asklepios, bearded and wearing a wreath of laurel leaves in his hair. The reverse is stamped with an incuse square containing Asklepios' coiled snake, magistrates' names, and the ethnic ΚΩΙΩΝ, usually in abbreviated form. There is considerable variety in the form and information of these legends, some of which even record an abbreviation for a constitutional office or body. On the flan below the incuse square appears a letter or a combination of letters.

There is no longer any reason to consider these coins reduced drachms. Their standard weight, as obtained from a frequency analysis of 194 dependably weighed specimens (fig. 1), is, to the nearest

[1] I am indebted to the American Numismatic Society for providing me with the opportunity to undertake this study at the Society's 1963 Summer Seminar and to Margaret Thompson, whose generous assistance and advice was indispensable in the study's every phase. Grateful acknowledgement is also due to Lucy Turnbull, Hansjorg Bloesch, Colin Kraay, Kenneth Jenkins, Georges Le Rider, Jacques Yvon, Eberhard Erxleben and Peter Berghaus for help in collecting materials and to William Calder III and Sterling Dow for suggestions on epigraphical matters.

.05, 2.05 gms.[2] This figure is almost exactly two-thirds the weight of second-century Koan drachms, 3.05 gms.,[3] and can only mean that, on the Rhodian standard traditionally in use at Kos, our Asklepios coins are most certainly tetrobols.

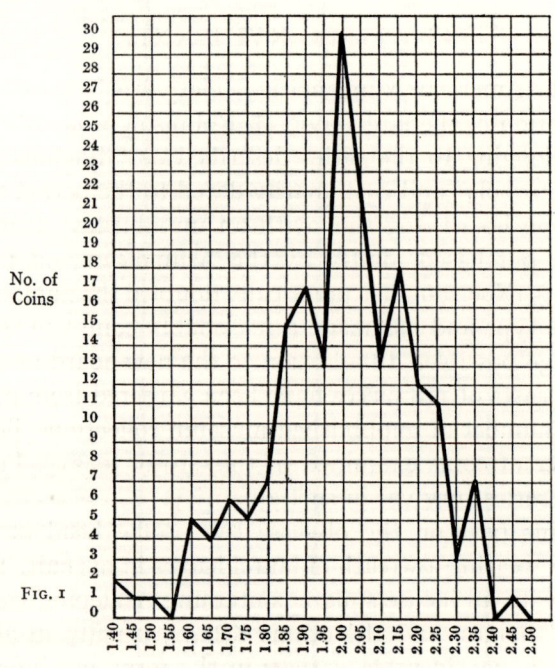

Fig. 1

[2] The frequency table shows a larger grouping at the 2.00 gm. mark, but taking into consideration a factor for wear and Hill's principle that the true weight is where the curve first jumps to a high peak (*NC*, 1924, 80), the heavier weight (2.05 gm.) is preferable.

[3] Frequency distribution of 21 of the drachms dated by Head to 190–166 B.C. (*BMC* 76–83) showed the greatest groupings at 3.00–3.05 gm. For reasons stated above the higher figure would seem the more accurate. The weights of only 15 drachms of the type assigned to 166–88 B.C. (*BMC* 117–118) were available for analysis, and they spread so widely on a frequency scale that the standard could be estimated only from an average of the 11 more typical weights. This average, 3.03 gm., plus a one per cent factor for wear (most of the coins are in relatively fine condition), gives a standard of about 3.05 gm. Admittedly, the sample number of both series of rare drachms provides an inadequate foundation for any firm conclusions as to their weight standards, but the approximations arrived at are dependable enough to allow safe comparison with the weights of our tetrobols.

Although Head reasonably assigned these tetrobols and the incuse Koan drachms (*BMC* 117–118) to the years 166–88 B.C., he was mistaken in implying that the two coinages, which have no magistrates' names in common, were minted contemporaneously.[4] Indeed the names on the tetrobols do not correspond to names on any other Koan coinage, bronze or silver, indicating that when the tetrobols were minted, they were minted exclusively, without larger or smaller denominations. The incuse drachms must have been earlier than the tetrobols and, as Head plausibly deduced, were probably first struck after 166 B.C. in imitation of the restored incuse drachms of Rhodes.[5]

A hoard from Kalymna, published by E. S. G. Robinson (*NC* 1936, 190 ff.), confirms Head's association of the Koan and Rhodian incuse drachms and establishes the relative chronology of the major second century coinages of Kos. The deposit contained pre-166 drachms of Rhodes and Kos and pre-166 bronze of Kos in worn or somewhat worn condition; post-166 drachms and hemidrachms of Kos and hemidrachms of Rhodes in fine to FDC state of preservation; and silver of Kalymna with and without magistrates' names, the latter slightly rubbed and the former very fine. Robinson dates the inscribed Kalymnian coins, of which two issues are recorded, ca. 125 B.C. and suggests that the hoard was buried "shortly before 100 B.C." This date seems unnecessarily late. All the Koan and Rhodian coins could have been minted in the first half of the second century. The fact that only pre-166 bronze and only a few issues of post-166 silver are present would point to an earlier period of deposit. As Robinson comments, the Kalymnian coins with magistrates' names look earlier than the date he assigns them; some reverses show the dotted frame which characterizes Koan silver of the third century. Now that Segre[6] has demonstrated that Kalymna had become fully integrated

---

[4] *BMC* xcvi.
[5] *BMC* xcvi and cix–cx. The heavy financial losses incurred by Rhodes in 166, which provide a plausible explanation for the revision of the weight and appearance of the Rhodian drachms, are explicitly documented by a statement in Polybios, xxx. 31. Head's chronology for the series is also confirmed by the Oreos hoard of ca. 173 B.C. (Noe 771) which contained nearly 600 Rhodian drachms of the type dated before 166. The absence of any of the later incuse drachms suggests that ca. 173 they were not yet in circulation.
[6] *Annuario*, 1944–45, pub. 1952, 12–17, 25–26 and 86. From the collected Kalymnian inscriptions Segre concluded that Kalymna had begun to be politi-

into the Koan state after 190 B.C., all the Kalymnian pieces must have been struck prior to that date and those with the magistrates' names possibly in 191–190 B.C. during the brief period when Kalymna asserted her independence. In any case it is unlikely that the Kalymna hoard was buried much after 150 B.C. and it may have been in the ground before that date.

As Robinson notes, the absence of any Asklepios tetrobols in the hoard indicates that they were not minted until after the incuse drachms and related hemidrachms had ceased to be struck. This earlier Koan series was probably produced for a limited period of some twenty years after 166,[7] giving our tetrobols a *terminus post quem* of ca. 145 B.C.

For the next two or three generations the only historical events of any importance involving Kos were connected with the Mithradatic War, and there is no certainty that these would have affected the Koan domestic economy sufficiently to have caused a change in minting policies. It is true that in 88 the Koans remained hostile to Mithradates until he reached the island, but they apparently succeeded in appeasing him by delivering up the treasures which had been entrusted to their keeping by Kleopatra and affluent Jewish bankers.[8] One questions whether Mithradates, with such vast plunder in hand, would have antagonized the Koans by further extensive confiscations from public and private resources at a time when he was trying to win over the various Greek states by acts of patronage as well as by threats. A few years later, in 82 B.C., Kos may have been rewarded for her fidelity to Rome by some privilege granted by Sulla, but about this we cannot be certain.[9]

---

cally absorbed by Kos in the last decades of the third century but rebelled in 191 when Kos and Rhodes sided with Rome against Antiochos. After Antiochos' defeat in 190, Kalymna was completely incorporated into the Koan polity and this situation prevailed at least into the first century. It may have been Kalymna's bid for autonomy in 191 B.C. that inspired the distinctive and rare silver issues with magistrates' names and star symbol.

[7] That is, for no more than 20 issues. The magistrates' names listed by Paton-Hicks (*The Inscriptions of Cos*, 1891, nos. 139–144 and 219–227) can now be supplemented for a total of nine on the drachms and thirteen on the hemidrachms. Five names appear on both denominations, giving a present record of seventeen separate issues for the series.

[8] Tacitus *Ann.* vi.14; Appian *Mithr.* 23 and 115; Josephos *A.J.* xiv, 7,2.

[9] Paton-Hicks, xxxix–xl.

The historical situation provides no conclusive reason for a break in the coinage which might serve as a *terminus ante quem* for the tetrobol series, and there is no way of establishing a burial date for the two lots of hoard coins which are associated with no other coinages.[10] Nevertheless, as Head remarks, it is scarcely likely that the Asklepios silver went on after the Mithradatic War. Apart from considerations of style, there is the circumstance that it is a substantial coinage[11] and its largest issues, which are not represented among the hoard coins, are the latest in date. It is quite improbable that such sizable strikings would have been put out in the post-Mithradatic period.

The present record gives us a total of 34 issues, determined by the magistrates' names on the reverses, and although there are perhaps a few issues which remain unknown, it seems unlikely that much new material will be added in the future. We cannot be certain that the issues were minted annually, or indeed at any regular interval, but the overlapping of obverse dies and the recurrence of magistrates' names strongly suggest that this was a compact coinage of rather limited duration and that it did not span the entire period between 145 and 88 B.C. Further than this we cannot go. Until additional hoard or other evidence turns up, the only safe chronological conclusion is that our Asklepios tetrobols were struck sometime in the second half of the second century B.C. and may have continued into the opening decades of the first century.[12]

---

[10] The interment of two hoards might be linked with Mithradates' occupation of Kos but there is good reason to believe that the American and English lots are actually two parts of a single hoard (see pp. 100 f.). Furthermore, the deposit seems to have been a savings accumulation rather than a currency hoard and there is, therefore, no need to postulate a military threat as the reason for its burial.

[11] See the Table of Issues on pp. 88 f. for the record of obverse dies. The fact that the proportion of known specimens per die is so low for almost all issues makes it clear that the coinage was originally much more extensive than the surviving record would indicate.

[12] It is impossible to restrict this dating from the prosopographical data. The inscriptions which list great numbers of Koan citizens come from the end of the third century and from the beginning of the second, at least two or three generations earlier than our coins. There are in fact very few prosopographically informative inscriptions which can be securely dated after the first decades of the second century. One exception is the list of Koans who served in the navy of Aulus Terentius Varro against Mithradates in 82 B.C. (*JÖAI*, 1898, 31–34). The only one of its names which corresponds to a name on our coins

One wonders why the Koans decided to discontinue their conventional drachm-hemidrachm coinage and replace it with the curious minting of a tetrobol fraction. The answer must lie in the coins' ingenious bi-standard convertibility: on the Koan-Rhodian standard the coins are tetrobols but on the Attic standard they have the weight of hemidrachms.[13] In the second century the widespread minting of posthumous Alexander and Lysimachos tetradrachms and the popular New Style issues of Athens gave the Attic standard, to which they were all struck, an international character. At Rhodes and at Kos during this time most of the large silver being produced was of Attic weight,[14] for the Rhodians had stopped minting their own tetradrachms at least by 166 although they continued to strike abundant issues of drachms on their traditional local standard. The older Rhodian tetradrachms, however, undoubtedly continued to circulate along with the Attic money, presenting problems of exchange which the citizens of Kos met by minting for local transactions a fractional coin adaptable to both standards: eight of the Asklepios pieces equal an Attic tetradrachm and six a Rhodian. In the late Hellenistic period a minor state in the southern Aegean needing a small change currency could hardly have solved the bi-standard problem more neatly.

The following Table of Issues presents the statistical record of the coinage. The 34 known issues are of three kinds: those bearing two

is the name of the ναύαρχος of the fleet, Εὔδαμος, who was probably a Rhodian (*JÖAI*, 1891, Beiblatt, 92). Most of our magistrates' names are common and can be found on inscriptions of all periods. Notable exceptions are Θευφαμί(δας), a name which according to the major Greek prosopographies does not appear anywhere in the Greek world except on these coins; and 'Ανθεσ... which is otherwise unknown at Kos. Three of the names appear only once each in Koan inscriptions: Λόχος, in a dedication dated by Segre (*Annuario*, 1944–45, no. XXVIII = Paton-Hicks no. 60) to the middle part of the first century B.C.; Δεινίας, as monarchos in an undated decree published by Paton (*Rev. Ét. Gr.*, 1896, 419, no. 7); and Γενοκ(λῆς), partially restored in another undated decree Paton-Hicks no. 9). See also n. 63.

[13] Head (*BMC* xcvi) recognized this. Paton (Paton-Hicks, 314) labeled the coins Attic hemidrachms. The Rhodian standard in actual practice during the Hellenistic centuries (stater = ca. 13 gm.) was nearly equivalent to the Cistophoric standard (stater = ca. 12.5 gm.). The Athenian New Style tetradrachms were struck to a standard of 16.75–16.90 gm.

[14] Rhodes issued Alexanders as did Kos. The latter mint also put out a tetradrachm coinage with autonomous types on the Attic standard (*ZfN*, 1928, 124, nos. 77–78).

magistrates' names (21 issues), those with one magistrate's name (5 issues), and those with one name together with an abbreviation for an official title or body, ΠΡΟΣ-ΠΡΟΣΤΑΤ (6 issues) or ΒΟΥ (1 issue). The names and abbreviations are written within the reverse incuse square on either side of the coiled snake, usually from the bottom of the incuse to the top. In four exceptional issues (1–3 and 14) the writing is from top to bottom and in one issue (12) the writing usually runs in a different direction on each side of the snake.

The earlier coinages of Kos were regularly inscribed with the full ethnic ΚΩΙΟΝ or, after 166, ΚΩΙΩΝ above a single magistrate's name. This format was retained in our earlier one-magistrate issues where the full ethnic could be written alongside the snake in place of a second magistrate's name or a magisterial abbreviation; however in the two-magistrate issues and the ΒΟΥ and ΠΡΟΣΤΑΤ issues, the ethnic was of necessity abbreviated ΚΩΙ, ΚΩ, or ΚΩΝ and located below the snake in the incuse. (The exception is coin 14b which has an unabbreviated ethnic squeezed into this space.) In the late one-magistrate issue, issue 34, the traditional formula was naturally revived but in reverse order, with name preceding ethnic. Apparently the Koans became accustomed to seeing the ethnic below the names on the long series of two-magistrate coins and had forgotten that in earlier times the ethnic was always in first position.

Since the ancients did not as a rule abbreviate by syncopation, the contracted ΚΩΝ should be regarded more as a vocalic representation of the full ethnic ΚΩΙΩΝ (Κῷων) than as an abbreviation proper. It shows that by the second half of the second century the citizens of Kos no longer pronounced the iota of the substantive adjective Κῶιος and did not articulate between the two omegas of its genitive plural. Thus ΚΩΝ is used like a full ethnic in the one-magistrate issues 11 and 34 in preference to ΚΩΙΩΝ, although room for the more complete spelling was available. The syncopated ΚΩΝ provided the most satisfactory solution to the problem of fitting a five-letter ethnic in a small space and one would expect it to be used on all the coins; but, as is seen from the Table of Issues, it was in fact employed less commonly than the abbreviations ΚΩΙ or ΚΩ.

The table also shows the vagaries of the puzzling letters at the bottom of the reverses. The letters, in relief outside of the protecting

TABLE OF ISSUES

Solid lines indicate die linkage.
Dotted lines indicate close stylistic affinity.

On l. and r. of Snake	Below Snake	Below Incuse	No. of known Obvs.	No. of known Revs.	Total Collected	Total no. in Hoards	No. in DMR Hoard	No. in Noe 276 Hoard
1. ΑΝΔΡΟΣΘΕ/ΒΟΥ	ΚΩ	Δ	2	2	2	1		1
2. ΚΛΕΩ/ΠΡΟΣ	ΚΩ	Δ	1	1	1			
3. ΦΙΛΙΩΝ/ΠΡΟΣΤ	ΚΩΙ	Δ	1	1	1			
4. ΠΡΟΣΤ/ΝΙΚΙΑΣ	ΚΩ	Δ	2	3	5	1	1	
5. ΠΡΟΣΤΑΤ/ΙΠΠΟΚΡΑ	ΚΩΙ	Δ	3	3	5	5	4	1
6. ΠΡΟΣΤΑ/ΕΥΔΑΜ	ΚΩΙ	Δ	4	4	4	2	1	1
7. ΠΡΟΣΤΑ/ΘΕΥΔΟΤ	ΚΩΙ	Δ	5	4	7	4	2	2
8. ΚΩΙΩΝ/ΑΡΙΣΤΟΚ		Δ	2	5	11	11	9	2
9. ΚΩΙΩΝ/ΑΡΙΣΤΩΝ		ΠΙ	2	2	3	1	1	
10. ΚΩΙΩΝ/ΝΙΚΟΜΗ		ΠΙ	1	1	1	1	1	
11. ΚΩΝ/ΝΙΚΩΝ		ΠΙ	2	2	4	2		
12. ΚΩΙΩΝ/ΑΝΘΕΣ		Α	4	6	9	3	1	1
13. ΑΓΗΣΙ/ΑΡΙΣΤΟ	ΚΩΙ	Α	2	6	9	6	6	2
14. ΠΑΡΜ/ΑΓΗΣΙ	ΚΩΙΩΝ, ΚΩΙ, ΚΩ	Δ	2	4	6	4	3	1
15. ΑΛΚΙΔΑΜ/ΔΕΙΝΙΑΣ	ΚΩΙ	Δ	3	6	7	4	3	1
16. ΑΓΗΣΙΑ/ΘΕΥΦΑΜ	ΚΩΙ	Δ	4	7	11	6	3	3

TETROBOLS OF KOS

17. ΑΛΚΙΔΑΜΟ/ΑΓΗΣΙΑΣ	ΚΩΝ	Δ	3	3	4	4	4	
18. ΝΙΚΟΜΗΔ/ΘΕΥΦΑΜΙ	ΚΩΙ, ΚΩΝ	Δ	4	5	6	5	4	1
19. ΛΟΧΟΣ/ΠΑΡΜΕ	ΚΩ	Δ	4	5	5	4	3	1
20. ΠΑΡΜΕ/ΓΕΝΟΚΛΗ	ΚΩ	Δ	4	3	5	1		1
21. ΝΙΚΟΜΗ/ΑΡΙΣΤΟ	ΚΩ, ΚΩΝ	Δ	5	10	10	4	2	2
22. ΘΕΥΦΑΜ/ΑΓΗΣΙΑ	ΚΩ	Δ	2	2	6	4	3	1
23. ΑΡΙΣΤΟΚ/ΛΟΧΟΣ	ΚΩΙ, ΚΩ	Δ, Ε	5	9	9	8	5	3
24. ΝΙΚΟΣΤ/ΔΕΙΝΙΑΣ	ΚΩ	Ε	5	5	6	3	2	1
25. ΤΕΙΣΑ/ΑΛΚΙΔΑ	ΚΩ, ΚΩΝ	Ε	4	4	5	3	3	
26. ΦΙΛΟΦΡ/ΜΕΝΩΝ	ΚΩ, ΚΩΝ	Ε, Δ	6	8	10	5	4	1
27. ΔΕΙΝΙΑΣ/ΝΙΚΟΣΤΡ	ΚΩ, ΚΩΝ	Δ, Ε	7	10	10	5	4	1
28. ΠΑΡΜΕ/ΛΟΧΟΣ	ΚΩ	Ε	1	1	2	1	1	
29. ΗΛΙΟΔΩ/ΕΥΑΡΑΤ	ΚΩΙ, ΚΩ, ΚΩΝ	Η, Ν	13	16	18			
30. ΤΙΜΟΓ/ΕΥΔΑΜ	ΚΩΙ	Η	2	2	2			
31. ΝΙΚΑΡΧΟΣ/ΑΣΚΛΗΠΙ	ΚΩΝ	Η	2	2	2			

Δ on Obv., star on Rev.

32. ΤΙΜΟΞΕΝ/ΕΚΑΤΑΙΟΥ	ΚΩΙ	Δ	5	9	10			
ΕΚΑΤΑΙΟΣ/ΤΙΜΟΞΕΝ	ΚΩΙ	Δ	3	4	4			
33. ΕΚΑΤΑΙ/ΤΕΙΜΟΣ	ΚΩΙ	?	1	1	1			
34. ΑΝΔΡΟΣ/ΚΩΝ		Δ	8	14	14			
		Totals	124	170	215	98	71	27

incuse square, were especially susceptible to rubbing and on many of the extant coins have been worn away entirely. The difficulty of obtaining an accurate reading of the letters is further complicated by careless die engraving and the inherent ambiguity among several of the letter forms, particularly between deltas and alphas.[15] As reverses struck from the same die demonstrate (see esp. nos. 8 c 1–3, PLATE XIX, 6–8), the letters were cut in the reverse dies themselves, not added with a second stamp.

The most common letter in this position is Δ. In issues 32–34 deltas occur on the obverse below Asklepios' head as well as on the reverse. Presumably, this is nothing more than duplication. Π appears in three one-magistrate issues (9–11) and A in the one-magistrate issue 12 and the two-magistrate issue 13.[16] Epsilons occur in the later, extensively linked two-magistrate issues 23–28, and in issues 23, 26 and 27 occur together with deltas. Some of these epsilons lack a middle horizontal stroke and have the appearance Ϲ.[17] On the reverses of three issues (29–31) which are not represented in the hoards and therefore should be even later than the epsilon issues, there is usually the letter H; although N sometimes appears and on one coin (30 b, PLATE XXIV, 10) a ⊓, which could be a pi but is more likely an eta whose upper half, as occasionally happens with the letters on other coins (see esp. 9 b, 10, 32 k, and 34 i, PLATES XIX, 15, 17; XXIV, 16, 20), has disappeared at the edge of the incuse square. Apparently, if the letters were not cut far enough below the incuse part of the die, their tops tended to be obliterated in the striking process.

These letters must be related to the minting of the coins, but beyond that little more can be said with confidence. Several possible interpretations can be rejected. The letters cannot stand for months in the Koan year or localities on the island; and their behavior and distribution make it extremely improbable that they represent work-

---

[15] In the catalogue all ambiguous triangular letters have been listed as deltas (with a dot below) unless an unmistakable alpha occurs elsewhere in the issue.

[16] Issues 17 and 19 have reverses with alpha-like letters, but it is probable that they are carelessly cut deltas.

[17] In some instances the weak middle bar may have disappeared with wear but in others it seems that the bar was intentionally omitted, either to reproduce the simpler three-stroke epsilon form (which is commonly used in many of these coins' legends) or the Hellenistic form of the alphabetic numeral digamma or six. For a use of this numerical digamma at Kos see Paton-Hicks no. 43.

shops.[18] Perhaps the most profitable line of approach is to consider these letters alphabetical numerals or, what is much the same thing, letters indicating positions in a sequence. We have A (1), Δ (4), E (5), Ϲ (6), possibly Z on its side (7), and H (8). Short diagonal lines to the lower left or right of the letter on two reverses (4b and 18c, PLATES XVIII, 5; XXI, 15) could be accidental marks caused by a slip of the die-engraving tool or they could be marks signifying that the letters were intended to be alphabetic numerals. There are of course difficulties with the interpretation of the letters as numerals: ΠΙ cannot be fitted into the series unless it be dubiously read as the numeral 6 in the earlier acrophontic numeral system whose pi's are elsewhere always inscribed in the older form Γ, not Π as they are in the legends of our one-magistrate issues; the readings of Ϲ as a numerical digamma and N as a zeta curiously turned on its side are at best questionable; and beta (2) and gamma (3) are missing from our coins altogether. But even if all or most of our letters are numerals, there is still no way of knowing what they mean.

The letters on our tetrobols may have served the same purpose as the isolated letters on earlier second-century Koan coinages: K, KE, and Δ on the post-166 B.C. drachms and A on the contemporaneous hemidrachms. These letters could be numerals also, but they certainly cannot indicate a sequence.

The behavior of the deltas and epsilons in the seven closely linked issues (22–28) is diagrammed in figure 2. The latest obverse die in issue 22, a delta issue, continued in use with epsilon reverses in the two successive issues: issue 23, a delta and epsilon issue, and issue 24, solely an epsilon issue. All the other obverse dies which continued to be used for two or more issues were always employed with epsilon reverses, even in issue 27 which is predominately a delta issue. It is hard to see what all this means. The letters simply defy any straightforward, convincing interpretation.

Since magisterial titles do not commonly appear on Greek coinages until Imperial times, the abbreviations ΠΡΟΣΤΑΤ and ΒΟΥ are among the most interesting features of our tetrobols. As Paton and Head recognized, ΠΡΟΣΤΑΤ refers to the Koan προστάται, a five-member board, comparable to the board of prytaneis at Athens and Rhodes,

---

[18] As Head conjectured (*BMC* xcvi).

which was responsible for administering the most important business of the state.[19] Paton and Head[20] thought the abbreviations should be expanded in the singular, προστάτ(ης), as the title of the man whose name appears with it.[21] This is certainly the most obvious restoration

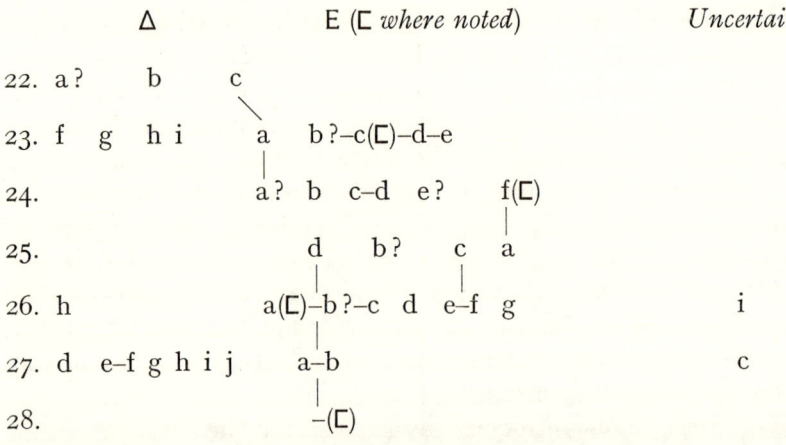

FIG. 2. Obverse dies are referred to by the letters assigned them in the Catalogue. Vertical connecting lines trace the progression of dies used in more than one issue. Coins whose reverse letters are missing or uncertain are classified with a question mark if their letters can be conjectured.

[19] The prostatai are frequently mentioned in the preamble of decrees as the Koan probouleutic executives. More scattered epigraphical references inform us that the prostatai presided in various religious, financial and judicial proceedings. S.v. προστάτης in Paton-Hicks; Segre, *Annuario* 1944–45; and R. Herzog, *Heilige Gesetz von Kos* in *Abhandl. d. Preuss. Akademie der Wissenschaften, Phil. hist. Kl.*, 1928. For the number of prostatai at Kos see M. Segre, *Riv. Filol.*, 1933, 368. The tenure of the prostatai is uncertain. Segre, the only scholar who has committed himself on this point (*Annuario*, 1944–45, 40), believed that they were rotated monthly, like the more numerous prytaneis at Athens; but his opinion is based on dangerously elaborate restorations in Kalymnian inscriptions, which in any case refer to Kalymnian not Koan prostatai. It is more probable that Kos followed the constitutional precedent of Rhodes, which rotated her similar five-member board of prytaneis semiannually (Hiller von Gaertrigen, *P-W*, Suppl. V., 1931, 767).
[20] Paton-Hicks 304 and *BMC* xcvi.
[21] Abbreviations as titles could precede proper names (as on our issues 4–7) or follow them (as on issues 1–3). Inscriptions use both word orders in mentioning a man and his title. On Greek imperial coins titles usually precede names.

but it is not the only one possible. In the twenty or thirty Koan inscriptions which make reference to the prostatai, a single prostates is never mentioned; it is always the full board of prostatai who are said to be doing one thing or another. Constitutional authority was invested in the prostatai collectively, making it unlikely that an individual prostates ever acted officially on his own. For this reason we would be justified in expanding ΠΡΟΣΤΑΤ in the plural and restoring the legends to read προστάτ(αι καὶ) δεῖνα or, at least in issues 4 through 7 in which abbreviation precedes proper name, προστάτ (αι τοὶ σὺν) δεῖνι, the prostatai under so and so.[22]

The BOY in the heretofore unknown issue 1 presents similar problems of interpretation. It must stand either for βουλευτής or βουλά;[23] and although again the former restoration is the most natural, membership in the boula must have been so common that it is difficult to imagine why any man who was a bouleutes would take any pride in advertising it. We do not know how large the Koan boula was. It probably had well over a hundred members and in any case it was certainly large enough for any politically-minded citizen to be a member at least once in his lifetime. A more reasonable restoration of the legend involves expanding BOY to denote the legislative body as a whole, allowing us to read 'Ανδροσθέ(νης καὶ) Βου(λά). But a fuller discussion of the significance of these ΠΡΟΣΤΑΤ and BOY legends is best postponed until after the other issues provide what clues they can.

About half of the magistrates' names which appear in the two-magistrate issues occur in more than one issue. For example, Hagesias appears in issues 13, 14, 16, 17 and 22; Parmeniskos in issues 14, 19, 20 and 28; Alkidamos in issues 15, 17 and 25; Theuphamidas in issues 16, 18 and 22. These recurrent names occur sometimes as the first of the two names, sometimes as second. There are three pairs of issues

---

[22] The legend ΙΜΥΡΝΑΙΩΝ ΠΡΥΤΑΝΕΙΣ on a roughly contemporary gold stater from Smyrna (Head, *HN*, 1911, 593) furnishes an excellent parallel for a coinage issued in the name of a full executive body.

[23] BOY cannot be an abbreviation for a proper name. No known Koan name begins with these three letters, and even if one did, it is almost certain that a longer abbreviation would have been used. On the two coins of issue 1 there is room for several more letters. BOY on the other hand was a common abbreviation for βουλευτής or βουλή in the inscriptions of the Hellenistic and Imperial East (M. Avi-Yonah, *Abbreviations in Greek Inscriptions, The Near East 200 B.C.–A.D. 1100*, 1940, 54).

bearing the same two names but in a different order: issue 16 (Hagesias/Theuphamidas) and issue 22 (Theuphamidas/Hagesias); issue 19 (Lochos/Parmeniskos) and issue 28 (Parmeniskos/Lochos); issue 24 (Nikostratos/Deinias) and issue 27 (Deinias/Nikostratos). There is no reason to believe that such paired issues were minted consecutively. Die linkage in fact proves that the paired issues 24 and 27 are separated from each other by two other issues, and stylistic criteria indicate that the other two pairs are not contiguous either.

Issue 32 presents a possible exception. Nine of its known reverses are inscribed Timoxenos/Hekataios, five are inscribed Hekataios/Timoxenos. No die linkage exists between the two types of coins, but their stylistic features (star on reverse, delta on obverse) are identical, suggesting that they were struck consecutively. There is as yet no way of knowing whether the two types represent two independent issues or, as they are classified in our Catalogue and Table of Issues, two independent series within a single issue. In any case it is unlikely that we have here a single issue whose two names were freely interchangeable. Consistency in the order of names in all the other two-magistrate issues[24] indicates that there was some significance attached to the order in which the names were recorded.

Repeated attempts to place the unlinked two-magistrate issues in a sequence which would bring the names into some kind of fixed relationship have been singularly unsuccessful, and permit no other conclusion but that the names occur at random, quite as the Table of Issues shows.

Most Greek coinages, when they are inscribed with magistrates' signatures, bear the name of only one man, who is usually thought to be either an eponymous magistrate or some kind of minting official. Neither identification, however, will fit the names on our tetrobols. The eponymous magistrate at Kos was the monarchos. Now the monarchos might be the person mentioned with the prostatai in the

[24] Single exceptions occur in issues 13 and 29. The names on one reverse die in issue 13 (13g) and on one reverse die in issue 29 (29q) are inscribed in a different order than the names on the other reverses in the issues. The order of names on these two exceptional reverses may or may not have been altered intentionally, but in either case the two reverses should not be classified as belonging to separate issues since they are unique and are linked by the obverse dies used with them to regularly inscribed coins in issues 13 or 29.

ΠΡΟΣΤΑΤ issues and the magistrate in the one-magistrate issues, but the monarchos could not be either magistrate of our two-magistrate issues simply because a man could be monarchos at Kos only once in his lifetime and his name therefore could appear in first or second position on only one issue. As I have indicated, recurrent names are sometimes in the first position, sometimes in the second; therefore neither position can be considered as reserved for the annual monarchos. The repetition of names within the two-magistrate issues also allows us to discard Head's conjecture[25] that these names are the names of prostatai. It is unlikely that a citizen of democratic Kos could have been a prostates more than once. Moreover, the BOY issue demonstrates that the legends are not to be associated with the prostatai exclusively.

There are three reasons why the magistrates on our coins cannot be minting officials. In the first place, it is improbable that the distinguished Koan prostatai would have been burdened with overseeing a technical operation like the minting of coins. This was a duty that would have been charged to a minor magistracy or board, not to the men who administered the state's business at large. Secondly, the random behavior of magistrates' names in the two-magistrate issues cannot be reconciled with regular magistracies of any kind. Constitutional offices imply order and system in their tenure, and order and system are missing altogether in our two-magistrate issues. Finally, even if at Kos the hypothetical office of mint magistrate could have been held by the same person more than once, it would hardly have been so popular a post that a man would want to hold it three, four, or even five times.

A third explanation for the names appearing on a number of Greek coinages and the one which has commanded the most serious attention in recent years is the identification of the men as wealthy citizens who voluntarily contributed to a λειτουργία for the coins' production. The magistrates' names which are prefaced by διά or παρά on several Greek imperial coinages are almost certainly the names of such private donors,[26] and the peculiar behavior of unprefaced names on the late Hellenistic coinages of Athens and Ilium has permitted

---

[25] *BMC* xcvi.
[26] Head, *HN* (1911), lxvii.

strong arguments to be advanced in favor of a similar interpretation for these names.[27]

This numismatic evidence becomes all the more convincing in the light of Rostovtzeff's observations on the importance of liturgy financing in Hellenistic times. Liturgies are most commonly thought of in terms of the trierarchy and choregia of classical Athens, but as inscriptions show and as Rostovtzeff has emphasized,[28] this kind of financing was increasingly relied upon in later times and indeed in the Hellenistic period must have constituted an important part of the small states' actual income. Many specific magistracies became *de facto* liturgies and actually were known as λειτουργίαι;[29] the rich citizens to whom these burdensome positions regularly went were expected to pay for the costs of administration out of their own pockets. As Rostovtzeff says, it was only natural in the post-classical age, when times were often hard, that Greek cities were forced to draw more and more on the resources of their wealthiest members.

From Hellenistic Kos itself an exceptionally large number of liturgy inscriptions have survived. These consist primarily of ἐπίδοσις lists, records of citizens who contributed toward a specific project or cause and the amount each of them donated. There are at least six ἐπίδοσις inscriptions: a monumental roster of hundreds of citizens who contributed emergency funds during the Cretan War in the last decade of the third century;[30] a fragmentary list also connected with this war;[31] an early second-century list of donors towards the construction and furnishing of a library;[32] a roughly contemporary list of deme members who financed the building of an Aphrodision;[33] an

---

[27] M. Thompson, *The New Style Silver Coinage of Athens* (1961), 584–599; and A. R. Bellinger, *ANSMN* VIII (1958), 23–24. Monetary liturgies have been discussed also in relation to coinages of Kolophon (J. G. Milne, *NNM* 96, 26–29), Eretria (W. Wallace, *Phoenix*, 1950, 21–26), and Cabyle in Thrace (T. Gerassimov, *ANSCent*, 276).

[28] *Social and Economic History of the Hellenistic World* (1941), 619–621 and 1463–1464.

[29] *OCD*, s.v. Liturgy.

[30] Paton-Hicks no. 10 (*SGDI* 3624). Discussions of its date and the dates of Paton-Hicks nos. 387 and 404 (nn. 33 and 36 below) are cited by L. Robert, *BCH*, 1935, 423, n. 3.

[31] Paton-Hicks no. 11 (*SGDI* 3625).

[32] L. Robert, *BCH*, 1935, 421–424.

[33] Paton-Hicks no. 387 (*SGDI* 3722).

unpublished list of contributors towards the Asklepieia, ca. 260 B.C.;[34] and an undated list of subscribers for an unknown undertaking.[35] To these might be added an early second-century list of citizens who donated funds for some religious purpose[36] and three inscriptions whose identity as ἐπίδοσις lists is probable but uncertain.[37] Yet another inscription from the time of the Cretan War informs us that the Koan navy was outfitted by means of ship liturgies or τριηραραχίαι.[38]

Since liturgical financing is attested at Kos perhaps better than anywhere else in the Hellenistic world, we have excellent reason to believe that it holds the key to the identification of the men named on our tetrobols. Like the Koans who contributed to the emergency war fund, the navy, the library and other such civic purposes, the men whose names appear on our coins were citizens who contributed to the cost of the minting and who received in recognition of this service the honor of having their names inscribed on the coins' reverses. No other identification can satisfactorily explain the irregular behavior of names in our two-magistrate issues and the questions raised by the legends in the ΠΡΟΣΤΑΤ and ΒΟΥ issues.

Our two-magistrate issues would be strikings for which the expense of the monetary liturgy was split and made less onerous. The frequent recurrence of names is understandable if we identify these repeating donors as the very wealthiest members of the state, men who were called upon to contribute whenever it was difficult to find new donors. The relative size of the two contributions towards a single issue would be reflected in the order in which the two donors names' were recorded; the name of the citizen who gave the larger sum was inscribed in the first position, that of the donor who made up the difference was recorded below. The one-magistrate issues would be those

---

[34] Mentioned by Herzog, *Heil. Ges.*, 38.
[35] Paton-Hicks no. 12 (*SGDI* 3626).
[36] Paton-Hicks no. 404 (*SGDI* 3735).
[37] R. Herzog, *Koische Forschungen* (1899), nos. 12 (ca. 300 B.C.) and 220 (undated); A. Maiuri, *Nuova Silloge Epigrafica di Rodi e Cos* (1925), no. 454 (first century B.C. ?).
[38] Segre, *Rev. Filol.*, 1933, 365–378. In addition to the τριηραρχία, the regular Koan liturgies, as listed by Herzog (*Heil. Ges.* 46) were the λαμπαδαρχία, the χοραγία, and the offices of ἀγωνοθέτης for the Dionysia and the Asklepieia, γυμνασίαρχος, ὑπογυμνασίαρχος and παιδόνομος.

financed by a single contributor, and it is interesting to note in this connection that four of the earlier one-magistrate issues (8-11) seem to be among the smallest in the tetrobol series. Finally the issues bearing magisterial abbreviations would be those financed, at least in part, by the prostatai or bouleutai.

The case for a contribution by the full board of prostatai is a strong one, since we know from the lengthy subscription list pertaining to the Cretan War that the board of prostatai did in fact participate in extraordinary state liturgies in the same way as private citizens. In the inscription, among the usual entries giving donors' names and amounts, there occurs the entry προστάται τοὶ σὺν Χ[α]ρίνῳ, 500 drachms.[39] Charinos, by whose name the board was identified, was the ἐπιστάτης of the prostatai.[40] The word order of this entry is particularly relevant to our issues 4-7 in which ΠΡΟΣΤΑΤ precedes name, for by analogy it is quite possible that the proper names on these issues are the names of similar ἐπιστάται, that the legends of these issues should be expanded to read προστάτ(αι τοὶ σὺν) δεῖνι, and that the expense of minting these issues, like the 500 drachms for the Koan war chest, was met by the prostatai collectively. We cannot, however, insist on this restoration too emphatically as the name of Nikias in issue 5 was short enough to be recorded in full and it will be noted that it appears in the nominative and not in the dative. And, too, the word order on the other ΠΡΟΣΤΑΤ issues, 2 and 3, does not lend itself to this restoration.

Another identification for the proper names on issues 4-7, and one which fits issues 2-3 as well, is that they are names of private contri-

---

[39] Paton-Hicks no. 10 (see n. 30), lines b 29-30. 500 drachms, a typical contribution, is rather small when divided among five men. The largest contribution in this list is 7000 drachms; the average ran from one hundred to five hundred drachms. The modesty of the sum given by the prostatai indicates that they were men of ordinary means, democratically chosen with little or no regard to their economic status. If the prostatai still consisted of ordinary citizens in the latter part of the second century it is likely that their contributions to a monetary liturgy would have been split with another donor, as is suggested below. Another explanation for the smallness of their contribution, however, is that each of the prostatai might have privately contributed more substantial amounts under their own names; Charinos' name does not appear elsewhere in the list, but then large sections of the list are missing.

[40] For his title, see Herzog, *Koische Forschungen*, no. 3.

butors who shared the coinage liturgy with the prostatai. In issues 2-3 we restore δεῖνα (καὶ) προστ(άται), in issues 4-7 προστάτ (αι καὶ) δεῖνα. Likewise, our Androsthenes of issue 1 could have been a citizen who donated only part of the issue's expense, the boula itself furnishing the rest. Thus, restoring Ἀνδροσθέ(νης καὶ) βου(λα), we need not cope with the mystery of why Androsthenes would have wanted to advertise his membership in the boula. Primarily for this reason the καὶ δεῖνα restorations are to be preferred for all the magisterial legends (see n. 39). They permit us to classify the magisterial issues with the common two-magistrate issues as issues financed by two donors. It must be admitted, however, that ΠΡΟΣΤΑΤ and ΒΟΥ could be simply abbreviations for titles and that the magisterial issues were financed by single donors who held a state office and who desired recognition of it on their coins: issue 1 by Ἀνδροσθέ(νης) βου(λευτής), issue 2 and 3 by δεῖνα προστ(άτης), and issues 4-7 by προστάτ(ης) δεῖνα. On the other hand, the issues with name preceding abbreviations (1-3) were perhaps financed by individual office holders, the issues with name following abbreviation (4-7) by the full board of prostatai, distinguished by the name of their ἐπιστάτης.

Regardless of how we restore these magisterial legends, the only plausible connection between the names and offices on the coins and the coinage itself remains the financial one. These citizens and governmental bodies must have been in some way responsible for the emissions. As explained above, this could not have been an administrative responsibility involving the supervision of the minting process. In view of the impossibility of associating recurrent names with state offices or deliberative bodies, it is equally unlikely that the responsibility was a merely legal one in that these were the men who authorized the striking of the individual issues. The only satisfactory interpretation of this responsibility is that it was the far more fundamental economic responsibility of putting up the money to make the minting possible.

Surviving inscriptions demonstrate that the Koan state depended heavily on its citizens to finance public undertakings. With a considerable amount of confidence we can now conclude that in the second half of the second century B.C. the state also relied on its citizens to help finance its coinage.

THE HOARDS

The two right-hand columns in the Table of Issues indicate the similarity in composition of the two unpublished tetrobol hoards. Not counting the six issues which are represented by a single coin, every issue (excepting 13 and 25) which appears in the one hoard appears in the other. The hoards' similarity becomes even more striking when we consider that the three largest issues in the tetrobol series (29, 32 and 34) are conspicuously absent from both hoards. Issue 29, compared with all other known issues, was in fact huge, having been minted from at least 13 obverse dies, and its tremendous output is reflected in its large number of surviving coins, a total which is all the more impressive since it was not augmented by the hoard material which practically doubled the number of known coins of most issues. By the same token, the sizes of issues 32 and 34 must have been second and third only to 29. The absence of coins from these three largest issues is overwhelming testimony to the identical nature of the two hoards and, incidentally, implies that the three large issues were struck after the hoards' burial (see p. 102).

The hoards do differ in the number and in the relative condition of the pieces they contain. With only two or three exceptions, the 27 coins[41] in the smaller Ashmolean-British Museum hoard are very handsome specimens. Several of the coins are in mint state (20 b, 21 d and 22 c 1, PLATE XXII, 2, 6, 9) and most of the others show only minimal signs of rubbing. All but two (18 b and 19 b, PLATE XXI, 14, 19) were well struck. By contrast, the 71-piece Robinson hoard[42] contains only one or two pieces whose condition is as fine as the average coin in the smaller hoard (9 a and 10, PLATE XIX, 14, 17). Most of the Robinson coins show a fair amount of wear, and some are quite defaced owing to much handling or, more commonly, to faulty striking (esp. 17 c, 27 d, and 27 g, PLATES XXI, 11; XXIII, 19; XXIV, 2).

Since the smaller hoard is composed of consistently finer pieces and since both hoards are otherwise surprisingly similar, it would appear

---

[41] Of the 28 coins cited in Noe, one of the Ashmolean pieces has been lost.
[42] Robinson's records indicate that one of the Mississippi tetrobols from his collection (8 d 2) should be added to the 70 ANS hoard coins.

that the two hoards are actually two parts of a single hoard which a dealer had split in order to realize a higher profit. His selection of the most handsome pieces was sold to the Ashmolean and British Museums in 1935 while the residue eventually came into Robinson's hands. We do not know exactly when or under what circumstances Robinson purchased his hoard, but it was probably not until the late 1940's.[43] This involves a difference of about fifteen years in the times of acquisition but poses no serious objection to the theory of a single hoard. It is quite possible that Robinson's coins were in the possession of a third party during the war years between discovery and eventual disposition. On the other hand, it is most unlikely that chance would have brought to light, within a limited period of time, two hoards which are identical except for the qualification that the one is smaller and more select. We may confidently conclude that there was only one hoard.

The state of wear of the hoard coins is fairly uniform throughout. No one issue or group of issues is composed exclusively of FDC or worn coins. Most issues contain coins with a moderate amount of rubbing and perhaps one or two examples in notably better or worse condition. The exceptionally fine or exceptionally worn pieces occur with equal frequency in both early and late issues. This means that wear is of no help in determining the sequence and it suggests that the hoard should be classified as a savings hoard, stored up piece by piece over a number of years as its owner had a surplus coin to put away. If the hoard were a currency deposit, an emergency burial of pieces in current circulation, we should expect to find a more marked differentiation in wear between issues, a more uneven representation of issues generally, and probably other coinages mixed with the tetrobols.

THE SEQUENCE OF ISSUES

The reasoning behind the arrangement of issues in the Catalogue and the Table of Issues requires some fairly detailed explanation. The issues are fundamentally grouped according to their presence or ab-

---

[43] Robinson, as his surviving papers show, began to prepare a study of the hoard in the early 1950's. A fragmentary draft of the study contains the vague statement that he purchased the hoard "several years" before then.

sence in the two hoard lots. As explained above (p. 100) the three large issues (29, 32 and 34) which were not represented among the hoard pieces must have been struck after the hoard's burial. Issue 29 is distinguished by the eta's on most of its reverses; issue 30, which is linked to issue 29 by two common obverses, and issue 31 are also eta issues. These three issues compose the first post-hoard group. A second post-hoard group consists of issues 32–34, all of which have deltas on the lower edges of their obverses (as well as on their reverses) and enigmatic star symbols behind the snake on their reverses. The lateness of this group is confirmed by the word order in the legends of the one-magistrate issue 34, which, in contrast to the legends on all other third and second century Koan coinages and the one-magistrate tetrobols associated with the hoard, is inscribed with the ethnic *below* the magistrate's name (see p. 87).

Within the issues minted before the hoard's burial there are two extensive groups of linked issues, issues 5–11 and issues 22–28. The reverses of the ΠΡΟΣΤΑΤ issues in the 5–11 group are inscribed with deltas and the simple abbreviation of the ethnic KΩI, whereas many reverses in the 22–28 group bear the sequentially later epsilon and the more sophisticated form of the ethnic, KΩN. It is likely therefore that the 22–28 group, a two-magistrate group, is later than the 5–11 group and that it should indeed be assigned to the very end of the hoard issues, i.e., after all the delta issues in the hoard series, where its epsilons (and numerical digammas?) fit neatly before the etas (and zeta?) of issues 29–31 (see p. 91).

All of the other two-magistrate issues in the hoard series are assigned positions between the early 5–11 group and the later 22–28 two-magistrate group. Issues 15 and 16 are linked and are placed early among the two-magistrate issues since their legends employ the simpler KΩI spelling of the ethnic. Five other two-magistrate issues are located between the 15–16 and 22–28 groups in no particularly significant order. Three of these unlinked issues (18, 20 and 21) are stylistically associated with issues 22–28 as some of their obverse dies (18 b, 20 b and 21 b, PLATES XXI, 14; XXII, 2, 5) are distinguished by the same curved sideburn cuttings that distinguish several obverse dies in the 22–28 group (22 c, 24 a; 24 f, 25 a; 25 d, 28 and 26 g—PLATES XXII: 9,13; XXIII: 3, 4; 11, 16 and 17).

ΠΡΟΣΤΑΤ issues 5–7 are linked by a common obverse die and the last (7) is linked to issue 8, a one-magistrate issue, by another common die. Issues 9–11 are firmly connected with issues 5–8 by the lettering technique in their legends. Beginning in issue 5 and continuing through issue 8, letters were not cut linearly but outlined with punched dots which were then connected with fine incised lines. The only other tetrobols whose reverses were inscribed in this way are those in issues 9–11, one-magistrate issues which naturally enough should follow the one-magistrate issue 8.

Since die linkage proves that the three largest ΠΡΟΣΤΑΤ issues (5–7) were minted consecutively, it follows that all the ΠΡΟΣΤΑΤ issues were probably minted in succession and that the three unlinked ones should be placed in positions 2 through 4. The legends in the two earliest ΠΡΟΣΤΑΤ issues (2–3) are inscribed from the top of the incuse square to the bottom and with the magisterial abbreviation following proper name. The BOY issue is characterized by the same arrangements and is therefore placed in position 1. Since the only earlier Koan coinage with a vertical legend, the post-166 Apollo hemidrachm coinage, was inscribed from the top of the reverse to the bottom, we have some justification for considering issues 1–3, also inscribed in this way, the earliest in the tetrobol series.

Issues 12–14 present special problems that make their assignation the most tenuous in the entire sequence. Issue 12 is a highly irregular one-magistrate issue. Two of its legends (12 h and i) are inscribed from the top of the incuse square to the bottom; the other four are inscribed from bottom to top in front of the snake, from top to bottom behind the snake. And the order in which the ethnic and proper name are recorded is transposed in several legends. Another unique feature of the issue is to be found in the engraving of its snakes' tails. In all other issues these extend straight back and usually intersect the name inscribed on the left of the incuse; most of the tails in issue 12, however, are bent downwards at a right angle to avoid intersecting the inscription. The letter on all the reverses of the issue is an unmistakable alpha; on one of the reverses (12 a and d) the alpha is inscribed inside of the incuse square below the snake.

Issues 13 and 14 are associated with issue 12, though not with each other. Issue 13 is a regular two-magistrate issue, related to issue 12 through the alphas on its reverses and through stylistic affinities between one of its obverse dies and an obverse die in issue 12. Since all of the epsilon, and pi-iota issues are known to have been minted consecutively, the two alpha issues should have been also. The obverse dies 12a–c (PLATES XIX, 20, XX, 1–2) and 13e–g (PLATE XX, 10–11) are strikingly close in general appearance and in the style in which their beards are cut. Issue 14, another two-magistrate issue, is associated with issue 12 through three of its reverses (14a–c) which are inscribed from top to bottom and by the distinctive "hair-pin" form of the omega on reverses 14a–c (PLATE XX, 12–15). The only other tetrobols on which this same kind of open omega appears are 12a and 12d (PLATES XIX, 20; XX, 3). The ethnic of 14b is spelled out in full, a possible indication of an early date for this issue but more likely the work of an unenlightened die cutter.

These three atypical strikings would seem to fit best in the middle of the sequence between the one-magistrate and two-magistrate issues. Admittedly this is a somewhat arbitrary placement based on category; but since die linkage, whenever it exists, shows that issues of a particular type were in fact struck in succession, this criterion may be regarded as a fairly reliable guide to the issues' relative chronology.

THE CATALOGUE

Coins from the Robinson or Ashmolean-British Museum hoard lots are distinguished by "DMR" or "Noe 276." The second column gives the readings of the inscriptions to left and right of the reverse snake; notations regarding the direction of the writing and the technique of engraving, although not repeated, apply to succeeding coins until negated by another notation. The third column gives the readings, if any, in the space within the incuse square below the snake. The last gives the readings on the flan below the incuse. Letters are dotted only when they are almost completely obliterated or when there is some real question as to their identity or presence in the legend. All dies are consistently fixed in the twelve o'clock position. Weights are expressed in grams. With reference to the plates, horizontal lines showing die linkage are used only when the linkage is between issues.

Obv.: Laureate head of Asklepios r.
Rev.: Coiled snake with inscription to l., r. and usually below; all in incuse square. Letter or letters outside incuse in field below.

ONE MAGISTRATE WITH BOY

1.
   a. Similar   ΑΝΔΡΟΣΘΕ[44]/ΒΟΥ   ΚΩ   Δ
                                downward
      BM (Noe 276), 2.24, PLATE XVIII, 1
   b. Similar   ΑΝΔΡΣ/ΒΟΥ   ΚΩ   Δ
      ANS, 1.75, PLATE XVIII, 2

ONE MAGISTRATE WITH προστάται ABBREVIATION

2.   Similar   ΚΛΕΩ/ΠΡΟΣ   ΚΩ   Δ
      BMC 128, 2.00, PLATE XVIII, 3

3.   Similar   ΦΙΛΙΩΝ/ΠΡΟΣΤ   ΚΩΙ   Δ
      BMC 131, 1.84, PLATE XVIII, 4

4.
   a. Similar   ΠΡΟΣΤ/ΝΙΚΙΑ upward   ΚΩ   no trace
      Cast at Winterthur

---

[44] This is Jenkins' reading. The omicron is a mere dot.

b. Same die as 4a   Similar   KΩ   ,Δ
　　　　(1) ANS (DMR), 2.07, Plate XVIII, 5
　　　　(2) BMC 130, 2.07
　　c. Similar   ΠΡΟΣΤ/ΝΙΚΙΑΣ   KΩ   Δ
　　　　(1) BMC 129, 1.92, Plate XVIII, 6
　　　　(2) Paris 1216, 1.78

5.
　　a. Similar   ΠΡΟΣΤ/ΙΠΠΟΚΑ̣   KΩΙ   Δ
　　　　　　　　　　　　in dots
　　　　(1) BM (Noe 276), 2.18, Plate XVIII, 7
　　　　(2) ANS (DMR), 2.31, Plate XVIII, 8
　　b. Same die as 5a ΠΡΟΣΤΑΤ/ΙΠΠΟΚΡΑ   KΩΙ   Δ
　　　　　　　　　　　　not in dots
　　　　ANS (DMR), 1.84, Plate XVIII, 9
　　c. Similar   Same die as 5b
　　　　ANS (DMR), 2.03, Plate XVIII, 10
　　d. Similar   ΠΡΟΣΤ/ΙΠΠΟΚΑ̣   KΩΙ   Δ
　　　　ANS (DMR), 2.23, Plate XVIII, 11

6.
　　a. Same die as 5d ΠΡΟΣΤΑ/ΕΥΔΑΜ   KΩΙ   Δ
　　　　　　　　　　　　in dots
　　　　Ashmolean (Noe 276), 1.59, Plate XVIII, 12
　　b. Similar   Similar   Δ
　　　　ANS (DMR), 2.05, Plate XVIII, 14
　　c. Similar   Similar   Δ
　　　　BMC 125, 1.99
　　d. Similar   Similar   Δ̣
　　　　Weber 6648, 1.83

7.
　　a. Same die as 5d ΠΡΟΣΤΑ/ΘΕΥΔΟΤ   KΩΙ   Δ
　　　　and 6a[45]
　　　　ANS (DMR), 2.06, Plate XVIII, 13
　　b. Similar   Same die as 7a
　　　　Berlin
　　c. Similar   Same die as 7a-b
　　　　BMC 127, 1.99
　　d. Similar   ΠΡΟΣΤ/ΘΕΥΔΟΤ   KΩΙ   Δ
　　　　BMC 126, 2.17
　　e. Same die as 7d ΠΡΟΣΤΑ/ΘΕΥΔΟΤ   KΩΙ   Δ
　　　　(1) Ashmolean (Noe 276), 1.92, Plate XVIII, 15
　　　　(2) ANS (DMR), 1.70, Plate XIX, 1
　　f. Similar   Similar   uncertain
　　　　Ashmolean (Noe 276), 1.98, Plate XIX, 2

[45] This die was fairly fresh in the minting of 5d but had lost its sharpness by the time 6a and 7a were struck. The die break above the crown of the head had widened in the interval between the striking of 6a and 7a.

ONE MAGISTRATE

8.
  a. Same die as 7f   ΚΩΙΩΝ/ΑΡΙΣΤΟ Recut: traces   Δ
                                    of ΚΩΙ below snake
     ANS (DMR), 2.44, PLATE XIX, 3
  b. Same die as 7f   ΚΩΙΩΝ/ΑΡΙΣΤΟΚ   Δ
     and 8a
     (1) ANS (DMR), 1.96, PLATE XIX, 4
     (2) BM (Noe 276), 2.18, PLATE XIX, 5
  c. Similar   ΚΩΙΩΝ/ΑΡΙΣΤΟ   Δ
     (1) ANS (DMR), 1.97, PLATE XIX, 6
     (2) BM (Noe 276), 2.19, PLATE XIX, 7
     (3) ANS (DMR), 2.04, PLATE XIX, 8
  d. Same die as 8c   Similar   Δ
     (1) ANS (DMR), 2.22, PLATE XIX, 9
     (2) Mississippi (DMR), 2.25, PLATE XIX, 10
     (3) ANS (DMR), 2.00, PLATE XIX, 11
  e. Same die as 8c–d ΚΙΩΩΝ/ΑΡΙΣΤΟ   Δ[46]
     (1) ANS (DMR), 2.01, PLATE XIX, 12
     (2) ANS (DMR), 2.15, PLATE XIX, 13

9.
  a. Similar   ΚΩΙΩΝ/ΑΡΙΣΤΩ   ΠΙ
     ANS (DMR), 1.62, PLATE XIX, 14
  b. Same die as 9a?[47] Same die as 9a
     BMC 121, 2.01, PLATE XIX, 15
  c. Similar   ΚΩΦΝ/ΑΡΙΣΤΩΝ   ΠΙ
     Berlin, PLATE XIX, 16

10. Extremely close ΚΩΙΩΝ/ΝΙΚΟΜΗ   ΠΙ
    to die 9a–b in
    appearance and
    cutting
    ANS (DMR), 1.80, PLATE XIX, 17

11.
  a. Similar   ΚΩΝ/ΝΙΚΩΝ   ΠΙ
     Boston 2028, 1.72
  b. Similar   Same die as 11a
     ANS (DMR), 1.87, PLATE XIX, 18
  c. Same die as 11b Similar   ΠΙ
     (1) BM (Noe 276), 2.15, PLATE XIX, 19
     (2) BMC 124, 2.03

---

[46] Appears on e(1) only. Faulty striking is probably responsible for the absence of any traces on the flan of e(2).

[47] The A? at the lower edge of the obverse (noted in *BMC*) was not intended to appear on the coin. It may result from an imperfection on the anvil surface picked up by the excessively wide flan of the coin.

12.
   a. Similar   ΑΝΘΕΣ downward/   A (below
                        ΚΩΙΩ[Ν] upward, not   snake in
                        in dots   incuse)
       ANS, 1.77, Plate XIX, 20
   b. Same die as 12a Similar   A (below
       ANS (DMR), 2.06, Plate XX, 1   incuse)
   c. Same die as 12a–b Similar   A
       BM (Noe 276), 1.61, Plate XX, 2
   d. Similar   Same die as 12a
       BMC 120, 1.85, Plate XX, 3
   e. Same die as 12d Same die as 12b
       BMC 119, 2.05
   f. Same die as 12d–e Same die as 12c
       Berlin, 1.41
   g. Same die as 12d–f ΚΩΙΩΝ downward/   A
                                ΑΝΘΕΣ upward
       ANS, 1.86, Plate XX, 4
   h. Similar   ΑΝΘΕΣ/ΚΩΙΩΝ   off flan
                       downward
       Ashmolean (Noe 276), 1.91, Plate XX, 5
   i. Similar   ΚΩΙΩΝ/ΑΝΘΕΣ   no trace
       Copenhagen 664, 1.98

TWO MAGISTRATES

13.
   a. Similar   ΑΓΗΣΙ/ΑΡΙΣΤΟ upward ΚΩΙ   A
       (1) ANS (DMR), 2.06, Plate XX, 6
       (2) Berlin
   b. Same die as 13a ΑΓΗΣΙ/ΑΡΙΣΤΟ   ΚΩΙ   Ạ
       (1) ANS (DMR), 2.15, Plate XX, 7
       (2) ANS (DMR), 1.81, Plate XX, 8
   c. Same die as 13a–b Similar   Λ (= Ạ)[48]
       Berlin
   d. Same die as 13a–c ΑΓΗΣΙ/ΑΡΙΣΤ   ΚΩΙ   Λ (= A)
       ANS (DMR), 2.19, Plate XX, 9
   e. Similar   Same die as 13d
       BM (Weber 6649), 1.94
   f. Same die as 13e ΑΓΗΣΙ/ΑΡΙΣΤΟ   ΚΩΙ   Ạ
       ANS (DMR), 2.10, Plate XX, 10
   g. Same die as 13e–f ΑΡΙΣΤ/ΑΓΗΣΙΑ   ΚΩ   Λ (= A)
       ANS (DMR), 2.25, Plate XX, 11

---

[48] Alphas with the horizontal bar omitted commonly occur in the tetrobol legends.

14.
  a. Similar   ΠΑΡΜ/ΑΓΗΣΙ   ΚΩΙ   Δ
                    downward
    BM (Noe 276), 1.97, Plate XX, 12
  b. Same die as 14a ΠΑΡΜ/[ΑΓΗΣΙ]   ΚΩΙΩ̣Ν̣ no trace
    Berlin, Plate XX, 13
  c. Similar   ΠΑΡΜ/ΑΓΗΣΙ   ΚΩΙ   Δ
    (1) ANS (DMR), 2.16, Plate XX, 14
    (2) ANS (DMR), 2.05, Plate XX, 15
    (3) Paris 1224, 1.97
  d. Same die as 14c ΠΑΡΜΙ̣/ΑΓΗΣΙ   ΚΩ   Δ
                    upward
    ANS (DMR), 2.13, Plate XX, 16

15.
  a. Similar   ΑΛΚΙΔΑ/ΔΕΙΝΙΑΣ   ΚΩΙ   Δ̣
    Ashmolean, 1.88
  b. Same die as 15a ΑΛΚΙΔΑΜ̣/ΔΕΙΝΙΑΣ ΚΩΙ   Δ
    (1) *BMC* 135, 1.98
    (2) ANS (DMR), 2.08, Plate XX, 17
  c. Similar   ΑΛΚΙΔΑ/ΔΕΙΝΙΑΣ   ΚΩΙ   Δ
    Ashmolean (Noe 276), 1.90, Plate XX, 18
  d. Same die as 15c ΑΛΚΙΔΑ/ΔΕΙΝΙΑ   ΚΩΙ   Δ̣
    ANS (DMR), 2.06, Plate XX, 19
  e. Same die as 15c–d ΑΛΚΙΔΑ/ΔΕΙΝΙΑΣ ΚΩΙ   off flan
    ANS (DMR), 1.75, Plate XX, 20
  f. Similar   ΑΛΚΙΔΑ/ΔΕΙΝΙΑΣ   ΚΩΙ   uncertain
    Paris 1213, 1.91, Plate XXI, 2

16.
  a. Same die as   ΑΓΗΣΙΑ/ΘΕΥΦΑΜ ΚΩΙ   Δ
    15 c–e[49]
    BMC 132, 2.02, Plate XXI, 1
  b. Same die as 15f[50] Similar   Δ
    BM (Noe 276), 2.11, Plate XXI, 3
  c. Similar   Similar   Δ̣
    ANS (DMR), 2.13, Plate XXI, 4
  d. Same die as 16c ΑΓΗΣΙ/ΘΕΥΦΑΜ   ΚΩΙ   Δ̣
    (1) ANS (DMR), 2.27, Plate XXI, 5
    (2) Ashmolean (Noe 276), 1.95, Plate XXI, 6
    (3) BM (Noe 276), 2.24, Plate XXI, 7
    (4) Berlin

---

[49] The many fine cracks in the die in front of Asklepios' face seem to be more numerous and pronounced on 16a than on 15d and e. They had not developed prior to the striking of 15c.

[50] 15f is too heavily rubbed to allow any statement as to the sequence in which 15f and 16b were struck. The sequence is fixed by the other die common to issues 15 and 16 (see n. 49).

e. Same die as 16c–d Similar   no trace
   Formerly in DMR Coll.
f. Same die as 16c–e Similar   ΚΩ   Δ
   ANS, 2.29
g. Similar   Same die as 16f
   ANS (DMR), 1.97, Plate XXI, 8
h. Same die as 16g ΑΓΗΣΙΑ/ΘΕΥΦΑΜ   ΚΩΙ   Δ
   Copenhagen 660, 1.96

17.
a. Similar   ΑΛΚΙΔΑΜΟ̣/ΑΓΗΣΙ̣Α̣   ΚΩΝ   no trace
   ANS (DMR), 2.35, Plate XXI, 9
b. Same die as 17a ΑΛΚΙΔ̣Α̣/ΑΓΗΣΙΑΣ   ΚΩΝ   Δ̣ (Α?)
   ANS (DMR), 2.03, Plate XXI, 10
c. Similar   ΑΛΚΙΑ̣ΜΟ/ΑΓΗΣΙΑΣ   ΚΩΝ   Δ
   ANS (DMR), 2.16, Plate XXI, 11
d. Similar   Same die as 17c
   ANS (DMR), 1.90, Plate XXI, 12

18.
a. Similar   ΝΙΚΟΜΗΔ/ΘΕΥΦΑΜΙ   ΚΩΙ   Δ
   ANS (DMR), 2.33, Plate XXI, 13
b. Similar   Similar   Δ
   BM (Noe 276), 2.17, Plate XXI, 14
c. Similar   ΝΙΚΟΜΗ/ΘΕΥΦΑΜΙ   ΚΩΝ   Δ ⸜
   ANS (DMR), 1.91, clipped, Plate XXI, 15
d. Same die as 18c ΝΙΚΟΜΗ/ΘΕΥΦΑΜ   ΚΩΝ   Δ
   ANS (DMR), 2.19, Plate XXI, 16
e. Same die as 18c–d ΝΙΚΟΜΗ̣Δ̣[51]/ΘΕΥΦΑΜΙ ΚΩΝ[52]   Δ
   Paris 1215, 2.03
f. Similar   Same die as 18e   no trace
   ANS (DMR), 1.99, Plate XXI, 17

19.
a. Similar   ΛΟΧΟΣ/ΠΑΡΜΕ   ΚΩ   Δ̣ (Α?)
   ANS (DMR), 2.37, Plate XXI, 18
b. Same die as 19a Similar   Δ̣ (Α?)
   BM (Noe 276), 2.00, Plate XXI, 19
c. Similar   Similar   Δ
   ANS (DMR), 2.16, Plate XXI, 20
d. Similar   Similar   Δ
   ANS (DMR), 1.98, Plate XXII, 1
e. Similar   Similar   Δ
   Paris 1217, 1.84

---

[51] The last three letters are joined together as in a monogram.
[52] In retrograde.

20.
   a. Similar   ΠΑΡΜΕ/ΓΕΝΟΚ   ΚΩ   Δ̣
      BMC 147, 1.90
   b. Similar   Same die as 20a
      Ashmolean (Noe 276), 2.10, Plate XXII, 2
   c. Similar   Similar   Δ
      (1) Paris 1223, 1.79
      (2) Berlin
   d. Similar   ΠΑΡΜΕ/Γ̣ΕΝΟΚ̣ΛΗ̣   ΚΩ̣   Δ
      BMC 146, 1.99, Plate XXII, 3

21.
   a. Similar   ΝΙΚΟΜ/ΑΡΙΣΤ   ΚΩΝ   Δ
      ANS (DMR), 2.14, Plate XXII, 4
   b. Same die as 21a ΝΙΚΟΜΗ/ΑΡΙΣΤ   ΚΩΝ   Δ
      BM (Noe 276), 2.26, Plate XXII, 5
   c. Same die as 21a–b ΝΙΚΟΜ/ΑΡΙΣΤ   ΚΩΝ   Δ
      BMC 139, 2.13
   d. Similar   ΝΙΚΟΜΗ/ΑΡΙΣΤΟ   ΚΩ   Δ
      Ashmolean (Noe 276), 2.15, Plate XXII, 6
   e. Same die as 21d ΝΙΚΟΜ/ΑΡΙΣΤ   ΚΩ   Δ
      ANS (DMR), 2.23, Plate XXII, 7
   f. Same die as 21d–e ΝΙΚΟΜΗ/ΑΡΙΣΤΟ   ΚΩ   Δ
      ANS, 1.96
   g. Similar   ΝΙΚΟΜ/ΑΡΙΣΤΟ̣   ΚΩ   Δ
      Formerly in DMR Coll.
   h. Similar   ΝΙΚΟΜΗ/ΑΡΙΣΤΟ   ΚΩ   Δ
      von Aulock 2762, 2.19
   i. Similar   ΝΙΚΟΜ/ΑΡΙΣΤ   ΚΩ   Δ̣
      Ratto, Feb. 1928, 689 (Pozzi 2661), divergent
      wts. 1.99 and 2.08
   j. Same die as 21i ΝΙΚΟΜ/ΑΡΙΣΤΟ   ΚΩ   Δ̣
      Berlin

22.
   a. Similar   ΘΕΥΦΑΜ/ΑΓΗΣΙΑ   ΚΩ   off flan
      ANS (DMR), 2.03, Plate XXII, 8
   b. Same die as 22a Similar   Δ
      (1) Berlin
      (2) BMC 133, 2.03
   c. Similar   Same die as 22b
      (1) Ashmolean (Noe 276), 2.05, Plate XXII, 9
      (2) ANS (DMR), 1.91, Plate XXII, 10
      (3) ANS (DMR), 2.08, Plate XXII, 11

23.
   a. Same die as 22c ΑΡΙΣΤΟ/ΛΟΧΟΣ   ΚΩΙ   Ε
      Ashmolean (Noe 276), 1.98, Plate XXII, 12

b. Similar   ΑΡΙΣΤΟΚ/ΛΟΧΟΣ   ΚΩΙ   off flan
ANS (DMR), 2.01, PLATE XXII, 14
c. Same die as 23 b   Similar   Ḙ
ANS (DMR), 2.28, PLATE XXII, 15
d. Same die as 23 b–c   Similar   E
ANS (DMR), 2.11, PLATE XXII, 16
e. Same die as 23 b–d   Similar   Ḙ[53]
BMC 138, 2.04
f. Similar   ΑΡΙΣΤΟ/ΛΟΧΟΣ   ΚΩΙ   Δ
BM (Noe 276), 2.35, PLATE XXII, 17
g. Similar   Similar   Δ
ANS (DMR), 1.86, PLATE XXII, 18
h. Same die as 23 g   Similar   ΚΩ   Δ̣
Ashmolean (Noe 276), 2.00, PLATE XXII, 19
i. Similar   Similar   ΚΩΙ   Δ
ANS (DMR), 2.17, PLATE XXII, 20

24.
a. Same die as 22 c   ΝΙΚΟΣΤΡΑ/ΔΕΙΝΙΑΣ   ΚΩ   off flan
    and 23 a[54]
Ashmolean (Noe 276), 2.18, PLATE XXII, 13
b. Similar   ΝΙΚΟΣΤΡ/ΔΕΙΝΙΑΣ   ΚΩ   E
ANS (DMR), 2.24, PLATE XXIII, 1
c. Similar   Same die as 24 b[55]
BMC 137, 2.07
d. Same die as 24 c   Similar   E
ANS (DMR), 2.16, PLATE XXIII, 2
e. Similar   Similar   uncertain
Mississippi, 2.13
f. Similar   Similar   Ɛ
Paris 1214, 1.87, PLATE XXIII, 3

25.
a. Same die as 24 f[56]   ΤΙΣΑΧ/ΑΛΚΙΔΑ   ΚΩ   E
BMC 134, 1.65, PLATE XXIII, 4
b. Similar   ΤΕΙΣΑ/ΑΛΚΙΔ   ΚΩ   off flan
ANS (DMR), 2.04, PLATE XXIII, 5

[53] Head's reading, Δ, is less likely.
[54] There are no die breaks which determine the sequence of strikings from this die. The three 22 c coins were struck from a reverse die that was earlier (as its wear indicates) used with another obverse die (22 a–b). It seems therefore that die 22 c–24 a was first cut during the minting of issue 22. The rest of the striking sequence, 23 a before 24 a, is required by the linkage of issue 24 to issue 25 (see n. 56).
[55] Head wrongly read H for the letter below the incuse.
[56] The sequence in which 24 f and 25 a were struck can be determined only from the circumstance that issue 24 is linked to two issues which must be earlier (see n. 54).

TETROBOLS OF KOS

    c. Similar   ΤΕΙΣΑ/ΑΛΚΙΔ   ΚΩ   E
       (1) ANS (DMR), 1.89, PLATE XXIII, 6
       (2) ANS (DMR), 1.99, PLATE XXIII, 7
    d. Similar   Similar   ΚΩΝ   E
       ANS, 2.19, PLATE XXIII, 11

26.
    a. Same die as 25d ΦΙΛΟΦΡ/ΜΕΝΩΝ   ΚΩ   ⌐
       ANS (DMR), 2.12, PLATE XXIII, 12
    b. Same die as 25d Similar   no trace
       and 26a
       ANS (DMR), 2.16, PLATE XXIII, 13
    c. Same die as 25d ΦΙΛΟΦ/ΜΕΝΩΝ   ΚΩ   uncertain
       and 26a–b?
       Fitzwilliam (Grose), 8547, 2.19
    d. Similar   Same die as 26a   uncertain[57]
       BMC 155, 1.91
    e. Same die as 25c ΦΙΛΟΦ/ΜΕΝΩΝ   ΚΩ   Ẹ
       (1) BMC 154, 1.97, PLATE XXIII, 8
       (2) ANS (DMR), 2.18, PLATE XXIII, 9
    f. Same die as 25c ΦΙΛΟΦΡ/ΜΕΝΩΝ   ΚΩ   E
       and 26e[58]
       Ashmolean (Noe 276), 1.98, PLATE XXIII, 10
    g. Similar   ΦΙΛΟΦ/ΜΕΝΩΝ   ΚΩ   E
       ANS (DMR), 2.12, PLATE XXIII, 17
    h. Similar   ΦΙΛΟΦΡ/ΜΕΝΩΝ   ΚΩΝ   Δ
       BMC 153, 1.98
    i. Similar   Similar   ΚΩ   uncertain
       Berlin
       Not illustrated ΦΙΛΟΦ/ΜΕΝΩΝ   ΚΩΝ   no trace
       Hunter 12, 1.46

27.
    a. Same die as 25d ΔΕΙΝΙΑΣ/ΝΙΚΟΣΤ   ΚΩ   Ẹ (⌐?)
       and 26a–c
       BMC 136, 2.02, PLATE XXIII, 14
    b. Same die as 25d, ΔΕΙΝΙΑΣ/ΝΙΚΟΣΤΡ   ΚΩ   E
       26a–c and 27a
       Lockett 2930 (Naville VII, 1539)
       Hirsch XXV, 2414), 2.03, PLATE XXIII, 15
    c. Similar   ΔΙΝΙΑΣ/ΝΙΚΟΣΤ   ΚΩ   uncertain
       BM (Noe 276), 2.23, PLATE XXIII, 18

---

[57] The traces are ambiguous but suggest Δ rather than E. Head's H? is certainly mistaken.

[58] A U-shaped configuration of three lines behind Asklepios' brow indicates that 25c (1) and (2) were the first strikings from this die. On these coins the three lines are distinctly articulated. On 26e (2) and f the two left-hand lines have merged.

d. Same die as 27c Similar   ΚΩΝ   Δ̣
   ANS (DMR), 2.34, Plate XXIII, 19
e. Similar   ΔΕΙΝΙΑΣ/ΝΙΚΟΣΤΡ   ΚΩΝ   Δ
   ANS (DMR), 2.05, Plate XXIII, 20
f. Same die as 27e   ΔΕΙΝΙΑΣ/ΝΙΚΟΣΤ   ΚΩΝ   Δ
   ANS (DMR), 1.99, Plate XXIV, 1
g. Similar   ΔΙΝΙΑΣ/ΝΙΚΟΣ⫽   ΚΩ   Δ
   ANS (DMR), 2.18, Plate XXIV, 2
h. Similar   ΔΙΝΙΑΣ/ΝΙΚΟΣΤ   ΚΩ   Δ
   Mississippi, 2.34, Plate XXIV, 3
i. Similar   Similar   uncertain
   Mississippi, 1.69
j. Similar   ΔΕΙΝΙΑΣ/ΝΙΚΟΣΤ   ΚΩΝ   Δ̣
   Ashmolean, 1.95

28. Same die as 25d, ΠΑΡΜΕ/ΛΟΧΟΣ   ΚΩ   Ϲ
     26a–c and
     27a–b[59]
     (1) ANS (DMR), 1.83, Plate XXIII, 16
     (2) Copenhagen 663 (W. de Molthein 2455), 1.88

29.
a. Similar   ΗΛΙΟΔΟ/ΕΥΑΡΑΤ   ΚΩ   Η
   (1) BMC 141, 1.94
   (2) ANS, 1.71
b. Same die as 29a   ΗΛΙΟΔΟ/ΕΥΑΡ⫽   ΚΩΙ   Ḥ
   Paris 1225, 2.04
c. Similar   ΗΛΙΟΔ/ΕΥΑΡΑ   ΚΩΙ   Η
   Bourgey, Dec. 1909, 196
d. Same die as 29c? Same die as 29c
   Mississippi, 1.98
e. Similar   ΗΛΙΟΔ/ΕΥΑΡΑ   ΚΩΙ   Ν
   Winterthur, 1.90, Plate XXIV, 4
f. Same die as 29e   ΗΛΙΟΔ/ΕΥΑΡ⫽   ΚΩΙ   Ṇ or Ḥ
   Weber 6650, 1.98
g. Similar   ΗΛΙΟΔΩ/ΕΥΑΡΑΤ   ΚΩΙ   Ḥ
   BMC 142, 2.09
h. Similar   Similar   off flan
   Ashmolean, 1.83
i. Similar   Similar   ΚΩΝ   uncertain
   BMC 144, 1.58, Plate XXIV, 5

---

[59] The disfigured appearance of 28 (1) shows that it must have been one of the very last coins to be struck from this die. The rest of the striking sequence, 25d to 26a–c to 27a–b, is fixed by other die linkage which sets issues 24, 25 and 26 in order (see nn. 56 and 58).

TETROBOLS OF KOS

   j. Similar   HΛIOΔ/EYAPAT   KΩI   no trace
      Ashmolean, 2.10
   k. Similar   Similar   H
      Copenhagen 622, 1.70
   l. Similar   Similar   no trace
      Kress 122, 404
   m. Similar   HΛIOΔ////EYAPAT   KΩI   H
      Ball VI, 342
   n. Similar   HΛIOΔ/EYAPA   worn   no trace
      Paris 1226, 1.99   away
   o. Similar   HΛIOΔ/EYAPAT   KΩI   H
      BMC 143, 2.13, PLATE XXIV, 6
   p. Similar   HΛIOΔ/EYAPA   KΩI   H
      Platt, Fx. Pr., Coll. A, 503, PLATE XXIV, 8
   q. Same die as 29p   EYAPA/HΛIOΔΩ   KΩI   H
      BMC 140, 1.89, PLATE XXIV, 9

30.
   a. Same die as 29o   TIMOΓ/EYΔA   KΩI   H
      BMC 148, 1.84, PLATE XXIV, 7
   b. Same die as   TIMOΓ/EYΔAM   KΩI   ⊓ (H?)[61]
      29p-q[60]
      Paris 1222, 2.09, PLATE XXIV, 10

31.
   a. Similar   NIKAPXOΣ/AΣKΛHΠI   KΩN   no trace
      BMC 145, 2.02, PLATE XXIV, 11
   b. Similar   NIKAPXO/AΣKΛHΠ   KΩN   H
      ANS, 1.68, PLATE XXIV, 12

32.
   a. Similar,   TIMOΞ/EKATAI   KΩI   Δ
      Δ beneath head   with star behind
      or presumably   snake
      off flan except
      where noted
      ANS, 1.94, PLATE XXIV, 13
   b. Same die as 32a   TIMOΞEN/EKATAIOY[62]KΩN   off flan
      BMC 149, 2.00
   c. Same die as 32a-b   TIMOΞE/EKATAI   KΩI   Δ
      Lockett 2931 (Naville VII, 1540), 1.91

---

[60] There is no way of being sure of the order in which 29o–30a or 29p and q–30b were struck. It is possible that issue 30 precedes 29.

[61] See p. 90.

[62] A full name in the genitive appears only here and on 32h. The rarity of these exceptions probably means that they are of no particular consequence. Hekataios is spelled in the nominative on 32l.

d. Similar　　　　　TIMOΞ/EKATAI　　　ΚΩΙ　Δ
   (1) Berlin
   (2) Paris 1219, 1.87
e. Same die as 32d TIMOΞ/EKATA　　　ΚΩΙ　Δ
   BMC 151, 1.63, Plate XXIV, 14
f. Similar　　Similar　　　　　　　　　　　　Δ
   BMC 150, 1.89, Plate XXIV, 15
g. Same die as 32f TIMOΞE/EKATAI　　ΚΩΙ　Δ
   Paris 1220 (Waddington 2739), 2.01
h. Similar　　　　T]IMOΞEN/EKATAIOY ΚΩΙ　Δ
   Paris 1227, 2.10
i. Similar except　TIMOΞE/EKATAI　　ΚΩΙ　Δ
   no trace of letter
   Weber 6651, 2.09
j. Similar　　　　　EKATAIO/TIMOΞE　　ΚΩΙ　Δ
   Paris 1221 (Waddington 2740), 1.82
k. Same die as 32j EKATAI/TIMOΞE　　ΚΩΙ　Δ
   Ashmolean, 1.85, Plate XXIV, 16
l. Similar　　　　　EKATAIOΣ/TIMOΞEN ΚΩΙ　Δ
   Copenhagen 661, 1.49
m. Similar except no EKAIT/TIMOΞ　　ΚΩΙ　Δ
   trace of letter
   Berlin, 1.75

33. Similar　　　　　EKATAI/TEIMOΣ[63]　ΚΩΙ　uncertain
    BMC 152, 1.64, Plate XXIV, 17

[63] Head read the second name in this legend as IEINOΣ, a name or part of a name without parallel in the prosopographies. The initial letter is almost certainly T, not I (as a small flake at the bottom of the stem superficially suggests). The fourth letter could be either N or M. The final letter, although the lower half is missing, is best read as Σ; the slant of the vertical stroke makes Γ a less likely alternative.

This coin is classified in a separate issue only with a good deal of hesitation. TEIMOΣ might be an erroneous variant for TIMOΞ in which case the coin would belong to issue 32. The spelling Τειμ- for Τιμ- is possible, but at Kos it is never used for the common name Τιμόξενος. The final sigma in the abbreviation is even more disturbing. Misspellings and omitted letters do occur in the tetrobols' legends (see esp. 1b, 17a and c, and 25a), but there are none quite so patently unreasonable as the engraving of a sigma in place of a xi. On the other hand, the name Τιμόστρατος existed at Kos (Paton-Hicks no. 10, line a 60) and another Τιμοσ- name (Τιμοσθένης) was common elsewhere. Either of these names could be the one abbreviated here. Or if the final letter of the abbreviation is a gamma rather than a sigma, the restored name would be Τειμογένης, a freqent variant for Τιμογένης, the second name in issue 30. Any of these latter possibilities is stronger than the reading of TEIMOΣ as a unique variant for TIMOΞ.

TETROBOLS OF KOS

ONE MAGISTRATE

34.
- a. Similar   ΑΝΔΡΟ/ΚΩΝ   Δ
  Hirsch XIII, 3978, 1.82, PLATE XXIV, 18
- b. Same die as 34a   ΑΝΔΡΟΣ/ΚΩΝ   Δ̣ (A?)
  BMC 122, 1.67
- c. Same die as 34a–b   Similar   Δ̣
  ANS, 1.84
- d. Same die as 34a–c   Similar   no trace
  Berlin, 2.35
- e. Same die as 34a–d   ΑΝΔΡ/ΚΩΝ   Δ
  Berlin
- f. Similar   ΑΝΔΡΟ/ΚΩΝ   Δ
  Münzhandl. Basel 10, 342 (Hess 207, 589), 1.72
- g. Same die as 34f   Similar   Δ
  von Aulock 2761 (Ball Fx Pr 39, 574), 1.41
- h. Same die as 34f–g   ΑΝΔΡ/ΚΩΝ   Δ
  ANS, 1.60, PLATE XXIV, 19
- i. Similar[64]   Similar   Δ
  BMC 123, 2.26, PLATE XXIV, 20
- j. Similar   Similar   Δ
  Weber 6647, 2.00
- k. Similar   Similar   off flan
  Formerely in DMR Coll.
- l. Similar   ΑΝΔΡΟ/ΚΩΝ   Δ
  Berlin
- m. Similar   Similar   Δ
  Ratto, Apr. 1927, 2071, 2.02
- n. Similar   Similar   no trace
  Florange-Ciani, Feb. 1925, 567
- ? Similar   Illegible   no trace
  Paris 1218, 1.78

JOHN KROLL

[64] The letter below Asklepios' head was probably intended as a delta even though it has the appearance of an alpha. There is, however, no basis for the sigma in Head's reading: ΑΣ.

PTOLEMY PHILOMETOR AND ATHENS[1]

(SEE PLATES XXV–XXVII)

The first half of the second century before Christ was literally a golden age for Athens. Her days of political and commercial supremacy might be only a stirring memory, but her prestige as the pre-eminent center of Greek culture remained undiminished. An association with Athens still confered its own peculiar distinction and in recognition of this the rulers of the various Hellenistic kingdoms, from Pontus to Numidia, visited the city, competed in her festivals and vied with each other in munificent donations of money and public buildings. Whether it was chiefly self-glorification or the glory of Athens that prompted the gifts concerned no one, least of all the recipient. Physically and economically the city prospered from the friendly rivalry of her royal patrons.

Among the major benefactors of Athens the Pergamene dynasty clearly deserves first place. Attalos I provided military support during the Second Macedonian War and demonstrated his personal interest in the city and her institutions by participating in the Mysteries, laying out the Lakydeion and donating sculptural groups for the south wall of the Acropolis. For her part Athens responded with high honors, including the compliment of a new tribe named Attalis. The sons of Attalos maintained the family tradition. All four entered horses and won prizes in the Panathenaic contests and all received the city's highest award for services to Antiochos IV, but it was the two older brothers who made outstanding contributions. Eumenes II erected a great stoa on the southern slope of the Acropolis and some years later Attalos II, who had studied in Athens and received Athenian citizenship, donated another impressive stoa extending along the eastern side of the central market square. Colossal statues of the two bene-

---

[1] This article owes its existence to Professor Benjamin D. Meritt, who called my attention to the body of epigraphical material relating to the statue of Ptolemy and to the gap in the celebration of the Ptolemaia with its implications for the New Style chronology.

factors were set up, possibly on the western approach to the Acropolis below the Propylaea.

Antiochos IV of Syria, like his Pergamene contemporaries, contributed substantially to the beautification of Athens. During his residence there in 176/5 B.C. he had been given not only Athenian citizenship but the affection of the demos, a feeling which he warmly reciprocated. As king he dedicated a gilt aegis with a head of Medusa, set up on the south wall of the Acropolis above the theater, and began the construction of a new and grandiose temple to the Olympian Zeus on the site of the unfinished Peisistratid structure. Statues of Epiphanes were erected in the city and undoubtedly other honors, of which we have no record, were voted him.

Another royal benefactor was the king of Egypt, Ptolemy VI Philometor, and indeed there is a strong possibility that his generosity to Athens was greater than has hitherto been realized. Of special pertinence is an inscription (*IG* II² 983) which concerns the erection of a bronze equestrian statue of a Ptolemy beside the old temple of Athena Polias. This was interpreted by Koehler in his earlier publication of the text as referring to the statue of Soter II mentioned by Pausanias (I. 8.6ff.) but as Ferguson pointed out,[2] the statue of that king stood before the Odeion in the Agora and was almost certainly a standing figure, since it was paired with a statue of his daughter Berenice, while the Ptolemy of our text was on horseback and on the Acropolis. Ferguson thought the equestrian statue probably represented Ptolemy VI but that it might commemorate one of his immediate predecessors, Epiphanes or Philopator. Kirchner, citing Ferguson's arguments, assigned the inscription to the middle of the second century.

The decree in question is illustrated on PLATE XXV (B)[3] together with another inscription (A) recently discussed by Pritchett (*Hesperia* 1947, 188f.). This second text belongs to the archonship of Speusippos, assigned to 177/6 B.C. by Dow in his publication of the inscription

---

[2] *Klio* 1908, 338 ff.

[3] I am indebted to Dr. Markellos Mitsos, Director of the Epigraphical Museum at Athens, for photographs and permission to reproduce *IG* II² 983, and to Professor Meritt for the same courtesies with respect to the two Agora inscriptions.

{The Speusippos stone has been cropped for reproduction but the text is intact.

(*Prytaneis* 65). Pritchett, however, would transfer Speusippos to 149/8, or at least to the period between 157 and 145, citing as chief evidence for the new date the distinctive style of lettering found on Prytaneis 65 and on many inscriptions of the mid-second century,[4] a style "characterized by a sigma the bottom stroke of which begins mid-way of the third hasta, by an epsilon with a vertical hasta which extends above and below the horizontal strokes, by a tau with a horizontal stroke which extends more to the left than to the right of the upright, by an omega in the form of a horseshoe without feet the left portion of which is frequently lower than the right, by a pi with the horizontal hasta extending beyond the perpendicular strokes, by a fully-formed mu having the four hastas resting on the line, and by a phi which roughly resembles a crossbow. The alphas are sometimes open at the top and exhibit a slightly curving horizontal hasta."

One of the inscriptions listed by Pritchett as an example of this type of writing is a stone from the Agora dated by the archonship of Lysiades to the mid-second century B.C. (PLATE XXVI, C).[5] Lysiades figures prominently in the discussion that follows and his contribution to the epigraphical argument is thus highly pertinent but for the moment it will suffice to point out that the Ptolemaic inscription, which Pritchett does not include in his citation of comparative material, has letter forms practically identical with those found on the Speusippos and Lysiades inscriptions. This is perhaps most noticeable with reference to the horseshoe omega and the crossbow phi but all the distinctive shapes described by Pritchett are present.[6] Clearly the Ptolemaic text belongs to the middle of the second century and the Ptolemy in question must be Philometor.

The erection of a statue in a position of prominence on the Acropolis certainly commemorated some outstanding benefaction on the part of Philometor. We have no explicit record as to the nature of the gift, but Homer Thompson has suggested an interesting possibility in this

---

[4] Of the twenty-three inscriptions listed by Pritchett, almost all fall within the period between 170 and 135 but a few extend the chronological limits to ca. 200–120 B.C.

[5] Published by B. D. Meritt, *Hesperia* 1942, no. 58.

[6] It will be noted that the two long inscriptions (B and C), in which there is considerable repetition of letters, show variation in the writing. The forms discussed by Pritchett are not used consistently in either text.

connection, namely that the Ptolemaion may be the creation of Ptolemy VI.[7]

Concerning this building we know very little. Pausanias (I. 17.2) describes the gymnasium of Ptolemy as being not far from the Agora and close to the Theseion and says that it took its name from the founder, whose bronze statue was there along with statues of Juba the Libyan and Chrysippos of Soli. Ephebic inscriptions of the late second and first centuries B.C. make it certain that a library and lecture facilities formed part of the gymnasium complex, and the fact that many of these stones were used in the construction of the "Valerian Wall" suggests at least that the Ptolemaion was in this general area.[8] There is no indication as to which Ptolemy was the donor. Judeich[9] assigns the structure to Ptolemy II but the attribution is little more than conjecture based on honors paid to Philadelphus and Arsinoe and on the importance of the Serapis cult at Athens in the mid-third century.[10] Far more plausible is the association with Ptolemy III proposed by Ferguson (*Hellenistic Athens*, 239 ff.) since the inauguration of the Ptolemaia and the creation of the new tribe Ptolemais ca. 224/3 B.C.

---

[7] *Hesperia* 1950, 322 f., with citation of the honors paid to Philometor and the importance of the Ptolemaic cult in the mid-second century. References to the Ptolemaion are compiled by R. E. Wycherley in *Agora III: Literary and Epigraphical Testimonia*, 142–144. The fact that no mention of the gymnasium occurs before the middle of the second century is perhaps significant.

[8] Citation of the pertinent texts is to be found in W. Judeich, *Topographie von Athen* (ed. 2, 1931), 353 and C. Pelekidis, *Histoire de l'éphébie attique* (Paris 1962), 263 f. The latter work contains the most recent discussion of the Ptolemaion and in this connection a misinterpretation should be noted. Pelekidis states that we do not know with certainty which Ptolemy was the founder of the gymnasium and then goes on to say that Pausanias tells us it concerned Ptolemy II Philadelphus. This is an error; the Pausanias text makes no reference to a particular Ptolemy.

The boundary stone of a gymnasium mentioned by Pelekidis adds nothing to our information on the Ptolemaion. M. and E. Levensohn in publishing it (*Hesperia* 1947, no. 2) note that it cannot be associated with a specific gymnasium, and its place of discovery, at the entrance to the Odeion of Herodes Attikos, almost certainly indicates that it had been moved from its original location.

[9] Op.cit., 92 and 353.

[10] The latter argument is in any case of dubious validity. As Sterling Dow has shown ("The Egyptian Cults in Athens," *Harv. Theological Rev.* 1937, 187 ff.), it is unlikely that official adoption and popular support of the Serapis cult antedated 229 B.C.

attest a close connection between Euergetes and Athens. The basic motivation for these honors, however, was surely political; they expressed Athenian gratitude for the pledge of Egyptian support against any threat from Macedon. Undoubtedly they may also have reflected the city's thanks for the gift of a gymnasium, but this is merely supposition. Nothing in the present record provides any firm link between the Ptolemaion and the third century.[11]

There are, on the other hand, certain considerations pointing to a second century date for the building and to Philometor as its founder. Little weight can be put on the description of Athens given by Herakleides the Critic since the work is of uncertain date.[12] Even if one accepts Ferguson's arguments for the end of the third century, the omission of the Ptolemaion is not proof that it did not exist at that time. As Ferguson notes, Herakleides was commenting on things which impressed him and he may have seen nothing remarkable in another gymnasium, but he does mention the three older gymnasia—Academy, Lykeion and Kynosarges—and one might suppose that a new and elaborate building in the same category would have been worth a reference if only by way of contrast.

[11] Ferguson argues that it must have been in existence before the death of Chrysippos, ca. 208–204 B.C., since his statue was erected there. But we know nothing more than that Pausanias saw a statue of the philosopher in that location in the second century A.D. Was it a Hellenistic work or a later copy? Assuming the former, had it been set up there originally or moved from another site? If a statue was erected shortly after Chrysippos' death, and there is no certainty that this was the case, the logical place for it would have been the Lykeion where he lectured (Diogenes Laertius VII. 7. 185) and a statue put up there might well have been transferred to the Ptolemaion after the new city gymnasia began to take over the functions of the earlier foundations. There must in any case have been more than one statue of Chrysippos in Athens since Cicero (*De finibus* I. 11. 39) and Diogenes Laertius (VII. 7. 182) mention a seated statue in the Kerameikos.

[12] Ferguson (*Hell. Athens*, 239, 261 ff. and especially 464 ff.) makes out a strong case for the period ca. 205 B.C. but others have put Herakleides as early as the beginning of the third century and as late as the first. The commentary of Jacoby (*F. Gr. Hist.* 369) gives only a broad dating, s. III/II, while the recent study of Friedrich Pfister (*Die Reisebilder des Herakleides*, Österreich. Akad. Wiss. Sitzungsb. 227/2 [Vienna 1951], 44 ff.) maintains that on the basis of the fragments no closer approximation than 275–200 B.C. is possible. Pfister, however, considers it likely that Herakleides was the pupil of Lykon mentioned with his father Demetrios in the philosopher's will, and such an association would seem to imply a *floruit* rather late in the third century.

More significant is the "climate" of the second century as compared with that of the third. During the earlier period, overshadowed as it was by the ever-present threat of Macedonian intervention, building activity in Athens had been minimal. The times were not propitious for the expenditure of public funds on construction projects and there was no tradition of foreign benefactors willing to endow civic edifices. After the decisive defeat of Philip at Cynoscephalae the situation was entirely different. Athens was able at last to look forward to an era of peace and prosperity under Roman protection; the public works which had been neglected or postponed could now be undertaken with confidence in the future. In the Macedonian invasion of Attica in 200 B.C. the three outlying gymnasia had been destroyed. Repairs were made in due course but the establishments had outlived their usefulness. Athens was developing in a different direction and the old gymnasia were inconveniently located. There was need for other gymnasia in the city itself so one of the first improvements of the new century was the Diogeneion.[13] Other projects were contemplated as funds became available. A passage in Polybius (XXVIII. 19.4) suggests that Athens met the problem realistically by soliciting contributions for her construction program. Eumenes provided a stoa for the theater area. Antiochos undertook to complete the Zeus temple. The city itself began work on a remodelling of the market square. Pharnaces of Pontus was reminded that he had promised a subsidy, and this money no doubt helped to finance the Middle Stoa on the south side of the Agora.[14]

Now it was Ptolemy's turn, but in this case the timing was poor. An embassy from Athens with regard to a gift (Polybius, above) was at

---

[13] Its date must be late third or early second century. Graindor (*Musée Belge* 1922, 220) and Wachsmuth (Pauly-Wissowa, *RE*, s.v. Diogeneion) would place its construction early in the second century, and this date accords well with the destruction of the suburban gymnasia in 200 B.C.

[14] References to this building will be found in the new guide to the excavations: H. A. Thompson, *The Athenian Agora* (ed. 2, Athens 1962), 24, 105 f., 207 and 213. See also M. Thompson, *The New Style Silver Coinage of Athens*, 714 n.

No one of the various royal and civic projects involved in this vast Athenian building program (Diogeneion, Stoa of Eumenes, Zeus temple and Middle Stoa) can be precisely dated, but it seems highly likely that the earliest structure was started shortly after the turn of the century and the latest within a few years of 170.

Philometor's court when Antiochos invaded the country in 170 B.C. For the next six years Egypt was in a state of almost continuous crisis, threatened by Syria and weakened by the struggle for power between Philometor and his younger brother Euergetes. It was not until 163 that Philometor gained control as sole ruler. During the years of comparative calm that followed, the young king was able to restore political stability, initiate reforms and carry on an extensive building program in Upper Egypt. The contribution to Athens which had been impossible in 170 was now feasible and desirable. Other Hellenistic monarchs had constructed, or were constructing, impressive monuments to their greater glory and the embellishment of Athens. It would be surprising if Ptolemy had failed to respond to the Attalid and Seleucid challenge.

Certainly at this time Athens was paying notable tribute to Egypt and the Ptolemaic cult. This is reflected not only in the erection of the statue discussed above but also in the remarkable splendor of the festival observances. References to proclamations at the Ptolemaia are frequently encountered in second century inscriptions but there is only one mention of the actual celebration. This occurs in *IG* II² 1938 with a record of over sixty-one hieropoioi in charge of the games. The archon is Lysiades whose date must fall within a few years of 150 B.C.[15]

Further evidence of the importance of the Ptolemaic cult in Athens during the middle of the second century B.C. is provided by the

---

[15] The exact year of Lysiades' archonship is uncertain. Ferguson first assigned him firmly to 152/1 (*Klio* 1909, 337 ff. and *Hell. Athens*, 339) but later shifted him tentatively to 148/7 (*Athenian Tribal Cycles in the Hellenistic Age*, 30). This second date is the one generally given to Lysiades in the archon lists of the second century, most recently in Pelekidis (*Hist. éphébie attique*, 300).

It had seemed to me significant that an issue of coinage with a Ptolemaic symbol was struck in 152/1, and in my study of the New Style money (pp. 605 f.) I argued that the coins substantiated Ferguson's original date for the archon. The coincidence of dates is still definitely attractive, but I no longer feel that it is a decisive factor in either the numismatic or the epigraphical chronology. Almost certainly the special observance of the Ptolemaia was not limited to Lysiades' archonship. One assumes that Ptolemy's gift to Athens, whatever its nature, was recognized by a statue and by unusually elaborate celebration of the Ptolemaic festival. We have a specific record of this only for the archonship of Lysiades but it is highly likely that similar pomp marked each observance of the international Ptolemaia between the date of Philometor's donation and his death in 146 B.C.

coinage. In 152/1 the mint magistrate Aphrodisios placed a cornucopiae as his badge on the coinage. Had this been the simple horn of plenty found on Greek coins of many mints and many periods there would be nothing remarkable about his choice. Such representations appear as symbols on the rare drachms of the final Old Style period at Athens and on three early issues of New Style money.[16] Aphrodisios' symbol, however, was an elaborate double cornucopiae with fillet almost identical with the reverse type of the Arsinoe issues of Ptolemy II and his successors, a coin type distinctively Egyptian in origin and connotation.[17]

The close connection between Athenian symbol and Ptolemaic type can readily be seen from the illustrations at the bottom of PLATE XXVII.[18] In particular the mirror image of the New Style reverse (7), simulating the die itself, shows the fidelity with which the diecutter

---

[16] For the Old Style issue, see Svoronos, *Les monnaies d'Athènes*, pl. 23, 35. The New Style coins (PLATE XXVII, 1–3) are from the issues of 193/2, 180/79 and 160/59 (Thompson, nos. 14, 115a, 421d). On the last of these the cornucopiae is combined with spears of grain but the horn itself is a simple device.

The single cornucopiae is also found as a symbol on both pre-New Style and New Style bronze (as PLATE XXVII, 4–5, from the ANS and Yale collections) and as a type on the "kollyboi" (Svoronos, pl. 18, 99–100, 112).

[17] Athenaeus (XI. 497b, c) describes the drinking-horn as first fabricated in the reign of Ptolemy Philadelphus as an attribute for statues of Arsinoe, which show the queen carrying such an object filled with fruits. This origin for the simple rhyton is, of course, impossible, but G. Kramer (*Über den Styl und die Herkunft der bemalten griechischen Thongefässe* [Berlin 1837], 126f.) suggests that Philadelphus may have been responsible for the creation of the double horn.

As a coin type the double cornucopiae with fillet is peculiarly Ptolemaic. It is used, in combination with the head of the deified Arsinoe, on an impressive series of gold octadrachms and silver dekadrachms initiated by Ptolemy II after the death of his queen. This Arsinoe money continued to be struck under later rulers; octadrachms and tetradrachms of gold formed part of the coinage of Ptolemy VI (Svoronos, τὰ Νομίσματα τοῦ Κράτους τῶν Πτολεμαίων, pls. XV ff. and E. T. Newell, *Royal Greek Portrait Coins*, 106). Even on non-Egyptian coinages the device is linked with the Ptolemies. Philometor's daughter Cleopatra was the wife of three Seleucid kings, and both Philometor and his brother Euergetes actively intervened in the dynastic struggles of Syria. It was during this period of strong Egyptian influence that the double cornucopiae appears as a Seleucid coin type.

[18] The gold tetradrachm is assigned to the early years of Ptolemy VIII by Svoronos (no. 1500) but is more likely an issue of Ptolemy VI. Both it and the Athenian tetradrachm (Thompson, no. 546i) are in the ANS collection.

copied his model. Note the orientation and shape of the horns, the volutes at the terminal point, the two prominent spikes above the rim and the pendent grapes on either side. Only the arrangement of the fillet is different; limitations of space forced the engraver to substitute a stiff bow with ties for the fluttering ribbons of the Egyptian coins.

Aphrodisios' Egyptian cornucopiae device is involved with the broader problem of the significance of the symbols found on the New Style silver. This has been dealt with in some detail elsewhere[19] and only a few observations need be repeated here. There can, I think, be no question about their being personal badges in that selection was the unrestricted prerogative of the magistrates whose names appeared in first place on the coinage. Where we can make a definite association of man and symbol, the personal connection is even closer; the device is a direct allusion to the magistrate's name, his origin, his family or his accomplishments. In many cases the relationship between magistrate and badge is obscure. If we could identify the men concerned and knew something of their background, we might well find that most, or all, of their symbols were personally significant, but as it is we cannot rule out two alternate possibilities. The device may have had reference to a contemporary event with which the magistrate had no direct connection or it may have been a random selection made simply to conform to the tradition of placing symbols on the coinage.

It should be noted, however, that the more distinctive the symbol the greater the probability that it was meaningful. A banal emblem such as a prow or a bunch of grapes might be the fortuitous choice of an unimaginative man; an unusual device almost certainly carried a message. This is true of the racing quadriga of Mikion, the trophy on prow of Themistokles, the griffin of Teian Apellikon, the Three Graces of Eurykleides, the elephant of Antiochos and the star and crescents of King Mithradates. It should also be true of the Ptolemaic cornucopiae of Aphrodisios.

In defining the exact nature of the message Aphrodisios was conveying, we are handicapped by the fact that we know little or nothing about the man. He may be the Aphrodisios of Azenia whose son is

[19] Thompson, 600–607.

mentioned in a roster of noblemen of the last quarter of the second century, but even assuming that identification to be correct, we have no information on the activity or career of Aphrodisios of Azenia which would explain the Ptolemaic symbol on his coinage. Working from the name alone, we can nevertheless make certain significant deductions. The Egyptian symbol cannot be a mere canting badge such as we find in some other connections. Nor is it at all likely that it reflects a direct association with Egypt on the part of either the magistrate or his family. Aphrodisios is a common Athenian name; there is no reason to suppose that our Aphrodisios was of foreign extraction.[20] Furthermore, it is noteworthy that the device appears only during Aphrodisios' second term in office. Three years earlier he had used the commonplace symbol of Nike for his money. All of this strongly suggests that the Ptolemaic symbolism had a specific rather than a general connotation, that it was connected less with the man himself than with some special occasion coinciding with his second tenure as mint magistrate. The obvious and, I think, the only tenable connection is with the Ptolemaic cult and its ritual observances.

This association is of considerable importance for the chronology of the New Style coinage. The Ptolemaia were celebrated in Athens from about 224 B.C. Inscriptions specifying the proclamation of honors at the Dionysia, the Panathenaia, the Eleusinia, and the Ptolemaia are numerous in the early and middle second century, the latest dating from 127/6. Then there is a gap. In 122/1, in 118/7, in 116/5 and again in 106/5 the formula includes only the first three festivals. There is no mention of the Ptolemaia. Later—in decrees of 101/0, 96/5 and ca. 94/3—all four festivals are enumerated.[21] The record is altogether clear and straightforward. Between 122 and 105, at a minimal reckon-

---

[20] Kirchner's record of second century Athenians named Aphrodisios (*Prosopographia Attica*) can be supplemented by a new archon, assigned tentatively to 170/69 B.C. (*Hesperia* 1947, no. 64).
[21] Pelekidis (op.cit., 300) lists the inscriptions mentioning the Ptolemaia and Ferguson (*Klio* 1908, 338) those omitting that festival. The archon dates of Ferguson, Pelekidis and Meritt (*The Athenian Year*, 235 ff.) are to some degree divergent; the years cited here are those of Meritt.

In discussing the Ptolemaia, Ferguson outlines their history at Athens as follows: a period of great popularity in the last quarter of the third century and the first half of the second; a disappearance ca. 150 due to the animosity aroused in the Greek world by the atrocities of Euergetes; a revival under the

ing, the Ptolemaic cult had fallen into such disfavor that the Ptolemaia had ceased to be celebrated.

Any suggested revision of the 196–87 B.C. chronology of the New Style series must take the coinage of Aphrodisios into account. On the lower chronology recently advocated by David M. Lewis,[22] this issue would date from 119/8, a time when the Ptolemaia were no longer being celebrated. Against this background the Egyptian device is incongruous and inexplicable. Had our magistrate's name been Ptolemaios instead of Aphrodisios or his antecedents less clearly Athenian, there would be no problem. The Ptolemaic symbol would be an understandable choice at any time, like the elephant of Antiochos or the Teian griffin of Apellikon. For a coinage struck before 126 or after 102 there would again be no problem. Any celebration of the Ptolemaia would suffice to explain the symbolism. For a coinage struck in 119/8 it is, under the circumstances, an extremely peculiar if not incredible device.

On the other hand, it was a particularly felicitous choice for the coinage of 152/1. At this time the Ptolemaic cult was at its apogee. Toward the middle of the century a bronze equestrian statue of Ptolemy VI had been erected on the Acropolis. That this commemorated Ptolemy's gift of a gymnasium and library seems highly likely, but in any case such signal recognition must surely have been inspired by signal benefactions. During this same period and undoubtedly in further acknowledgement of Ptolemy's generosity to Athens, the Ptolemaia were celebrated with unusual magnificence. For this we have the combined testimony of the epigraphical and numismatic records.

MARGARET THOMPSON

---

oligarchic government of 103–88 in response to the pro-Greek policy of Soter II; a final disappearance at the time of the Mithradatic War and Sullan occupation of the city. Ferguson's theory that the Ptolemaia disappeared ca. 150 can no longer be accepted since the festival is now known to have been observed in 127/6. One assumes that there was a period of gradual decline before the celebration was abandoned ca. 126–123 B.C.

[22] "The Chronology of the Attic New Style Coinage," *NC* 1962.

HERCULES-MELQART ON A COIN OF FAUSTUS SULLA

(See Plate XXVIII)

One of the more puzzling coins in the Roman Republican series is S 880–81.[1] The obverse shows a young man with diadem (Plate XXVIII, 1); the reverse, Diana in a biga (Plate XXVIII, 2). This coin forms the counterpart to S 879 with the bust of Diana on the obverse (Plate XXVIII, 3), on the reverse the famous scene of the elder Sulla receiving Bocchus and Jugurtha (Plate XXVIII, 4). The identity of the young man on the obverse of S 880–81 has been variously suggested as Bocchus, Jugurtha or Hercules, and it is with these three possibilities that this paper is concerned.

The moneyer, Faustus Sulla,[2] was in many ways characteristic of his age and typical of the lesser sons of famous fathers. Born in 86 B.C., he was still a child at his father's death in 78. He was bothered early in life by bids for the restitution of property appropriated by his father, but successfully avoided the legal pursuit of his claimants. In 63 he served under Pompey in the East, where he particularly and profitably distinguished himself in the capture of the temple at Jerusalem (Joseph. *BJ* 1.149, 154; cf. *AJ* 14.69, 73). He won other rewards as well. We know, for example, that the tiara of Mithridates passed into his hands (Plut. *Pomp.* 42.3). There was reason for his diligence: he was obliged upon his return to produce for the Roman populace the games promised by his father's will (Cic. *Sull.* 54f.). As moneyer, probably in 62,[3] he struck S 879 and 880–81. In 54 as

---

[1] Numbers refer to the type numbers of E. A. Sydenham, *The Roman Republican Coinage* (London, 1952), henceforth abbreviated as S.

[2] For references relating to the life and career of Faustus Sulla see F. Münzer, "Cornelius (377)," *PW* and T. R. S. Broughton, *The Magistrates of the Roman Republic* (New York, 1951–52), henceforth abbreviated as *MRR*.

[3] Since the coin is the only evidence for the date, one would like to use the closing date of a hoard as a decisive indicator, but there are no hoards from the 60's, according to H. A. Grueber, *Coins of the Roman Republic in the British Museum* (London, 1910), henceforth abbreviated as G, cxii, 1.411 ff. (cf. Ap-

quaestor, he struck coins in honor of Pompey. At the outbreak of the Civil War, he cheerfully hoped through it to restore his desolated fortunes. After some confusion about his sphere of action, Sulla accompanied Pompey to the East, but after Pharsalus he fled to Africa, and after Thapsus he planned to flee to Spain, but fell into Caesarian hands and was killed.

The problematic obverse of S 880–81 shows the head of a young man; on some examples of the coin, he seems very young. He faces right and wears a diadem, with long ends fluttering out behind his head. His hair is short, lumpily curly, and characterized by a prominent erect forelock. He has sideburns, which on some specimens have been worn away completely or worn to such an extent that they are no longer recognizable. The face is fat and fleshy, in contrast to the sharp outline of the head. The man wears a cloak which lies remarkably high on his neck, and its collar creates a pronounced diagonal, below which are broad, parallel markings as if to indicate a furry material. The cloak is tied under his chin in a knot with short ends, which, on one of the best coins, seem to be paws.

The obverse legend reads FEELIX (G 1.472 n.), which corresponds to the FAUSTUS of the reverse. Both refer to the Sullan family, and thus offer no clue toward the identity of the head, a problem that has occupied a number of numismatists over a considerable period of time, as the following résumé of identifications shows:[4]

---

pendix). T. Mommsen, *Geschichte des römischen Münzwesens* (Berlin, 1860), 624, n. 457, T. Mommsen–Duc de Blacas, *Histoire de la monnaie romaine* (Paris, 1870), 2.484, n. 1, and E. Babelon, *Description historique et chronologique des monnaies de la République romaine* (Paris, 1885–86), henceforth abbreviated as B, 1.420, offered 64 as an approximate date without special explanation. Grueber suggested 62, apparently as a likely date for Sulla to have been moneyer and one to which the coinage falls by comparison with contemporaneous issues (1.471, nn. 1, 2). Sydenham followed Grueber and proposed 63–62 (p. 145, n. 879), which is impossible since in 63 Sulla was in the East. Either 64 or 62 is possible, but the latter seems more probable. A. Alföldi, "Studien zur Zeitfolge der Münzprägung der römischen Republik," *RSN* 36 (1954), 5–30, associates both issues of Faustus Sulla for stylistic reasons, but would place S 879–81 in 56 and S 882–84 in 55.

[4] The authors cited treat the problem in the following works:
    P. Seguin, *Selecta Numismatica Antiqua* (Paris, 1684), 218f.
    J. Eckhel, *Doctrina Numorum Veterum* (Vienna, 1795), 5.192f.
    E. Q. Visconti, *Iconographie grecque* (Milan, 1826), 3.293 n.

Seguin	Jugurtha	1684
Eckhel	Bocchus	1795
Visconti	Hercules	1826
Riccio	Hercules	1843
Duchalais	Hercules	1849
Cavedoni	Hercules Callinicus	1854
Mommsen	Jugurtha?	1860
Müller	Bocchus	1862
Mommsen-Blacas	Jugurtha?	1870
Babelon	Jugurtha	1885
Serafini	Hercules	1897
Grueber	Hercules	1910
Alföldi	Jugurtha	1951
Sydenham	Hercules	1952

Scholarly opinion has always wavered about the identification of this coin, since no absolutely convincing evidence has turned up to solve the problem. Bocchus, Jugurtha, or Hercules? The first two must obviously be considered together, for both come from the same historical scene.

In 106 the war against the Numidian king Jugurtha had already been languishing a number of years, even after the arrival of Marius

G. Riccio, *Le monete delle antiche famiglie di Roma* (Naples, 1843), 72 f.
A. Duchalais, "Mémoire sur les monnaies antiques frappées dans la Numidie et dans la Mauretanie," *Mémoires de la société des antiquaires de France* 19 (1849), 404–67.
C. Cavedoni, *Ragguaglio storico archeologico de' precipui ripostigli antichi di medaglie consolari e di famiglie romane* (Modena, 1854), 75, n. 55.
Mommsen, 624.
L. Müller, *Numismatique de l'ancienne Afrique* (Copenhagen, 1862), 3.36 f.
Mommsen-Blacas, 2.485.
Babelon, 1.421.
C. Serafini, "L'arte nei ritratti della moneta romana repubblicana," *BCAR* 25 (1897), 3–34.
Grueber, 1.472.
Alföldi, "Komplementäre Doppeltypen in der Denarprägung der römischen Republik," *Schweizer Münzblätter* 2 (1951), 1–7.
Sydenham, p. 146.

as supreme commander in Africa.[5] Then the Romans managed to inflict a decisive defeat upon the combined forces of Jugurtha and his dubious ally, his father-in-law Bocchus, King of Mauretania. The latter asked the Romans for terms. In an interview in 105 between Bocchus and the elder Sulla, at this time a resourceful junior officer, Sulla urged that Bocchus arrange the surrender of Jugurtha to the Romans. Bocchus agreed, but afterwards wondered if he might not better betray Sulla to Jugurtha. Abiding by his promise, however, he handed over Jugurtha. The war ended. Marius triumphed gloriously. Jugurtha, after figuring ignominiously in the procession, died in prison. Bocchus with insufferable pride dedicated on the Capitoline a gold representation of his surrender of Jugurtha to Sulla (Plut. *Sull.* 6.1, *Mar.* 32.2). The elder Sulla adapted this scene for his signet (Val. Max. 8.14.4; Plin. *HN* 37.8), and Faustus later used the motif of the ring for the reverse of S 879.

This brief survey of events makes the reasons for the identification of the type as Bocchus or Jugurtha clear. Eckhel (5.192f.) thought it natural that the younger Sulla should represent Bocchus on the coinage in honor of his father. Müller (3.36f.) also believed the head to be that of Bocchus because of the royal diadem and the cloak, an article of Mauretanian costume. Two points should, however, be noted. First, Bocchus' intentions towards Sulla were at best ambiguous (Sall. *Iug.* 108.3, 113.2–4; Plut. *Sull.* 3.3), and one can hardly imagine why the family would want to honor this man, although the transaction in which he participated ultimately redounded to Sulla's credit. Nor can one imagine that the presence of the foreign king on their coin would have pleased the Roman people. Second, there are no portraits of Bocchus to verify the identification. The figures on the reverse of Faustus Sulla's companion-coin are much too small to show individual character, and Bocchus himself lacks any personal coinage,[6] which might display the royal head.

Seguin, Mommsen, Mommsen-Blacas, and Babelon considered Jugurtha a more probable candidate than Bocchus. Mommsen thought the royal portrait might derive from Bocchus' dedication piece. Alföldi feels very strongly that the head is that of Jugurtha,

---

[5] For the historical background see *CAH* 9.116–39 and *MRR* for 106 and 105.

[6] J. Mazard, *Corpus Nummorum Numidiae Mauretaniaeque* (Paris, 1955), 59.

since this coin and its counterpart illustrate his theory of cross-related types: the reverse of S 879 represents Bocchus and Jugurtha before Sulla, and therefore the obverse of S 880–81 must represent Jugurtha.[7] Babelon's explanation (1.421) has resulted in some numismatic confusion. He identified the head on Sulla's coin as that of Jugurtha on the basis of the resemblance between it and that of a coin formerly thought to be Numidian (PLATE XXVIII, 5). The portrati head of the latter coin is then sometimes identified as Jurgutha on the basis of its resemblance to Sulla's coin!

The head on the non-Roman coin faces left. The man's hair is short, with a prominent forelock similar to that of Sulla's coin, and he wears an intertwined wreath-diadem that is tied behind his head with fluttering ends, again like Sulla's coin. He too has sideburns. His profile is singular, especially the sharp, curved nose with its high bridge, but, in spite of a superficial similarity, this coin cannot portray the same man as the Roman coin.[8] Furthermore, since the non-Roman coin is no longer classified as Numidian, but as part of the Barcid series in Spain and prior to Jugurtha,[9] it cannot serve as proof for the Jugurtha identification of the Roman coin.

Moreover, there is little likelihood that the younger Sulla would late in the 60's place on the obverse of his coin an enemy conquered forty years earlier. Rome's problems in these later years were primarily domestic and, insofar as they were foreign, certainly not African. Faustus may well have wanted to commemorate the glorious deeds of his father, but for such a purpose the submission scene on the reverse of S 879 is far more satisfying than the proud, youthful, and prosperous head of the obverse of S 880–81.

In any case, the Romans, perhaps as a consequence of the long tradition of Roma obverses, generally reserved that position for the

---

[7] Alföldi, "Doppeltypen," 1–7, believes that the types of some denarii are cross-related in their meaning, so that the obverse of coin A is to be associated with the reverse of coin B, and reverse A with obverse B. This necessitates, of course, the possession of both coins for the understanding of their message.

[8] S. Gsell, *Histoire ancienne de l'Afrique du Nord* (Paris, 1928), 2.329, n. 3.

[9] L. Charrier, *Description des monnaies de la Numidie et de la Mauretanie* (Macon, 1921), 18, points out that no specimens of this coin have ever been found in Numidian territory; cf. E. S. G. Robinson, "The Punic Coins of Spain and Their Bearing on the Roman Republican Series," *Roman Coinage* (Oxford, 1956), 43 f.

gods. Among mortals, even Romans, until the very end of the Republic, appeared rarely on the coinage; and foreigners more rarely still: apart from the Bocchus-Jugurtha-Sulla reverse (S 879), the supposed Philip V of Macedon (S 551),[10] Perseus (S 926), and Aretas (S 912) are the only instances. The last two are shown in appropriately humble attitudes, and one can explain the regal pose of Philip by the fact that the moneyer thought himself honored by his family's social connection with the king. One must remember too that Philip, a nobler enemy than Jugurtha, enjoyed friendly relations with the Romans after his defeat. This coin, incidentally, is the only one of the "royal" coins that antedates Sulla's. Thus neither the immediate political situation nor precedent proves upon investigation to be a good argument for the presence of Jugurtha upon the obverse.

The case of Hercules is the most complex. Visconti thought the head was that of Hercules, simply because it resembled other representations of the young Hercules (3.417 n.). Riccio favored Hercules on the basis of "modern scholarship" and the known devotion of Sulla and his family to the god (73). Duchalais presented a more interesting interpretation. Although this Hercules is uncommon, he found a similar type at Tyre, and he explained Sulla's type as follows: "... nous savons qu'Hercule, d'après les traditions africaines, était père de Syphax, tige de la race des rois de Mauretanie et de Numidie; il est donc tout naturel que Faustus ait été choisir, pour en parer les pièces qu'il a fait frapper, le dieu principal de la nation numidique, comme pour indiquer que ce dieu avait passé aux Romains (417)." The Numidian god would then have come over to the Romans by the rite of *evocatio*, but this was no longer in practice during the first century B.C. (*PW* 6.1152f.), when respect for the ancestral religion had largely disappeared. Therefore the allusion that Duchalais suggested would have been too subtle for the contemporaries of Sulla to grasp. Cavedoni identified the portrait as that of a young Hercules Callinicus by reason of its similarity to the representation on an Etruscan mirror (75 n. 55).[11] Serafini accepted Cavedoni's Hercules,

---

[10] According to G 2.277 n. this Philip V does not resemble other portraits of the king.

[11] E. Gerhard, *Etruskische Spiegel* (Berlin, 1845–97), 3.130f., 2. pl. 137.

Grueber was hesitant (1.472 n.), and Sydenham decided in favor of Hercules without comment.

Since neither Bocchus nor Jugurtha is a likely or probable identification, Hercules remains. It must be admitted immediately that the head, if Hercules', is unlike every other Hercules in the Republican coinage, although it shows affinities with a coin in the Romano-Campanian series (S 6; PLATE XXVIII, 6). On the other hand, the Hercules types display considerable variety,[12] and thus the head may be that of Hercules. If we make this assumption, two questions present themselves: (1) why did the younger Sulla wish Hercules to figure on this coin, and (2) which Hercules does the coin show?

To answer the first, it is necessary to consider the character of the Roman Hercules. Whatever his origin and background,[13] he arrived early and was first honored in the Forum Boarium. Although the legend of the establishment of the Ara Maxima there, after his heroic encounter with the local villain Cacus, is in the best tradition of Hercules of the twelve labors, the nature of the god was apparently soon affected by the business world around him. Whether because he had completed long voyages with efficiency, or because he possessed "mercurial" skill in discovering profit, merchants turned to him for aid. In good fortune they sacrificed to him at the Ara Maxima a tenth of their gain (Plaut. *Bacch.* 665f., *Stich.* 232, 386, *Truc.* 562; Dion. Hal. 1.40.6; cf. Plut. *QR* 18).[14] Among the first of these may have been Octavius Herrenus, a flute-player who went into business and prospered (Macr. 3.6.11), but the most lavish occasions, the dedications of Sulla (Plut. *Sull.* 35.1), Lucullus (Diod. 4.21.4; cf. Plut. *Luc.* 37.4), and Crassus (Plut. *Crass.* 2.2), came in the late Republic.

Out of this custom of dedicating a tenth to Hercules upon the successful completion of business ventures grew the custom of dedicating

---

[12] Head covered by the lion's skin, S 775, 882–83; head without the lion's skin, 563, 604–5, 791, 1139; Hercules and the Nemean lion, 768; Hercules in a chariot, 429, 511; with trophy, 970, 971; standing, 1051, 1140; playing the lyre, 810.

[13] For greater detail see G. Wissowa, *Religion und Kultus der Römer* (Munich, 1912) and J. Bayet, *Les Origines de l'Hercule romain* (Paris, 1926) as well as the articles in *PW*, *Dar.-Sag.*, and Roscher's *Lex*.

[14] The sacrifice of the tenth was, however, not peculiar to Rome but was prevalent throughout Italy. See, for example, the engaging inscription of the Vertuleii from Sora (*CIL* 1².2.1531).

a tenth of the booty or of otherwise showing kindly attentions to the god upon the successful completion of military ventures. Hercules also participated in the celebration of triumphs (Ath. 4.153c, 5.221f), when it was customary to carry a statue of the god in triumphal garb in the procession (Plin. *HN* 34.33). The reverses of the coins of C. Antius Restio (S 970, 971) perhaps reflect this practice; Hercules is shown full figure, walking, holding his club and a trophy, while the lion's skin hangs over one arm. Hercules probably figured more importantly in the lives of the generals than the surviving evidence indicates, but even so the list of generals whom we know to have paid reverence to him in one way or another is impressive: M. Minucius Rufus (*CIL* 1².2.607); Q. Fabius Maximus (Strab. 6.3.1; Plin. *HN* 34.40; Plut. *Fab.* 22.5-6; cf. Dio 42.26.1);[15] M'. Acilius Glabrio (Liv. 36.30.3); P. Cornelius Scipio Nasica (Liv. 38.35.4); M. Fulvius Nobilior (Cic. *Arch.* 27; Eumen. *Panegyr.* 4.7; Macr. 1.12.16; Plin. *HN* 35.66; cf. Plut. *QR* 59); L. Aemilius Paulus (Plut. *Aem.* 17.6, cf. 19. 2-3; Fest. 282 L, cf. Plin. *HN* 35.19);[16] P. Cornelius Scipio Aemilianus (Plin. *HN* 36.39; cf. App. *Lib.* 135); L. Mummius (*CIL* 1².2.626; cf. 632);[17] L. Cornelius Sulla (Plut. *Sull.* 35.1; Ov. *Fast.* 6.209-12);[18] L. Licinius Lucullus (Diod. 4.21.4; Plin. *HN* 34.93); M. Aurelius Cotta (Memnon 35.7-8 *FGrH* 3 B 363 f.); Cn. Pompeius Magnus (Vitr. 3.3.5; Plin. *HN* 34.57).[19]

With the devotion of generals to Hercules must also be considered the power of the legend of Alexander at Rome.[20] Hercules had traveled vast distances, almost from end to end of the known world. Alex-

---

[15] For Fabian devotion to Hercules on the basis of their descent from the god see Münzer, s.v. "Fabius," *PW* and note 16 below.

[16] Cf. the sacrifice of his son, Q. Fabius Maximus Aemilianus, to Hercules in Spain (App. *Iber.* 65) and the building by his grandson, Q. Fabius Maximus Allobrogicus, of a temple to Hercules in Gaul after a victory over the Celts (Strab. 4.1.11).

[17] The identity of this Munius with the victor at Corinth has often been questioned, most recently by B. Riposati, "Postilla all'epigrafe reatina di Lucius Munius," *Epigraphica* 12 (1950), 137-49.

[18] See S. B. Platner and T. Ashby, *A Topographical Dictionary of Ancient Rome* (London, 1929), 256.

[19] Ibid. 255f.

[20] Cf. A. Bruhl, "Le souvenir d'Alexandre le Grand et les Romains," *MEFR* 47 (1930), 202-21 and J. Gagé, "Hercule–Melqart, Alexandre et les Romains à Gadès," *REA* 42 (1940), 425-38.

ander, a devoted worshipper of Hercules, at the time of his death entertained hopes, according to some, of conquering the West as he had already conquered the East. The relationship between the hero-god and the hero-king was thus established. Now the Romans, in the very period in which their generals were demonstrating special regard for Hercules, were also moving widely about the known world. The similarity between Hercules, Alexander, and the Roman generals was too obvious to be missed and doubtless fostered the popularity of Hercules, particularly when independent-minded generals became a regular feature of Roman political life.

Of all the generals Pompey displayed the greatest inclination towards being a second Alexander.[21] He was thought to resemble Alexander (Plut. *Pomp.* 2.1–2; Sall. *Hist.* 3.88M). He emulated Alexander's conquests and his policies in founding cities (App. *Mith.* 115) and in employing a private historian, Theophanes of Mytilene (Cic. *Arch.* 24; Strab. 13.2.3). His very name, Pompeius Magnus (Plut. *Pomp.* 13.3ff., *Crass.* 7.1, *Sert.* 18.2, *Moral.* 206E; Plin. *HN* 7.96; Dio 37.21.3),[22] demonstrates his admiration, while his triumph was a veritable parade of his passion for Alexander (Plut. *Pomp.* 45, cf. 46.1–2; Plin. *HN* 7.95–99; App. *Mith.* 116–17; Dio 37.21.2; cf. Vell. Pat. 2.40.4, 53.3). In fact, Pliny, although of course much after the event, not only equates Pompey with Alexander but maintains that his deeds are almost on a par with those of Hercules and Liber (Plin. *HN* 7.95). It is doubtless in view of this that Faustus Sulla in 54, by that time Pompey's son-in-law, struck coins (S 882–83) with an obverse of Hercules in the lion's skin and a reverse of four wreaths. The obverse, so unusual in the iconography of Hercules during the Republic, is certainly intended to recall the coins of Alexander (G 1.489 n. 1). Finally, one should remember that the Pompeian watchword at Pharsalus was *Hercules Invictus* (App. *BC* 2.76).

Hercules, however, could not save his friends from defeat at the hands of Venus Victrix, and Antony's regard for him (Plut. *Ant.*

---

[21] This is treated extensively by M. Gelzer, *Pompeius* (Munich, 1959), 54, 78, 92f., 97ff., 124ff.
[22] J. P. V. D. Balsdon, in his review of Gelzer's *Pompeius*, suggested that Pompey used the cognomen Magnus freely only after his Alexandrian feats in the East, *Historia* 1 (1950), 299.

4.1-2, 36.4, 60.2, *Comp. Demetr. et Ant.* 3.3; App. *BC* 3.16; Strab. 14.1.14; S 1103) ruined his future with Augustus.[23] Thus attention to Hercules as the bringer of luck, commercial or military, is shown primarily during the Republic, especially during the last one and one-half centuries of its existence. With the Empire, Hercules at first disappeared from prominence, and when he later returned, it was in the character of a savior-god.

The coins with Hercules types bear out very well the military significance of the god, for instead of portraying the general himself, an unknown practice at this time, the moneyer advertised the god to whom the general owed the prosperous outcome of his endeavors. Some coins commemorate past achievements, but others, particularly in the late Republic, allude to contemporary generals. In the former category are coins in honor of an Aurelius Cotta (S 429), M'. Acilius Glabrio (S 511), Fulvius Nobilior (S 810), and Sulla (S 880-81); in the latter, those for Marius (S 563?, 604-5), Sulla (S 768), and Pompey (S 882-83, 939, 1051).

The character of the Hercules types is also revealing. Whereas the head on the quadrans in the earliest Republican coinage wore the conventional lion's skin, the subsequent heads were revised to a less traditional type. Between these portrait styles, however, came the coins on which Hercules poses on the reverse as *triumphator* (S 429, 511); on the first of these (PLATE XXVIII, 7), Hercules, dressed in the lion's skin, drives a biga of centaurs, but already on the second (PLATE XXVIII, 8) he has usurped the place of Jupiter, Mars, and Victory in the triumphal quadriga. Hercules driving the centaurs has comic antecedents, and the god may have presided over the *ludi plebeii* in the Circus Flaminius, but these festival aspects[24] are overshadowed by the probability of a reference to M. Aurelius Cotta, legate of L. Scipio in 189 (Liv. 37.52.1-2; cf. Polyb. 21.18.1; B 1.240) or, more likely, to M. Aurelius Cotta, who as legate in 203-200 took action against Philip V of Macedon (Liv. 30.26.4, 42.1-10, 31.3.2-6,

---

[23] Augustus' animosity towards Hercules and its effects are discussed by R. Schilling, "L'Hercule romain en face de le réforme religieuse d'Auguste," *RP* 16 (1942), 31-57.

[24] For the centaurs s.v. "Herakles," Rosch. *Lex.*, 2191, 2244 f.; for Hercules' association with various games cf. 2978 ff. See also F. Matz, "Belli facies et triumphus," *Festschrift für C. Weickert* (Berlin, 1955), 52.

HERCULES-MELQART

5.5–9).²⁵ The models for the centaur type seem in any case to be Macedonian.²⁶ Furthermore, any doubts about the meaning of this type are allayed by the coin for M'. Acilius Glabrio, which is only slightly later. Livy tells us that Glabrio sacrificed to Hercules on Mt. Oeta (36.30.3), after which he defeated Antiochus at Thermopylae in 191. Upon his return to Rome, he enjoyed a splendid triumph (Liv. 37.46.2–4). The presence of Hercules on the coin doubtless alludes to these events, and his military importance is indicated both by his triumphant bearing and by the trophy that he carries. Curiously, the trophy should belong to Mars (cf. S 472, 490, 565), but Hercules tends more and more to replace Mars on the coins as elsewhere: Mars merely stands for the facts of war, but Hercules indicates success.

Upon these types follow two approximately contemporaneous²⁷ issues of revised heads, the first (S 563) from a non-Roman, the second (S 604–5) from the Roman mint.²⁸ Both present the same peculiar pose; the figure is viewed from behind, but since the head is turned, once to the left and once to the right, a profile is presented. On the earlier, and artistically superior, coin (PLATE XXVIII, 9), Hercules appears older and more godlike. He is bearded, and he wears a laurel wreath tied behind with dangling ribbons. On his right shoulder rests his club. The later Hercules is younger and coarser (PLATE XXVIII, 10). He is beardless and short-haired, and he carries his club on his left shoulder. In both cases the lion's skin is hung over the shoulders, and the appearance of the lion's head on the shoulder with the club is quite remarkable. This, together with the pose, for which S 564 seems to be the only Republican parallel, relates these coins with more than accidental significance.

---

[25] From the fact that the moneyer of this coin, M. Aurelius Cot(t)a, may have been the father of the Cotta who so brutally sacked Heracleia in Bithynia and carried off the Hercules statue from its agora (Memnon 35.7–8, *FGrH* 3B, 363f.), one may wonder if the Aurelii had some private concern for Hercules beyond his normal military value. Probably, however, the statue was simply the best statue to loot in Heracleia.

[26] Matz, 46.

[27] See *MRR*, Appendix I, for a conspectus of dates for the moneyers Ti. Quinctius and P. Cornelius Lentulus Marcelli f.

[28] Sydenham assigned the latter to an auxiliary Italian mint, p. 85, cf. p. 86, n. 606.

The reverses are also important. The first shows two galloping horses with a naked rider, a link with the biga and quadriga types discussed above. The second shows Roma in military costume being crowned by the Genius of the Roman people.[29] This first numismatic instance of the Genius type,[30] to which the Cornelii Lentuli were so partial,[31] is thought to refer to the Gallic victories of Marius (G 2.233 f. n. 3), since M. Claudius Marcellus, the father of the moneyer, P. Cornelius Lentulus, served under Marius at Aquae Sextiae in 102 (Plut. *Mar.* 20.4, 21.1). If this second coin pertains to Marius, one may perhaps assume the same for the first. An allusion to Marius, with his universal military reputation, would be appropriate just before or during the Social War, when crisis demanded all the aid of the Roman Hercules against his Marsic counterpart (cf. S 631), and the Genius type would be most apt on a coin in honor of Marius, whose military reforms made his army the first that really represented the whole Roman people.[32]

Sulla too was honored by coins on which Hercules appeared. S 768 (PLATE XXVIII, 11) shows very handsomely the struggle of Hercules with the Nemean lion, a theme familiar in art and legend,[33] but unique on Republican coins. This coin, struck by an obscure C. Poblicius in the late 80's or early 70's, is explained by Grueber (xc) as possibly commemorating the victory of Sulla over the forces of Marius at the Porta Collina (App. *BC* 1.93; Plut. *Sull.* 29). There was a temple of Hercules outside this gate (Liv. 26.10.3), and from its neighborhood comes the inscription of Publicia, wife of a Cn. Corne-

---

[29] See Wissowa, 175 ff. The Genius of the Roman people, although offered state sacrifice in 218 (Liv. 21.62.10) and granted a temple before 43 (Dio 47.2.3), achieved its greatest popularity in the Empire, when the genius of the people and that of the emperor became closely related, but the concept of the genius of the army may go back to Republican times.

[30] Cf. E. Rink, *Die bildlichen Darstellungen des römischen Genius* (Diss. Giessen, 1933), 41 ff.

[31] J. Gagé, "Les Cornelii Lentuli et 'le genius Populi Romani'," *Congrès international de numismatique de Paris II* (Paris, 1953), 219–27. Cf. S 752, 791.

[32] Alföldi, "The Main Aspects of Political Propaganda on the Coinage of the Roman Republic," *Roman Coinage*, 93 f., suggests that the Genius type indicates anti-senatorial feeling.

[33] Cf. R. Bräuer, "Die Heraklestaten auf antiken Münzen," *ZFN* 28 (1910), 35–112 and F. Brommer, *Herakles. Die zwölf Taten des Helden in antiker Kunst und Literatur* (Münster, 1953).

lius, who dedicated and decorated an *aedes* of Hercules (*CIL* 1².2.981).[34] Her dedication precedes the coin by a short time only, and even if it does not pertain to the Porta Collina temple, it indicates a family concern for Hercules that the moneyer may well have shared. On the other hand, if Publicia's inscription refers to the Porta Collina temple, what better moment to think of restoring it than just after Sulla's victory?

Since it is now clear that during the late Republic successful generals especially favored Hercules, and that he appeared on coinage intended to honor them, it is obvious why Faustus wanted Hercules to figure on this coin. While his father's devotion to the god was of personal rather than familial character, the son might nonetheless have wished to continue the cult as an act of filial piety.[35] The younger Sulla had other contacts with Hercules as well. After his father's death, he became the ward of Lucullus (Plut. *Luc.* 4.4), another worshipper of Hercules. Most recently he had campaigned with Pompey, whose pretensions to being a second Hercules as well as a second Alexander were probably well defined by 63. Finally, he might have wanted to thank Hercules for his own luck in the East. He was only in his early 20's, and certainly not in a class with the great generals, but if Hercules had become the god of successful military operations, with possibly more emphasis on their successful than on their military aspect, Faustus would have been only somewhat presumptuous in his display of appreciation. The Roman public who saw the coin could surely have made the correct association between Hercules and Faustus, and they might even have interpreted the appearance of Hercules as an indication that their long awaited games were at last forthcoming with all the magnificence of such celebrations (cf. Dio 37.51.4).

We can then consider the second question: which Hercules does this coin show? The various proposals made in the past are suggestive, for the individual objects adduced as parallels to the coin themselves

---

[34] For the difficulties imposed by the distance, one kilometer, of the inscription from the gate, see bibliography cited by Platner-Ashby, 251.

[35] Faustus also honored Diana and Venus (S 879, 880–81, 884), although it must have been difficult for him to treat with due respect all the gods from whom his father derived his *felicitas*; cf. J. P. V. D. Balsdon, "Sulla Felix," *JRS* 41 (1951), 1–10.

display a strong resemblance. The Hercules Callinicus of the Etruscan mirror is a young man, with the club in his right hand, lion's skin over his left shoulder. His face shows traces of sideburns, and he wears a diadem in his short, curly hair.[36] On the obverse of a Romano-Campanian coin (S 6; PLATE XXVIII, 6)[37] appears a similar young Hercules with sideburns and diadem. The club lies over the shoulder, and the lion's skin is represented by a knot and one paw. One might also compare a coin of Populonia (*BMC Italy* 24; PLATE XXVIII, 12), almost identical in pose and attributes, except that the lion's skin is missing, and a coin of Capua (*BMC Italy* 1, 2; PLATE XXVIII, 13), but it too lacks the lion's skin, and the club lies behind the neck.

The young diademed Hercules of this Etrusco-Italian group shares certain characteristics with the two main types of the Barcid series in Spain.[38] The face of both types is in profile, the head laureate,[39] and the club rests on the farther shoulder, rather in the manner of S 563 and 604–5, but once an older, bearded man is represented, once a young man with traces of a sideburn. The head always faces left.

It is, however, to the representations of Hercules-Melqart on a long series of Tyrian coins (*BMC Phoenicia* 233 f.) that the head on Sulla's coin bears the greatest resemblance. The head is strong, but rather conventional, with a fleshy face, and faces right (PLATE XXVIII, 14–16). A laurel wreath is tied around the short, curly hair. More significant for the relationship between this type and that of Sulla is the lion's skin cloak. It is knotted under the chin, and the lion's paws are quite distinct in the better specimens of the coin, but mere blobs on the poorer. The comparison of the better and the poorer specimens leads

---

[36] This youthful Hercules, first suggested by Cavedoni (75 n. 55), has several parallels among Etruscan mirrors. Hercules is represented as bearded only three times according to Gerhard (5.75); often wears a diadem (3.134 f., 2. pl. 140; 3.174 ff., 2. pl. 181; 5.73 ff., pl. 60; 5.78 f., pl. 61.1); twice wears a laurel wreath (3.141 f., 2. pl. 151; 4.86 f., pl. 342); twice receives a wreath (3.156 ff., 2. pl. 165; 4.87, pl. 343.1; cf. 3.135, 2. pl. 141; 4.90 f., pl. 345).

[37] The similarity between Sulla's coin and Italian coins was suggested by Grueber 1.472 n.

[38] Robinson, 39 f.

[39] Although the laurel wreath symbolizes victory and on Roman coins of the Republic occurs more frequently (S 563, 775, 1139), than the diadem (S 880–81), both appear indifferently in Hercules representations elsewhere. Perhaps the wreath is favored for the purer Hercules-Melqart and the diadem for the Etruscan Hercules.

one to believe that the ends of the cloak on the Roman coin are also paws. Moreover, the collar lies high on the back of the neck and forms the same sharp diagonal as on the Roman coin, with the same "furry" markings below. The Tyrian head has the same sideburns as the Roman, and the relief shows the same inclination to wear away at this point.

Since these Tyrian coins definitely, and the Barcid coins probably, represent Hercules-Melqart, it seems likely that the shadowy figure of this god lies behind the above-mentioned similarities in the coins and mirrors. Melqart,[40] whose name means "king of the city," that is, Tyre, is a latecomer to the Canaanite pantheon. He is first mentioned in an Assyrian text. His origins are obscure, but he seems to be an amalgam of Ba'al and Yam, which may account for his double nature as fertility god and god of the sea. Nonetheless, however vague his personality, he was the god whom Tyrian colonists took with them everywhere: to Cyprus, to Thasos, to Africa and to Spain. As he traveled about the Mediterranean, Melqart acquired new features, and it was probably the Cypriotes who bestowed on him the Herculean attributes,[41] which led to his ultimate equation with Hercules.[42] Alexander's destructive siege of Tyre in 332 (Diod. 17.40; Curt. 4.7–20; Arrian *Anab.* 2.15.8–24.6) and his subsequent festivities there dedicated to Hercules (Diod. 17.46; Curt. 4.19; Arrian *Anab.* 2.24.6) doubtless also contributed to the transformation of Melqart. Thus it is in the definitely Hellenized form of Hercules that the head of Melqart appears on the coinage of Tyre from the beginning of the autonomous era in 126 B.C. until the late second century A.D. During this long span of time, the head retained its essential identity, although the tendency was towards greater crudeness of execution.

In Africa, Melqart was naturally most revered at Carthage. This city always sent a tenth of its revenue to the temple in Tyre (Diod. 20.14.2) and after successful wars a part of the booty (Just. *Epit.*

---

[40] E. Meyer, s.v. "Melqart," Rosch. *Lex.*; Gsell, *Histoire* (Paris, 1929), 4.301–13; R. Dussaud, "Melqart," *Syria* 25 (1946–48), 205–30 and "Melqart, d'après de récents travaux," *RHR* 151 (1957), 1–21.

[41] This point, with particular emphasis on coins, is discussed by Dussaud, "Melqart," *Syria* 25 (1946–48), 205–30.

[42] For example, the bilingual inscription from Malta *IG* 14.600; Hdt. 2.44; Arrian *Anab.* 2.16.1; Cic. *Nat. D.* 3.42; Diod. 20.14.1.

18.7.7), while in times of emergency it tried to propitiate the god (Diod. 20.14.3). Carthaginian devotion is also attested by the number of names that are compounds of Melqart, for example, Hamilcar and Bomilcar. Thus it is no surprise that the enterprising Barca family adhered to the cult (Liv. 21.21.9, cf. 41.7; Sil. Ital. 3.14 ff.) and consequently gave Melqart the prominent obverse position on their Spanish coinage.[43]

Etruscan contacts with Melqart are also quite obvious. Initially, the Etruscans and Carthaginians were closely associated, even allies. The Carthaginians probably settled a colony at one of the ports of Caere, and Etruscans must have been present in Carthage, where an Etruscan inscription has been found.[44] Since the Carthaginians were such great mixers and amalgamators, Bayet concludes, "Dans ces conditions, il apparait également impossible que les Carthaginois n'aient pas influencé, ou complété, certains Hercules italiques, et surtout étrusques; et qu'ils aient introduit dans la péninsule, toute pénétrée déjà d'hellénisme, leur Melqart pur et non modifié."[45] Thus the Etrusco-Italian Hercules, and perhaps the Hercules of S 563 and S 604–5, may well be of Carthaginian derivation and a near relative of Melqart.

If then it is Hercules-Melqart who figures on the coins of Sulla, one can explain his presence there quite easily. In 63 Sulla was with Pompey in the East. The episode at Jerusalem was the most celebrated event of the entire year, which Pompey had devoted to regulating the confused affairs of the defunct Syrian kingdom, the new Roman province of Syria. When he returned to Pontus at the end of the season, he placed M. Aemilius Scaurus in charge of Syria and Palestine (App. *Syr.* 51; Joseph. *AJ* 14.79). This man, Sulla's step-

---

[43] From the rather individualistic types Robinson inferred that the Barcids had, in Hellenistic fashion, indulged in a certain amount of self-portraiture (39 f.), and he proposed that the coin formerly identified as Jugurtha might really represent a younger Barcid (43 f.).

[44] Bayet, 82–5; cf. M. Pallottino, *Gli Etruschi* (Rome, 1940), 78–87 for Etruscan-Carthaginian relations. Cf. the evidence for trade contact in E. Boucher, "Céramique archaïque d'importation," *Cahiers de Byrsa* 3 (1953), 11–85. The Etruscan inscription found at Carthage was formerly thought to be a dedication to Melqart, but E. Benveniste has argued otherwise in "Notes étrusques," *SE* 7 (1933), 245–49.

[45] Bayet, 85.

brother, shared the family talent for profiteering, but he apparently treated Tyre with great kindness, for the city honored him as its *patronus* in an inscription dating from the 60's (*IGRP* 3.1102). Perhaps Sulla was with Scaurus at Tyre; from the warmth of their relationship later, when Sulla in 54 helped extricate Scaurus from a legal scrape (Ascon. 28 C), one might guess that the two had already been associated abroad. Sulla's coin would then be still more of a family testimonial than previously imagined.

Yet even without Scaurus, Sulla would certainly have become aware of the god of Tyre, simply by virtue of the coins with his portrait. Not only does the long duration of the type increase the probability of Sulla's having seen it, but we know furthermore that these coins circulated in Palestine as well as Tyre.[46] Having seen and possibly possessed the coin, and having already heard of the god, Sulla would surely have identified Melqart with Hercules in that bland manner with which the later Romans considered all acceptable foreign gods as variant forms of their own. Once he had made the Hercules-Melqart equation, no obstacle barred the adoption of the head as the type for his own issue in Rome in the following year. Taking into account both the non-numismatic reasons for Sulla's wish to represent Hercules and the numismatic prototype, which he might very recently have seen, one arrives at the conclusion that the likelihood of Sulla's coin representing Hercules borders on certainty.

One last point must be added. Under Trajan, at the time of Hercules' revival on the coinage,[47] in addition to full figure reverses of Hercules, obverses reminiscent of the Republican busts appeared, but especially reminiscent of the Melqart types (*BMC Empire* 3.1062 ff., 1071 ff.). Moreover, among the Trajanic restorations are S 563 and 880–81, of which the first shows Spanish affinities and the second probably represents Hercules-Melqart. This is interesting, because Trajan was born at Italica, not far from Gades, site of one of the

---

[46] For a list of hoards in Palestine containing coins from the mint of Tyre see S. P. Noe, *A Bibliography of Greek Coin Hoards*, NNM 78 (New York, 1937), 346.

[47] Except for the Hercules of M. Durmius of 18 B.C. and the Hercules Adsertor of Galba (*BMC Empire* 1.11, 294 n.), Hercules was absent from the imperial coinage until the time of Trajan.

oldest and most famous of all Hercules-Melqart sanctuaries. Therefore, the Punic nature of the Trajanic types is likely to reflect deliberate policy.[48]

APPENDIX: THE DATE OF S 880–81

Grueber (1.412 ff.) cited as relevant for the period 72–50 the following four hoards:

San Gregorio di Sassola approx. closing date 52–early 51
Compito approx. closing date 51
Cadriano approx. closing date 50–early 49
San Cesario approx. closing date 50–early 49

Of these the San Gregorio hoard contained no coin of the type S 880–81,[49] and thus the Compito hoard is the first to bear on the problem,[50] but, with a closing date of 51,[51] its bearing is slight.

Sydenham's entries in his Table of Finds (lv) appears eminently helpful:

Ossero approx. closing date 68[52]
Compito approx. closing date 62
Casaleone approx. closing date 59

However, closer inspection shows these entries to be somewhat misleading. The Ossero hoard contained no example of Sulla's coin,[53] and Sydenham and Grueber agree that its most recent coins fall into the

---

[48] P. L. Strack, *Untersuchungen zur römischen Reichsprägung des zweiten Jahrhunderts. Teil I. Die Reichsprägung zur Zeit des Traian* (Stuttgart, 1931), 95 ff. The imperial cult of Hercules with particular reference to its development under Trajan is discussed by J. Beujeu, *La Religion a l'apogée de l'Empire. La Politique religieuse des Antonins.* (Paris, 1955), 80–87.

[49] L. Cesano, "Ripostiglio di monete famigliari rinvenuto a S. Gregorio di Sassola presso Tivoli," *NSA* (1903), 604–20.

[50] Grueber's Table of Finds (3.22–3) contains an error, for according to S. T. Baxter, "Osservazioni sopra un ripostiglio di monete consolari scoperto nelle colline di Còmpito nell'agro lucchese," *Periodico di numismatica e sfragistica* 6 (1874), 109–20, the coin FEELIX:FAUSTUS, S 880–81, was found in the hoard.

[51] Baxter, 111, suggested 54 as a closing date; T. Mommsen, "Denarschatz von Compito," *ZFN* 2 (1875), 352–56, proposed 58–54; but Grueber's 51 seems the most likely.

[52] Grueber estimated the closing date as about 73 (1.364).

[53] F. Salata, *Il ripostiglio di denari della repubblica romana scoperto ad Ossero* (Parenzo, 1899).

late 70's. The hoard's value for the present problem is therefore limited. Next, one must consider the same Compito hoard that Grueber dated to 51. If Sydenham's date were correct, this hoard would be crucial evidence. However, his date is impossible on the basis of dates after 62 that he himself assigned to some moneyers represented in the hoard. For example, P. Fonteius P. f. Capito (S 900) and L. Furius Brocchus (S 902), both assigned to ca. 61. Concerning the Casaleone hoard,[54] Grueber did not include it in his work, and, although this hoard too contains the S 880–81 type, its date is again too late to be significant. Sydenham's date 59 is too early for the same reason as in the case of the Compito hoard. Moneyers after 59 are, for example, P. Plautius Hypsaeus (S 910, 911), M. Aemilius Scaurus and P. Plautius Hypsaeus (S 912, 913) both 58, and L. Roscius Fabatus (S 915) ca. 58. It is noteworthy that the joint issues of Scaurus and Hypsaeus are among the few that can be dated exactly (S p. 151 n.).

LYDIA H. LENAGHAN

[51] L. Rizzoli, "Casaleone—Tesoretto monetale scoperto nei fondi dei signori Romanin-Jacur," *NSA* (1908), 91–97.

AN UNPUBLISHED COIN IN THE NAME OF TETRICUS II

(See Plate XXIX)

The Ashmolean Museum recently acquired an antoninianus, in the name of Tetricus II, which prompts some reconsideration, at least, of old problems. Details are as follows:

Obv.: IMPCPESTETRICVSCAVG Bust r., rad., dr.
Rev.: SPESP—VBLICA Spes advancing l., flower in raised r., l. holding up drapery; in exergue, P
Æ. 2.924 gm. 20 mm. Dies ↑↑

The object of this note is to attempt some judgement of the authenticity of the coin, which in turn involves discussion of the nature of the association of the two Tetrici, father and son. That association has long been recognized as problematical. Most recently G. Elmer wrote of Tetricus II:[1]

"Im Jahr 274 ist er zusammen mit seinem Vater Konsul. Das führt uns ins Jahr 273 als das Jahr, in dem er die Cäsarenwürde erhalten hat; denn auch bei den Thronfolgern war es üblich, in dem Jahr, das ihrer Ernennung folgte, das Konsulat anzutreten.

... Er ist nur Thronfolger und niemals Augustus gewesen. Die Münzen, auf denen er den Titel Augustus führt, sind keine staatlichen Erzeugnisse, sondern gleichzeitige Fälschungen. Einige andere Münzen, auf denen Tetricus Vater und Sohn gemeinsam dargestellt sind, führen die Umschrift *impp... augg=imperatores... augusti*. Aber auch aus diesen Stücken darf man nicht schließen, daß er gemeinsam mit seinem Vater Augustus gewesen wäre, denn seinem Brustbild fehlt immer der Lorbeerkranz, der in dieser Zeit das eigentliche Zeichen der Augustus würde ist. Die Umschrift *imperatores... augusti* an Stelle von *augustus et caesar* kommt im 3. Jahrhundert auch sonst vor."

Arguments of this nature had been present long before, in the mind of Eckhel,[2] when he wrote the masterly paragraph in the *Doctrina* headed *Vtrum Augustus?*

---

[1] In "Die Münzprägung der gallischen Kaiser in Köln, Trier und Mailand," *Bonner Jahrbücher* 146, p. 75.
[2] *Doctrina Numorum Veterum*, pars II, Vol. vii (2nd ed., 1828), p. 459f.

"Tetricum filium fuisse Augustum, probat Bandurius[;] I. ex numis inscriptis: IMPP. TETRICI. AVGG., aut similiter, quos recitatos vide in numis patris. II. ex titulo IMP. ejus nominibus in binis numis praefixo. III. ex numo ejus postremo mox producto,[3] in cujus antica sub finem additur A., quod ait notare Augustum. Addo ergo his fortius argumentum aliud ex numo musei Caesarei:

– – – – TETRICVS. AVG. *Caput radiatum puerile.*
SALVS. AVG. *Salus stans.* Æ. III.

Addo denique testimonium Vopisci, eum a patre in Gallia nuncupatum imperatorem adserentis.

Argumenta haec ut valida in speciem videri possunt, tamen collatum Augusti titulum non satis evincunt. Nam I. in numis aureis, quorum praeconium propter operis nitorem, et quia haud dubie in ipsa principis sede, atque adcuratius cusi sunt, solum est audiendum, Augustus nunquam dicitur, nisi in consortio patris. At vidimus alias, non raro manifestos Caesares per causam praesentis Augusti patris participasse honorem Augusteum sibi indebitum, cujus exempla dedimus in Maximino et Maximo, et alibi. II. Si vere Augustus fuit, cur in iisdem his numis ejus caput constanter est nudum, cum tamen patris constanter sit laureatum? Sane hoc aevo caput nudum indubitatum est Caesaris indicium. III. Obvii sunt Tetrici jun. numi, in quorum antica is Caesar tantum dicitur, at in aversa scriptum SALVS. AVGG. ... etc. ut ergo his in numis τὸ AVGG. Tetricum jun. nequaquam Augustum probat, etsi illum quoque complectatur, ita neque in aliis. IV. Titulum *imperatoris* non semper probare etiam Augustum, satis supra in moneta Salonini disserui. Quod si revera Augustus dicitur in aeneis, iisque paucissimis, et explicate in unico tantum, facile istud tribui potest monetarii ignorantiae titulorum vim non satis percipientis, praecipue cum operis ruditas, quae plerosque Tetricorum aeneos inter barbaros jure ablegat, abunde doceat, ab imperitissima eos manu fuisse elaboratos. Denique Trebellius et Victor, qui utramque ejus fortunam prodidere, eum Augustum nunquam, quod memorare certe non neglexissent, sed Caesarem solum appellant."

It has seemed worth while to reproduce Eckhel's comments in full: lucid, moderate and yet cogently constructed, they supply the foundation for Elmer's subsequent view (and for his exclusion of all 'Augustus' coins of Tetricus II unassociated with his father) as well as for the attitude taken by P. H. Webb.[4]

---

[3] That is to say, a coin described with obv. C. PIV. TETRICVS. A., *Caput radiatum*, and rev. SOLI.CONSER., *Centaurus arcum tenens* (Æ. III. [Banduri]).
[4] *RIC* V (2), p. 399. J. de Witte, *Recherches sur les empereurs qui ont régné dans les Gaules* (Lyons, 1868), did not address himself to the problem.

There can, however, be no doubt that the question in some ways still remains a puzzling one, to which neither historical nor epigraphical evidence has offered a clear solution. As Eckhel observed, the historical sources show variation. In the *Scriptores Historiae Augustae, Aurelian*, xxxii, we read: "inter haec (i.e., Aurelian's triumph) fuit Tetricus ... adiuncto sibi filio, quem imperatorem in Gallia nuncupaverat." But it is stated in the *Tyranni triginta, Tetricus Senior*, xxiv, 1, that "Victoria sive Vitruvia Tetricum ... Augustum appellari fecit filiumque eius Caesarem nuncupavit," while in *Tetricus Junior*, xxv, 1, it is recorded of Tetricus II that "hic puerulus a Victoria Caesar est appellatus;" and Aurelius Victor, *de Caesaribus*, xxxiii, 14, wrote: "interim Victoria ... Tetricum imperatorem facit ... filioque eius Tetrico Caesarea insignia impartiuntur." Of the four sources, then, three agree that Tetricus II was created Caesar. But it will be noted that these three comments are all directed to the moment of his father's elevation as emperor by Victoria, and not to the subsequent period of their association; and it will be noted, as being of equal importance, that the passage in the life of Aurelian refers explicitly to the period at the end of their rule. There is, in fact, no contradiction; and the only lack of definition that can be criticized lies in the alternative use of *Augustus* and *imperator* to describe the original position of Tetricus I (*SHA Tyr. trig.* and Aurelius Victor), coupled with the use of *imperator* to describe that of Tetricus II at the time of their downfall (*SHA Aurelian*). It may well be that the terms had become complementary to each other, and so interchangeable.

Epigraphical evidence, so far as it goes,[5] is more straightforward. Milestones, with the possible exception of one, style Tetricus II *nobilissimus Caesar*: he also appears as *princeps iuventutis*—a style appropriate to a Caesar—and even as *dominus noster*. This led Stein to conclude that he was never Augustus, and in forming this conclusion he emphasized the fact that the coins never show him as laureate, while also dismissing the fact that they do often (i.e., by association) style him Augustus. Needless to say, however, if Tetricus II received the formal style of Augustus only a very short time before his father capitulated to Aurelian it is unlikely, to say the

[5] Cf. Paully-Wissowa, *Real-Enc.* s.v. Esuvius, col. 704f.

least, that milestones would have immediately reflected the change of status.

Historical and epigraphical sources, therefore, agree in indicating that the original rank of Tetricus II was that of Caesar. But the possibility is not ruled out that *SHA Aurelian* is correct in stating that he was Augustus when Aurelian took over. Attention must now be turned to the coins. These may appear to substantiate Eckhel's more important contentions.

(i) Aurei never style Tetricus II *Augustus* in his own right, i.e., never *nisi in consortio patris*; and sometimes even a double-headed obverse can show the title, in the singular, applying to his father alone.[6]

(ii) Antoniniani, though few in number, tell a similar story.[7]

(iii) On previously known coins with the portrait of Tetricus II and the title *Augustus* the head of Tetricus II is always bare.[8]

(iv) There are many coins with obverse showing Tetricus II as Caesar and with reverse legend ending in AVGG, thus seeming to associate him with his father but also apparently differentiating his rank.[9]

(v) There are, as Eckhel implied, coins of Tetricus II which give him, individually, the title *imperator*. Some of those previously recorded[10] are doubtless open to suspicion, but probably not all. Eckhel declined to allow that the *praenomen imperatorium* necessarily connoted the rank of Augustus.

Nevertheless the criticisms of both Eckhel and Elmer are themselves open to some question.

(a) *Superior evidence of gold* (Eckhel). This argument is of course valid only when gold is being produced. If at the moment of the downfall of the Tetrici gold coinage was for one reason or another suspended or impossible the argument loses all force.

(b) *Contemporary forgeries* (Elmer). There seems to be no reason except that of convenience for stigmatizing as contemporary

---

[6] See *RIC*, Tetricus I, nos. 204–211—not all, of course, certainly authentic.
[7] See *RIC*, Tetricus I, nos. 212–3, with de Witte, op.cit., no. 6a.
[8] See notes 6 and 7 above.
[9] See *RIC*, Tetricus I, nos. 225, 232, 238a, 244, 254–9, 263, 266, 270–1.
[10] See *RIC*, Tetricus I, nos. 236, 250, 253, 290–1.

forgeries coins showing Tetricus II as Augustus in his own right. By whom and for what purpose would they have been made? If forgeries at all, they would with far more probability belong to a much later age.

(c) *Moneyers' ignorance* (Eckhel). This argument would be admissible if coins of Tetricus II as Augustus in his own right were obviously of barbarous style; but this has not been substantiated.

(d) *"Augustus" and "imperator"* (Eckhel, Elmer). It is stated that the laurel wreath is the proper sign of an *Augustus*. But the laurel wreath is in fact the mark of an *imperator*. There are coins, showing Tetricus I laureate and Tetricus II bare, with legend IMPP ... AVGG. These *could* show, first, that the son possessed an imperium subordinate to the father's, and secondly that the son was, like his father, *Augustus*. Historical sources have indicated that Tetricus I, an undoubted *Augustus*, could be equally described as *imperator*: the coins suggest that Tetricus II, also described historically as *imperator*, could likewise have been *Augustus*.

Until now, of the coins that have styled Tetricus II *imperator* and *Augustus* in his own right,[11] only very few have been critically examined; and their authenticity has not been felt to lie heavily in the scales. It is at this point that we must turn our attention to the coin just acquired by the Ashmolean. While this might well divide opinion on the constitutional grounds already sketched, considerations of fabric and style cannot easily be dismissed. The coin is a struck coin, and its fabric is that of a neat and well produced antoninianus of the period. But it does not fail to display also the characteristic imperfections of that period, (1) disparity between the quality of the obverse and reverse dies, (2) a reverse surface which, as with so many other pieces of the same period, is cracked and 'folded' as the result of striking an insufficiently prepared blank, and (3) an edge which, altogether devoid of any suspect vertical cracks, is rough, lumpy and coruscated in the manner of innumerable Tetrican coins. The style is best studied in connection with that of another coin which shares a reverse die with the Oxford coin:

[11] See n. 10.

Obv.: IMPPTETRICIPIIAVGG Jugate busts r. of Tetricus I, rad., cuir., and Tetricus II, bare-headed and (?) dr.

Rev.: SPESP-VBLICA etc., precisely as on the Oxford coin. Schulman, 5 March 1923 (Vierordt), 2422 (illustrated), ex Consul Weber (2358). Present location unknown. Described as billon, i.e., Æ; no weight or die-axis given, though the dies may have been ↑↑.

The hand that made the obverse die for the Vierordt coin quite certainly also made that of the Oxford coin. The lettering on each shows fairly large forms, slender and even sinuous strokes, and some irregularity: while it is well balanced it is not particularly neat. In regard to portraiture both coins show the same plain treatment, with an expression that is a little empty and hair that is treated in loose strokes. The neat appearance of each obverse is due to tidy if not incisive portraiture well struck up from carefully (but not exactly) centred dies. Both obverses show to advantage in comparison with the single common reverse: of banal style, this is a little worn, especially where the letters S and P occur in the legend.

It may, of course, be argued that the Vierordt coin is itself dubious. Coming from the Consul Weber collection, sold in 1909, it could be regarded as having first appeared—for it does not seem to have been recorded earlier—at a time when forgery was becoming more skilled, more academic and more discriminating.[12] This view would, however, be more attractive if half a century had produced more than a single known specimen of the double-headed issue and if more than one specimen were known of the die-linked, single-headed issue. If these coins are the result of forgery, it was forgery of an unusually subtle kind. Intimate knowledge of the conventions of the rare double-head series had to be combined with nicely judged understanding of the position of Tetricus II as *imperator* and *Augustus*. Then again, the head of Tetricus II, while that of a manifestly young man, is shown maturing to a degree distinctly greater than on most of his coins. Finally, since the two coins are linked by a common reverse die, it would have been necessary for a forger to produce (a) two obverse dies of exactly similar style—no easy task; and (b) a reverse showing just

---

[12] And sometimes a good deal better than the standard of the "Geneva forgeries," for which cf. R. A. G. Carson, *Num. Chron.* 1958, pp. 47 ff.

that inferiority of style which is amply demonstrated by numberless issues of the reign. Considered together, these were formidable obstacles for a forger; and it seems far more likely that both coins are genuine, even though the only certain proof—recorded inclusion in an uncontaminated hoard—is still lacking.

If the coins are genuine they are evidence for the fact that the mint which produced them regarded the two Tetrici as *Impp ... Pii Augg* simultaneously, while also regarding Tetricus II individually as *Imp ... C Aug*. The joint style has other parallels, as has been seen; and it was from this joint use of **AVGG**, combined with the son's bare head, that Eckhel sought to show that while **AVGG** included Tetricus II it does not show that he was ever Augustus. But the individual *Imp ... C Aug* of the Oxford coins and its radiate head— different levels of *imperium* produce a bare-headed son only when he is shown with his father—constitute a statement that he was Augustus. If so, it was in all probability right at the end of the Tetrican reign. The intrusive letter **C** before the **AVG** of the Oxford coin can only stand for *Caesar*: no other signification is conceivable at that point in the obverse legend, and though this intrusion appears to be unique for the reign it is understandable enough. The only dated double-headed coins with *Impp ... Augg* show Tetricus I as Cos. III, i.e., probably A.D. 273.[13] It must be concluded that after an uninterrupted previous period of coinage in the name of Tetricus II as *Caesar* (even though his father's reverses often showed *Augg*) his advancement to the overt and personal rank of Augustus took place at the very end of their imperial adventure, and that, in this particular mint at least, it was not felt at once to terminate his previous status as Caesar. In short, it is not impossible to reconcile the literary and epigraphical with the numismatic evidence, if this last is accepted, and to conclude of Tetricus II that he was "first Caesar and then, for a very short period, Augustus."[14]

The final question—that of the identification of the mint—is much less easy to approach. No record seems to exist elsewhere of the letter P as an exergual mark for the Tetrican series: it may be no more than

---

[13] Cf. Paully-Wissowa, loc.cit., and *RIC* V (2), pp. 402 ff., as against Elmer, op.cit., p. 74 (A.D. 274).
[14] *CAH* XII, p. 306.

an officina mark. Portraiture, and still more the lettering, links the Vierordt and Oxford coins with the groups given by Elmer to Cologne.[15] How far this attribution is correct it is difficult to say, for both portraiture and lettering are also similar to those of Lyons, a stylistic source of which Webb was clearly aware.[16] In spite of Elmer's work on the coinages of the Gallic emperors it is probable that more work remains to be done on the mint-attributions.

This newly discovered coin thus raises problems which are serious and complicated. Its authenticity cannot easily be rejected out of hand; and, should it be accepted, or even suspended in the balance, there are important points which arise for resultant consideration.

C. H. V. SUTHERLAND

[15] Op.cit., pl. 11, 7–9, 12; pl. 12, 21–2.
[16] *RIC* V (2), p. 380 and pl. 15, 3.

A SIXTH CENTURY HOARD OF MINIMI FROM THE WESTERN PELOPONNESE

(See Plate XXX)

The hoard described here was acquired for the American Numismatic Society by Miss Katharine M. Edwards in the course of her sojourns in Greece during the 1920's. Nothing further is known of provenience except that it was purchased in the village of Zacha, a mountain town lying above the Alpheus valley in the west central Peloponnese, about 16 miles distant from the Ionian coast. Half the coins are distinctly black in appearance; the other half show a greenish brown patina. Most of the catalogue is comprised of coins from the latter group. The darker specimens are for the most part illegible. The existence of two such distinct colorations would normally provoke suspicion that we are not dealing with a single, self-contained body of evidence. However, the internal composition of the deposit and the frequency of the various issues represented leave no doubt that we have to do with a homogeneous grouping. The difference in the appearance of the coins may be explained by the accident of position in the soil.

In tabulating the contents of the hoard we have ignored about 60 fragments of metal, which crumble upon contact and merely serve to record the poor quality of the alloy used to manufacture some of the coins. The hoard also contains two flat, round pebbles which are hardly distinguishable from the worn specimens. Other than these oddities, the total number of coins comes to 1179, distributed as follows:

Total Æ 3	77	Æ 3 legible	5	Æ 3 illegible	72
Total Æ 4	1102	Æ 4 legible	508	Æ 4 illegible	594
Total of Hoard	1179	Total legible	513	Total illegible	666

All the Æ 3 coins have been cut down. Of the 5 legible Æ 3 three are from the fifth, the remaining two (511, 512) from the sixth century. Of the illegibles only one belongs definitely to the sixth century.

Among the 594 illegible Æ 4 we have included 21 of extremely thin flan, some with two or three tabs on the edge, which do not seem to have received the imprint of a die. Such specimens found also in other deposits in the Balkans[1] confirm the existence of the irregular moneyer operating beyond the pale of Roman control. At the same time, the recurrence of the type implies a certain rationale. The coins may have been minted by a barbarian tribe finding itself in Greece long enough to need currency but not in a position to use the Roman money.

Fully 182 of the remaining Æ 4 illegibles, in addition to some listed in the catalogue (9, 51, 61), have been mutilated in some fashion. Many of these are the larger Æ 4 of the late fourth or early fifth century, such as the common **SALVS REIPVBLICAE**, Victory dragging captive, of Valentinian II and Arcadius. A good number, however, are from the second half of the fifth century. Halved coins of Leo[2] show the practice to have begun fairly early. The process initiated toward the middle of the century of cutting down the older Æ 3 still in circulation in an effort to make them conform in a general way to a new reduced weight and module is well attested from other hoards as well as in the Zacha material. The habit appears to have become so ingrained that it continues into the sixth century, provoked by the conspicuous difference in size between the Æ 4 of the period of Marcian and Leo and those of Anastasius and his successors. The lone large Æ 3 bronze of Baduila (511) also has been drastically cut down by a chisel from its original size. The coin shows practically no wear and must be among the king's last issues. Whether it was cut down in Italy, its place of mintage, or upon its importation into Greece, is open to question.

The hoard invites comparison with two other recently published deposits, both from the Greek peninsula. The Yale hoard has a burial date in the late 60's of the fifth century, in the reign of Leo. The

---

[1] See "A Bronze Hoard of the Period of Leo I," *Museum Notes* IX (1960), pp. 143, 144, and *A Bronze Hoard of the Period of Zeno I*. *NNM* 148, New York, 1962, p. 1, both published by us. These two works will be referred to as Y and V. The first is the property of Yale University. Its deposition is "somewhere on a line running from Corinth through Dalmatia" (Y, p. 148). The second was unearthed in the vicinity of the Thessalian town of Volo.

[2] Y, p. 142.

contents of Volo point to a deposition in the reign of Zeno, sometime between August 476 and April 491. As we move down in time through the three hoards, we find progressively fewer remains of the coinage of the early fourth century. At Zacha such Æ 3 are hardly in evidence: only 3 (1-3) compared with 65 out of 515 coins in the Yale hoard and 38 out of 1064 at Volo. The life of the coinage of the House of Constantine can thus be estimated as roughly 175 years.

It is noticeable that Zacha shows no coins definitely ascribable to Arcadius. Two specimens of Honorius appear (5, 6). This fact, plus the relatively heavy concentration from the period of Valentinian III, would justify our placing the hoard, even were its provenience not known, to the west of both the Yale and Volo deposits, which are poor in Honorius and fuller in the coins of Arcadius, his brother ruling in the east.

The two coins from the mint of Heraclea (2, 51), probably the least productive of the Roman minting centers in the east, compare with the three found in the Yale deposit, whereas none of the 1064 legible specimens in the Volo hoard can be assigned to this mint. If the absence of representation at Volo is not purely accidental, the output from Heraclea may have supplied the immediate vicinity and the hinterland.[3] Cities on or near the coast such as Volo, Corinth, Thessalonica, or Athens seem to look east rather than west for their commercial ties. Constant barbarian forays from the north helped isolate the Greek littoral from the ever shifting political pattern in the interior at the same time that the capital city of Constantinople was becoming the focal point of Byzantine authority and drawing the various provincial centers within a single radius of control.

A number of Peloponnesian hoards of small bronze reaching down into the sixth century is known, but only summary listings of their contents have been published. Only in recent years has care been taken through more detailed excavation reports and analyses of the coinage from such disparate regions as North Africa, Cyprus and Palestine,[4] to enlist the support of numismatics in helping to supply the

---

[3] So too M. Thompson, *The Athenian Agora. Volume II. Coins from the Roman through the Venetian Period*, Princeton, 1954, p. 6.
[4] For the North African material see particularly J. Lafaurie, "Trésor de monnaies de cuivre trouvé à Sidi Aïch (Tunisie)," *Revue Numismatique* VIe Série, II

historical record of the end of the ancient world. Our knowledge of the monetary history of the period has not yet advanced to the point where we can trace out economic patterns or relate numismatic formulae to specific political events. The number of unpublished specimens at Zacha and in other deposits warns that a fairly complete list of coin types still eludes us. Without it we are not in a position as yet to give a coherent picture of the coinage of the Empire from the reign of Anastasius to that of Justinian or Justin II. Much more evidence needs to be collected before we can engage even in meaningful speculation. We have therefore limited ourselves in the pages which follow mainly to a descriptive analysis of the hoard.

There is no reason to suppose a shrinkage in the number of coins circulating in the Peloponnese for the fifth and most of the sixth century. Although the history of the area for this period is extremely spotty,[5] the volume of coinage found in the excavations at Corinth and Olympia, together with the few recorded hoard deposits, makes it clear that the region continued to be regularly supplied with small bronze change for its daily transactions. In addition to an unpublished hoard from Palaiochori in the central Peloponnese mentioned by Bon,[6] the Corinth excavations have yielded three deposits, all of a composition similar to the Zacha material. A find of 1930 included, together with the usual Æ 3, the following coins:

(1959–60), pp. 113–130, and bibliography cited therein; for Cyprus, D. H. Cox, *Coins from the Excavations at Curium, 1932–1953*. NNM 145, New York, 1959; Palestine, H. Hamburger, "Caesarea Coin Finds and the History of the City," *Bulletin of the Jewish Palestine Exploration Society* XV (1950), pp. 78–82 and, by the same author, "Minute Coins from Caesarea," *Atiqot. Journal of the Israel Department of Antiquities* I (1954), pp. 115–138. The most numerous of the hoards of the period come from Italy but have not received the attention of scholars following the careful researches of L. Cesano, "Della moneta enea corrente in Italia nell' ultima età imperiale romana e sotto i re ostrogoti," *Rivista Italiana di Numismatica* XXVI (1913), pp. 511–551, and XXXI (1918), pp. 96–100, "Ancora della moneta enea corrente in Italia nel V–VI secolo d. C." See also A. Levi, "Sessa Aurunca. Tesoretto di monetine di bronzo bizantine (follari o nummi)," *Notizie degli Scavi di Antichità*, Serie Quinta, XVI (1919), pp. 356–358.

[5] The fullest recent discussion of the history of the Peloponnese for this period is A. Bon, *Le Péloponnèse Byzantin jusqu' en 1204*, Paris, 1951.

[6] Op.cit., p. 17, note 3.

28 Theodosius II
15 Marcian
32 Leo
38 Zeno
40 Various Victory types
148 Monogram of Anastasius.

A "shop find" from the Corinthian Agora discovered in 1933 contained *inter alia*:

7 Theodosius II
4 Marcian
1 Aelia Zenonis
15 Victory reverses
5 Palm tree reverses
66 Monogram of Anastasius
18 Christogram reverse
63 Justinian I, including monogram, Ꙙ or VOT in wreath
1 Huneric
1 Theodoric
1 Athalaric
1 Theodahad
11 Baduila.

J. M. Harris mentions a hoard found in 1937 which yielded:

6 Marcian
3 Leo
9 Zeno
48 Victory types
92 Anastasius
6 Justinian.[7]

[7] K. M. Edwards, "Coins found at Corinth during the years 1930-1935," *Hesperia* VI (1937), pp. 248, 249; J. M. Harris, "Coins found at Corinth," *Hesperia* X (1941), p. 145. O. Broneer records a hoard found at Isthmia which contained 270 bronze coins, of which 61 were "very small coins—of the fifth and sixth centuries:" "Excavations at Isthmia, 1954," *Hesperia* XXIV (1955), p. 136. The Athens Dipylon hoard contained out of a total of 598 pieces, 472 late imperial or Byzantine small bronzes which I. Svoronos describes as "badly worn and useless:" *Journal International d' Archéologie Numismatique* XII (1909–10), pp. 6–9.

Of particular interest are the coins found in the course of the excavations at Olympia, about 15 miles northwest of Zacha. As at Corinth the volume of coinage drops practically to zero by the end of the sixth century. The coins were described in good detail, but without illustration or indication of weight, by A. Postolakas, Keeper of the Greek National Numismatic Museum, in the late nineteenth century.[8] His catalogue does not distinguish between hoards[9] and excavation finds. Nevertheless, the description and the quantity of the various specimens allow us to trace a picture which can be compared with Zacha. In the list which follows we have included a cross reference to the *British Museum Catalogue*,[10] which did not use the material, and have indicated the number of identical specimens in Zacha:

Anastasius monograms 9[11]

Justin I[12]

VOT XIII	1	
VOT XIIII	4	*BMC* 29, 91; Z 1 (391)
Christogram	4	*BMC* 37, 159; Z 11 (344–354)
Cross w/ pellets	2	*BMC* 38, 173 or 41, 201; Z 8 (332–339)

---

[8] Νομίσματα ἐν τῷ Ἐθνικῷ Νομισματικῷ Μουσείῳ Κατατεθέντα Ἔτει Ἀκαδημαϊκῷ ͵αωπγ´,-αωπδ´, Athens, 1885, pp. 57–66.

[9] F. Adler in *Olympia, Ergebnisse der von dem deutschen Reich veraushalteten Ausgrabung*, Berlin, 1897, p. 97, refers without further description to two hoards of small bronze buried one in 565 and the other in 576. R. Weil in the same volume, pp. 128, 129, notes that Olympia has yielded more than 20 hoards, most from late antiquity, inasmuch as the region was safe from war in the classical period. He classes the hoards of small bronze under three groupings: 1) hoards of Justinian I without coins of the German kingdoms; 2) hoards of Justinian with Vandalic and Ostrogothic pieces; and 3) hoards reaching down to Justin II.

[10] Unless otherwise specified, all references in this article are to W. Wroth, *Catalogue of the Coins of the Vandals, Ostrogoths and Lombards (and the Empires of Thessalonica, Nicaea and Trebizond) in the British Museum*, London, 1911, cited by page and number. Friedländer refers to I. Friedländer, *Die Münzen der Vandalen*, Leipzig, 1849; Kraus to F. F. Kraus, *Die Münzen Odovacars und des Ostgotenreiches in Italien*, Halle, 1928.

[11] The form of the monogram is not specified throughout.

[12] Postolakas' reasons for assigning these coins to Justin rather than Justinian are unclear.

Justinian

1)	VOT XIII	2	*BMC* 28, 86; Z 2 (388, 389)
2)	⩓	1	*BMC* not; Z not
3)	Ă	5	*BMC* 34, 141; Z 18 (355–372)
4)	⩓ or ⩓	10	*BMC* not; Z 11 (399–409)
5)	⩨	1	*BMC* not; Z not
6)	N	1	*BMC* 36, 154
7)	✢	1	*BMC* 36, 157 *var.*; Z not
8)	✢	2	*BMC* not; Z not
9)	✢	3	*BMC* liv, note; Z 7 (392–398)
10)	monogram	1	
11)	lion	1	*BMC* 26, 65; Z not
12)	star	5	*BMC* 38, 165; Z not
	"Various unusual monograms"	6	

Ostrogoths

Athalaric monogram	7	*BMC* 66, 47; Z not
Theodahad monogram	1	*BMC* 74, 15; Z not
Baduila		
DN REX B	4	*BMC* 90, 28; Z 37 (461–497)
monogram	3	*BMC* 89, 24; Z 14 (447–460)
lion	3	*BMC* 94, 50; Z 13 (498–510)

Vandals

Hilderic cross	2	*BMC* 14, 9; Z not
Gelimer		
monogram	1	*BMC* 16, 4; Z 1 (416)
palm tree[13]	13	*BMC* 26, 68; Z 24 (418–441)
"Vandalic"		
N IIII	1	*BMC* 7, 12; Z 1? (417)
Victory	1	*BMC* 20, 21; Z 15 (317–331)

---

[13] Postolakas claims to read the name **GEL AMER** on one of these coins. If this is correct, we have a clear assignment of these issues to a particular monarch, such as was not available to Wroth, who classed them under a general Vandalic heading.

Except for the surprisingly small number of monogram reverses, the coins from Olympia, in addition to presenting some new types, show a pattern strikingly similar to the Zacha hoard. Not only are we confronted with parallel examples of the royal mintages, but the large number of coins of Justinian type 4 is very noticeable. The geographical range in which some of these types occur, however, has been vastly expanded in recent years by new evidence from Palestine and Cyprus.[14] Among the coins found in the sand dunes of Caesarea, H. Hamburger reported in 1954 a number of coins of types 3, 4, 8 and 12, as well as others with a cross potent reverse of the type found in Z 332–338. From his illustrations it is evident that the coins are well made and can in no instance be considered degenerate copies of Roman originals. Whether the coins were minted on the spot or derived from a larger minting center such as Antioch can not presently be determined from the evidence. An impressive number of imperial coins, particularly with a variety of monogram reverses, has appeared in Cyprus also. This phenomenon is too widespread to merit our dismissing most of the sixth century types as east Mediterranean imitations. Egypt would of course continue to imitate, as she had in the fifth century, and Vandal piracy would play a role in momentarily disrupting a particular coast-line. Yet the consistency of formulae and types on the small bronze coinage of the sixth century over so wide an area as Italy, Greece, Cyprus, and Palestine can more easily be explained as an indication of continued Roman influence in these regions. An organized scheme of operations which for the moment may only be hinted at need not surprise us. As more evidence becomes available, it may in the future be possible to ask and answer such questions as the relationship of the petty bronze to the large folles of the period and to probe more deeply into the time-table by which the reform started by Anastasius was brought to completion in the various provinces of the East Roman Empire. Erratic though the pattern of the coinage may appear at first glance, there are factors which warn us against believing in the collapse of the monetary system. It is on the face of it extremely unlikely that men of the caliber and vision of Anastasius and Justinian, whose control over every department of government and practically every expression of

[14] See note 4.

Roman life can be attested in detail, would neglect such a valuable public instrument as the coinage. Further, the material from Zacha is well enough preserved to admit of certain distinctions. Not only the Romans, but the Vandals and Ostrogoths as well, worked from specific mints with specific patterns of operation. The study of the Yale and the Volo hoards has established that there were coins circulating in the fifth century which fall so far below even the wide spectrum of style within the official mint that they only can be considered productions of an irregular moneyer in a more unsettled area. From the Zacha hoard it becomes clear that the distinction extends to the sixth century and applies not merely to the Roman but also to the royal mintages. The highly deviant specimens which we have labelled imitations of the standard Vandal and Ostrogothic currency (433–441, 496, 497, 509, 510) suggest political and economic conditions fluid enough to have produced irregular money derived from a Vandal or Ostrogothic model. The existence of such copies also, by contrast, underlines the measure of authority which these Germanic tribes must have enjoyed in those areas firmly in their control.

One of the more vexing problems to confront the student of the numismatic history of the period is the proper assignment of the monogram reverses. At Zacha as in most other finds (they are in short supply at Olympia) the monogram types form by far the largest segment of the currency of the period. 225 coins out of a total of 514, that is to say, almost half the coins in the hoard, show various forms of a monogram reverse. These have to be distributed over a seventy to eighty year period ranging from 491 to the date of deposition of the hoard. It is clear that Anastasius, following the pattern of the coinage of his predecessors, inaugurated his reign with an issue of small bronze bearing on the reverse a monogram which incorporated the Greek letters of his name in the genitive case. The hoard shows six varieties of this basic pattern (1–6 in the Table). The use of the Greek instead of the Latin alphabet appears to be an innovation begun in the reign of Leo. It is to be interpreted as a step in the transformation of Rome into Byzantium.[15] The formula, however, exists in very great supply (149 coins). To explain it, we should be forced to assume that most of the collecting was done during the reign of Anastasius, an expedient

[15] See the discussion in V, pp. 11, 12.

which the generally steady progression of the various types in the hoard does not seem to admit. The same monogram, at least in what we take to be its initial form ⋈ , had as early as Sabatier[16] been assigned to Justinian. Its use on the capitals of St. Sophia and other mid-sixth century churches as well as on Byzantine silver attributable on other grounds to Justinian[17] puts the ascription beyond question. We shall therefore be justified in distributing the 149 coins between the two emperors, Anastasius and Justinian. Because Justinian is later in time and rules over a longer period, most of the specimens are no doubt his, although we can not be sure which.

The use of this particular monogram device on the monumental art of the period and on silver objects, proved through their various control marks to have been manufactured under strict supervision and with imperial sanction, means that we are dealing with an official Roman formula. The same formula on the bronze coinage suggests that the specimens in question are the official Roman issues of the day minted at Roman mints according to Roman standards for use in Roman territory. The wide spectrum of style betrays not so much the irregular moneyer as the debasement of artistic standards within the mint itself. It reflects difficulty in procuring competent die-cutters and even possibly losses of a proper metal supply because of barbarian incursions. Further, what talent remained had long since turned its attention to the more decorative arts.

Once we realize that the coins in the hoard are Roman and not "Vandalic" imitations, the nature of Anastasius' reform and the various problems connected with his introduction of large folles need to be reconsidered. Clearly, at least in some areas of the Empire, small bronze continued to be minted by Roman authority after this date. The assignment of particular types to their respective mints and the date of change in each instance are questions which only additional hoard evidence can solve. Does Antioch, for example, mint the monogram type only for Anastasius or for Justinian as well?

[16] J. Sabatier, *Description Générale des Monnaies Byzantines Frappées sous les Empereurs d'Orient Depuis Arcadius Jusqu' à la Prise de Constantinople par Mahomet II*, Paris, 1862, p. 83 and pl. I, 30.
[17] E. C. Dodd, *Byzantine Silver Stamps. Dumbarton Oaks Studies Seven*, Washington, 1961, p. 13.

What rôle does Thessalonica play? Nicomedia? Cyzicus? Most importantly, the need for currency by the Justinianic armies in the West is probably supplied by local mints set up for the purpose in Italy. These added minting centers affect Greece too, so that the contents of the Zacha hoard result from two influences: 1) Roman types imported from Italy along with coins of the Vandals and Ostrogoths, and 2) coinage minted in the older established centers in the East. In the absence of mint marks ascription is difficult. The mint mark begins to be crowded off the field under Leo and does not appear on most of the coins of Zeno. However, the form of monogram may be of help. In discussing the material from the Volo hoard, we called attention to the fact that some forms of monogram appear to belong only to particular mints.[18] In effect, the monogram comes to take on the functions of the mint mark as a sign of the issuing center. It is likely that, as additional evidence becomes available, such analysis will yield useful distinctions. Waage claims for Antioch, for example, a form ⋈ which does not appear at Zacha.[19]

Monograms 1 through 6 in the Table have some form of cross bar in the lower left segment which forms the letter A (**A** or **A**) and makes it possible to read **ANACTACIOV** or **IOVCTINIANOV**. The bar is lacking in the next four. As Dodd points out,[20] the forms can be read as **IOVCTINOV**. At least 56 coins in the hoard show these forms. Either the first (518–527) or the second (565–578) bearer of the name is a possibility. The assignment of some of these forms on Byzantine silver stamps to Justin II seems incontrovertible. Here again we are before an official imperial formula. If Justinian, who certainly had a mind of his own, can use Anastasian formulae, Justin II might equally well borrow his from Justin I. The pattern of coinage in the hoard requires that Justin I be well represented. Not only do these monograms correspond to the letters of his name; if, as we contend, the coins in question are official Roman issues, the tradition of Roman coinage would demand a continuing mintage with a distinctive signature for each reign. The propriety of using the same formula does not arise

---

[18] V, pp. 15, 16.
[19] D. B. Waage, *Antioch-on-the-Orontes, IV, Part II. Greek, Roman, Byzantine and Crusaders' Coins*, Princeton, 1952, no. 2063.
[20] Op.cit., pp. 13, 14.

for Justin I, who would simply be developing a new type different from that of Anastasius, but only for Justinian and Justin II, choosing, for whatever reasons, to retain the monograms of their predecessors. The sequence of issues in the hoard suggests the ascription of the four monograms to Justin I. Although it would be theoretically possible to divide the 56 coins in question between Justin I and Justin II, as we have done for Anastasius and Justinian, the disproportionately large representation of Baduila (61 coins) and the extremely fresh condition of his coins, particularly the lion series (498–508), require that the deposition be fixed somewhere close to the end of his reign (541–552).

METROLOGICAL ANALYSIS

The Zacha hoard is perhaps most important to historians because it leads us from the turbulent fifth century through the first half of the sixth century, and its contents confirm a fact that is well known among numismatists though it has not yet been incorporated into the body of secondary historical literature. Historians since J. B. Bury have usually followed the texts of John Malalas of Antioch and Marcellinus Comes of Constantinople in their reconstruction of the monetary reform of Anastasius.[21] From these brief notices of that reform it seemed as though there was "a calling in or demonetization of the existing currency" of small bronzes.[22] In place of the small bronze minimi of the fifth century, it was believed that only heavy,

---

[21] Johannes Malalas, *Chronographia*, Bk. XVI, O 117 (ed. Bonn, p. 400, ll. 16–21); Marcellinus Comes, *Chronicon, sub anno* 498 (MGH, AA, XI [= *Chronica Minora*, II], p. 95).

[22] The standard study of these texts from the philological standpoint is R. P. Blake, "The Monetary Reform of Anastasius I and Its Economic Implications," *Studies in the History of Culture, The Disciplines of the Humanities, Dedicated to Waldo Gifford Leland*, Menasha, Wisconsin, American Council of Learned Societies, 1942, pp. 84–97, also reprinted in *Numismatic Review* IV (1947), pp. 35–42. Cf. J. B. Bury, *History of the Later Roman Empire from the Death of Theodosius I to the Death of Justinian*, London, 1939, I, pp. 446–7. Also see E. Stein, *Histoire du Bas Empire*. II. *De la disparition de l'Empire d'Occident à la mort de Justinien (476–565)*, Paris-Bruxelles-Amsterdam, 1949, p. 205; and G. Ostrogorsky, *History of the Byzantine State*, trans. by Joan Hussey, New Brunswick, 1957, pp. 59–60.

reformed bronzes were in circulation within the Byzantine state after the reform. The excavation finds and the hoards, however, prove conclusively that such was not the case. Minimi continued to be issued well into the reign of Justinian, and they retained their value as coin. This is clearly the case though they seem not to occur very often in hoards jointly with the new bronzes of larger module and heavier weight.

The Zacha hoard does not add materially to our knowledge of the fifth century bronze currency. There are too few coins of the pre-reform period contained in this hoard to clarify any of the problems that concern the period prior to the reign of Anastasius. Results from the study of the Yale hoard and the Volo hoard have shown that the minimi from the reign of Arcadius through that of Leo I were issued at a theoretical weight of 1.14 grams or one Roman scruple.[23] There may have been a slight increase in the weight of these coins during the reign of Marcian, but it can have been of only slight significance. To all intents and purposes the fifth century minimi were issued before A.D. 475 at a standard of one Roman scruple. During the twenty-month reign of Basiliscus, however, there was a reduction in the weight

---

[23] The weight of the Roman pound is traditionally given as 327.45 grams. F. Hultsch, *Griechische und römische Metrologie*, 2nd ed., Berlin, 1882, pp. 155–161, treats the earlier studies of this problem by Cagnazzi, Letronne, Böckh and Mommsen. Hultsch accepts the traditional weight. The evidence for the weight of the Roman pound is almost purely numismatic. Most recent attempts to arrive at the weight of the Roman pound have used the solidus as a starting point. A. Luschin von Ebengreuth, "Der Denar der Lex Salica," *Sitzungsberichte der Kaiserlichen Akademie der Wissenschaften in Wien*, Phil.-hist. Klasse, Band 163, Abh. 4, pp. 59–89, has constructed the most complete frequency table for the solidus and its fractions. He listed 459 weights for the solidus. L. Naville, "Fragments de métrologie antique," *Revue suisse de numismatique* XXII (1920–22), pp. 42–60; "La livre romaine et le denier de la Loi Salique. Réponse à M. Dieudonné," op.cit., pp. 257–63; and *Les monnaies d'or de la Cyrénaique*, Geneva, 1951, pp. 108, 9, has argued that the weight of the pound was actually somewhat lower, i.e., 322.56 grams. P. Grierson, "Coinage and Money in the Byzantine Empire 498– c. 1090," Settimane de Studio del Centro Italiano di Studi sull'alto Medioevo, VIII (21–27 aprile, 1960), *Monete e Scambi nell'alto Medioevo*, Spoleto, 1961, p. 415, suggests a weight of about 325 grams. A similar weight was proposed by Cagnazzi, but it has been rejected by most authorities. There was, in addition to the twelve ounce pound, a fourteen ounce pound which was used in fulfilling mining leases. H. L. Adelson, *Light Weight Solidi and Byzantine Trade During the Sixth and Seventh Centuries*, NNM 138, pp. 11–14.

of the minimi to approximately five carats (0.94 grams). At that point the text of the *Theodosian Code* (XI, 21, 2), which stipulated that twenty-five pounds of bronze were to be equivalent to a solidus, was changed so that twenty pounds of bronze were made equal to a solidus. The text in the *Justinian Code* (X, 29, 1) records that change. The process of decline, however, was not arrested at that point. In the reign of Zeno the weight of the bronze coinage went still lower. It probably reached a theoretical weight of four and one half carats (0.84 grams). There would then have been 384 coins struck from the pound of metal. This much is clear from the metrological evidence of the earlier hoards.

In the sixth century the decline in the weight of the small bronzes apparently reached the nadir. It is impossible in the present state of our knowledge to distinguish the coinage of Anastasius with a monogram from that of Justinian. A total of 149 coins in the Zacha hoard may be attributed to either Anastasius or Justinian. These coins have an average weight of 0.61 grams, but many of the coins are in very poor condition. These pieces were probably issued at a theoretical weight of four carats (0.76 grams), and 432 coins were struck from a pound of raw metal.

There are in this hoard, in addition, nineteen coins (298–315) with monograms which cannot be attributed with any degree of precision to one of the early sixth century emperors. The majority of these coins must have been issued by Anastasius or Justinian. If they are included in the frequency table, the resultant figures remain virtually unchanged.

The monogram attributed to Justin I appears on 56 coins. A frequency curve drawn from these coins reveals an average weight of 0.63 grams. The characteristics of this curve are so close to that of the coins attributed to Anastasius or Justinian that they must have been issued on the same standard.

It is therefore possible to construct a frequency curve from the 224 coins with identifiable Byzantine sixth century monograms.[24]

---

[24] Coin 340 is omitted because the monogram is quite different from the others and has a star above it. The barbarous specimens (341–3) have been omitted because they are obviously not of official Roman origin. The inclusion of the few coin fragments does not materially alter the results, but their ex-

The average weight remains 0.61 grams while the mean deviation is 0.12 grams and the standard deviation is 0.15 grams. There can be no doubt that all of these coins were struck to a single standard with slightly better accuracy than the fifth century minimi. The theoretical weight must have been 0.76 grams or four Roman carats.

The monogram coins can be compared with two other groups in the hoard. There are forty-seven coins attributed to Justinian in this hoard which bear types other than the usual monogram. Though the average weight of these coins is only 0.57 grams, or 0.04 grams lighter than the monogram series, there is little doubt that they were meant to be issued at the same standard. If the standard were as low as three and one half carats, over one-quarter of the coins would be overweight even in their present worn state. In addition, there are eleven coins of the Christogram type which are attributed to either Justin I or Justinian. The range of weight in this series extends between 0.38 and 1.00 grams. Since only eleven coins are scattered over that range, any frequency curve would be meaningless. Nevertheless, it is significant that the average weight of this series is also 0.57 grams. Thus they appear to fit into the Byzantine sixth century system though they are less accurately struck.

There are in addition some few coins from the Vandals and Ostrogoths in this hoard. Any deductions based on these few coins must be considered quite conjectural, but in the absence of more detailed metrological studies and larger hoards that have been scientifically published, it is not amiss to state these conjectures. Of the twenty-two pieces of supposedly Vandalic origin in this hoard only six may be assigned to specific Vandal kings. The remaining sixteen are simply placed under the classification "Vandalic." If we are correct in assigning these sixteen anonymous pieces to the Vandalic series (see note 13), then these twenty-two coins reflect a standard of bronze coinage which is precisely that of the sixth century Byzantine imperial issues. Since the earliest of the Vandalic royal coins in this group is that of Thrasamund (A.D. 496–523), this is what we should

---

clusion would be difficult because many of the remaining coins appear to be clipped (see supra, p. 160). In our treatment of the Yale hoard (Y, pp. 143,4) and the Volo hoard (V, pp. 18,19) we have pointed out the difficulties in segregating the clipped specimens.

have expected. The average weight of the "Vandalic" series is 0.57 grams. Thus they share precisely the same average weight as the forty-seven coins of Justinian. Nevertheless, this result is conjectural not only because of the few coins involved but also because of the questionable character of the attribution of some of these coins to the Vandals. It must be remembered constantly that Wroth's original attribution of masses of fifth and sixth century minimi to the Vandals has been under constant revision, and that there has been a continuous decline in the number of small bronze types that can be classified with certainty as Vandalic.

In the case of the Ostrogothic coins the attributions are more certain and the coins more numerous, particularly for the reign of Baduila. The metrological study of these coins reveals an unsuspected monetary reform for which there is no literary evidence. A frequency distribution constructed from the total of sixty-three Ostrogothic coins of certain attribution assumed a bi-modal form.[25] This can only be the result of a change in the standard at some time during the reign of Baduila. The lion coinage of Baduila almost certainly was struck in Rome after the capture of the city in A.D. 549. It was issued in imitation of a lion coinage of Justinian. This hoard does not contain any of the lion coinage of Justinian for comparison. Justinian's lion type was issued at Rome after A.D. 539. The capture of Rome in 536 cannot be assumed as the date for the issuance of these coins with a frontal bust, if the dating of the reform in portraiture, which is based on the large dated bronzes of the year twelve from the mint of Constantinople, is accurate (see note 80). Justinian's small lion type must have been issued between 539 and the reconquest of the city by Baduila in December, A.D. 546. It is quite unlikely that they were issued by the Byzantines in the years 547–9 when they held the city for the second time. During this later Byzantine occupation most of the city lay in ruins and devoid of population. Belisarius, as we know from Procopius, even had difficulty providing new iron gates to replace those destroyed by Baduila after the Byzantine army entered

---

[25] Coin 446 was not included because the attribution was quite uncertain. Nos. 496,7 and 509,10 were omitted as contemporary imitations. The Æ 3 fragment (511) was omitted as was the unidentifiable Ostrogothic fragment (512).

HOARD OF MINIMI 175

the city in A.D. 547. The Byzantine army was continually in desperate need of financial support until the arrival of Narses. The only alternative to a date between 539 and 546 for the issuance of the lions of Justinian is that Narses first issued the lion type after the death of Baduila in A.D. 552. In that case they would have been copying an Ostrogothic type originated by their most successful enemy. Such a suggestion is unlikely in the extreme.

From the facts stated above it is evident that the lion coinage of Justinian should most probably be dated in the period A.D. 539–546. The two pieces in the *British Museum Catalogue* are distinctly heavier than the other minimi attributable to Justinian.[26] The first weighs 15.6 grains (1.01 grams) and the second 17.7 grains (1.08 grams). They are undoubtedly in a better state of preservation than most minimi, but even so the weights are quite high. The three coins of Baduila of the lion series in the same catalogue have weights that are equally high.[27] They are 15.6 grains (1.01 grams), 18.5 grains (1.20 grams), and 15.2 grains (0.99 grams). The average weight of these three coins in the British Museum is therefore 1.07 grams. On the other hand, the average weight of the nine DN REX/B coins in the same catalogue is only 0.71 grams.[28] The four Baduila coins with monograms listed in the *British Museum Catalogue* have an average weight of 0.75 grams.[29] Thus from this catalogue alone it should have been obvious, though it was not noticed, that the lion series is one-third heavier than the other coins of Baduila. Not one of the lion series in the *British Museum Catalogue* weighs less than 15.2 grains

---

[26] *BMC* 113, 35–6. Lorenzina Cesano, "Della moneta enea corrente in Italia nell'ultima età imperiale romana e sotto i re Ostrogoti," *Rivista Italiana di Numismatica*, XXVI (1913), p. 515, gives an average weight of 0.89 grams for the nine specimens from the Castro dei Volsci hoard and an average weight of 1.01 grams for the pieces in the British Museum.

[27] *BMC* 94, 50–52. L. Cesano, op.cit., p. 518, gives the average weight of 206 specimens as 0.66 grams. She gives the average weight of the pieces in the British Museum as 1.02 grams. She noted (p. 521, n. 15) that they were heavier than the other coins of Baduila.

[28] *BMC* 90, 28–36. L. Cesano, op.cit., p. 518, gives the average weight of 272 specimens as 0.67 grams. She gives the average weight of the specimens in the British Museum as 0.69 grams.

[29] *BMC* 89, 24–27. L. Cesano, loc.cit., gives the average weight of 158 specimens as 0.73 grams and the average weight of the coins in the British Museum as 0.74 grams.

while not one of the small bronzes of other types weighs as high as 15 grains.[30]

The results of a metrological study of the Ostrogothic coins from the Zacha hoard confirm the data from the *British Museum Catalogue* The fifty-two coins of the Ostrogothic kings Theodoric and Baduila, apart from the lion type, have an average weight of 0.67 grams. They were probably struck to a standard of four and a half carats and a theoretical weight of 0.84 grams. In effect this means that 384 coins were struck from the pound of raw metal and that the Ostrogoths continued the bronze coinage on the same standard as that which had prevailed during the reign of Zeno. It was during the reign of Zeno that the Ostrogoths entered Italy upon the urging of the Emperor. At some point between 549 and 552 Baduila, in his moment of triumph, increased the weight of the bronze nummi. This was probably done in imitation of the lion coinage of Justinian, which was also heavy.

Only eleven coins of the lion series of Baduila are present in the Zacha hoard. The average weight of these eleven specimens is 0.73 grams. It should, however, be remembered that one of these coins weighs only 0.39 grams and that several others show signs of having been reduced in size. Many reasons may be conjectured for this, but they would remain hypothetical. The best preserved specimens are not too far below the excellent coins in the British Museum. Since there are so few coins spread over the range from 0.37 grams to 1.05 grams, a frequency curve is not really applicable. Nevertheless, if we calculate the degree of dispersion of the weights, the mean deviation is 0.21 grams and the standard deviation is 0.23 grams. The coefficient of variation is quite high at 31.45 per cent. Under these conditions it is obvious that the average weight of these coins is well below the theoretical weight at which they were issued. These facts indicate that the coins must have been struck at the same standard as those of Basiliscus. The theoretical weight was probably intended to be five carats (0.94 grams). It is quite unlikely on the basis of the evidence

---

[30] The average weights given by L. Cesano from the Castro dei Volsci hoard would indicate that the monogram type was actually slightly heavier than the other two. Since only the average weights are given and there is no description of the individual coins, it is impossible to check her results.

TABLE OF METROLOGICAL ANALYSES

	No. of Coins	Average Weight	Mode	Median	Mean Deviation	Standard Deviation	Coefficient of Variation
Yale hoard (pre-Zeno)	371	0.92	0.75	0.91	0.24	0.29	31.72
Volo hoard (pre-Zeno)	810	0.88	0.87	0.88	0.21	0.26	29.43
Volo hoard (Basiliscus)	36	0.79	0.71	0.76	0.18	0.22	28.34
Volo hoard (Zeno)	110	0.62	0.52	0.58	0.19	0.24	39.03
Zacha hoard							
Anastasius or Justinian Monograms	149	0.61	0.60	0.60	0.11	0.13	23.05
Anastasius or Justinian & Indeterminate Monograms	168	0.60	0.60	0.60	0.11	0.14	23.97
Justin I Monograms	56	0.63	0.57	0.60	0.14	0.18	27.73
Anastasius and Sixth Century Byzantine Monograms	224	0.61	0.57	0.60	0.12	0.15	24.94
Christogram	11	0.57			0.13	0.18	30.86
Justinian without Monogram	47	0.57	0.54	0.56	0.12	0.14	25.40
Vandalic	22	0.57	0.57	0.58	0.13	0.16	28.74
Ostrogothic (excluding lion type)	52	0.67	0.57	0.65	0.12	0.15	21.78
Baduila (lion type)	11	0.73			0.21	0.23	31.45

before us that the theoretical weight was intended to be as high as the standard of the earlier fifth century pieces, i.e., one scruple (1.14 grams).

The economic and historical problems arising from these studies of the minimi of the fifth and sixth centuries cannot be treated within the compass of this study of a single hoard. It is sufficient to point out that there was an economic revival evident within the Byzantine Empire during the last years of Zeno which continued through the early part of the sixth century.[31] Anastasius is described by Procopius as "the most provident and at the same time the most businesslike of all emperors," and he left 320,000 pounds of gold in the treasury on his death.[32] The lightening of the bronze currency during his reign was not a measure caused by necessity, but a conscious financial policy. It must also be borne in mind that the light series of reformed folles, which was apparently the earliest, had a theoretical weight of about 9.2 grams. Since these coins were worth forty nummi, the effect of the reform was to lower the theoretical weight of the nummus still further. The minimi of the sixth century cannot have been considered nummi. They would have been grossly overweight. The explanation for their issuance must await a broader study of the economic history of the period.

NUMBER OF COINS FOR EACH HEADING IN THE CATALOGUE

Regular Issues

Constantinian Æ 3	3
Theodosius I Æ 4	1
Honorius	2
Arcadius, Honorius, or Theodosius II	2
Theodosius II	5
Period of Theodosius II	18
Period of Valentinian III	10
Valentinian II, Theodosius I, Arcadius, Honorius (Valentinian III)	2
Marcian	8
Valentinian II, Valentinian III, or Marcian	1
Libius Severus	1

[31] Cf. G. Downey, *A History of Antioch in Syria from Seleucus to the Arab Conquest*, Princeton, 1961, p. 501.
[32] Procopius, *Anecdota*, XIX, 5–7.

Leo	20
Zeno	2
Basiliscus	1
Zeno or Basiliscus	1
Basiliscus and Marcus or Leo and Verina	1
Roman, Illegible	2
Anastasius or Justinian	149
Justin I	56
Indeterminate monograms, Anastasius through Justinian	19
Sixth century	24
Justin I or Justinian	11
Justinian	47
Thrasamund	4
Hilderic	1
Gelimer	1
"Vandalic"	16
Theodoric	4
Athalaric?	1
Baduila	61
Ostrogothic	1
Uncertain	1
Total:	476

Barbarous Issues

Late fourth, early fifth century	1
Arcadius, Honorius, or Theodosius II	1
Period of Theodosius II	7
Valentinian II, Theodosius I, Arcadius, Honorius (Valentinian III)	1
Marcian	1
Leo	1
Sixth century	3
Justinian	9

Imitations of Royal Coinages

"Vandalic"	9
Baduila	4
Total:	37

CATALOGUE*

CONSTANTINIAN

Æ 3

Reverse illegible

1. *Obv.*: ..CON...
   7–13   .35

FEL TEMP REPARATIO

Soldier l., spearing fallen horseman[33]

*2. *Obv.*: DN...   3.   8–14 ↑ .47
   ...IO
   9–11 ↑ .55 ..HA[34]

THEODOSIUS I

Æ 4

SALVS REIPVBLICAE C. 30

Victory running l., dragging captive

4. *Obv.*: DNTHEO...
   10–11 ↓ 1.24 P|

---

* Obverse legend and type, when recorded, are preceded by *Obv*. Busts are draped and pearl diademed, facing right, unless otherwise indicated. Three dots indicate an indeterminate number of illegible letters. The line below the reverse legend records the size in millimeters, the die position, and the weight in grams. A "cf." preceding the reference to the standard catalogues indicates not an identification but an approximation to the type.

An asterisk preceding the number means the coin is illustrated in the Plates.

For those monograms of the Emperors Marcian through Basiliscus which appear in the hoard we have used the reference to the Table of Monograms which appears on page 89 of our *A Bronze Hoard of the Period of Zeno I*. *NNM* 148, New York, 1962.

[33] The type occurs from Constantius II through Julian II. Nos. 10–24 in Y; 3–8 in V. Y p. 159, n. 2 and V p. 45, n. 3 should be corrected to read "—Constantius II."

[34] The third letter of the mint-mark is an H; in which case, the coin was minted at Heraclea. However, the notorious confusion of H with N in the lettering of the period makes Nicomedia a possibility. So also with coin no. 51.

HONORIUS
Reverse illegible[35]

5. *Obv.*: DNHON...
    10–11 ↓ 1.26

6. *Obv.*: ...ONO...
    10–11 ↓ .81

LATE 4th, EARLY 5th CENTURY: BARBAROUS
VOT X MVLT XX within wreath[36]

7. 8–10 ↓ .31 SM..

ARCADIUS, HONORIUS, OR THEODOSIUS II
GLORIA ROMANORVM

Three emperors, standing, with spears; two outer resting hands on shields; central figure slightly smaller[37]

8. ...R...
   6–11 ↑ .79

CONCORDIA AVGGG around cross

9. *Obv.*: ...VSP...[38]
   ...GGG   .MKA
   6–10 ↓ .37

---

[35] Possibly same as no. 4.
[36] The type is found for Gratian, Valentinian II, Theodosius I, and Arcadius. Y 85; V 68–70.
[37] The module of the specimens depicting two or three emperors (8, 10) falls between Æ 3 and Æ 4 size. Pearce has plausibly argued that a distinction was originally intended (J. W. E. Pearce, "Corrections and Additions," *Roman Coinage*, London, 1933, p. 4; also "A Late Roman Hoard from Southwest Asia Minor," *Numismatic Chronicle* 5th Series XV (1935), pp. 21–24) and that such specimens represent a third intermediate denomination. There is unfortunately no agreement on what to call them. Pearce originally listed them as Æ 4, then as "Æ 3 small" (*Roman Coinage*, p. 22). R. A. G. Carson and J. P. C. Kent, *Late Roman Bronze Coinage*, London, 1960, refer to them as Æ 3. In V and here we have called them Æ 4, the size into which they were quickly absorbed. The inadequacy of the traditional nomenclature for the metrological problems of the late Roman period is acute.
[38] The coin is severely cut down.

ARCADIUS, HONORIUS, OR THEODOSIUS II: BARBAROUS

GLORIA ROMANORVM

Two emperors standing, holding spears and leaning on shields

10. 7–10 ↓ .52[39]

THEODOSIUS II

Anepigraphic. Cross in wreath. *Sab.* 32

11. *Obv.*: ...DOSIVS... |
    9–10 ↑ .79   SMKA
12. *Obv.*: ...SIVSPFAVG |
    10–11 ↓ .85   CON
13. *Obv.*: ...EOD...
    10–11 ↑ .96
14. *Obv.*: ...ODOSI...
    10–13 ← .77

Reverse illegible

15. *Obv.*: .NTHEO...
    9–11   .66

PERIOD OF THEODOSIUS II[40]

16. *Obv.*: .N...
    11–13 ↘ .85
17. *Obv.*: ...PFAVG
    10 ↑ .93
18. *Obv.*: ...FAVG
    11 ↑ .84
19. *Obv.*: ...AVG
    12 ↓ .71

20.	12–13	↑	.87 CON	21.	7–10	↓	.47 ANT
22.	11–12	↑	.93	23.	9–10	↑	.75
24.	10–11	↓	.66	25.	10	↓	.66
26.	9–10	↓	.58	27.	8–10	↓	.49
28.	9–11	↖	.48	29.	10–11	↘	.70
30.	10–12	←	.53	31.	9–10		.92
32.	10–11		.77	33.	9–10		.70

---

[39] See note 37.

[40] The majority of coins in this group are undoubtedly Theodosian, but the type is known also in a rare issue of Valentinian III (R. A. G. Carson and J. P. C. Kent, *Late Roman Bronze Coinage* A.D. *324–498. Part II, Bronze Roman Imperial Coinage of the Later Empire* A.D. *346–498*, London, 1960 [=CK], no. 867). Since the hoard is closer to Italy than either Y or V, it is possible that one or more coins under this heading belong to the latter emperor.

PERIOD OF THEODOSIUS II: BARBAROUS

Anepigraphic. Cross in wreath

34. 10–11 ↑ .69   35. 9–10 ↙ .86
36. 9 ↙ .78   37. 10–11 ↘ .72

Same, in reel border

38. 8 ↓ .42   39. 8–9   .49

Anepigraphic. Cross potent in wreath

40. 8–9   .57

PERIOD OF VALENTINIAN III[41]

VOT XX in wreath

41. 10–11 ↓ .88 $\overline{..S}^{\perp}$

VICTORIA AVGG

Victory running l., with wreath and palm

*42. ...AVG.
    11–13 ↘ 1.56

SALVS REIPVBLIC(A)E

Victory running l., dragging captive

43. ...CAE   44. 10–12 ↓ .91
    11–12 ↙ 81.

Victory running l., with wreath and palm[42]

45. 10–11 ↑ 1.10   46. 11   ↓ .82
47. 10   ↓ .84   48. 9–10 ↓ .75
49. 10–11 ↓ .87   50. 8–12   .44

---

[41] These coins all have a distinctive style which is characteristic of the later pieces of Honorius and of Valentinian III from the mint of Rome. The relief is high, but the outlines of the type are not sharp, with the result that the figures appear thick and heavy. Y 259 ff; V 258 ff.

[42] Either VICTORIA AVGG or SALVS REIPVBLIC(A)E is possible. Y 269–280; V 265–272.

VALENTINIAN II, THEODOSIUS I, ARCADIUS, HONORIUS, (VALENTINIAN III)

SALVS REIPVBLICAE

Victory running l., dragging captive

51. Obv.: ...AVG   52. SALVS...
    SALVS...   10–12 ↑   .49
    7–12 ↓   .45   SMHA[43]

VALENTINIAN II, THEODOSIUS I, ARCADIUS, HONORIUS, (VALENTINIAN III): BARBAROUS

SALVS REIPVBLICAE

Victory running l., dragging captive

53.   11–12   .42

MARCIAN

⛨ (V 5) within wreath

54. Obv.: DNMARC...
    9–10 ↓   .77

⛨ or ⛨ (V 1 or 7) within wreath

55. Obv.: DN...
    10–11 ↙   .98

⛨ (V 7) within wreath

56. Obv.: ...AV.
    10   ↙ 1.02   NIC

Indeterminate monogram within wreath

57. Obv.: ...N...   58.   10–11 ↑ 1.23
    10–11 ↑   .89
59.   9–10 ↑   .94   60.   9–10   1.10
61.   7–10   .71[44]

---

[43] The coin has been halved. For the mint mark see note 34.
[44] Halved.

MARCIAN: BARBAROUS

Barbarous monogram within wreath[45]

62. *Obv.*: ...∽....
    9–10 ↓ .63

VALENTINIAN II, VALENTINIAN III, OR MARCIAN

Reverse Illegible

63. *Obv.*: ...NVSPFA..[46]
    9–11   .47

LIBIUS SEVERUS[47]

℞ᶜE (V 1)

64. 8 ↗ .49

LEO I

Anepigraphic. Lion crouching l., looking r. *Sab.* 19

65. *Obv.*: .NL...   66. 7–8 ↑ .61 C̄ON
    7–8 ↓ .77 C̄ON
67. 7–8 ↙ .95   68. 9–11   .83

NᔆE (V 1) within wreath. *Sab.* 18

69. *Obv.*: DNL..   70. *Obv.*: ...PA..
    6–7   1.07   7 ↓ 1.03
71. *Obv.*: ...AVG   72. *Obv.*: ...O
    6–7 ↑ .84   4–7 ↓ .90
73.   6–7 ↑ .90   74.   6–7   .84

---

[45] Possibly an attempt at V 12.
[46] The coin is pierced.
[47] The monogram was first identified by I. Friedländer (*Die Münzen der Ostgothen*, Berlin, 1844, pp. 5f.) as that of Ricimer. The bust on the obverse is Libius Severus III, to whose reign (461–465) the piece must be assigned. CK assigns the type to the mint of Rome (no. 871, 872). Y 502; V 1059–1062.

$\stackrel{s}{\mathsf{NE}}$ or $\stackrel{s}{\mathsf{NE}}$ (V 1 or 2) within wreath. *Sab.* 18

75. 6   ↓ 1.07   76. 6   ↓ .82

$\stackrel{s}{\mathsf{NE}}$ (V 2) within wreath. *Sab.* 18

77. *Obv.*: ...AVG   78. 10   .77
    7   ↑ 1.16

$\stackrel{\circ}{\mathsf{KE}}$ (V 5) within wreath. *Sab.* 18

79. *Obv.*: ...NISP...   *80. *Obv.*: ...OSP...

    10   ↑ 1.04   10–11 ↓ .80 ..$\overline{\mathsf{NA}}$[48]

Anepigraphic. Figure in long robes, nimbate, standing facing, holding globe surmounted by cross in r., and scepter transversely in l.[49]

Cf. *Sab.* 15

81. *Obv.*: ..LEO...   82. 10–11 ↑ 1.18 b|E
    10–11 ↑ 1.06 b|E

83. 10–11 ↓ 1.02 "|E   84. 10–11 ↙ .58

Same type, barbarous

85. 9   ↙ .41

[48] If the third letter of the mintmark is truly N, we have a rare instance of what must have been the early issue of Leo with the longer version of the mint mark, SMNA, before it was changed to NIC. Another example with the same obverse legend and apparently the same form of monogram on the reverse is listed by J. W. E. Pearce and M. E. Wood, "A Late Roman Hoard from Dalmatia," *Numismatic Chronicle* 5th Series XIV (1934), p. 276 (pl. VII, 26).

[49] The identification of the figure is a matter of dispute. Despite difficulties in accounting for b|E in the reverse field, ascription to Leo's wife, Verina, seems more attractive than to Basilissa Eudoxia, the member of the Theodosian house who was released from Vandal captivity in 461. The latter event might call for a commemorative issue, but would not *prima facie* require continued reference over a number of years such as the abundance of the type in the coin finds would indicate. We should, however, prefer to suspend judgment pending further evidence. An ivory in Florence showing a female figure in the same pose and with the same attributes may represent the same figure. It is illustrated in H. Pierce and R. Tyler, *L'Art Byzantin*, vol. II, Paris, 1934, pl. 27, and, most recently, in J. Beckwith, *The Art of Constantinople*, London, 1961, fig. 48, but assigned to the Empress Ariadne (d. 515).

ZENO

⊠ (V 4) within wreath

86. 8–10   .52

𝈕𝐸 (V 5) within wreath

87. *Obv.*: .NZEN...
   8–9 ↓ .80

BASILISCUS

𝈕𝐵 (V 1) within wreath[50]

88. *Obv.*: ...I...S...
   10–11 ↓ .73

ZENO OR BASILISCUS

Indeterminate monogram[51]

89. 7–8   .39

BASILISCUS AND MARCUS OR LEO AND VERINA

Two emperors enthroned[52]

*90. 10–11 ↑ 1.15

ROMAN, ILLEGIBLE[53]

91. *Obv.*: ...PFAVG   92. *Obv.*: ...AVG
   10   .70   9–11   .71

[50] V 1023–28; CK 2284–6. *BMC* 31, 109 (pl. IV, 8) is probably a monogram of this type which has been printed upside down and attributed to Marcian. Nos. 1 and 2 under Basiliscus in the Table of Monograms in V should be reversed.

[51] The coin is badly enough damaged that it is impossible to decide between Zeno V3 and Basiliscus V2 for the form of monogram.

[52] The coin is quite heavy but must be placed in the latter part of the fifth century. It is either an example of the last coinage of Leo (V 887; CK 2276) with two emperors seated, facing, nimbate, each with transverse scepter, or a similar type depicting Basiliscus and Marcus. The type, first published in V (1042), shows them each not with scepter but with possibly a globe. This particular specimen is in such poor condition that it adds nothing to our knowledge of the issue.

[53] Fabric and style of lettering assign these to the early fifth century.

ANASTASIUS OR JUSTINIAN[54]

🜍 (Z 1) in reel border   BMC 32, 128; CK 2288

93.	Obv.:	...AVG			94.	9	↑	.83
	8–9	↑	.54					
*95.	9	↑	.79		96.	9	↑	.76
97.	8	↑	.75		98.	8–9	↑	.71
99.	9–10	↑	.67		100.	9	↑	.66
101.	7–8	↑	.65		102.	8–10	↑	.61
103.	8–10	↑	.60		104.	9	↑	.58
105.	8–9	↑	.58		106.	9	↑	.57
107.	8–9	↑	.56		108.	9	↑	.50
109.	10	↓	1.03		110.	9–11	↓	.96
111.	10–11	↓	.76		112.	8–10	↓	.76
113.	8–9	↓	.65		114.	9	↓	.63
115.	8–9	↓	.60		116.	10	↓	.57
117.	9–10	↓	.56		118.	9–10	↓	.56
119.	8–9	↓	.55		120.	7–11	↓	.53
121.	7–10	↓	.52		122.	8–9	↓	.50
123.	8	↓	.48		124.	7–8	↓	.44
125.	8–9	↓	.43		126.	8	↓	.39
127.	7	↓	.34		128.	9	↗	.75
129.	8–10	↖	.75		130.	9–10	↖	.87
131.	7–9	↖	.41		132.	9	↙	.65
133.	9–10	↙	.54		134.	8–9	↙	.44
135.	9	↙	.63		136.	10	↘	.56
137.	8–9	←	.54		138.	9–10		.89
139.	8		.80		140.	8–9		.69
141.	8		.68		142.	9		.64

[54] Two coins found in the Italian Monte Roduni hoard with this monogram yielded the obverse inscription **DNANASTA** (Friedländer, p. 42). The attribution has been accepted and confirmed by later scholarship. The reverse type seems always to have been minted with a reel border. Since it is most likely that Justinian availed himself of the same formula (see above, p. 167), one should like to have some means of distinguishing, such as is not presently available. No coin with Justinian's name on it has come to our attention.

In the monogram series which follows (nos. 93–316) we have separated the coins showing a reel border from those which, if it existed, have it off flan.

143.	7–8		.62	144.	9	.58
145.	8–9		.58	146.	8–10	.58
147.	9–10		.48	148.	8–9	.42
149.	8		.38			

⚕ (Z 2) in reel border[55]

150.	9–10	↑	.50

⚕ (Z 3) in reel border

151.	9	↓	.49

⚕ (Z 4) in reel border

152.	8–9	↑	.77	153.	8–9	↓	.83
154.	8–11	↓	.73	155.	8–10	↓	.63
156.	8–9	↗	.78	157.	8		.36

⚕ or ⚕ (Z 1 or 4)

158.	8–9	↑	.65	159.	9	↑	.58
160.	8–9	↑	.58	161.	8–9	↑	.57
162.	7–8	↑	.55	163.	8	↑	.54
164.	7–8	↑	.49	165.	7–8	↑	.46
166.	7	↑	.27[56]	167.	8–9	↓	.94
168.	8	↓	.76	169.	8–9	↓	.64
170.	7–9	↓	.61	171.	8–9	↓	.51
172.	9–11	↗	.90	173.	9–10	↗	.73
174.	8–9	↗	.70	175.	7–8	↗	.67
176.	9	↗	.60	177.	8–9	↗	.52
178.	8	↗	.46	179.	9–11	↙	.78
180.	9	↙	.76	181.	7–8	↘	.31[57]
182.	9	←	.36	183.	9–10		.75
184.	9–10		.75	185.	8–10		.55
186.	8–9		.46	187.	7–9		.40[58]

[55] Unless the form is merely a caprice of the die-cutter, the double A can only be Anastasius, not Justinian.
[56] This is a coin fragment.
[57] Fragment.
[58] Fragment.

Same, in reel border

188.	Obv.: ...AVC			189.	Obv.: ...V.			
	8–10	↓	.67		8–10	↑	.56	
190.	9–10	↑	.69	191.	8–9	↑	.64	
192.	8–10	↑	.62	193.	8–10	↑	.60	
194.	8	↑	.59	195.	8	↑	.46	
196.	9	↓	.77	197.	8–9	↓	.76	
198.	9–10	↓	.76	199.	8–11	↓	.74	
200.	10–11	↓	.71	201.	9–11	↓	.68	
202.	8–10	↓	.67	203.	7–8	↓	.59	
204.	9	↓	.57	205.	9–10	↓	.55	
206.	7–8	↓	.46	207.	8	↗	.62	
208.	8–9	↗	.61	209.	7	↗	.53	
210.	8–10	↗	.42	211.	8–9	↖	.63	
212.	9–10	↖	.61	213.	7–9	↙	.60	
214.	9–10	↙	.54	215.	9–10	↘	.52	
216.	7–8	→	.48	217.	8–10		.85	
218.	8–9		.70	219.	9–10		.67	
220.	9		.59	221.	8–10		.51	
222.	7–9		.40	223.	9–10		.38	

𐤍 (Z 5) in reel border

224.	8	↑	.59	225.	7–8	↑	.33	
226.	8–9	↓	.52	227.	8	↓	.39	

Same, in wreath

*228.   9–10   →   .86

𐤍 (Z 6)

229.	Obv.: ...AVC			230.	10–12	↑	.68	
	9–11	↑	.55					
231.	7–8	↑	.55	232.	8–9	↑	.60	
233.	8–9	↓	.72	234.	8–9	↙	.55	
235.	7–10		.60	236.	8–9		.60	

HOARD OF MINIMI

Same, in reel border

237.	Obv.: ...V.			238.	7–10	↓	.37	
	8–9	↘	.46					
239.	9		.81	240.	8–10		.70	
241.	8–9		.51					

JUSTIN I[59]

Ņ̃ (Z 1) BMC 33, 135

242.	9–10	↑	.83	243.	8–9	↑	.57	
244.	8–9	↑	.52	245.	8–9	↓	.50	
246.	8–9	↓	.47	247.	8	↓	.36[60]	
248.	8–9	↗	.80	249.	8–9	↗	.46	
250.	9–10	↙	.72	251.	9–10		1.00	
252.	8–9		.72					

Same, in reel border

253.	10–11	↑	.84	254.	8–10	↑	.82	
255.	8–9	↑	.63	256.	9	↑	.57	
257.	9–10	↑	.55	258.	8–9	↑	.41	
259.	10–12	↓	.84	260.	8	↓	.70	
261.	8–9	↓	.56	262.	8–10	↓	.55	
263.	8–9	↓	.41[61]	264.	9	↗	.62	
265.	9–10	↙	.65	266.	9–10	↙	.65	
267.	9–10	↙	.64	268.	9–10	↘	.52	
269.	8		.55	270.	8		.54	
271.	7–9		.37[62]					

Ņ̃ (Z 2)

272. 8–9 → .50

---

[59] For the assignment of the next four monograms to this emperor see above, p. 170. BMC 33, 135–138 gives the monogram to Anastasius, but there are no accompanying inscriptions. It does not appear as a separate form in Sabatier or Kraus or in Friedländer's description of the Monte Roduni find.
[60] Fragment.
[61] Fragment.
[62] Fragment.

13*

Ņ (Z 3)

273.	Obv.:	...FAVG			274.	8–9	↑	.77
		9	↗	.56				
275.		8–9	↑	.41	276.	9–10	↓	1.07
277.		8	↓	.76	278.	8–9	↓	.57
279.		7	↓	.52	280.	8–9		.62

Same, in reel border

281.	Obv.:	...AVG			282.	9–10	↑	.90
		8–10	↓	.66				
283.		8–9	↑	.67	284.	8	↑	.61
285.		8–9	↑	.54	286.	8–9	↓	.91
287.		8–9	↓	.41	288.	8–9	↓	.35
289.		9	↗	.73	290.	8–9	↙	.59
291.		9	↙	.43	292.	9–10		.93
293.		8		.68	294.	9–10		.66
295.		8		.54	296.	7–8		.48

Ņ (Z 4)

297. 10   ↗ 1.09

INDETERMINATE MONOGRAMS, ANASTASIUS THROUGH JUSTINIAN[63]

298.	8	↑	.61	299.	7–9	↓	.41
300.	9–10		.88	301.	8–9		.54
302.	7		.44	303.	6–7		.44

Same, in reel border

304.	Obv.:	...AV.			305.	8–10	↑	.83
		10	↑	.54				
306.		8	↑	.60	307.	8–10	↑	.52[64]

[63] The monograms under this heading are not completely on flan and do not permit closer identification.
[64] Fragment.

308.	10	↓	.92		309.	8–9	↓	.41[65]
310.	8	↙	.41		311.	8	→	.62
312.	7–8	→	.44[66]		313.	8–9		.68
314.	8		.65		315.	8–9		.63[67]
316.	8		.38					

SIXTH CENTURY

Victory advancing l., with wreath and palm[68]   *BMC* 20, 21

317.	8–9	↙	.42 *↧		318.	8	↖	.23
319.	7–9	↗	.29		320.	9	↘	.48
321.	8–9	↙	.47		322.	8	↙	.43
323.	8	↙	.39		324.	8	↙	.36
325.	8	←	.36		326	7–8		.30
*327.	8–9		.51		328.	8–9		.46
329.	7–9		.34		330.	8–9		.33

Victory standing front, wreath in each hand cf. *BMC* 22, 42

331.   9–10   ↑   .66

[65] Fragment.
[66] Fragment.
[67] Fragment.
[68] The coins under this heading have been assigned to the sixth century on two counts: 1) style and fabric; and 2) equivalent specimens do not appear in significant amounts in the fifth century Volo and Yale hoards. The Victory types are more barbarized than on specimens of the late fifth century. The lines of the drapery are finely and symmetrically drawn but seem to exist as geometric designs in their own right and not as the dress pattern itself. Both the thickness and the diameter of the coins are considerably less than coins of the fifth century; in fact, they fall short of many of the sixth century monogram types, for example. The completely erratic die positions also rouse suspicion. The coins may possibly be imitations minted in Italy from a theme which is common on the gold coinage of the period but had not been used on the bronze since early in the fifth century. The sum of these factors leads us to refer more of the Victory types than has previously been done to the sixth century instead of the fifth, or at least to keep in mind that distinctions can and should be made. Most of the fifth century specimens found at Zacha seem in their general characteristics imitative of the coinage of Valentinian III and have been so entered in the catalogue. If so, Italy is again a likely source of mintage. Needless to say, the poor quality of the coins in question, 317–331, renders the exact identification of the stance of the Victory figure sometimes ambiguous.

Cross potent in reel border[69] BMC 38, 173
Pellet in each of two lower segments

332.	Obv.: Traces of letters				333.	Obv.: Dots for inscr.		
	9–10	←	.46			8–9	↙	.34
334.	8–9	↓	.35		335.	7	↙	.24
336.	9	↗	.48		337.	8	→	.29
*338.	8	→	.65					

Cross pattée in wreath[70] BMC 41, 201
Pellet in each of two lower segments

*339. Obv.: Traces of letters
    9–10 ↑ 1.02

Ŋ̊ (Z 1) in reel border[71]

340. Obv.: Traces of letters
    9–10 ↙ .86

Indeterminate monograms, barbarous[72]

341	Obv.: Traces of letters				
	10–11	.72	342.	8–10	.40
343.	8–9	.35			

[69] As in the case of the Victory figures, the style and fabric of these coins suggest that they be assigned to the sixth century. The relief on the reverse is high and sharp. The strong linear effect of the cross, its lines filling the whole of the reverse field, is very similar to the impression made by coins 392–410, which can on other grounds be assigned to Justinian. The flans are quite thin.

[70] The reverse of this coin is surprisingly well made: the details of the wreath carefully drawn and the cross well centered. It is of heavier weight than the preceding specimens. The severe economy of line with which the obverse bust is drawn and the carelessness in the treatment of the obverse legend mark the coin as belonging to the sixth century. This discrepancy between the artistic quality of obverse and reverse is characteristic of the bronze coinage of the period.

[71] Cf. BMC 36, 154. The BMC specimens lack the star and the projection from the lower part of the right leg.

[72] The form of monogram is not clearly enough preserved to merit illustration or conjecture. Assignment is on stylistic grounds.

JUSTIN OR JUSTINIAN (?)

☧ (Z 1) Christogram in reel border[73]   BMC 37, 159

344. Obv.: IVS...
    9–10 ↑ .57
346. Obv.: Traces of letters
    7–10 ↑ .62
348. Obv.: Traces of letters
    7–8 ↑ .38
350. Obv.: Traces of letters
    7–8 ↗ .39
352. 8–9   .75
354. 7–8   .39

*345. Obv.: Traces of letters
    8–9 ↑ .66
347. Obv.: Traces of letters
    7   ↑ .51
349. Obv.: Traces of letters
    8–9 ↘ 1.00
351. 8–10 ↑ .53
353. 7–9   .49

JUSTINIAN I

Ⱥ (Z 1) in reel border[74]   BMC 34, 141

*355. Obv.: IVSTI...
    9 ↖ .84

356. Obv.: IVSTI...
    10–11 ↗ .57

---

[73] Coins with a Christogram reverse have generally been assigned to Justinian. The lone specimen in the Monte Roduni find (Friedländer, pp. 43, 52) reads only IVS—. Those listed in the BMC have garbled legends which suggest Justinian. A coin in the Italian Castro dei Volsci hoard reads simply IVS... (L. Cesano, "Della moneta enea corrente in Italia nell' ultima età imperiale romana e sotto i re ostrogoti," *Rivista Italiana di Numismatica* XXVI (1913), p. 515, no. 225). Sabatier lists the type but does not attempt an ascription. The Zacha specimens are on the whole more poorly made than the other coins of Justinian in the hoard. In some instances the obverse is anepigraphic. Postolakas assigned the type to Justin I but does not record a legend (see above, p. 164). Since a Christogram appears on the larger bronze of Justin (W. Wroth, *Catalogue of the Imperial Byzantine Coins in the British Museum*, Volume I, London, 1908, p. 16, 40–48 (pl. III, 10), it is at least theoretically possible that some of our coins belong to him. For the Ravenna silver coins of Justinian with a Christogram see BMC 117, 69–71.

[74] Four examples of the type were unearthed at Monte Roduni (Friedländer, p. 43). One of the 19 specimens listed by L. Cesano from Castro dei Volsci reads IVS..INIA (op.cit., p. 515, nos. 158–176). The coins are very common and have been found throughout the eastern Mediterranean: 1 at Antioch (Waage, op.cit., no. 2055); 1 at Cyprus (Cox, op.cit., no. 642); 51 at Athens (Thompson, op.cit., no. 1718); 7 at Corinth (K. M. Edwards, *Corinth. Volume VI. Coins 1896–1929*, Cambridge, Massachusetts, 1933, no. 760); 12 at Caesarea (H. Hamburger, "Minute Coins from Caesarea," *Atiqot. Journal of the Israel Department of Antiquities* I (1954), p. 136, no. 113); and 5 at Olympia (Postolakas type 3; see above, p. 165).

357.	9–10	↑	.66		358.	8	↑	.54
359.	8–9	↑	.42		360.	8–9	↖	.54
361.	8–9	↖	.37		362.	8–9	↗	.68
363.	8–9	↙	.56		364.	8–9	←	.48
365.	9	←	.44		366.	8	←	.47
367.	9–11	←	.68		368.	9	←	.77
369.	9–10	→	.67		370.	9–10	→	.63
371.	10–11		.82		372.	8–9		.59

Same, barbarous

373.	9	↑	.41		374.	7	↑	.59
375.	9–11	↓	.52		376.	9–10	↙	.51
377.	9–11	↖	.36		378.	9	→	.33[75]
379.	7–8		.47		380.	7–9		.28[76]

⃞ (Z 2) in wreath[77] BMC 33, 140

381. *Obv.*: IVSTIN...
    10   ↙   .85

382. *Obv.*: IVSTI...
    8–9   ↑   .71

*383. *Obv.*: ...IANVS
    9–11   ↓   .59

⃞ (Z 3) in reel border BMC 33, 139

*384. *Obv.*: Traces of letters
    8   ↓   .46

385. *Obv.*: Traces of letters
    8–9   ↓   .37

386.   8–9   ↓   .77[78]

387.   9   ↖   .76

---

[75] The coin is pierced.
[76] Pierced.
[77] Sabatier, vol. I, p. 86 (pl. I, 26) gave this and the following monogram to Anastasius, incorrectly. The name of Justinian has been read on the Monte Roduni specimens of both types (Friedländer, pp. 43, 52), corroborated also by the Castro dei Volsci coins (Cesano, op.cit., p. 515, nos. 177–222).
[78] The monogram on this coin is practically a mirror image of the type: ⃞.

HOARD OF MINIMI

VOT XIII(I) in wreath[79] *BMC* 28, 86

388. *Obv.*: Traces of letters
9–10 ↑ .69

389. *Obv.*: Traces of letters
10–11 ↓ .88

Same, barbarous

390. 8–9 ↓ .25

VOT XIIII in wreath *BMC* 29, 91

*391. *Obv.*: Traces of letters
9–10 ↑ .64

⳨ (Z 4) in wreath[80] *BMC* liv, note; *Friedländer*, 43

392. *Obv.*: IVSTI...
Emperor, nimbate, facing front,
holding *globus cruciger* in r.
8–10 ↗ .46

393. *Obv.*: IVS...
Same as No. 392
5–10 ↓ .36[81]

*394. *Obv.*: Same as No. 392
8–10 ↑ .54

395. *Obv.*: Same as No. 392
8–9 ↓ .37

396. *Obv.*: Same as No. 392
9–10 ↗ .59

397. *Obv.*: Same as No. 392
10 ↙ .62

398. *Obv.*: Same as No. 392
9 ↙ .48

---

[79] The assignment of this and the following type to Justinian is confirmed by the reading of the emperor's name in the *BMC* recorded specimens.

[80] The type has been noted in three examples from Monte Roduni (Friedländer, p. 43) and three from Olympia (type 9 above, p. 165), and no doubt represents an imperial issue. Although the facing bust does not appear on the large bronze of Justinian before A.D. 538, this need not apply to the Æ 4. Examples of a facing bust for Anastasius have been recorded on Byzantine silver stamps. As Dodd points out (op.cit., p. 9, note 35), we are not dealing with an individual likeness of an Emperor but rather with "a formal type-portrait adopted by Anastasius and used by his successors." The adoption of the facing bust on the coinage should be viewed in the same light as Justinian's adoption of the monogram of Anastasius. It serves both as a convenient abstract symbol of imperium as well as a definition of the name of the particular ruler.

[81] Fragment.

⚐ (Z 5) in reel border[82]

399. *Obv.*: IV...
Emperor, facing front, nimbate
8–9 ↘ .55

400. *Obv.*: Same as No. 399, but bust flanked by cross on either side: †|†
7–8 ↑ .44

*401. *Obv.*: Same as No. 399 †|†
7–9 ↓ .66

402. *Obv.*: Same as No. 399 †|†
8–9 ↓ .36

403. *Obv.*: Same as No. 399 †|†
7–10 ↗ .48

404. *Obv.*: Same as No. 399 †|†
8–9 ↗ .79

405. *Obv.*: Same as No. 399 †|†
9–10 ↗ .62

406. *Obv.*: Same as No. 399 '''|†
8 ↗ .45

407. *Obv.*: Same as No. 399 †|'''
8–9 ↓ .45

408. *Obv.*: Same as No. 399
7–9 ↑ .37

409. *Obv.*: Same as No. 399
8–12 ↘ .54

ϙ†ρ (Z 6) in reel border[83]

*410. *Obv.*: Same as No. 399
7–10 ↓ .44

VANDAL ROYAL COINAGE
THRASAMUND
Victory running l., holding wreath[84]

*411. *Obv.*: DNRC...
9–11 ↓ .62

412. *Obv.*: DNR...
10 ↖ .40

413. *Obv.*: ...IASI
9–10 ↖ .58

414. 9–10 ↗ .55

---

[82] Examples of the type have appeared so far at Olympia (10; see above, type 4, p. 165) and at Caesarea (6; H. Hamburger, op.cit., p. 136, no. 114). It is a moot point whether the formula should be read as the letter A or as a triangle with one projecting side. The obverse in most cases seems to be anepigraphic.

[83] Unpublished. Its attribution to Justinian is on stylistic grounds.

[84] The assignment oj these coins to Thrasamund seems to us confirmed by the recent study of M. Troussel, "Les Monnaies Vandales d' Afrique Découvertes de Bou-Lilate et du Hamma," *Recueil des Notices et Mémoires de la Société Archéologique du Départment de Constantine* LXVII (1950–51), pp. 147–192. The letters are held to stand for *Dominus Noster Rex*. Cf. a similar type with obverse legend —ASI (cf. our coin 413) assigned by Sabatier (vol. I., p. 218, no. 6) and by Wroth (*BMC* 21, 37) to Thrasamund.

HILDERIC

Reverse illegible, in wreath

415. *Obv.*: HILD...
    9–10   .66

GELIMER

⦗⋈ (Z 1) in wreath *BMC* 16,4 *Var.*

*416. *Obv.*: Traces of letters
    10–11 → .88

"VANDALIC"

N I (?) in reel border[85]

417. 10 → .89

Palm tree with fruit, in reel border[86] *BMC* 26, 68

418. *Obv.*: Traces of letters		419. *Obv.*: Traces of letters	
9 → .79		7–8 ↓ .37	
420. *Obv.*: Traces of letters		421. *Obv.*: Traces of letters	
7–8 ↗ .29		9–11 ↙ .63	
422. *Obv.*: Traces of letters		*423. Traces of letters	
9–10 ↙ .59		9 ↘ .46	
424. *Obv.*: Traces of letters		425. *Obv.*: Traces of letters	
8–9 ↘ .43		7–11 ← .68	
426. *Obv.*: Traces of letters		427. *Obv.*: Traces of letters	
9–10 ← .57		7–8 ← .48	
428. *Obv.*: Traces of letters		429. *Obv.*: Traces of letters	
9–10 .72		8–9 .71	
430. *Obv.*: Traces of letters		431. *Obv.*: Traces of letters	
8–9 .57		7–9 .45	
432. *Obv.*: Traces of letters			
7–8 .30			

---

[85] The piece is too worn to permit of an exact description and it is quite possible that part of the type is off flan. In any case, the specimen is unpublished. Small bronze with N̄ IIII are known in the Vandal series (*BMC* 7, 12), but the formula is always in two lines.

[86] For the possible attribution of this common type to Gelimer see above, p. 165, note 13. The obverse on these coins is very crudely done.

Imitations[87]

433.	8–9	↓	.37		434.	8–10	↖	.50
435.	8–9	↗	.51		436.	7–8	↙	.44
437.	7–9	↙	.38		438.	8	↘	.50
439.	6–8		.41		440.	8–9		.37
441.	7–8		.35					

OSTROGOTHIC ROYAL COINAGE

THEODORIC

⟨monogram⟩ (Z 1) in reel border *Kraus* 96,80

442. 9   ↓   .71

⟨monogram⟩ (Z 2) in reel border *Kraus* 96,80 *Var.*

443. *Obv.*: Traces of letters
   8–9 ↑ .54

Indeterminate monograms in reel border

444. 8   .45   445. 8–9   .52

ATHALARIC(?)[88]

MỊ
IA in reel border

*446. *Obv.*: ATH...
   9 ↗ .63

---

[87] The obverse is in all instances anepigraphic.
[88] Unpublished. The reading of the first I on the reverse is doubtful and the ascription to Athalaric, who is not otherwise represented in the hoard, is open to question.

BADUILA

⟨monogram⟩ (Z 1) in wreath[89] BMC 89,24; Kraus 196,69

447. Obv.: ...PFAVG
    9–10 ↓ .82
448. Obv.: ...AVG
    8–9 ↓ .62
449. Obv.: ...AVG
    9 ↓ .59
450. Obv.: ...AVG
    7–10 ↓ .42
451. Obv.: ...AVG
    8–10 ↙ .75
452. Obv.: ...VG
    9 ↖ .49
453. 10–11 ↓ .87
454. 9–10 ↓ .70
455. 10 ↓ .83
456. 8 ↑ .69
457. 8–9 ↑ .66

⟨monogram⟩ (Z 2) in wreath

458. 9–10   .76
459. 9   .64

⟨monogram⟩ (Z 3) in wreath

*460. Obv.: ...TASI...
    9–10 ↗ .52

$\overline{DN}^*_B REX$ in wreath BMC 90,28; Kraus 196,71

461. Obv.: ...SAVG[90]
    9–10 ↑ 1.06
462. 8–9 ↑ .75
463. 7–8 ↑ .61
464. 9–10 ↑ .42
*465. 9 ↓ .64
466. 8–9 ↗ .76
467. 9–10   .57

[89] The obverse of these pieces shows the head of Anastasius, who remains on Baduila's bronze until replaced by a portrait of the king himself. There is no evidence that Baduila ever struck bronze with the head of Justinian, who was after all his enemy. Reference to such coins at Sessa Aurunca in Italy (A. Levi, "Sessa Aurunca. Tesoretto di monetine di bronzo bizantine follari o nummi," *Notizie degli Scavi di Antichità*, Serie Quinta, XVI (1919), p. 357) bearing the monogram of Baduila with the legend DN IVSTINIANVS PP AC is suspicious. Silver pieces with the head of Justinian are extremely rare and are to be assigned to the very beginning of the reign before the change (see *BMC*, p. 85).

Coins 447–495 and 511 were struck at Baduila's capital, Ticinum (See Kraus, op.cit., p. 183; *BMC*, pp. 89ff.).

[90] These coins have the bust and legend of Anastasius on the obverse.

$DN^*_B REX$ in wreath

468.	9	.77	469.	8–9	.59
470.	9–10	.44			

$\overline{DN}_B REX$ in wreath Kraus 197,73

471.	Obv.: ...AVG			472.	9	↑	.87
	8–9	↓	.76				
473.	8–9	↑	.61	474.	9–10	↓	.73
475.	8–9	↓	.71	476.	10–11	↘	.62
477.	8–9	←	.51	478.	9–10		.45

$DN_B REX$ in wreath Kraus 197,74

479.	Obv.: ...AS...			480.	Obv.: ...SAVG		
	8–9	↓	.67		8–9	↖	.58
481.	Obv.: ...SAVG			482.	Obv.: ...AVG		
	10	↙	.75		9	↑	.55
483.	Obv.: ...AVG			484.	8–9	↑	.65
	8	↓	.41				
485.	9–10	↑	.64	486.	10	↓	1.00
487.	10	↓	.86	488.	9–10	↓	.47
489.	8–9	↗	.60	490.	8–9	↗	.48
491.	8		.79	492.	10		.79

$DN_B \underline{REX}$ in wreath

493.	Obv.: ...AV.		
	8–9	↓	.69

$\overline{DN}_B REX$ in wreath

494.	9–10	.75

HOARD OF MINIMI

$\overline{DN}$ REX in wreath
B

495. 9–10 ↓ .60

Imitations

$\overline{DN}\overset{*}{\underset{B}{}}REX$ in wreath

496. *Obv.*: ...RIA2   497. *Obv.*: Traces of letters
     9–10 ↓ .70   9–10 ↓ .83

Lion advancing r., within wreath[91] *BMC* 94,50; *Kraus* 198,80

498. *Obv.*: DNB ADVI..   *499. *Obv.*: DNB ADVI..
     Bust of Baduila, beardless,   Same as No. 498
     facing, wearing crown and robes   10–12 ↓ .93
     9–10 ↑ .51
500. *Obv.*: DNB...   501. *Obv.*: DNB...
     Same as No. 498   Same as No. 498
     9–11 ↑ 1.01   11–12 ↓ 1.05
502. *Obv.*: DNB...   503. *Obv.*: ..B A...
     Same as No. 498   Same as No. 498
     9–11 ↓ .76   9–10 ↗ .53
504. *Obv.*: ...VILA   505. *Obv.*: Same as No. 498
     Same as No. 498   9–10 ↑ .92
     9   ↙ .37
506. *Obv.*: Same as No. 498   507. *Obv.*: Same as No. 498
     9–10 ↑ .52   9   ↓ .62
508. *Obv.*: Same as No. 498
     9–10 ↓ .51

Imitations

509. *Obv.*: Same as No. 498   510. *Obv.*: Same as No. 498
     6–8 ↑ .26   7   ↗ .22

[91] Minted at Rome (see Kraus, op.cit., p. 183; *BMC*, p. 94). Wroth points out that these coins are on the model of the small bronze of Justinian also minted at Rome with the same reverse (*BMC* p. 94, n. 1 and pl. XVI, 9, 10).

Æ 3[92]

[DN]   in wreath   *BMC* 91,38; *Kraus* 196,68
[BADV]
ELA
REX

*511. 10–14 ↓ 1.29

OSTROGOTHIC

Æ 3

Unidentifiable fragment, in reel border[93]

512. ...A
    9–13   .88

UNCERTAIN

Æ 4

Lion standing l., looking back; no border[94]

*513. * above lion   ⊥
    11   ↓ 1.19

HOWARD L. ADELSON AND GEORGE L. KUSTAS

---

[92] A 10-nummi piece which has been severely cut down.

[93] The piece has been severely cut down so that further identification is impossible. Perhaps same as preceding.

[94] The bust is badly gouged. Although the legend cannot be read there are enough traces of letters remaining to make it certain that this is not a coin of Leo. Likewise, it can not be assigned to Baduila, whose lion series shows consistently a facing bust on the obverse and a lion striding right. The same description applies to the coins of Justinian minted at Ravenna. The coin is very well made and shows traces of a mint mark. It should possibly be assigned to the late fifth or early sixth century and considered an Italian imitation of Leo's issues with standing lion types.

TABLE OF MONOGRAMS IN THE ZACHA HOARD

MARCIAN

V_1 V_5 V_7

LIBIUS SEVERUS

V_1

LEO I

V_1 V_2 V_5

ZENO

V_4 V_5

BASILISCUS

V_1

ANASTASIUS OR JUSTINIAN

Z_1 Z_2 Z_3 Z_4 Z_5 Z_6

JUSTIN I

Z_1 Z_2 Z_3 Z_4

SIXTH CENTURY

Z_1

JUSTIN OR JUSTINIAN (?)

Z_1

JUSTINIAN I

Z_1 Z_2 Z_3 Z_4 Z_5 Z_6

GELIMER

Z_1

THEODORIC

Z_1 Z_2

BADUILA

Z_1 Z_2 Z_3

THREE MORE HOARDS
OF BYZANTINE COPPER[1] COINS
(See Plates XXXI–XXXIX)

Two hoards of Byzantine coins belonging to the University of Nebraska have been loaned me for study by the Rev. I. C. G. Campbell, the University's Curator of Coins and the donor of the hoards. They are here published with his permission and with my great gratitude for his generosity and his patience in what neither of us expected to be so long an operation. Correspondence about them with Mr. D. M. Metcalf of Oxford, England, makes it clear to me that a more searching analysis of details and more recorded weights would yield more information, but as it is apparent that I am not going to have the time that such further study would demand, I must content myself with this brief presentation, somewhat supplemented by notes that I have transmitted to him on particular points which he raised. I hope they will be useful for his further researches in a field where he has no superiors and fewer competitors than he could wish.

The third hoard here presented was aquired near Troy in the 30's.

ISTANBUL HOARD A OF 1946

In 1946 Mr. Campbell acquired in Istanbul a large hoard of scyphate coins extending from John II to Alexius III. He had good reason to believe that it was actually found in the city and that it was complete. For the most part the types are familiar but the flans are distinctly smaller than those published by Wroth: 20–23 mm. as against about 30 mm. The difference in the diameter of the dies themselves is only between ca. 16 mm. for the specimens in the hoard and ca. 18 mm. for the published examples, but it is enough to show that they were

---

[1] I have abandoned the convention of calling these coins bronze since analysis shows that they are predominantly copper.

prepared for different sized flans. There is no sign of these having been cut down after striking. Except for the earliest pieces the metal is copper which has been silvered as is plainly visible on many of them. John continued to use billon for these small coins as he did for the larger ones of Wroth's Types 5, 6 and 7. One of his specimens, however, seems to have been silvered copper so that perhaps we may conclude that the new fashion came in at the end of his reign. The flans are neatly made and the dies are competently cut. The inscriptions never appear complete and seldom appear at all but the coins as a whole look neither barbarous nor degenerate. Their fabric is exactly like that described for a much smaller group, the Istanbul Hoard of 1933, *Greek and Byzantine Studies*, 1958, pp. 169–171. That also consisted of coins of Manuel I, Andronicus I, Isaac II and Alexius III, and therefore supports the evidence of the present hoard.

The combination of the two and the fact that this fabric appears so rarely elsewhere makes a prima facie case for the theory that they were struck at the capital. It is, however, by no means clear what their relation is to the large flans published by Wroth and heretofore considered the standard scyphate issues of base metal. We have no convincing published evidence for the provenance of those, but if they also are not products of the mint of the capital we must find some other origin for what are the most impressive examples of this class. If they do all come from the same city we must explain the simultaneous issue of two strictly parallel series. The explanation that comes to mind first is that of two different denominations, and this may indeed be the true one. Remarks on that possibility with regard to different types may be found in Bellinger and Metcalf "A Hoard of Byzantine Scyphate Bronze Coins from Arcadia," *NC*, 1959, pp. 155–164 (but see the comment on p. 163, nos. 195–201).

Whatever the ultimate decision, the first step is the assembly of as much evidence as possible. The contents of the Istanbul Hoard A of 1946 is as follows.

John II, 1118–1143

1–7.   Bust of Christ bearded nimbate facing. Almost obliterated.

Rev.: Bust of John in crown, jewelled collar and divitision,[2] holding in r. cross, in l. *globus cruciger*. On one specimen ΠΤ, on one Δ. The full inscription should be, according to Wroth, ΙѠΔЄСΠΟΤΤΠΦVΡΟΓΝΤ but our ΠΤ shows that there must have been variations.

PLATE XXXI, 1

These are like Wroth's Type 6 (*BMC*, pp. 562f., nos. 53–56) except for the size of the flans. The metal of six of them appears to be billon, as in the BM; one is copper that has been silvered.

Manuel I, 1143–1180

8–10. Bust of Christ beardless nimbate facing. Almost obliterated.

Rev.: Bust of Manuel in crown, jewelled collar, divitision and chlamys decorated with jewels, holding in r.

---

[2] It is impossible to be certain about the names of the garments. Our fullest information comes from Chapter 46(37) of Book I of the *Book of Ceremonies* of Constantine Porphyrogenitus which is well summarized by James D. Breckenridge, "The Numismatic Iconography of Justinian II," *NNM* 144, 1959, pp. 31f., 35–38. In the 10th century it would seem that there were three imperial garments of capital importance: the divitision, the chlamys and the loros. The first was a long tunic, the second a cloak fastened by a fibula on the right shoulder, the third a long narrow scarf worn around the body, one end generally falling over the left wrist. The divitision might be worn alone or with either of the others. All were essentially civilian garb, the third being a development of the ancient *consular trabea*. It is assumed that the garments that appear on these coins are forms of one or other of these three, though we hear also of two more called sagion and tzitzakion whose form we do not know, and the scaramangion seems to have been either a substitute for the divitision or the same article under a different name. But the illustrations do not exactly coincide with the descriptions. The divitision is said to have been decorated but its richness consisted chiefly in its woven or embroidered ornament. On the coins, however, the emperor is sometimes shown standing in a long robe decorated with three rows of jewels (e.g., *BMC*, pl. LXVI, 6–11). It is the upper part of such a robe which appears on the coins of John, our nos. 2 and 3. This is worn with a loros, also jewelled, which crosses it like a broad belt and is draped over the emperor's left wrist. Whether the long garment is a form of divitision or went by another name we cannot say. It is known that by the 14th century the names divitision and chlamys had given place to saccus and mandyas. Codinus, *De Officialibus Palatii Constantinopolitani* XVII, Bonn, p. 93, ll. 19f. ἐνδύεται ἐπάνω τοῦ σάκκου καὶ τοῦ διαδήματος μανδύαν χρυσοῦν. Cantacuzenus in *Historia* I. 41, Bonn, p. 200, l. 6 calls the saccus ἡ πορφύρη. Further research may provide more information about 12th century regalia and we may have to abandon the use of 10th century terms.

labarum, in l. *globus cruciger*. On one specimen MA, on two HΛ.

PLATE XXXI, 2

These bear the same relation to Wroth's Type 9 (*BMC*, p. 574, nos. 34–39) that the preceding ones do to Type 6 of John. The fact that there are only three specimens and that their obverses are much more worn than those of Manuel's other types gives ground for regarding this as his earliest issue, almost exhausted by the time the hoard was buried.

11–86. To l. and r. IC XC. Christ bearded nimbate seated on throne without back.

PLATE XXXI, 3

Rev.: MANYHΛ to l. ΔЄCΠOT to r. (never complete and seldom legible at all). On l. Manuel in crown, jewelled collar, divitision and loros with star of jewels, holding in r. *labarum*, in l. *globus cruciger*. To r. Mother of God nimbate crowning him. Beside her head to l. MP to r. ΘV. In 15 cases the jewels on the loros take the form ⁚ (XXXI, 4), in one ✳ (XXXI, 5); in all the others it is ∴ (XXXI, 6).

PLATE XXXI, 4–6

This is the smaller counterpart of Wroth's Type 11, Variety 1 (*BMC*, p. 575, nos. 40–47). The average wear is much less than on the preceding type.

87–105. Similar, but to l. and r. above seat of throne, stars.
Rev.: Same inscription and type. Jewel always ∴.

PLATE XXXI, 7, 8

This is the smaller counterpart of Wroth's Type 11, Variety 2 (*BMC*, p. 575, nos. 48–50). The degree of wear does not distinguish this from the preceding variety.

106–173. To l. and r. MP ΘV. Mother of God seated on throne with back.
Rev.: MANYHΛ upward on l. ΔЄCΠOTHC downward on r. Manuel in crown, jewelled collar, divitision, chlamys and loros, holding in r. *labarum*, in l. *globus* with patriarchal cross (on two coins the *globus* bears a plain cross).

PLATE XXXI, 9–11

BYZANTINE COPPER COINS 211

This is like Wroth's Type 13, Variety 1 (*BMC*, pp. 576f., nos. 56, 57). The condition does not justify any theory as to whether this is an earlier or later issue than nos. 11–86 and 81–105. In view of the numbers included in this hoard, however, it is a fair presumption that the four issues of Manuel involved were the only ones issued on these small flans or at least that, if Wroth's Type 12 was so issued, it was in small quantity and so early in the reign as to have been no longer in circulation by the time the hoard was buried. Wroth's Type 10 is so rare that it cannot be considered a normal emission of the capital.

Andronicus I, 1183–1185

174–181. To l. and r. M̅P̅ Θ̅V̅. Mother of God standing on dais.
Rev.: ΑΝΔΡΟΝΙΚΟC upward on l. ΔΕCΠΟΤΗC downward on r. (Inscription never complete and mostly illegible). On l. Andronicus in crown, jewelled collar, divitision and loros with jewelled star, holding in r. *labarum*, in l. *globus cruciger*. On r. Christ bearded crowning him.
PLATE XXXI, 12, 13
This is the smaller version of Andronicus' regular copper type (*BMC*, pp. 584f., nos. 5–9). Either he struck few coins in his short reign or they were recalled and restruck after his time.

Isaac II, 1185–1195

182–843. To l. and r. M̅P̅ Θ̅V̅. Mother of God seated facing on throne with back (XXXI, 14).
Rev.: To l. and r. ICAAKIOC ΔΕCΠΟΤΗC in columns. Isaac in crown, jewelled collar, divitision and loros, holding in r. cross, in l. *anexikakia*. The jewels on the loros generally have the form ∴ (XXXI, 15), but in 24 cases the design is ⦂ (XXXI, 16), in 5 it is a star (XXXI, 17). In 30 cases there is a star in the lower l. field (XXXI, 18).
PLATE XXXI, 14–18

844–894. Same type but back of throne decorated, in 34 cases with stars (XXXI, 19) to l. and r., in 13 cases with ·⁞· (XXXI, 20), in 4 cases with ·∴.
Rev.: Same. In one case the jewels on the loros form ⦂, on all others ∴.
PLATE XXXI, 19, 20

Nos. 182–843 correspond to Wroth's Type 4 (*BMC*, pp. 592, nos. 19–31) of which the last two specimens have stars on the back of the throne. It may be questioned whether this difference is of any more importance than the presence or absence of a star in the lower field of the reverse and, in the present state of our knowledge, we cannot say, but the constitution of the Arcadian Hoard (*NC*, 1959, p. 163) is well to bear in mind. There were only two coins of Isaac with stars on the throne's back and they of easily distinguished fabric and condition, marking them as strays in that hoard. There was one with ∴ on the throne like the rest of the hoard in appearance but 67 pieces had the throne undecorated. While it is possible that we have to do here with nothing more than the engraver's preference, as I believe to be the case with the variations of the jewels on the loros, we will do well to suspend judgment until we have more evidence in hand.

Alexius III, 1195–1203

895–1051. +KERO HΘEI. Bust of beardless Christ facing. To l. and r. IC XC (XXXII, 1, 2).
Rev.: On l. Alexius in crown, jewelled collar, divitision and loros with star (XXXII, 3), holding in r. *labarum*. On r. St. Constantine in crown, jewelled collar, divitision and jewelled loros, holding in l. *labarum*. They hold between them *globus cruciger*. Between their heads ʘ (for ὁ ἅγιος). The star on the emperor's loros has sometimes a simplified form ⁝⁝ (XXXII, 4, 5) or ∴ (XXXII, 6–8).

PLATE XXXII, 1–8

In publishing the large specimens of this type Wroth divides them into two varieties: 1, *BMC*, pp. 602f., nos. 15–19 without the name Comnenus; 2, *BMC*, pp. 603f., nos. 20–36. His inscriptions are very fragmentary and they are equally so on our smaller coins. To judge from the traces of letters very few of which would be visible at all in an illustration—any more than Wroth's are—the legend to the left was intended to be AΛEΞIω or AΛEΞIω ΔEC, to the right Tω KωNCTANTI. Of these elements KωN can be read with certainty (XXXII, 9, 10); in several cases there is an upright ω at the top followed by K, KT, KTω or KωN downward (XXXII, 11, 12); once a fairly clear but unintelligible ωHO (XXXII, 13). There is none that can be surely attributed to Wroth's Variety 2. As less than one out of five have any semblance of letters, however doubtful, I have not attempted to divide the issue on that basis.

PLATE XXXII, 9–13

1052–1088. Same type but no inscription except $\overline{\text{IC}}$ $\overline{\text{XC}}$ to l. and r.
Rev.: Same. PLATE XXXII, 14, 15

This is the only instance in which the type may have been modified in the interests of adapting it to a smaller flan. None of the obverses of Alexius' larger bronze has this simplified type, which reverts to Manuel's Type 9 (*BMC*, pl. LXX, 3). However, there is a similar distinction between the two varieties of Alexius' gold Type 1, the former (*BMC*, pp. 599f., nos. 1, 2) with no inscription but $\overline{\text{IC}}$ $\overline{\text{XC}}$, the latter (*BMC*, p. 600, nos. 3–7) with the addition of KЄRO HЄΘI. The type there is Christ seated but the analogy would be suggestively close if it were not for the inscriptions of the reverse. If they paralleled the gold, the copper of this group should be without the name Comnenus, but one of our coins certainly seems to read KOM—(XXXII, 16, 17?) and since no such inscription can be read on any coin of nos. 895–1051 the analogy of the gold holds for neither of these copper varieties.
PLATE, XXXII, 16, 17

ISTANBUL HOARD B OF 1946

In contrast to the homogeneity of the Istanbul Hoard A of 1946, a smaller but more diversified group was acquired by Mr. Campbell, also in Istanbul in 1946. It does not, however, show the characteristics which one would expect. The distinctive issues which compose the previous hoard are here represented by two coins only: Nos. 224 and 251. Nos. 1–7 are the only specimens of what we are accustomed to think of as the normal copper scyphates. On the other hand the presence of Manuel's coins of Fabric B (nos. 8–65) and of Theodore's coins (nos. 252–448) parallels the Troad Hoard, while the prominence of Manuel's Fabric C connects this hoard with that from Arcadia (*NC*, 1959, pp. 155–164). This combination of Fabric B and Fabric C is somewhat surprising since they give every indication of issuing from different mints. It is possible that this is a modern conflation of two different hoards but it is equally possible that it is an ancient collection made by a traveller in different places. It does not seem likely that the collection was made in Constantinople itself no matter how the coins finally got there.

Alexius I, 1081–1118

1. Christ bearded seated on throne with back. Details obscure.

Rev.: Inscription illegible. Half-length figure of Alexius in divitision and jewelled chlamys, holding in r. short cross, in l. *globus cruciger*.   PLATE XXXIII, 1

BMC, p. 543, nos. 14–21, Type 4.
The flan is thin with rough edges, the obverse much worn. Traces of silvering.

John II, 1118–1143

2. To l. and r. I̅C̅ X̅C̅. Bust of Christ bearded. Details obscure.
    Rev.: IѠ ΔЄCΠOTT Π[. Half-length figure of John in divitision decorated with three rows of jewels, holding in r. short cross, in l. *globus cruciger*.   PLATE XXXIII, 2, 3
    BMC, p. 562, no. 53, Type 6.
    Flan fairly regular, both sides worn; traces of silvering.

3. Same type.
    Rev.: Inscription]VPOΓ[. Same type.
    PLATE XXXIII, 2, 3
    Less worn but with no traces of silvering. The style seems rougher.

Manuel I, 1143–1180

The coins of Manuel in this hoard may be divided into three general classes by fabric.

A. Flans large and smooth with traces of silvering. The inscriptions are small and clear but not wholly visible since the coins show signs of much wear. The workmanship is good and is like that of the issues of Alexius I and John II.

B. Flans large but irregular and with no trace of silvering; the edges are frequently bevelled. The inscriptions are large and clear. The workmanship is good.

C. Flans irregular and varying in size, sometimes very small. There is no trace of silvering. There is seldom any legible inscription. The types are poor and carelessly struck.

BYZANTINE COPPER COINS

FABRIC A

4, 5. Bust of Christ beardless. Worn and obscure.
Rev.:]HΛ ΔЄC. Half-length figure of Manuel in divitision and chlamys decorated with a star, holding in r. *labarum*, in l. *globus cruciger*. PLATE XXXIII, 4
BMC, 574, nos. 34–37, Type 9.

6. To l. and r. I̅C̅ X̅C̅. Christ seated on throne without back.
Rev.: Above M̅P̅ to r. Θ̅V̅ ΔЄCΠ. On l. Manuel in divitision and loros decorated with ⁖ holding in r. *labarum*, in l. *globus cruciger*. To r. Virgin crowning him.
PLATE XXXIII, 5, 6
BMC, p. 575, nos. 40–47, Type 11 but BMC has M (MP no. 43) instead of M̅P̅.

7. Similar type but stars to l. and r. above seat of throne.
Rev.: To r. ΘY ΔЄCΠ. Similar type but loros has ⁖ and Manuel holds cross. PLATE XXXIII, 7, 8
BMC, p. 575, nos. 48–50, Type 11, but no mention of cross instead of *labarum*.

FABRIC B

8–41. To l. and r. I̅C̅ X̅C̅. Christ bearded nimbate seated on throne with back. In six cases there is a cross within the nimbus and one pellet in the limbs of the cross (generally one limb visible); in two cases the cross bears ⁖.
Rev.: On l. upward MANOVHΛ on r. downward ΔЄCΠOTHC. Manuel in divitision, chlamys and loros, holding in r. sword downward, in l. *globus cruciger*.
PLATE XXXIII, 9–15
Variations of the inscriptions occur: Six times MANOVH ΔЄCΠOTHC. Three times MANOVHΛ ΔЄCΠOTHC. Once MANΧHΛ ΔЄCΠOTH. These may be considered normal. There are also abberations whose misplaced, malformed or omitted letters prove nothing except the general ineptitude of the diesinkers. The only thing that needs to be recorded is the fact that the great majority of inscriptions are wrong or imperfect.
Not in BMC. The flans are ca. 25–30 mm. in diameter, the dies ca. 15–20 mm. There is no sign of silvering.

42–60. Same type. In eight cases there is a cross with a pellet in its limbs within the nimbus.
Rev.: On l. upward ΔЄCΠOTHC on r. downward MANOVHΛ. Same type. PLATE XXXIV, 1–4

The normal inscriptions are: Three times ΔЄCΠOTHC MANOVHΛ. Five times ΔЄCΠOTH MANOVHΛ. As in the preceding group more often than not the final C of ΔЄCΠOTHC is omitted. In five cases also the form ΔЄCΠOTIC appears.
Sabatier II, p. 209, no. 14, pl. LVI, 1. Not in *BMC*. The fabric is identical with that of nos. 8–41.

61–64. Same type. One with pellet in limb of cross.
Rev.: On l. upward MANOVHΛ on r. downward O ΠOPΦHPOΓЄN. Same type.   PLATE XXXIV, 5–7
The inscription is never complete. It appears as:
OVHΛ   ΠOPΦHPOΓ
OVHΛ   ΠOPΦH
VHΛ   ΠOPΦHP
              O ΠOPΦH
Not in *BMC*. Same fabric.

65.   Same type.
Rev.: On l.]POΓЄΛHT on r.]NOVH. Double struck.
                                                PLATE XXXIV, 8
Not in *BMC*. Flan broader (38 mm.) and partly flattened. Nos. 8–65 obviously belong together, because of the identity of the types. There is at present no evidence as to the order of issue of the different varieties. If they were struck at the capital it seems surprising that they have not been published more often.[3] Manuel uses the title Porphyrogennetos on his gold (*BMC*, pp. 566–569, nos. 1–16) but not elsewhere on his copper. The substitution of H for V is an anticipation of the difficulty that the die-sinkers of Nicaea were to have with the spelling of that word (*BMC Vandals*, pp. 210–213, nos. 1–24).

FABRIC C

IST TYPE

66–68.   Christ seated on throne without back. Stars to l. and r. above seat of throne.

---

[3] Aside from Sabatier II, p. 209, no. 14, the type is recorded from:
Pergamum.   Kurt Regling, "Münzfunde aus Pergamon," *Blätter für Münzfreunde*, Oct.–Nov., 1914, Col. 5681; 1 of our nos. 8–41, 1 of our nos. 42–60, 1 that he records as with ΠOPΦVP[.
Corinth.   Katharine M. Edwards, *Corinth Vol VI, Coins*, p. 145, no. 143; 30 specimens of our first two varieties.
Athens.   Margaret Thompson, *The Athenian Agora Vol II, Coins*, p. 74, no. 1901, 1 specimen; 1 of a number of indications of difference between Athens and Corinth, *Greek and Byzantine Studies*, 1958, pp. 165f.

BYZANTINE COPPER COINS

Rev.: On l. Manuel in divitision and loros, holding in r. cross, in l. *globus cruciger*. On r. Virgin crowning him.

PLATE XXXIV, 9–11

These are the types of no. 7 but the appearence is quite different. The flans are irregular and there is no trace of silvering. The workmanship is poor.

69–71. Similar type.
Rev.: Similar but Manuel holds *labarum* instead of cross.

72–77. Similar type.
Rev.: Similar but what Manuel holds in r. cannot be distinguished.

78–81. Similar but stars not visible.
Rev.: Similar but Manuel holds cross in r.

82–87. Similar. Stars not visible.
Rev.: Similar but Manuel holds *labarum*.

88–91. Similar. Stars not visible.
Rev.: Similar but what Manuel holds in r. cannot be distinguished.

It is clear that nos. 66–91 form a single group. Although the types are those of no. 7 the superior fabric and workmanship of that piece sets it apart from these miserable coins, which are hardly possible to illustrate. It is to be doubted that the variation between cross and *labarum* in Manuel's hand marks a difference of issue though, of course, that is possible. Probably of more significance is the pair of stars above the seat of the throne which are noted in *BMC*, p. 575, nos. 48–50. The striking is so poor that it is frequently impossible to see them but there is no case where they are surely absent as they are on no. 6.

2ND TYPE

92–149. To l. and r. M̄P Θ̄V. Virgin seated on throne with back.
Rev.: In one case on l. upward MANO in two cases traces of letters; in one case on r. downward ΔЄCΠOT in one case ΔЄC. Otherwise no visible inscriptions. Manuel in divitision, chlamys and loros, holding in r. long cross, in l. *anexikakia*. PLATE XXXIV, 12–15

Cf. *BMC*, p. 577, no. 58 where the *anexikakia* is called sword. The fabric there is different and the inscription is in panels to l.

and r. These flans vary in diameter from 21 to 25 mm.; the figure of the emperor varies in height from 11 to 15 mm. The workmanship is invariably poor.

150–215.   Similar type.
Rev.: Similar type. The *anexikakia* cannot be distinguished though there is no sign of the *globus* shown on *BMC*, p. 577, nos. 56f. Probably they are just like nos. 92–149.

The still poorer appearance of nos. 92–215 makes it apparent that they succeeded nos. 66–91. Everything points to the operation of a mint without competent workmen putting out a great deal of money in a hurry.

Not clearly belonging to any of the above groups by fabric

216.   To l. IC. Christ seated on throne without back. To l. and r. stars above seat of throne.
Rev.: To r. ΔЄСΠΟΤ. Half-length figure of Manuel in divitision decorated with three rows of jewels, holding in r. short cross, in l. *globus cruciger*.   PLATE XXXV, 1, 2
Not in *BMC*. The obverse is very much like no. 8, though the condition makes any exact comparison impossible. The reverse type is borrowed from John II, Type 6 (nos. 2 and 3 above) but is quite unlike it. The figure is smaller and the inscription more careless and differently placed. Flan irregular. No trace of silvering.

217.   To l. IC. Same type.
Rev.: To r. ΔЄСΠ. Similar figure except that Manuel holds *anexikakia* in l.   PLATE XXXV, 3, 4
Not in *BMC*.

218, 219.   To l. MH. Virgin seated on throne with back.
Rev.: Inscription illegible. Emperor standing in divitision and loros, holding in r. short cross, in l. *anexikakia*.
PLATE XXXV, 5
Not in *BMC* but the types are very much like Manuel. Flan rounder, like no. 7 but smaller. No trace of silvering.

220.   Bust of bearded Christ. Beard represented by large dots. Very rough workmanship.
Rev.: Half-length figure of emperor in divitision, chlamys and loros, holding in r. short cross, in l. *globus cruciger*.

BYZANTINE COPPER COINS

There are traces to the right which might be a very badly misformed ΔЄC. PLATE XXXV, 6
Not in BMC, but cf. pl. LXX, 5, 6 for the reverse type.

Isaac II, 1185-1195

221–223. To l. and r. M͞P Θ͞V. Virgin seated on throne with back. Rev.: To l. ICAAKIOC in a panel, to r. ΔЄCΠOTHC in a panel. Isaac standing in divitision and loros, holding in r. cross, in l. *anexikakia*. In upper r. Manus Dei crowning him. PLATE XXXV, 7–12
The inscriptions are incomplete. They read:

```
IC      ΔЄC
AA      Π
KI

I       ΔЄC
A       ΠO
          T
          N

A       Π
I
        H
        C
```

BMC, pp. 592f., nos. 19–31.
The flans are ca. 27 mm. There is no trace of silvering.

224. Same type.
Rev.: To l. AA to r. Δ (very obscure). Same type.

```
Π
O
T
H
```

The types and inscription are the same but the flan is only 21 mm. and the fabric is quite different from the foregoing. It is just like the coins illustrated in *Greek and Byzantine Studies*, 1958, pl. 9, 5–7 and there are traces of silvering. The appearance of this and no. 251 is so distinctive as to suggest a different denomination intended or a difference in place of striking.

225–227. To l. I͞C and OЄMMA to r. X͞C and NYHΛ in panels. Bust of Christ bearded, nimbate, one pellet in cross.
The inscriptions are incomplete. The best preserved reads:

```
O
M       N
A       HΛ
```

Rev.: No legible inscription. Emperor in divitision, chlamys and loros, holding in r. *labarum*, in l. *globus cruciger*. The pearls of the loros beneath his l. hand are exaggerated.   PLATE XXXV, 13–16

A specimen of this type is assigned to Isaac II in *NC*, 1959, pp. 163f. because of the resemblance of the obverse type to Isaac's copper, *BMC*, pp. 594f., Type 6 and because of the emperor's pointed beard. We repeat the attribution here because there is as yet no surer one to offer. There are, however, reasons for being doubtful. 1) The bust of Christ on Isaac's bronze is beardless; this one is bearded. 2) The exaggeration of the jewels is a characteristic of gold of Alexius I (*BMC*, pl. LXIV, 3) The traces of inscription on the rev. suggest a reading downward to r. whereas that on the scyphate bronze of Isaac is normally in a panel. 4) The only traces that can possibly be interpreted as a letter look like M to the lower r. which might belong to Alexius III, *BMC*, pp. 603f., Type 4, Variety 2. The question cannot be settled until a really legible specimen is found.

Alexius III, 1195–1203

228–231.   To l. and r. IC XC; to l. upward +KERO to r. downward HΘEI (i.e. KYPIE BOHΘEI). Bust of Christ beardless nimbate ∴ in limbs of cross. The inscriptions are incomplete. The best preserved reads: RO Θ E I.

Rev.: No legible inscription. On l. Alexius in divitision and loros, holding *labarum* in r.; on r. St. Constantine in divitision and loros holding *labarum* in l.; they hold *globus cruciger* between them.   PLATE XXXVI, 1–4

BMC, pp. 602–604, nos. 15–36, Type 4. It is impossible to tell whether these belong to Wroth's Variety 1 or 2.

232–250.   Same type. Details obscure.
Rev.: Same type. Details obscure.

251.   To l. and r. IC XC. No other inscription. Same type.
Rev.: No inscription visible. Same type.
                                           PLATE XXXVI, 5, 6

Like no. 224 this is a small neat flan which bears traces of silvering. Not only its appearance but also the omission of the major inscription on the obv. sets it apart from nos. 228–250 and shows that it belongs with *Greek and Byzantine Studies*, p. 170, nos. 22, 23.

BYZANTINE COPPER COINS

Theodore Lascaris I, 1204–1222

252.   To r. $\overline{\Theta V}$. Virgin seated on throne without back.
Rev.: No inscription visible. On l. Theodore in divitision and loros, holding in r. *labarum*. On r. St. Theodore in military dress holding in l. spear. They hold long patriarchal cross between them.   PLATE XXXVI, 7
BMC Vandals, p. 208, nos. 4–9.

253.   Similar type. Very obscure.
Rev.: Traces of letters to l. and r. Similar type. Peculiar style and fabric. Flattened.   PLATE XXXVI, 8, 9

254–447.   To l. and r. $\overline{IC}$ $\overline{XC}$. Christ seated on throne without back. In 54 cases to l. and r. stars above seat of throne. In some further cases stars may have been on the die but in many cases they were certainly absent.
Rev.: To l. ΘЄΟΔШΡΟC ΔЄCΠΟΤΗC in panel, to r. ΚΟΜΝΗΝΟC Ο ΛΑCΚΑΡΗC. Sometimes stars in lower field l. or r. The inscription is never completely preserved, but all the elements of it are found. Theodore in divitision, chlamys and loros, holding in r. cross, in l. *anexikakia*. Above, Manus Dei crowning him.
PLATE XXXVII, 1–11
This type is like Sabatier II, p. 301, no. 1, pl. LXVI, 7 and *BMC Vandals*, p. 195, no. 4, pl. XXVI, 4 with some differences. Sabatier's emperor holds a scepter and *globus cruciger*, Wroth's a *labarum* and *globus cruciger*. Sabatier's inscription is given as ΘЄΟΔΟΡΟC ΔЄCΠΟΤΗC ΚΟΜΝΗΝΟC Ο ΔΥΚΑC; on the BM coin the words on the right are obliterated. The name Ducas accounts for the attribution by Sabatier and Wroth to Theodore Angelus Comnenus Ducas, Emperor of Thessalonica. But similar as is our type it cannot belong to that Theodore for our emperor certainly bears the name Lascaris, the family name of the two Theodores of Nicaea. The elder had married a daughter of Alexius III and without further right had adopted the name Comnenus which was much more distinguished than his own. Signor T. Bertelè, whose eminence in the field of later Byzantine numismatics is well known, calls my attention to further evidence of this borrowing of Theodore I: G. L. F. Tafel and G. M. Thomas *Urkunden zur älteren Handels- und Staatsgeschichte der Republik Venedig* II (*Fontes Rerum Austriacharum* XIII), pp. 205–207 and Heisenberg *Neue Quellen zur Geschichte des lateinischen Kaisertums*, 1923, II, p. 25. Whether this impressive combi-

nation of names was adopted on his first being crowned in Nicaea in 1206 or was a later confirmation of the security of his position we cannot say. His other copper type seems to bear only ΘΕΟΔШΡΟC and the silver, of which a considerable body has lately been published ("A Hoard of Silver Coins of the Empire of Nicaea," *Centennial Volume of the American Numismatic Society*, 1958, pp. 73–81) has no more than ΘΕΟΔШΡΟC ΔΕCΠΟΤΗC.

Uncertain Emperor

448.   To l. I]C to r. X[C. Christ bearded seated on throne without back. He is nimbate with one or two pellets in the limbs of the cross within the nimbus. To lower l. oval of dots whose function cannot be determined; it may have been decoration of the throne. The surface is pitted and corroded so that much of the detail is lost.

Rev.: No legible inscription except for marks on the lower r. which might include the letters ΔΕ. Emperor in divitision (?), chlamys and loros, holding in r. *labarum* in l. *globus cruciger*. Apparently double struck for the four pearls to the r. of the crown are repeated farther to the r. and above.   PLATE XXXVII, 12, 13

This does not seem to be any published type and it may be an unofficial issue. Not only has the oval of dots on the obverse no parallel but the emperor's undergarment which, if it is the divitision ought to extend to the ground, ends above the ankles giving the appearance of misunderstood military costume.

Signor Bertelè believes that this is a coin of John II and points out that it belongs with Ratto (1930), nos. 2101 and 2102.

449–469.   Illegible scyphate pieces of the same period as the rest of the hoard.

THE TROAD HOARD

A smaller hoard found in the Troad provides valuable evidence because its provenance is sure and it is reasonably certain that it is complete.

Manuel I, 1143–1180

FABRIC B

1–14.   To l. and r. I̅C̅ X̅C̅. Christ bearded nimbate seated on throne with back.

BYZANTINE COPPER COINS

       Rev.: On l. upward MANOVHΛ on r. downward ΛЄCΠO THC. Manuel in divitision, chlamys and loros, holding in r. sword downward, in l. *globus cruciger.*

                                    PLATE XXXVIII, 1-4

15.   Similar.
       Rev.: Similar but much smaller and carelessly drawn. Apparently overstruck on an earlier type.

                                       PLATE XXXVIII, 5, 6

This resembles the foregoing more than any other known type, but its appearance is so unlike that, in default of any recognizable inscription, it must be considered doubtful. It may be a local or unofficial issue.

16-23.   Similar.
       Rev.: On l. upward ΔЄCΠOTHC on r. downward MANOVHΛ. In one case the inscription on r. is MANχHΛ Δ. The final Δ is apparently a mere error. Same type.

                                    PLATE XXXVIII, 7-12

                      FLAT FABRIC

24.   To l. and r. I̅C̅ X̅C̅. Bust of Christ (beardless?) nimbate.
       Rev.: On l. upward MANOVHΛ (badly blundered and obscure). Manuel in divitision, chlamys and loros, holding in r. *labarum*, in l. *globus cruciger.*

                                  PLATE XXXVIII, 13, 14

This is like the coin attributed by Wroth to Manuel of Thessalonica, *BMC Vandals,* p. 199, no. 4, pl. XXVI, 9 (which is the one previously published by Sabatier, II, p. 303, no. 2, pl. LXVI, 10). The only difference between the types is that here the emperor holds a *labarum* in his right hand; on the published coin it is a long cross. All the other details, however, are so similar that there is no doubt that the emperor is the same. This also may be a local or unofficial issue but I agree with the opinion of Bertelè that it is a coin of Manuel Comnenus and not of Manuel of Thessalonica.

25.   Virgin seated. Very obscure.
       Rev.: No inscription legible. Manuel in divitision, chlamys and loros, holding in r. *labarum*, in l.*anexikakia.*

                                       PLATE XXXVIII, 15

Probably either *BMC*, p. 577, no. 58 or previous hoard nos. 92–149. This fabric is better than those but the details are not clear enough to be sure.

Except for nos. 15, 24 and 25 these all belong to the same series of Manuel already listed in the previous hoard, nos. 8–65. It is significant that they were found in Asia Minor together with coins of Theodore Lascaris and unaccompanied by any of the other types of Manuel whose abundance is so well known—unless no. 25 be an exception.

Isaac II, 1185-1195

26, 27.   To l. I̅C̅ and O[E]MMA to r. X̅C̅ [NΥHΛ] in panels. Bust of Christ (bearded?) nimbate.
Rev.: No inscription legible. Emperor in divitision, chlamys and loros, holding in r. *labarum*, in l. *globus cruciger*. The pearls of the loros beneath the l. hand are exaggerated. PLATE XXXIX, 1, 2
This is the type of nos. 225–227 of the previous hoard. The present specimens do not affect the uncertainty of its attribution.

Theodore Lascaris I, 1204-1222

28–31.   Virgin seated. Very obscure.
Rev.: No inscription visible. On l. Theodore in divitision and loros. On r. St. Theodore in military dress, holding in l. spear. They hold patriarchal cross between them.
PLATE XXXIX, 3–5
BMC Vandals, p. 208, nos. 4–9. Previous hoard no. 252.

32–140.   To l. and r. I̅C̅ X̅C̅. Christ seated on throne with back.
Rev.: To l. ΘEOΔWPOC ΔECΠOTHC in panel, to r. KOMNHNOC O ΛACKAPHC in panel. Sometimes stars in lower field l. or r. Theodore in divitision, chlamys and loros, holding in r. cross, in l. *anexikakia*. Above, Manus Dei crowning him. PLATE XXXIX, 6–10
Previous hoard nos. 254–447.

There is a gratifying proportion of rarities in this hoard but more important is its general composition. Of its total of 140 pieces, 131 belong to two issues (considering nos. 1–14, 16–23 as a single group);

22 of Manuel, 1143–1180, 109 of Theodore, 1204–1261. Now everybody knows that coins of Manuel are extremely common and it is not at all surprising to find them still circulating in the 13th century. But it is surprising to find that his coins in this hoard are not of the common types but almost all of a type practically unknown before. So also the great majority of the coins of Theodore belong not to the type already known from *BMC Vandals*, pp. 207–209, nos. 4–11 (5 of them from a single find in Cyprus) and *Greek and Byzantine Studies* Vol. I, pp. 163–168 (Piraeus, Corinth, Athens) but to an unknown one. The simplest explanation of these facts and, I believe, the correct one is that Manuel had a mint in Asia Minor which produced enough money for the district so that his successors did not need to supplement it with their own. But this regional money was not intended to move far from its place of origin, nor did it; hence its rarity in collections. In view of the similarity in style and fabric it is reasonable to suppose that the bronze of Theodore was issued from the same mint, and in the case of Theodore that mint was presumably Nicaea. We then have a workable hypothesis that Manuel had a mint at Nicaea the coins of which, like Theodore's, were sometimes used side by side with the products of other mints, as illustrated in the previous hoard, but may have been expected to satisfy the normal demands of a restricted region.

Why then is the earlier known type of Theodore so slightly represented here (nos. 28–31) and in the larger hoard (nos. 252, 253)? There are two available explanations: a difference in time or a difference in place. If the type with Theodore and St. Theodore was issued later its earliest specimens and those only might have been included with the large number of coins of Theodore alone. The condition of these few pieces does not favor this possibility; they seem rather more than less worn. It would be rash to rely too much on such an argument with coins like these but it is worth keeping in mind. If, on the other hand, Theodore had a second mint nearer the Aegean coast, that would explain why its products should have been carried as far as Corinth while at the same time they had some currency in such a district as the Troad.

We must not ignore the alternative: that the second type of Theodore was the product of Nicaea and that our coins were struck at a second mint in the interior which had previously been used by Manuel but not by his successors. It may be urged in favor of this that a second mint at Nicaea would have been unnecessarily close to Constantinople for Manuel, but it will be recalled that there were late Roman imperial mints at Heraclea, Cyzicus and Nicomedia as well as at Constantinople. It might be argued that the capital mint should be the source of the largest issue and that we now have far more specimens of our type than of the other, but a short time ago that would not have been true and in the future a single large hoard might reverse the picture. We can be sure that Theodore's coins were struck in Asia Minor and reasonably sure that one type of Manuel was also, but whether Theodore had one or more mints and which was Nicaea, we cannot settle definitely with the evidence in hand.

ALFRED R. BELLINGER

PLATE XXXI. 1, John II; 2–11, Manuel I; 12–13, Andronicus I; 14–20, Issac II.
PLATE XXXII. 1–17, Alexius III.
PLATE XXXIII. 1, Alexius III; 2–3, John II; 4–15, Manuel I.
PLATE XXXIV. 1–15, Manuel I.
PLATE XXXV. 1–6, Manuel I; 7–16, Issac II.
PLATE XXXVI. 1–6, Alexius III; 7, Theodore I; 8–9, Theodore I(?).
PLATE XXXVII. 1–11, Theodore I; 12–13, Uncertain Emperor.
PLATE XXXVIII. 1–15, Manuel I.
PLATE XXXIX. 1–2, Issac II; 3–10, Theodore I.

A MILIARESION OF ROMANUS III AND A NOMISMA OF MICHAEL IV

(See Plates XL–XLI)

One of the most beautiful coins in the Byzantine series is the miliaresion with the Virgin and infant Christ on the obverse and the emperor standing with patriarchal cross on the reverse. Encircling the figures on both sides is a hexameter verse, παρθένε σοι πολύαινε ὃς ἤλπικε πάντα κατορθοῖ, which begins on the side with the Virgin and thus denotes it as the obverse.

A choice example of this coin was recently added to the Byzantine collection of the American Numismatic Society and although it has been illustrated in the sales catalog[1] it seems desirable to publish it here with some additional comments. A full description of the coin is as follows:

Obv.: +ΠΑΡΘΕΝΕ COIΠΟΛVAINE

    The Virgin, draped and wearing nimbus, standing facing on footstool, holding infant Christ in l. arm and placing r. hand to her breast; Christ wearing nimbus, raises r. hand in benediction and holds scroll in l.; three linear borders ornamented with eight globules; M̄ Θ above, l. and r. in field.

Rev.: OCHΛΠIKEΠAN TAKATOPΘOI

    The emperor standing facing on footstool, bearded, wearing crown with cross and long jeweled robe with loros which is draped over l. arm, holds long patriarchal cross in r. hand and *globus* surmounted by patriarchal cross in l. hand; three borders ornamented as on obverse.

    2.91 gr. ↙ Plate XLI, 1

---

[1] *Münzen und Medaillen*, XXV (Nov. 17, 1962), no. 728. This specimen is of unusually small flan but it is not unique in this respect. Hirsch Cat. XXIV (1909), no. 3305 and Glendining Cat. (March 9, 1931), no. 672 illustrate specimens with small flans, and the gold coin of this type which is known only from Sabatier's collection is also of this small size. The weight is normal.

The coin is remarkable in many respects. The figure of the Virgin is common on Byzantine coins but this is the only instance on the coinage of the type known as Hodegetria (the Conductress) in which the Virgin, standing or seated, holds the infant Christ in her left arm and places her right hand to her breast.

The Hodegetria is well known in other art media,[2] however, and along with the types portraying the Theotokos, received a stimulus from the Council of Ephesus in 431 which upheld the title "Mother of God" for the Virgin. Though probably of Egyptian derivation it was introduced to Constantinople from one of the eastern centers, Antioch or Jerusalem.[3] One tradition records that Eudocia, the wife of Theodosius II, during her visit to Jerusalem in ca. 443, sent back to Constantinople an image of the Theotokos, reputedly painted by St. Luke and identified as the Hodegetria.[4] At any rate, it was an established form in Byzantine art at an early date and remained popular for centuries. The epithet Hodegetria is inscribed on several icons of the Virgin and thus has become the term commonly applied to this type. However, the same type does bear other epithets as well and there is reason to believe that the Virgin portrayed on this coin is the one known as Peribleptos. This question will be discussed below.

Also remarkable is the metrical inscription on the obverse and reverse of this coin. Only one other instance is known in the Byzantine series—that of an iambic trimeter legend on an issue of Constantine IX (1042–1055).[5] However, metrical inscriptions are common on Byzantine lead seals[6] and such verses or epigrams are well known from Byzantine literature[7] of the tenth and eleventh centuries. Iambic trimeter was the usual form on the seals and in the literature although a few hexameter verses are known too.

---

[2] For other examples of the Hodegetria, cf. G. Schlumberger, *L'épopée byzantine à la fin du dixième siècle* (Paris, 1896–1905), vol. I, pp. 33, 181 and 489; vol. II, p. 192; vol. III, frontispiece.

[3] Cf. O. M. Dalton, *Byzantine Art and Archaeology* (Dover ed., New York, 1961), pp. 386 and 673.

[4] *Enkyklopaidikon Lexikon*, vol. 9, p. 954, s.v. ὁδηγήτρια.

[5] W. Wroth, *Imperial Byzantine Coins in the British Museum* (London, 1908), vol. I, p. lvi; vol. II, p. 502, nos. 16–17.

[6] W. Froehner, "Bulles métriques," *Annuaire de la Société française de numismatique et d'archéologie* VI, 1882, 40–66; VIII, 1884, 312–42.

[7] Cf. K. Krumbacher, *Geschichte der byzantinischen Litteratur* (Munich, 1897).

The coin is attributed to Romanus IV in the standard catalogues but this is undoubtedly incorrect. It was first published in 1847 by Sabatier in his *Iconographie d'une collection choisie de cinq mille médailles* where it was attributed to John II Comnenus (1118–1143).[8] Two coins of this type were described, one of gold and one of silver, the former having a smaller flan. In a letter of Count de Salis to Sabatier in 1859,[9] de Salis stated his belief that the issue belonged to Romanus IV (1067–1071) and it is this latter attribution that appears in Sabatier's *Monnaies byzantines* (1862) and all successive catalogues.[10] However, as early as 1900 Hauberg pointed out the evidence of Danish imitations of this type which were issued in Skåne by Sven Estridsen before 1047.[11] The attribution to Romanus IV is then clearly impossible and Hauberg suggested Romanus III (1028–1034). The article was cited by Wroth but the evidence was not accepted and the coin was listed under Romanus IV. Since this evidence is not acknowledged in any of the standard catalogues it is perhaps worthwhile to review Hauberg's arguments and revaluate the evidence.[12]

The reverse type of the miliaresion, with the standing emperor holding a long patriarchal cross in his right hand and a *globus* surmounted by a patriarchal cross in his left hand, is found on Danish coins of Sven Estridsen, King of Denmark 1047–1075.[13] There can be

---

[8] J. Sabatier, *Iconographie d'une collection choisie de cinq mille médailles* (St. Petersburg, 1847), Byzantines Pl. Sup. XXIV, no. 32 (gold) and no. 33 (silver). However, F. de Saulcy describes the coin in his *Essai de classification des suites monétaires byzantines* (Metz, 1836), p. 246 and assigns it to John I Zimisces (969–976).
[9] *RN* 1859, 448.
[10] J. Sabatier, *Monnaies byzantines* (Paris, 1862), vol. II, p. 172, no. 6 (gold) and no. 7 (silver); Wroth, p. 525, Type 1; H. Goodacre, *A Handbook of the Coinage of the Byzantine Empire* (London, 1928), p. 253, no. 5.
[11] P. Hauberg, "De l'influence byzantine sur les monnaies du Danemark au xie siècle," *Congrès international de numismatique réuni à Paris, en 1900; Procès-verbaux et mémoires* (Paris, 1900), pp. 335–45.
[12] The evidence is accepted by Philip Grierson, however, in his article "Notes on the Fineness of the Byzantine Solidus" (*BZ* 54, 1961, p. 94) in reference to the nomisma of Michael discussed below.
[13] P. Hauberg, *Myntforhold og Udmyntninger i Danmark indtil 1146* (Copenhagen, 1900); cf. pl. VIII and pp. 213f.; no. 1 is of medallic size and a faithful reproduction of the type and nos. 4 and 9 are close derivatives; types 1 and 4 = nos. 5 and 6 on pl. XXVI in the Congress Proceedings.

no doubt that the type was copied from the Byzantine miliaresion in question. In the paper read at the International Numismatic Congress in Paris in 1900, Hauberg stated that the evidence of finds indicated that these imitations were issued by Sven before 1047 when he was a potentate in Skåne and contesting the throne with Magnus the Good.[14] The find evidence is listed and commented upon in Hauberg's study *Myntforhold* which appeared in the same year as the Congress Proceedings.[15] Five hoards (nos. 93, 97, 99, 100 and 101 listed on pp. 169–171) close with one or two specimens only of Sven Estridsen and presumably were deposited shortly after Magnus the Good's death in 1047. According to Hauberg, the issues of Sven included in these finds must date from the period of struggle for power between Magnus and Sven from 1044–1047.[16] These are types 4, 5, 6 and 8, of which 4 is a close derivative of the miliaresion. Type 1, the medallion and exact copy of the reverse of the miliaresion, is not known from any find, yet its analogies with type 4 must date it to the same period and it was undoubtedly the prototype of type 4.

The Danish evidence would seem to be conclusive in dating the coin before 1047 or shortly afterwards,[17] but other factors as well suggest an early date. There have been many reattributions in the Byzantine series as set forth by Wroth and for the eleventh century one can cite Grierson's "The Debasement of the Bezant in the Eleventh Century"[18] and "Notes on the Fineness of the Byzantine Solidus."[19] In these articles, certain gold issues of various emperors (Constantine, Romanus and Michael) are reattributed on the basis of the fineness of the gold. It can be noted that the tetarteron assigned

---

[14] "De l'influence ...," op.cit., p. 341.
[15] See note 13.
[16] *Myntforhold*, op.cit., p. 215.
[17] Cf. Brita Malmer, "En Vikingatida Silverskatt från Gandarve i Alva på Gotland," in *Gotländskt Arkiv*, 1957, p. 32. However, Hauberg's contention that the Byzantine prototypes were introduced by the Norwegian prince, Harald Hardråde, when he returned to Scandinavia in 1046 after several years' service in the Byzantine armies, has been criticized. Cf. Erik Moltke, "De danske runemønter og deres praegere," in *Nordisk Numismatisk Årsskrift* 1950, p. 2 and Brita Malmer, "A Contribution to the Numismatic History of Norway During the Eleventh Century," in *Commentationes de nummis saeculorum IX–XI in suecia repertis* (Stockholm, 1961), p. 356.
[18] *BZ* 47, 1954, 379–94.
[19] *BZ* 54, 1961, 91–97.

by Wroth to Romanus IV (p. 525, Type 3) belongs in fact to Romanus III.[20] These are gold coins, however, and they also bear the legend of a Romanus, neither of which is the case with our miliaresion. Nevertheless, Grierson believes that this coin also belongs to Romanus III and this has subsequently become quite apparent to me from a study of the style and from examination of the literary evidence.[21]

The miliaresion has a triple ringed border on both sides ornamented with eight globules on the center ring. This type of border was undoubtedly influenced by the Arab dirhem although the earliest miliaresion does not show these ornaments.[22] They first are noted on the silver coinage of Leo VI and, except for our miliaresion and another silver coin attributed to Romanus IV, are not evident after John I (969–976). If it can be expected that such ornamentation should fall within a more or less restricted chronological period, the miliaresion cannot be much later than the early eleventh century.

The weight of the coin is of some significance. It fits into the weight-group of silver coinage from the late ninth century down to the reign of Constantine IX (1042–1055).[23] With the succeeding silver coinage the weights have fallen considerably and are not restored until the time of Alexius I. In this case also, the miliaresion fits into the period before the mid-eleventh century.

An important factor is style. The form of the loros worn by the standing emperor is a common one on the late Byzantine coinage and is first noted on the gold coins of Romanus III. In the careful execution of the design and in the treatment of certain details, the miliaresion is most similar to these gold coins of Romanus III (PLATE XLI, 2). On both issues, the crown is identical in that the jeweled pendants on either side of the head terminate in two tear-

[20] *BZ* 47, 1954, 383.
[21] I am indebted to Philip Grierson who first suggested this to me in a letter.
[22] For the influence of the Arab dirhem on the Byzantine miliaresion, see George C. Miles, "Byzantine Miliaresion and Arab Dirhem: Some Notes on Their Relationship," in *ANSMN* IX, 1960, 189–218. Many of the early miliaresia were overstruck on dirhems but due to clipping, they do not show the Arab globules which are always outside the third ring.
[23] Wroth, vol. I, p. lxxvii; however, the data on the silver coinage are undoubtedly incomplete and may be subject to revision. For additional data on Constantine IX, cf. P. Grierson, "Coinage and Money in the Byzantine Empire 498–c.1090," in *Moneta e Scambi nell'alto Medioevo* (Spoleto, 1961), p. 430.

shaped beads rather than in three as in most other cases. The loros, also, on the miliaresion and on some of the gold specimens, is draped across the emperor diagonally while on all other emperors, it is perfectly straight.[24]

Above all, the literary evidence strongly favors an attribution to Romanus III who, according to Michael Psellus, was particularly devoted to the icon of the Virgin. Much of Psellus' account, actually, is concerned with Romanus' piety and the forms it took. The emperor was determined to build a church in honor of the Theotokos that would rival the church of St. Sophia built by Justinian I. This was the church of St. Mary Peribleptos, the building of which, according to Psellus, turned out to be "the cause of evil and the occasion for many injustices."[25] Romanus also was responsible for adorning St. Sophia and restoring the Church of the Holy Sepulchre in Jerusalem. Of special interest, however, in view of the figure of the Virgin on the coin and, particularly, of the hexameter verse accompanying the type—*Whoever puts faith in you, most glorious Virgin, is successful in all things*[26]—is another passage in Psellus. The sentiment expressed in this verse is reminiscent of Psellus' account of the near disaster suffered by Romanus in an ill-considered military venture. In a battle against the Arabs near Aleppo in 1030, the imperial forces were

---

[24] The only exception is found on the nomisma of Michael IV discussed below.
[25] Michael Psellus, *The Chronographia*, tr. E. R. A. Sewter (New Haven, 1953), III, 14.
[26] A similar sentiment is expressed on a miliaresion of Basil II and Constantine VIII (cf. Wroth, p. 476, Type 2 under John I). The legend, much abbreviated, reads Μήτηρ θεοῦ δεδοξασμένη ὁ εἰς σὲ ἐλπίζων οὐκ ἀποτυγχάνει — *Glorious Mother of God, he who puts his hope in you will not fail*. This remarkable miliaresion also portrays the Theotokos but of the type known as Nikopoia with the Virgin holding a medallion of Christ. Traditionally attributed to John I, it has recently been assigned to Basil II (Ph. Grierson, "A Misattributed Miliaresion of Basil II," in *Recueil des travaux de l'Institut d'Études byzantines, No. VIII₁. Mélanges G. Ostrogorsky I*, Belgrade, 1963, pp. 111–16). The occasion of the issue was in commemoration of a victory of Basil over Bardas Phocas in 989. The victory, surrounded by miraculous circumstances, was attributed to the intervention of the Mother of God. The parallels between this issue and our miliaresion are striking with respect to the legend and the portrayal of the Virgin and in view of her intervention at a critical moment in both emperor's lives. Romanus was undoubtedly aware of the earlier coin and, in a similar circumstance, was influenced in his choice of type and legend.

ambushed and Romanus was cut off from his troops, who were routed. Wandering around by himself, Romanus came upon some of his own men in flight who recognized him by the color of his sandals. Then, Psellus says, "... someone came up with the ikon of the Theometor, the image which Roman emperors habitually carry with them on campaign, as a guide and guardian of all the army. This alone had not been taken by the enemy. When the emperor saw this beautiful sight (he was particularly reverent in his veneration for this ikon) he immediately took heart, and holding it in his hands—but no words can describe how he embraced it, how he bedewed it with his tears, how heartfelt were the words with which he addressed it, how he recalled Our Lady's kindnesses in the past and those many times when She, his ally, had rescued and saved the Roman power in moments of crisis. From now on he was full of courage ..."[27]

Though defeated, Romanus miraculously escaped with his life and, collecting his forces, returned to Constantinople. It was at this time that the church of St. Mary Peribleptos was constructed and perhaps also this was the occasion for the beautiful miliaresion with its dedicatory inscription, so appropriate in the light of his recent good fortune.

Of great interest for this association of the miliaresion with the church of St. Mary Peribleptos are the several icons of the Virgin of the so-called Hodegetria type from the monastery of St. Clement at Ochrida. One of these icons bears the epithet "Peribleptos" (PLATE XL)[28] while two others are identified as "Hodegetria" and "Psychosostria" but, in any event, they are not labeled exclusively Hodegetria although all are of the Hodegetria type.[29] The earliest representation of this type of the Virgin to be inscribed with the epithet Hodegetria, illustrated in Kondakov, is somewhat later than the eleventh century and it is apparent that several epithets were used for the same type.[30] Furthermore, the epithet Peribleptos seems to have been first applied to the Virgin by Romanus III, if one can believe Psellus when he

---

[27] Psellus, op.cit., III, 10–11.
[28] Reproduced from V. J. Djurić, Icônes de Yougoslavie (Belgrade, 1961), no. 8.
[29] N. P. Kondakov, Ikonografia Bogomateri (Petrograd, 1915), vol. II, p. 237 and figs. 102, 115 and 116.
[30] Ibid., figs. 93, 94, 95, 96, 97, 99, 102 and 108; cf. also fig. 106 inscribed Η ΕΟΛΕVCΑ.

states, "It was his wish to honour the Theometor with some name of more than ordinary beauty. Unfortunately, he failed to notice that the epithet he gave her was in fact more suited to a woman than a saint ...."[31] In view of all this it would seem almost certain that the Virgin represented on this coin is the "Peribleptos" whom Romanus honored with a church.

Closely associated with this miliaresion, both in style and in the problem of its attribution is an uncommon nomisma, also in the collection of the American Numismatic Society and generally attributed to Michael VI. The description of the coin is as follows:

Obv.: +IhSXISREX RESNANTIHM

Christ, bearded, seated facing on throne without back, wearing nimbus, tunic and mantle; r. hand outstretched in benediction, in l. hand book of the Gospels with ∴ on cover; three borders of dots.

Rev.: +MI XAHL ΔESΠOΤ

The Archangel Michael, winged, standing l. facing, with tunic and mantle, holds *labarum* in r. hand along with the emperor who stands r. facing, with jeweled robe and loros; the *manus Dei* touches crown of emperor; three borders of dots.

4.38 gr. ↓ PLATE XLI, 3

This coin is even more rare than the miliaresion and although other specimens are known to exist in permanent collections, it apparently is not reproduced in sales catalogs.[32] The type with the Archangel Michael is unusual and marks his first appearance on the Byzantine coinage. That it is the Archangel Michael rather than another archangel is assumed from the name of the emperor.

The attribution of this coin has a history similar to that of the miliaresion. First published in Sabatier's *Iconographie* where it was attributed to Michael VII, it appeared later in Sabatier's *Monnaies byzantines* and all successive catalogs under Michael VI (1056–1057).[33] This coin also was imitated on the coins of Sven Estridsen which ap-

---

[31] Psellus, op.cit., III, 15.
[32] Grierson states (*BZ* 54, 1961, 94 n. 3) that he knows of only four specimens.
[33] *Iconographie*, Byzantines Pl. Sup. XXIV, no. 4; *Monnaies byzantines*, vol. II, p. 161, no. 2; Wroth, vol. II, p. 509, type 2; Goodacre, p. 236, no. 2.

pear in the early finds dated shortly after 1047.[34] Hauberg suggested Michael IV or V as a more likely attribution but the evidence was ignored for Michael as well as for Romanus.[35] Recently, Philip Grierson assigned it to Michael V (1041–1042) on the basis of the fineness of the gold.[36] It is my belief that the coin belongs to Michael IV (1034–1041).

The Danish imitations of this coin and of the Romanus coin are dated to the period 1044–1047. It is clear that the Danish issues were of about the same time and it is suggestive that the Byzantine prototypes were also nearly contemporary. Further, the two coins reveal a uniformity of style that must place them very close to each other. The form of the loros is identical in both cases even to the diagonal sweep across the emperor. There is a triple border on our nomisma which is also found on the definitely attributed series of Michael IV[37] (PLATE XLI, 4) but not on the issue assigned to Michael V or VI.[38] Grierson's data for the fineness of the gold show conclusively that the nomisma cannot belong to Michael VI but do not help in the choice between Michael V or Michael IV. Of the two specimens examined by Grierson, one shows a figure of $21\frac{1}{2}$ carats, the other $22\frac{1}{2}$. In comparison, those of Michael IV were 23, 22, $20\frac{1}{2}$, $21\frac{1}{2}$ and $19\frac{1}{2}$ carats.[39] The fact, however,

---

[34] Cf. Hauberg, *Myntforhold*, pl. VIII, types 7, 8 and 11 of which type 7 copies the obverse and reverse of the nomisma and types 8 and 11, the reverse only. Type 8 is included in the early finds mentioned above, pp. 230f.; type 7 = no. 3 on pl. XXVI in the Congress Proceedings.

[35] "De l'influence ...," p. 340 but in the *Myntforhold*, p. 128 he names only Michael IV.

[36] *BZ* 54, 1961, 94–95.

[37] Wroth, p. 496, nos. 1–5. The Dumbarton Oaks specimen also shows three rings while the line drawing in Sabatier's works shows two rings and is undoubtedly the source of Wroth's description.

[38] Wroth, p. 498, no. 1 (Michael V) which Grierson assigns to Michael VI (*BZ* 54, 1961, 94).

[39] *BZ* 54, 1961, tables II and III, pp. 93–95. The attribution to Michael IV means that Michael V is left without a coinage if Grierson's reattribution of Wroth, p. 498, no. 1 (Michael V) to Michael VI is correct (see n. 38 above). However, it would not be surprising that no coinage of the four-month reign of Michael V has survived to us. On the other hand, Grierson has not provided data on the fineness of this issue and, believing that such data would be helpful in determining the issuing authority of this coin, I tested the ANS specimen. The results were inconclusive, in my opinion, for the coin was of approximately 19 carat gold (specific gravity 16.5) which is a degree of fineness possible for either Michael V or VI if one can assume that the debasement initiated by Michael IV was continued by Michael V.

that Michael IV was Romanus' immediate successor and reigned for seven years while Michael V's reign extended for only four months is a consideration favorable to the attribution of the coin to Michael IV.

Once again the literary sources are most helpful for they reveal to us circumstances that explain the minting of this special issue. About Michael IV we learn from Psellus that he was a very devout man and a very sick man. He was afflicted with epilepsy and dropsy, and concern over his health dominated most of his actions. Psellus states, "He tried various methods, such as prayers and purifications, in the hope of being cured, but he was confident of ultimate recovery for one reason in particular—the building of a church in honour of the Anargyroi, in a suburb of the city, on the east side."[40] It was a magnificent structure, according to Psellus, and when it was finished Michael dedicated it as a monastery. Psellus also states, "The object of all this was, in some measure, to honour the Deity, but the emperor also hoped to propitiate the 'Servants of God'; perchance they might heal his affliction. It was all in vain, though, for the measure of his life was fulfilled, and his health still continued to break up."[41]

The Holy Anargyroi were the saints, Cosmas and Damian, physicians of the third century who accepted no pay for their services and who were martyred under Diocletian.[42] The fact that it is the Archangel Michael portrayed on this coin is consistent with the emperor's actions and beliefs for the Archangel Michael was particularly venerated as a healer.[43] His cult flourished in various places where springs with medicinal waters were said to have been caused by him and at Constantinople he was the great heavenly physician. Illustrative of his worship as a healer is this poem from the Palatine Anthology: "Here is kept divine help for wretched men afflicted in mind or body. For vexing trouble at once is put to flight, Michael, by thy name, thy image, or thy house."[44] It is reasonable to infer that honoring St. Michael on this coin was another attempt on the part of the ailing emperor to propitiate a saint whose healing powers were well known.

JOAN M. FAGERLIE

[40] Psellus, op.cit., IV. 31.
[41] Ibid., IV. 32
[42] *The Catholic Encyclopedia*, vol. IV, p. 403.
[43] Ibid., vol. X, pp. 275f.
[44] *The Greek Anthology* (Loeb Classical Library), tr. W. R. Paton, vol. I, Book I. 32.

THE STAVRATON:
EVIDENCE FOR AN ELUSIVE BYZANTINE TYPE[1]
(SEE PLATES XLI–XLII)

To Umberto Dorini and Tommaso Bertelè economic historians owe a special debt. The publication of Giacomo Badoer's account book[2] affords a view of commerce in the Byzantine capital shortly before its demise that is unique both in wealth of detail and range of interests. This is surely the most useful document to be made available in the field since Evans's edition of Pergolotti.[3]

For the numismatist the *Libro dei Conti* is a mixed blessing; or, rather, a blessing in disguise. The information it purveys is concealed behind Venetian orthography and some unusual terms. The accounts are kept in a "language" that has to be learned:[4]

> a di dito per el dito ser Carlo Chapelo per
> l'amontar de livre 10 de stravati grievi dadi
> a Critopulo de la zecha de so hordene, a perp.
> 22 car. 6 .... a c. 101 perp. 226. car. 6[5]

Further acquaintance with Badoer's columns elucidates both their manner and their contents. One phase, however, that does not readily offer a meaning is *stravati grievi*. Occurring rarely in the book,[6] on

---

[1] I am grateful to the staff of the American Numismatic Society, and in particular to Professor Howard Adelson, for much helpful advice in the preparation of this note. From the society's vault I have taken figures 1–4; figures 5 and 6 are after Laurent.

[2] Giacomo Badoer, *Il Libro dei Conti* (Rome, 1956).

[3] F. B. Pegolotti, *La Pratica della Mercatura*, ed. Allan Evans, Mediaeval Academy of America (Cambridge, Mass., 1936).

[4] Of one such difficulty the editors give forewarning: depending on the preceding verb, *per* in the text can mean "to" or "from"—an important distinction in business!

[5] Badoer, p. 179 (9 November, 1437).

[6] Bertelè, "L'Iperpero bizantino dal 1261 al 1453," *Rivista Italiana di Numismatica*, LIX (1957), p. 86, suggests that the phrase occurs often (spesso). Inspection of the account book revealed only four occasions on which it is employed. Bertelè's article is devoted to an elucidation of some of the problems raised by Badoer's text. It is more enlightening about the Palaeologan economic situation than it is about the actual currency of the period.

each occasion it describes coins weighed in bulk and then converted into the familiar *hyperpyra* and carats.

Evidently, in addition to his dealings in ginger, slaves, canvas, sugar, gold-leaf, horses, wine and other commodities, Badoer made a not insubstantial profit out of money itself. But we are concerned not so much with the *utilità* to which he put his specie as with the coins themselves. *Tornesi*, florins, aspers, *carlini* and ducats all appear: about none of these is there the darkness—unrelieved by Du Cange or any other lexicographer—that surrounds the *stravati*. The editor is of little help. Having established that the term refers to a silver coin "on which a cross is particularly visible,"[7] Bertelè abandons the problem. Certainly little more can be deduced from the text beyond the fact that *stravato* is a likely transliteration of σταυράτον and that this designation indicates an actual coin rather than a money of account.[8]

Is the name given to this coin-with-a-cross merely a piece of commercial *argot* used only in the capital towards the middle of the fifteenth century? No *stravato* appears in the list of one hundred and sixty-eight coins in the *Pratica della Mercatura*, written almost exactly a hundred years before Badoer closes his accounts, despite its author's long residence in the eastern Mediterranean in the service of the Bardi and his almost certain visits to his bank's branch in Constantinople.[9] The *lacunae* in Pegolotti's work have been justly observed,[10] but it is improbable that he would have omitted such a term had it been current commercial usage in his time. Again, if the *stavraton* was simply a local nickname for the *hyperpyron* it would be unlikely to occur in a foreigner's business accounts. *A fortiori*, it would not appear with the infrequency that it does in the *Libro dei Conti*, a rarity that suggests the author especially noted the coin by name rather than using it loosely as a synonym for the more usual designation.

---

[7] Ibid.

[8] Professor G. L. Kustas has suggested that *stavraton* could, by extension, indicate a crooked or bent coin. Its use in the context of Badoer's account, however, precludes such an interpretation.

[9] Evans, op.cit., pp. xx–xxi.

[10] P. Grierson, "The Coin List of Pegolotti," *Studi in onore di Armando Sapori*, I (Milan, 1957), 492.

That the name was not, in fact, confined to the mercantile world of the capital is indicated in a nearly contemporary Greek source, an anonymous document known to numismatists for nearly fifty years. On end-papers used to strengthen a thirteenth century codex of Aristides, Sokrates Kugeas discovered the personal *aide-memoire* and account-book of an important churchman of Thessalonika.[11] These notes cover a period from 1419 to 1437 and deal mostly with the cleric's ecclesiastical revenue. Being obviously incomplete, they give no impression of a formal account-book. For our purposes it is of greater importance that they record his petty receipts than that they present a thorough picture of his finances. It is our good fortune that he reveals himself to posterity as much concerned with secular things as was Giacomo Badoer. These receipts, while less systematic than the Venetian's, show where lay at least one Greek ecclesiastic's treasure and his heart also.

His piece-meal accumulation is lovingly recorded; with pleasure the cleric notes that between October, 1425 and November, 1426 he received a monthly increment of ten *stavrata*.[12] He uses the term often by itself, sometimes adjectively to qualify *nomismata*. The *hyperpyron* figures less frequently: where it does occur it is never accompanied by *stavraton*.

An entry of 1426 provides us with an exchange of twelve *stavrata* for one hundred aspers.[13] And this rate is sufficiently close to that given by Badoer—asp. 11 *a perparo*[14]—for us to be certain that the *stavraton* and the *hyperpyron* represent the same unit of value. When associated with the *nomisma*—as they are in both the Venetian and Thessalonikan texts—we are faced with the problem of three names for the same concept. Any solution must wait upon the numismatic evidence. However, since our two sources are not exactly con-

---

[11] "Notizbuch eines Beamten der Metropolis in Thessalonike," *Byzantinische Zeitschrift*, XXIII (1914–1919), pp. 143–163. In his notes, Kugeas determines the chronology of the entries and where they were written. This dating and location (Thessalonika and Constantinople) I have followed throughout.
[12] Ibid., p. 150.
[13] This passage is quoted by V. Laurent, "τὸ πολίτικον, monnaie divisionnaire de l'époque des Palaeologues," *Cronica Numismatica Si Arheologica* (Bucharest), CXIV (1940), p. 17, where he ascribes the passage to 1452. As far as I can determine, Laurent has been the only Byzantinist to make use of Kugeas's text.
[14] Badoer, p. 253 and passim.

temporary it is worth digressing to see what information can be gleaned from their differences.

We should expect variants of value for together the two account-books cover nearly a quarter of a century. To the Greek, in 1426, twelve and one half aspers were worth one *hyperpyron*. To Badoer, a decade later, the exchange rate was 11:1. Had the asper weakened or the *hyperpyron* strengthened ? At the same time, the ecclesiastic notes that the *hyperpyron* is worth one fourth of the Φλοριον βενέτικον.[15] For the ducat—which is undoubtedly the coin in question—the merchant would give not more than three *hyperpyra*. Thus on two separate, if related, exchanges the Greek currency seems to have hardened. This may only have been a temporary rallying but it nonetheless should give pause to those who have suggested a progressive and inflexible devaluation of the *hyperpyron* under the later Palaeologi.[16] Much more comparative study of the account-books needs to be done before we will be able to trace the Palaeologan monetary situation in its true complexity. But it is already evident that the postulate of an unswerving descent into fiscal and monetary chaos is a gross oversimplification. The capital, at least in the period of Badoer's accounts (1436–1440) remained a thriving commercial center. Written a hundred years after Nicephoros Gregoras[17] had recorded the daily decline of the *hyperpyron*, the Venetian text offers little or no substantiation for this *fin-du-monde* attitude.

Bertelè has pointed out that the few gold *nomismata* known of Manuel II's reign (1391–1423) are all of considerable weight (averaging 4.70 gr.) and high title, higher indeed than any gold since the Comnenian era.[18] They all bear the traditional iconography and nothing about them suggests the description *stavraton*. Furthermore, their good alloy would have given them a ratio of almost 1:1 in relation to

---

[15] Kugeas, p. 149. The description of ducats as Φλορια βενέτικα in this Byzantine text suggests some corrective to the general view that the Venetian coin dominated the commerce of the eastern Mediterranean, while the florin ruled only in the west. The good fortune of the *fiorino* in Byzantium is also suggested by the adoption of the Baptist motif on *nomismata* of John V Palaeologos.

[16] Cf. G. I. Bratianu, "L'Hyperpère byzantine et la monnaie d'or des republiques italiennes," *Etudes byzantines d'histoire économique et sociale*, Paris, 1938, pp. 225–237.

[17] *Hist. Byz.* (ed. Bonn), III, 52.

[18] Bertelè, "L'iperpero bizantino," p. 82.

the *ducato d'oro* while, as has been seen, our early fifteenth century texts suggest a rate of three or four to one. The inevitable conclusion is that the *hyperpyron*, if it is a coin and not a unit of reckoning, is silver. A unique passage in Badoer suggests as much: *l' utilità che ho fato di hi perperi grievi vendudi per arzento*.[19] The debased quality implied in this passage would account for their evaluation by weight although there is no intimation in the anonymous Greek's account that he ever took such a measure.

Weighing was, of course, normal procedure for transactions involving bronze and the great majority of cross-bearing Palaeologan coins are of this material. With the exception of Bellinger[20] and Whitting,[21] Byzantine numismatists have unjustifiably ignored the bronze and thus missed the sometimes close relations between its iconographical types and those on the precious metals.

The cross, for instance, has been regarded as an exceptional motif on later Byzantine issues. Only ten years ago Stewart suggested that the emblem, appearing on a fourteenth century bronze scyphate, was "of course not Byzantine but purely Western in origin" and that the coin was "a Latin-Byzantine hybrid."[22] The piece in question undoubtedly has an obverse motif closely connected with the Neapolitan *gigliati* and their Rhodian and Turkish imitations. But crosses akin to this had occurred on Byzantine bronze long before the Latin conquest. Bellinger presented at least fourteen different types of cross that appeared between the accession of Michael IV (1304) and the death of Alexius I Comnenus (1118).[23] And cruciferous issues of the thirteenth and fourteenth centuries held very close to these prototypes. In this way a bronze of Andronicus II's first period of lone rule (1282–1295) has a reverse with *crux ansata* and pellets (PLATE XLI, 1) that derives directly from a type of Andronicus I Comnenus.[24]

---

[19] P. 334 (18 January 1437).
[20] *The Anonymous Byzantine Bronze Coinage*, NNM 35 (New York, 1928).
[21] "The Anonymous Byzantine Bronze," *Numismatic Chronicle*. 6th series, XV (1955), pp. 89–99.
[22] "A Latin-Byzantine Hybrid," *Studies Presented to D. M. Robinson*, II (St. Louis, 1953), 251–260.
[23] Op.cit.
[24] Cf. J. Sabatier, *Description générale des monnaies byzantines* (Paris, 1862), pl. LVII, 14 and W. Wroth, *Catalogue of the Imperial Byzantine Coins in the British Museum*, II (London, 1908), 617, 11.

Following the re-taking of Constantinople by the Greeks, coins with cross motifs appear to be linked in series rather than created as novel, independent types without precedent or successor.

For example, the device on a flat bronze of Andronicus II and his grandson (PLATE XLI, 2)[25] is very like that on the scyphate *nomisma* of Michael VIII included in the Ratto sale.[26] From the same period of Andronicus's reign (1325–28) there exists in the cabinet of the American Numismatic Society an interesting variant (PLATE XLII, 3) on Wroth's scyphate with large cross and $\begin{smallmatrix}Β\boldsymbol{\Theta}\\Β\boldsymbol{\Theta}\end{smallmatrix}$.[27] On the A.N.S. coin the fabric is flat and the letters set at forty-five degrees, rather than upright, within the quadrants of the cross. Again unknown to Wroth, there exists from Andronicus II's second reign alone a bronze with the reverse legend ΒΟΗΘΕ ΚΥΡΙΕ enclosing a cross pattée (PLATE XLII, 4) identical with that on a silver *nomisma* of John V Palaeologos published by Sabatier and unrecorded since then.[28]

This last coin bears the legend πολιτικον and is used by Laurent to demonstrate that these issues were actual coins rather than tokens.[29] Of seven such *politika*, four carry crosses. One is of billon,[30] the others of silver (PLATE XLII, 5, 6). In the light of their existence, we must reconsider Bertelè's refusal to recognize the *stravati*.[31] The very rarity of cross-bearing types in silver is perhaps reflected in the infrequency with which they appear in Badoer. But the fact of their existence is attested to both by the documents and the coins themselves.

[25] Wroth, op.cit., p. 628,50. Nearly forty years ago, Bertelè published a flat bronze coin of Andronicus II with a cross similar to our figure 2. It dates, however, from this emperor's joint reign with Michael IX (1295–1320) and shows the co-emperors on the obverse with four rays in the center and a six ray star in each of the quadrants (*Zeitschr. für Numism.*, XXVI, 1926, pl. III, 79). Here Bertelè gives it to the reign of the two Andronici (1325–28) but A. Veglery and G. Zacos, "The coins of Andronicus II with the inscription 'Emperor of the Romans'," *Num. Circ.*, LXIX (1961), attribute it to the joint reign with Michael IX.
[26] *Monnaies byzantines et d'autres pays contemporaines* (Lugano, 1930), no. 2219.
[27] Wroth, op.cit., p. 627, 49.
[28] Sabatier, II, pl. LXII, 16.
[29] "το πολίτικον," p. 6.
[30] This coin appeared in the Cahn sale of May, 1932 (catalogue 75, no. 1749) where it is described as silver and attributed to John V Palaeologos.
[31] "L'Iperpero bizantino," p. 86.

All the silver coins illustrated are of the reign of John V (1341-1391), either alone or with his son, or else are anonymous issues. Thus there is no way of showing—except by the evidence here adduced—that they were current in the fifteenth century, in the Byzantium of Giacomo Badoer and the nameless cleric whose notes are so fortunately preserved. But the imperial government in this period did not attempt to withdraw older coins;[32] there is no *a priori* reason why some of these fifty year old coins should not come into the hands of our two sources. In the capital, in its last days almost ignorant of gold and desperately short of silver,[33] what survived would almost certainly have been employed in commerce.

Every cruciferous bronze that we possess dates from before the accession of John V (15 June 1341). Their silver successors, as we have seen, follow an iconographical tradition as old as the eleventh century.[34] To all of them, silver and bronze alike, the name *stavraton* could be equally applied. It was apparently used only for the silver to distinguish them from the more usual *nomismata*, those that did not bear the emblem. The account books still speak of the *hyperpyron*, but where this does not refer to a very rare gold minting,[35] the term probably represents a concept, an ideal standard like the carat, as much as a specific currency unit. The silver expression of this unit was that which bore a cross.

The conservative character of Byzantine money—the feature which makes its study at once so monotonous and so fascinating—showed itself for the last time when Palaeologan moneyers set upon their silver the crosses which had previously adorned the bronze. For the merchant, the ecclesiastic, indeed for anyone concerned with recording his transactions, the term *stavraton* graphically distinguishes this type of silver not only from other types but equally from the cross-bearing bronze. The difference in value is identified by name; for this reason Badoer specifies *stravati* when he receives them.

---

[32] R. S. Lopez and I. W. Raymond, *Medieval Trade in the Mediterranean World*, (New York, 1955), p. 15.
[33] R. S. Lopez, "The Dollar of the Middle Ages," *Journal of Economic History*, XI (1953), p. 229.
[34] Supra, p. 156.
[35] "L'Iperpero bizantino," p. 81.

There is a close parallel in the history of Venetian coinage. When the maritime republic first minted its silver *soldino* (ca. 1330), the coin was popularly called the *ginocchiello* for the kneeling doge on its obverse.[36] With equal justice, the name could have been applied to the *ducato d'oro* then familiar for more than forty years. But the descriptive epithet was reserved for the motif as now used on a coin of different material and value. When, some time after 1341, the cross was impressed on Byzantine silver instead of bronze an analogous situation arose. Some means of recording the change had to be found and the obvious choice was the new coin's salient feature. To name something is to distinguish it and the distinction is all the more important when otherwise confusion is likely. With the coin in his hand, Badoer knew immediately if it were silver or bronze, even though he might not know the quality of its content. But in a document intended for later use some record of this identification was necessary. In a city and a century where gold and silver were heavily alloyed, when the *nomisma* and the *hyperpyron* were quite other than they had been in more prosperous days, *stavraton*, to Greeks and Italians, meant a specific coin. Its name remains as a monument to that period of confusion and the evidence of one small effort at clarification.

ANTHONY CUTLER

[36] N. Papadopoli, *Le monete di Venezia* ... (Venice, 1893), I, 159.

A HOARD OF LEEUWENDAALDERS FROM AINTAB
(See Plates XLIII–XLIV)

In 1959 the American Numismatic Society acquired from Vassar College a lot of 115 Dutch Leeuwendaalders and half daalders which bore the unmistakable aspect of hoard specimens in that they were covered with a green copper compound. The earliest date was 1613 and the latest 1692 and the mints of all six provinces that had struck leeuwendaalders were represented as well as the three cities of Overijssel: Deventer, Kampen and Zwolle.

No one at Vassar knew where they had been found, how they had come to Vassar, how long they had been there or even whether they represented an entire hoard or only a part of one, but with the kind assistance of Mrs. Hilda Pratt Benedict, Vassar-Class of 1910, Mrs. Alfred Coons, Mrs. Daniel Dorman, Dr. Fred Field Goodsell, American Board of Commissioners for Foreign Missions, Miss Elsa Hasbrouck, Vassar-Class of 1909 and Mr. George T. Welch, Comptroller of Vassar College, to all of whom the author is greatly indebted, the actual history of the hoard was finally discovered.

As must be expected with events that took place more than fifty years ago the memories of all the parties that could give us information do not coincide in every detail, but by and large the facts could be established with sufficient certainty.

On the morning of February 17, 1906, the main building of the Girl's Seminary at Aintab (now Gaziantep), Turkey was destroyed by fire and as it had already become inadequate for the purposes of the growing school it was decided that a new building should be constructed on a nearby site. During the excavations for that building in the summer of 1906 the coins were found.

No eyewitness of the event appears to be living, at least not in the United States, but we are fortunate that the late Mrs. John Merrill, the acting principal of the school, recorded the discovery and ensuing events at the time. Mrs. Merrill wrote:

"A Wonderful Find

When the foundations for the new school building were being dug, the workmen came upon a large iron pot, shaped like a goldfish bowl, and filled with silver coins. The head workman sat on top of the jug to prevent the men from grabbing the coins, and sent word to Mr. Sanders. There were 1300 of the coins, most of them about the size of a silver dollar, the others of a half dollar. They were Dutch coins and many bore the date 1639! They had Latin mottoes around the edge, a lion on one side, and a shield and a head on the other. The larger number bore the words: *Confidens Domino Non Movetur*. When we came to America in 1908 we brought them with us and were able to sell most of them for belt buckles, pins, etc. to the people who contributed a dollar (or 50¢ for the small ones) to the new building. Who buried them and why remained a mystery."

The Mr. Sanders mentioned in Mrs. Merrill's story was Dr. Charles S. Sanders, President of Central Turkey College, a boy's school that was also located in Aintab and where the late Dr. Merrill taught. Eventually Dr. Sanders had to clear the hoard with the Turkish authorities as there was a law that all "antiquities" found in the Turkish Empire had to be delivered up to the government. In the case of the Lion Dollars, however, that had been found in Aintab it was finally decided by the authorities that coins sufficiently resembling them had been in circulation recently enough to permit the verdict that they were not antiquities.

As for the contents of the hoard the most important statement in Mrs. Merrill's account is that there were 1300 coins in the pot. Since she took charge of them and eventually sold most of them we must accept this statement as at least roughly accurate. In addition she states positively that all the coins were Dutch, that all had the lion on one side and "a head" (i.e., the knight) and a shield on the other, that all had Latin mottoes and that they were of two sizes, dollar and half dollar. This would confirm that all the coins in the pot were either leeuwendaalders or half daalders. As she says, most of them have the legend **CONFIDENS DOMINO NON MOVETUR** although there are some with other Latin mottoes as **DA PACEM IN DIEBVS NOST** which appears on some of the Zwolle coins in the Aintab Hoard.

This lot, in fact, represents the balance remaining of the hoard after the greatest part had been sold by Mrs. Merrill, the proceeds of those sales being used to support the Girl's School in Aintab.

In addition to the 115 pieces found at Vassar we have only been able to trace eight more of the 1300 coins; namely two daalders which have been made into pins and which are the property of the two daughters of Mrs. Merrill: Mrs. Coons and Mrs. Dorman, two which we acquired from Miss Ruth Blankenhorn, who was a student at Vassar at the time, one of them a daalder and the other a half daalder, both of which Miss Blankenhorn kindly donated to the ANS, and finally four pieces which are the property of Miss Harriet Norton, who had been a teacher at the school. Two of these are daalders, one a half daalder and one a testoon of Lorraine. Such testoons are occasionally found in Leeuwendaalder hoards in the Middle East, and the piece in question both by its aspect and Miss Norton's testimony came from the Aintab hoard. But there cannot have been many, as Mrs. Merrill does not mention quarter-size pieces.

Out of about 1300 pieces we have been able to catalogue only 123, and it is not even likely that this sample is in any way representative of the whole.

It is, of course, well known that the leeuwendaalders, at least from about 1620 on, were struck for circulation in the Levante and were struck in great quantities, the latter being to some extent supported by the fact that no two specimens in the hoard are from the same pair of dies. It is also known that they circulated well into the nineteenth century, as the Turkish authorities confirmed, and the thoroughly mixed aspect of the hoard would seem to indicate that it, too, circulated a long time before it was buried.

Even if we had the whole hoard, the end date would be meaningless for the determination of the burial date since leeuwendaalders were struck only in small quantities after 1700 and not at all after 1713 while they circulated for more than a century after that. The "large iron pot" which might have given some indication of the burial date has disappeared, but from the location in which the hoard was found, it might be conjectured that the hoard might have been buried in the latter part of the eighteenth or early in the nineteenth century during the internal disturbances with the Derebeys, or perhaps during the war between Sultan Mahmud II of Turkey and Mohammed Ali of Egypt when the latter's armies defeated the Turks at Aleppo in 1832 and advanced into Anatolia. Aintab is about 100 miles due north of Aleppo.

The principal reason that this remainder of the Aintab Hoard has been considered in such detail is that it contains a few pieces that have heretofore been unknown and also that this is the first time that any Near Eastern hoard of leeuwendaalders has been published in any detail at all; the only previous publications, namely, those of the Beyrouth Hoard and the Saida Hoard being of extreme brevity. The previously unknown pieces are the following:

a. Westfriesland Daalder 1674 (No. 15)

Previously unknown with a crowned lion in the shield on the obverse.

b. Gelderland Half Daalder 1643 (No. 44)

Flan rather small and while we read the date as 1643 it might conceivably be 1645 but either of these dates was previously unknown to van Gelder who listed under Gelderland only half-daalders of 1640, 1641 and 1646. The whole daalder for 1643 is listed but that for 1645 is not.

c. Kampen Daalder 163– (No. 68)

Date not legible in its entirety and from its position the 3 could conceivably have been a mint mark. This seemed a possibility especially since otherwise no leeuwendaalders of Kampen are known between the years 1597 and 1646. The ANS not having any similar coins of Kampen that could have been used for comparison, a rubbing was submitted to the Royal Cabinet at the Hague. Dr. van Gelder very kindly informed us that no mint mark other than the lys of the Wijntgens family could be expected since that family had been in charge of the municipal mint from 1590 until 1653 and that therefore the shape in question could be nothing else than a 3. Also it could not be ruled out that some leeuwendaalders could have been minted in Kampen in 1639 as there is a copper duit of 1639 and a schelling with the title of Ferdinand III. Furthermore the reversed N (И) which appears on the piece under discussion also appears constantly on schellingen of Kampen with the title of Emperor Mathias. There is however no evidence that the mint in Kampen operated in the thirties before 1639. In addition to its date the piece is also remarkable because of the two small wavy lines appearing in front of the lion in the shield on the obverse which represent the waves characteristic of the lion in the arms of Overijssel.

d. Kampen Daalder 1689 (No. 110)
This piece fills in the series listed by van Gelder under Kampen that runs from 1681 to 1693. The date 1689 has previously been known only in a gold specimen.

e. Zwolle Daalder 1633 (No. 112)
This piece has the lion in the shield on the obverse charged with the shield of Zwolle, a type previously unknown.

f. Zwolle Daalder 1639 (No. 113)
While there is a daalder in the hoard (No. 114) which corresponds to v. G. Zwolle III, i.e., with the large lion on the reverse not charged with the shield of the city, this other daalder of 1639 (No. 113) is different from any type previously listed by either Verkade or van Gelder. On the obverse the shield displays St. Michael with not one but two shields of the city and on the reverse the large lion is charged with the city arms. Thus, were it not for the different obverse the piece would fall under v.G. type Zwolle II, for which only the date 1637 had previously been listed. It may, however, be noted that the legend on the obverse has **A.L. IMP** as given in v. G. Zwolle III, while No. 114 which otherwise corresponds to that type has the legend ending with **ZWOLLE IMP**.

There never has been a complete catalogue of the dates and mints of leeuwendaalders and half-daalders and, in fact, until a few years ago many dates of the various mints for the coinage of which documentary evidence exists were unknown in actual specimens. Recently, however, a flood of leeuwendaalders and half-daalders has turned up on the European coin market. They are believed to have come from extensive but unpublished hoards which are being dispersed by Near Eastern coin dealers.

Dr. Enno van Gelder has been compiling a complete list of all known dates and mints (including those known only from the Aintab

Hoard, but excluding seignorial and foreign imitations) and has provided it for publication here in conjunction with this discussion. For this and much other assistance the author is most grateful to Dr. van Gelder.

Selected Bibliography

Enno van Gelder, H. "Leeuwendaalders," *De Geuzenpenning Munt—en Penningkunde*, VIII, ii (April, 1958), 13–16.
"Leeuwendaalders van Friesland," *Jaarboek voor Munt—en Penningkunde*, XLIV (1957), 57–59.
Munthervorming tijdens de Republiek 1659–1694, Amsterdam, 1949.
"Beyrouth Hoard," *Jaarboek voor Munt—en Penningkunde*, XXXVI (1949), 175.
Hasluck, F. W. "The Levantine Coinage," *Numismatic Chronicle* (1921), 39–91.
Schaetzen, Chev. M. "Monnaies Belges trouvées à Saida (Syrie)," *Revue Belge de Numismatique* (1925), 239.
Verkade, P. *Muntboek bevattende de Namen en Afbeeldingen van munten*, Schiedam, 1848.

CATALOGUE

INTRODUCTION

All coins have on the obverse a knight with a shield and on the reverse a large lion rampant. Except for the leeuwendaalders of Westfriesland of 1674 and Utrecht of 1646, the small lion in the shield appears to be uncrowned on all specimens listed although the preservation of some pieces leaves this not quite certain.

Equally the question whether the inner circle is dotted or solid is sometimes hard to decide. It may seem solid, but in some cases this might be due only to wear which caused the small dots to have been blurred into the aspect of a solid line. "Almost solid" describes this case.

The description of the legends does not take into account differences in interpunctuation, but does record fully differences in the abbreviation of words and accidental mistakes in spelling such as DON in place of DNO. The stops used after each word in the description do not mean that they are or are not on the coins or that there may not be double stops (:) on the coin. The description also does not go into the size of the small shield, the shape of its ornaments, the size and position of the large lion or other details of the design which are quite impossible to describe accurately. Suffice it to state that no two coins in the catalogue are of the same pair of dies.

The following abbreviations are used:

Mm.—Mint mark.

MMm.—Mint Master's mark.

*—Indicates the previously unknown specimens.

V.—Verkade. Coins are given a V. reference even if the abbreviations of the legends are not exactly as in Verkade, but not where there is a material difference in legend or design.

v.G.—The "Provisional List" compiled by Dr. van Gelder and appearing in conjunction with this discussion. Since this list does not take into account variations in abbreviation or punctuation, references to it have been handled in the same manner as references to Verkade.

THE AINTAB HOARD

Holland

1. 1662 Daalder. V. 49.1, v.G. II.
    Obv.: MO · ARG · PRO · CON – FŒ · BELG · HOL · Mm. Rose
    Knight looking right, inner circle dotted
    Rev.: CONFIDENS · DNO · NON · MOVETVR · date
    Inner circle dotted

Westfriesland

2. 1622 Daalder. V. 66.4, v.G. III.
    Obv.: MO · ARG · PRO · CON – FOE · BELG · WESTF
    Knight looking right, inner circle dotted
    Rev.: CONFIDENS · DNO · NON · MOVETVR no Mm.
    Inner circle dotted

3–4. 1633, 1637 Daalders. V. 66.4, v.G. III.
    Obv.: MO · ARG · PRO · CON – FOE · BELG · WESTF
    Knight looking right, inner circle dotted
    Rev.: CONFIDENS · DNO · NON · MOVETVR · MMm. Lys
    Inner circle dotted

5–8. 1637, 1640, 1641 (2) Daalders. V. 66.4, v.G. III.
    Obv.: MO · ARG · PRO · CON – FOE · BELG · WEST
    Knight looking right, inner circle dotted
    Rev.: CONFIDENS · DNO · NON · MOVETVR ·   date, MMm. Lys
    Inner circle dotted

9–11. 1642, 1643, 1647 Daalders. V. 66.4, v.G. III.
    Obv.: MO · ARG · PRO · CON – FOE · BELG · WES
    Knight looking right, inner circle dotted
    Rev.: CONFIDENS · DNO · NON · MOVETVR date, MMm. Lys

12.–13. 1649, 1650 (property of Mrs. Alfred Coons) Daalders. V. 66.4, v.G. III.
    Obv.: MO · ARG · PRO · CON – FOE · BELG · WEST ·
    Knight looking right, inner circle dotted
    Rev.: CONFIDENS · DNO · NON · MOVETVR ·   date, MMm. Lys
    Inner circle dotted

HOARD OF LEEUWENDAALDERS

14. 1670 Daalder. V. 66.4, v.G. III.
    Obv.: MON · ARG · PRO · CON – FOE · BELG · WESTF
    Knight looking right, inner circle solid
    Rev.: CONFIDENS · DNO · NON · MOVETVR ·   date,
    Inner circle solid   [MMm. Starfish

15–16. 1674,* 74 (?) Daalders. V. 66.4, v.G. III.
    Obv.: MON · ARG · PRO · CON – FOE · BELG · WEST
    Knight looking right, lion in shield clearly crowned in one specimen, indistinct in the other, inner circle solid
    Rev.: CONFIDENS · DNO · NON · MOVETVR ·   date,
    Inner circle solid   [MMm. Starfish

17–18. 1632, 1634 Half Daalders. V. 66.5, v.G. III.
    Obv.: MO · ARG · PRO · CON – FOE · BELG · WESTF
    Knight looking right, inner circle dotted
    Rev.: CONFIDENS · DNO · NON · MOVETVR ·   date, MMm. Lys
    Inner circle dotted

Zeeland

19–20. 1617 (property of Miss Norton), 16–– Half Daalders. V. 88.2, v.G. III.
    Obv.: MO · ARG · PRO · CON – FOE · BELG · ZEL · Mm. Castle
    Knight looking right, inner circle dotted
    Rev.: Mm. Castle CONFIDENS · DNO · NON · MOVETVR · date
    Inner circle dotted

Utrecht

21. 1646 Daalder. V. 107.4, v.G. III.
    Obv.: Mm. Shield. MO · ARG · PRO · CO – NFŒ · BELG · TRA
    Knight looking right, lion in shield crowned and with saltire on breast, inner circle dotted
    Rev.: CONFIDENS · DNO · NON · MOVETVR · date
    Inner circle dotted

22–25. 1685 (2), 1688 (2) Daalders. V. 107.4, v.G. III.
    Obv.: MO · ARG · PRO · CON – FOE · BEL · TRA · Mm. Shield
    Knight looking right, lion in shield uncrowned but with saltire on breast, inner circle dotted
    Rev.: CONFIDENS · DNO · NON · MOVETVR ·   date,
    Inner circle dotted   [Mm. within date

Gelderland

26. 1638 Daalder. V. 11.1, v.G. II.
    Obv.: Mm. Croix recroisée · MO · ARG · PRO · CO – NFOE · BELG · GEL
    Knight looking right, inner circle dotted
    Rev.: CONFIDENS · DNO · NON · MOVETVR · date
    Inner circle dotted

27. 1638 (property of Miss Norton), Daalder. V. 11.1, v.G. II.
    Obv.: MO · ARG · PRO · CO – NFOE · BEL · GEL
    Knight looking right, inner circle dotted
    Rev.: CONFIDENS · DON · NON · MOVETVR · date
    Inner circle dotted

28. 1639 Daalder. V. 11.1, v.G. II.
    Obv.: MO · ARG · PRO · CO – NFOE · BEL · GEL ·
    Knight looking right, inner circle dotted
    Rev.: CONFIDENS · DNO · NON · MOVETVR · date
    Inner circle dotted

29. 1639 Daalder. V. 11.1, v.G. II.
    Obv.: MO · ARG · PRO · CON – FEO · BELG · GEL
    Knight looking right, inner circle dotted
    Rev.: CONFIDENS · DNO · NON · MOVETVR
    Inner circle dotted

30–32. 1639 (property of Mrs. Dorman), 1640 (2) Daalders. V. 11.1, v.G. II.
    Obv.: MO · ARG · PRO · CON – FOE · BELG · GEL ·
    Knight looking right, inner circle dotted
    Rev.: CONFIDENS · DNO · NON · MOVETVR · date
    Inner circle dotted

33–36. 1641 (2), 1642, 1643 Daalders. V. 11.1, v.G. II.
    Obv.: MO · ARG · PRO · CO – FOE · BELG · GEL
    Knight looking right, inner circle dotted
    Rev.: CONFIDENS · DNO · NON · MOVETVR · date
    Inner circle dotted

HOARD OF LEEUWENDAALDERS

37. 1647 Daalder. V. 11.1, v.G. II.
    Obv.: MO · ARG · PRO · CON – FOE · BELG · GEL ·
    Knight looking right, inner circle dotted
    Rev.: CONFIDENS · DNO · NON · MOVETVR · date
    Inner circle dotted

38–40. 1647 (2), 1648 Daalders. V. 11.2, v.G. II.
    Obv.: MO · ARG · PRO · C – ONFOE · BEL · GEL ·
    Knight looking left, inner circle almost solid
    Rev.: CONFIDENS · DNO · NON · MOVETVR · date
    Inner circle almost solid

41–42. 1648 (2) Daalders. V. 11.2, v.G. II.
    Obv.: MO· ARG · PRO · C – ONFOE · BEL · GEL ·
    Knight looking left, inner circle dotted
    Rev.: CONFIDENS · DNO · NON · MOVETVR · date,
    Inner circle dotted   [Mm. within date

43–44. 1641 (donated by Miss Ruth Blankenhorn), 1643* Half Daalder. V. 11.3, v.G. II.
    Obv.: MO · ARG · PRO · CON – FOE · BELG · GEL ·
    Knight looking right, inner circle dotted
    Rev.: CONFIDENS · DNO · NON · MOVETVR · date
    Inner circle dotted

Overijssel

45–47. 1613 (?)(later than 12), 1617 (property of Miss Ruth Blankenhorn), 1643 Daalders. V. 139.3, v.G. II.
    Obv.: MO · ARG · PRO · CON – FOE · BELG · TRAN
    Knight looking right, inner circle almost solid
    Rev.: CONFIDENS · DNO · NON · MOVETVR · date
    Inner circle almost solid

48. 1633 Daalder. V. 139.3, v.G. II.
    Obv.: MO · ARG · PRO · CON – FOE · BELG · TRAN
    Knight looking right, inner circle almost solid
    Rev.: CONFIDENS · DON · NON · MOVEVR · date
    Inner circle almost solid

49. 1640 (property of Miss Norton), V. 139.3. v.G. II.
   Obv.: MO · ARG · PRO · CO – FOE · BELG · TRA
      Knight looking right, inner circle dotted
   Rev.: CONFIDENS · DNO · NON · MOVET
      Inner circle dotted

50–51. 1641, 1644 Daalders. V. 139.3, v.G. II.
   Obv.: MO · ARG · PRO · CON – FOE · BELG · TRA
      Knight looking right, inner circle dotted
   Rev.: CONFIDENS · DNO · NON · MOVETR · date
      Inner circle dotted (1644 almost solid)

52–56. 1677 (3), 1679 (2) Daalders. V. 139.3, v.G. III.
   Obv.: MO · ARG · CONFOE – BELG · PRO · TRANS
      Knight looking right, inner circle solid
   Rev.: CONFIDENS · DNO · NON · MOVETVR · date,
      Inner circle solid   [MMm. Rosette within date

57. 1681 Daalder. V. 139.3, v.G. III.
   Obv.: MO · NO · ARG · CONF – Œ · BELG · PRO · TRA
      Knight looking right, inner circle solid
   Rev.: CONFIDENS · DNO · NON · MOVETVR · date,
      Inner circle dotted   [MMm. Rosette within date

58. 1688 Daalder. V. 139.3, v.G. III.
   Obv.: MO · NO · ARG · CON – BELG · PRO · TRANS
      Knight looking right, inner circle dotted
   Rev.: CONFIDENS · DNO · NON · MOVETVR · date,
      Inner circle dotted   [Mm. Rosette within date

59. 1688 Daalder. V. 139.3, v.G. III.
   Obv.: MO · NO · ARG · CONF – BELG · PRO · TRANS
      Knight looking right, inner circle dotted
   Rev.: CONFIDENS · DNO · NON · MOVETVR · date,
      Inner circle dotted   [Mm. Rosette within date

60–61. 1688, 1692 Daalders. V. 139.3, v.G. III.
   Obv.: MON · ARG · CONF – BEL · PRO · TRANS
      Knight looking right, inner circle dotted
   Rev.: CONFIDENS · DNO · NON · MOVETVR · date,
      Inner circle dotted   [Mm. Rosette within date

HOARD OF LEEUWENDAALDERS

Friesland

62. Undated (ca. 1615–1625) Daalder. V. 124.2, v.G. IV.
    Obv.: MO · AR · PR · CO – NFOE · BEL · FRI
    Knight looking right, inner circle dotted
    Rev.: CONFIDENS · DNO · NON · MOVETVR ·
    Inner circle dotted

Deventer

63. 1664 Daalder. V. 150.3, v.G. II.
    Obv.: MO · ARG · CIVIT · – IMPER · DAVENT ·
    Knight looking right, inner circle dotted
    Rev.: CONFIDENS · DNO · NON · MOVETVR · date,
    Inner circle dotted   [MMm. Moor's head within date

64–67. 1687 (2), 1688 (2) Daalders. V. 150.3, v.G. II.
    Obv.: MO · ARG · CIV · IMP – BEL · DAVENTR
    Knight looking right, inner circle solid
    Rev.: CONFIDENS · DNO · NON · MOVETVR · date,
    Inner circle solid   [MMm. dog within date

Kampen

68. 163–* Daalder. V. 163.1, v.G. II.
    Obv.: MO · ARG · CIV · IMP – BELG · CAMPEN
    Knight looking right, inner circle almost solid (Behind the lion in the shield are the "waves" which characterize the arms of Overijssel)
    Rev.: CONFIDEИS · DИO · ИOИ · MOVETVR · date, Mm.
    Inner circle solid

69–70. 1648 (2) Daalder. V. 163.3, v.G. III.
    Obv.: MO · AR · CIVI · IMP – BELG · CAMPEN ·
    Knight looking left, inner circle almost solid
    Rev.: CONFIDENS · DNO · NON · MOVETVR · date,
    Inner circle dotted   [MMm. Lys within date

71–79. 1648 (7), 1649 (2) Daalders. V. 163.3, v.G. III.
    Obv.: MO · AR · CIVI · IM – P · BELG · CAMPEN
    Knight looking left, inner circle dotted

Rev.: CONFIDENS · DNO · NON · MOVETVR · date,
Inner circle dotted   [MMm. Lys within date
(one 1649 almost solid)

80–84. 1649 (4), 1650 Daalders. V. 163.3, v.G. III.
Obv.: MO · AR · CIVI · IM – P · BEL · CAMPEN
Knight looking left, inner circle almost solid
Rev.: CONFIDENS · DNO · NON · MOVETVR · date
Inner circle almost solid   [MMm. Lys within date

85–94. 1681 (2), 1682 (5), 1683 (3) Daalders. V. 163.1, v.G. III.
Obv.: MO · ARG · CIV · IMP – BELG · CAMPEN ·
Knight looking right, inner circle solid
Rev.: CONFIDENS · DNO · NON · MOVETVR · date,
Inner circle solid   [MMm. Horseman within date
(one 1683 dotted)

95–110. 1684 (7), 1685 (2), 1686, 1686 (later than 84), 1688 (4), 1689* Daalders. V. 163.1, v.G. III.
Obv.: MO · ARG · CIV · IMP – BELG · CAMPEN ·
Knight looking right, inner circle dotted (one 1686 almost solid)
Rev.: CONFIDENS · DNO · NON · MOVETVR · date,
Inner circle dotted   [MMm. Horseman within date
(one 1686 almost solid)

111. 1646 Half Daalder. V. 163.2, v.G. III.
Obv.: MO · ARG · CIVI · IMP – BELG · CAMPEN ·
Knight looking right, inner circle dotted
Rev.: CONFIDENS · DNO · NON · MOVETVR · date, MMm. Lys
Inner circle dotted   [within date

Zwolle

112. 1633* Daalder. v.G. I.
Obv.: MO · ARG · IMP · CIVI – ZWOL · A · L · IMP ·
                                      (i.e. *ad legem imperii*)
Knight looking right, in shield lion with arms of Zwolle on breast, inner circle dotted
Rev.: DA · PACEM · DOMINE · IN · DIEBVS · NOST ·
Lion with city arms on breast, dividing date, inner circle dotted

HOARD OF LEEUWENDAALDERS

113. 1639* Daalder. v.G. II.
    Obv.: MO · ARG · CIVITA – ZWOL · A · L · IMP ·
    Knight looking right, in shield St. Michael with two city arms of Zwolle, inner circle almost solid
    Rev.: rowel · DA · PACEM · DOMINE · IN · DIEBVS · NOST ·
    Lion with city arms on breast dividing date, inner circle dotted
114. 1639 Daalder. v.G. III.
    Obv.: MO · ARG · CIVITA – ZWOLL · IMP ·
    Knight looking right, in shield St. Michael with arms of Zwolle, inner circle dotted
    Rev.: rowel · DA · PACEM · DOMINE · IN · DIEBVS · NOSTR ·
    Lion without city arms dividing date, inner circle dotted
115. 1640 Daalder. v.G. III.
    Obv.: MO · ARG · CIVITA – ZWOL · A · L · IMP
    Knight looking right, in shield St. Michael with arms of Zwolle, inner circle dotted
    Rev.: rowel · DA · PACEM · DOMINE · IN · DIEBVS · NOST ·
    Lion without city arms dividing date, inner circle dotted
116. 1642 Daalder. V. 172.2, v.G. III.
    Obv.: MO · ARG · CIVITA – ZWOL · A · L · IMP ·
    Knight looking right, in shield St. Michael with arms of Zwolle, rowel in left field, inner circle dotted
    Rev.: rowel · DA · PACEM · DOMINE · IN · DIEBVS · NOST ·
    Lion without city arms dividing date, inner circle dotted
117–119. 1646 (2), 1648 Daalders. V. 172.4, v.G. III.
    Obv.: MO · ARG · CIVITA – ZWOL · A · L · IMP ·
    Knight looking right, in shield St. Michael with arms of Zwolle, inner circle dotted
    Rev.: rowel · DA · PACEM · DOM · IN · DIEBVS · NOST · date
    Lion without city arms, inner circle dotted
120. 1649 Daalder. V. 172.4, v.G. III.
    Obv.: MO · ARG · CIVITA – ZWOL · A · L · IMP
    Knight looking right, in shield St. Michael with arms of Zwolle, inner circle dotted
    Rev.: rowel · DA · PACEM · D · IN · DIEBVS · NOST · date
    Lion without city arms, inner circle dotted

121. 1652 Daalder. V. 172.4, v.G. III.
   Obv.: MO · ARG · CIVIT – ZWOL · A · L · IMP
   Knight looking right, in shield St. Michael with arms of Zwolle, inner circle dotted
   Rev.: DA · PACEM · DOM · IN · DIEBVS · NOS · date, MMm. Starfish
   Lion without city arms, inner circle dotted

122. 1685 Daalder. v.G. IV.
   Obv.: MO · ARG · CONFŒ – BELG · CIV · ZWOL ·
   Knight looking right, in shield lion, inner circle dotted
   Rev.: CONFIDENS · DNO · NON · MOVETVR · date, MMm. Starfish
   Lion without city arms, inner circle solid

Lorraine

123. (property of Miss Norton), Testoon of Nancy. Henri le Bon (1608–1624).
   Obv.: HENRI · D:G: · DVX · LOTH · MARCH · D:C · B · G
   Bust right
   Rev.: MONETA · NOVA · NANCEII · CVSA ·
   Crowned shield of Lorraine with eight quarters and center shield
   de Saulcy, p. 162.

SUMMARY OF HOARD

	Daalders	Half Daalders	Total
Holland	1	–	1
Westfriesland	15	2	17
Zeeland	–	2	2
Utrecht	5	–	5
Gelderland	17	2	19
Overijssel	17	–	17
Friesland	1	–	1
Deventer	5	–	5
Kampen	43	1	44
Zwolle	11	–	11
	115	7	122
Lorraine	Testoon		1
			123

HERBERT J. ERLANGER

A PROVISIONAL LIST OF DUTCH LION-DOLLARS

The type of the Dutch lion-dollar was created once for all by the die-engraver of the provincial mint of Holland in 1576:

Obv.: A warrior clad in contemporary armor stands three quarters to the left; his head covered by an open crested helmet is sharply turned to the right; with his right hand he holds a large shield with ornamental border, under which his feet appear; with his left hand he holds a slip of the light cloak that flows freely from his back; the shield displays the coat of arms of Holland, a lion rampant; legend MO[neta] NO[va] ARG[entea] ORDIN[um] HOL[landiae]

Rev.: A large heraldic lion rampant; legend CONFIDENS D[omi]NO NON MOVETVR

Only the very oldest lion-dollars struck in 1575 and early in 1576 show some slight hesitancies before the definitive type was established; the warrior of these early specimens wears armor of "antique" design and lacks the characteristic turn of the head. All later issues of Holland as well as of other provinces and towns show hardly any deviation from this prototype which was neither varied nor modernized in the course of more than a century.

The imitations by other provincial mints started in 1585; these took over the essential characteristics of the type, but usually replaced the elements peculiar to Holland by their own equivalents: the coat of arms in the shield on the obverse, the motto and the mint mark on the reverse. Later, the desire to produce as exact replicas as possible of the prototype brought back many of the original features to the lion dollars struck outside Holland: the plain lion in the shield, the CONFIDENS motto, and even the rose mint mark of Dordrecht. By a clever device legends of the type MO[neta] NO[va] ORD[inum] TRAI[ecti] AD VA[lorem] HOL[landie] produced an obverse legend beginning and ending with the same words as the original.

This conformity to the Holland prototype was more or less legalized in 1606 when the States-General accepted the lion-dollar as a general coin for all the provinces. Its new status found expression in the new obverse legend—similar to that of other denominations—MO[neta] ARG[entea] PRO[vinciarum] CONFOE[deratarum] BELG[icarum], followed by the name of the province. For the reverse the plain lion of Holland with the traditional motto was tolerated, whereas all other coins bore the crowned and armored lion of the United Provinces and the accompanying device "Concordia Res Parvae Crescunt." Besides that the date was shifted from the obverse to the reverse where it took the place of the rose mint mark.

The provinces adhered with hardly any exceptions to the new pattern, but the towns maintained individual variations much longer. Only after 1659, when they accepted a general supervision of the central authorities over their coinage, did they resign themselves to the same conformity; the municipal arms disappeared from the coins as well as local mottoes for reverse legends, while the obverse legends too were adapted to the general pattern suggesting coinage in the name of the United Provinces.

Apart from the differences in the heraldry and the legends mentioned before, the most notable exceptions to the uniformity of obverse design are:

a. in a few cases the lion in the shield on the obverse is crowned, probably the effect of a confusion with the crowned lion of the States-General;

b. one die-engraver, working both for the provincial mint of Gelderland and the municipal mint of Kampen, reversed the position of the warrior;

c. in the second half of the 17th century the crest on the warrior's helmet was almost universally suppressed;

d. after 1606 all provincial issues show the lion rampant, as prescribed in the ordinance of that year; the province of Utrecht only continues to use its own arms, but these being a lion rampant bearing a small saltire on his shoulder could hardly be distinguished from the general pattern.

The large lion of the reverse suffered still fewer attacks:

a. Zeeland replaced the lion rampant during a few years by its own lion issuant;

LIST OF DUTCH LION-DOLLARS

b. the town of Zwolle for a few years permitted the lion to be charged with the municipal arms and later added some new elements to the field such as a grassy ground or a date.

Before 1606 the place of the mint mark was at the top of the reverse; it was a fairly regular feature of the coins in so far as it was not replaced by the Holland rose. The latter abuse was made impossible by the new design of 1606 and from then onwards the usual place of the mint mark was at the end of the obverse legend. However, many provinces discontinued this mark altogether in the course of the century. On the other hand some provinces, and all of the towns, introduced eventually the use of a mintmaster's mark for which room was found at different places in the design. Utrecht alone ended by putting both a mint mark and a mintmaster's mark on the coins.

The following survey is a first attempt to list the lion-dollars struck by the provinces and towns of the Republic of the United Netherlands, excluding both the unauthorized imitations of a few Dutch *seigneuries* and the numerous lion-dollars struck abroad, especially in Germany and Italy.

For the sake of simplification in the description of the types and variations no stops have been indicated (saltires, crosslets or pellets before 1606, almost exclusively pellets after that date). For the same reason slight variations in the abbreviations of the legends or in the details of the design (e.g., the nature of the inner circles, the position of the shield and the decoration of its frame) have been neglected.

The list contains all the dates of lion-dollars (left hand column) and half lion-dollars (right hand column) known to the author either from specimens seen in public or private collections both in Holland and abroad or, for a small number, from descriptions in reliable catalogues and reports of hoards. However the list must of necessity remain incomplete as our knowledge of the series is continually expanding as a result of new information about Middle East hoards. Additionally, anyone having a date or mint of a lion-dollar or half lion-dollar that is not contained in this list is requested to communicate with the Koninklijk Penningkabinet at the Hague.

Holland

I *Obv.*: Warrior standing behind shield displaying the arms of Holland (lion rampant), date at the bottom of the shield; MO · NO · ARG – ORDIN · HOL(L)

Rev.: Lion rampant; rose CONFIDENS · DNO · NON · MOVETVR

undated	warrior in Roman armor with head turned to the left	emaciated bust (struck 1575)
1575	similar	similar
1576	similar	broad bust
1576		
1577	1577	
	1578	
1585	1585	
1586		
1589	1589	
1597		
	1598	
1601	1601	
1602		
1604	1604	
1605	1605	

II *Obv.*: Warrior standing behind shield displaying lion rampant; MO · ARG · PRO · CON – FOE · BELG · HOL rose

Rev.: Lion rampant; date CONFIDENS DNO NON MOVETVR

1606	1606
1607	
1608	1608
1609	
	1610
1611	
1612	
1616	1616
1617	1617
	1618
1622	1622

LIST OF DUTCH LION-DOLLARS

1623	1623
1624	
1625	
1626	
1627	
1628	
1632	
1633	
1634	1634
1635	
1636	1636
1637	
1640	1640
1641	1641
	1645
	1647
1648	1648
1649	
1650	1650
1651	
1652	1652
1655	
1662	
1663	
1664	
1666	
1668	
1674	
1680	
1683	
1684	
1685	
1687	

West-Friesland

I *Obv.*: Warrior standing behind shield displaying the arms of West-Friesland (two lions passant guardant), date at the bottom of the shield; MO NO ARG WEST – FRI VALOR HOL

Rev.: Lion rampant; rose CONFIDENS DNO NON MOVETVR

1588
1589

II *Obv.*: as obv. of I, except place of date
Rev.: Lion rampant; rose DEVS FORTITVDO ET SPES NOSTRA

1600		date at the bottom of the shield
1601		similar
1603		similar
undated		(struck ca. 1603)
	1603	date in the field divided by shield
1604	1604	similar
1605	1605	similar

III *Obv.*: Warrior standing behind shield displaying lion rampant; MO ARG PRO CON – FOE BELG WES(TFRIS)
Rev.: Lion rampant; date CONFIDENS DNO NON MOVETVR (usually mintmaster's mark before or after date)

1606		no mintmaster's mark
1609		no mintmaster's mark
1611		no mintmaster's mark
1612		no mintmaster's mark
1613		no mintmaster's mark
1613		mark: fleur-de-lis
1614		no mark
1615		mark: fleur-de-lis
1616	1616	fleur-de-lis
1617	1617	fleur-de-lis
1618		fleur-de-lis
1622		mark: rose
1622		no mark
	1623	no mark
1623	1623	mark: rose
1624	1624	rose
1626	1626	rose
1628		rose
1629	1629	rose

LIST OF DUTCH LION-DOLLARS

1629	1629	no mark	
1631	1631	mark: fleur-de-lis	
1632	1632	fleur-de-lis	
1633	1633	fleur-de-lis	
1634	1634	fleur-de-lis	
1635	1635	fleur-de-lis	
1636	1636	fleur-de-lis	
1637		fleur-de-lis	
1638	1638	fleur-de-lis	
1639		fleur-de-lis	
1640	1640	fleur-de-lis	
1641	1641	fleur-de-lis	
1642	1642	fleur-de-lis	
1643	1643	fleur-de-lis	
1644	1644	fleur-de-lis	
	1645	fleur-de-lis	
1646	1646	fleur-de-lis	
1647	1647	fleur-de-lis	
1648	1648	fleur-de-lis	
	1649	fleur-de-lis	
1649		mark: flower	
1650	1650	flower	
1651	1651	flower	
1652		flower	
1654	1654	flower	
1655		flower	
1661	1661	flower	
1662	1662	flower	
1664	1664	flower	
1665		flower	
	1666	flower	
1668		flower	
1670		flower	
1671		flower	crowned lion in shield on obv.
1674		flower	similar
1675		flower	similar
1677		flower	similar

1678		flower similar
1697		flower similar
1699		flower similar
1700		flower similar
1713		mark: stork similar

Zeeland

I *Obv.*: Warrior standing behind shield displaying arms of Holland (lion rampant), date at the bottom of the shield; MO NO ORD ZEL – AD VA ORD HOL

 Rev.: Lion rampant; castle CONFIDENS DNO NON MOVETVR

1589	1589

II *Obv.*: Warrior standing behind shield displaying arms of Zeeland (lion issuant above waves), date at the bottom of the shield; MO NO ARG – ORDIN ZEL

  Rev.: Lion issuant above waves; castle DOMINE SERVA NOS PERIMVS

1597	1597
1598	1598
1599	

III *Obv.*: Warrior standing behind shield displaying lion rampant; MO ARG PRO CON – FOE BELG ZEL castle

   Rev.: Lion rampant; date CONFIDENS DNO NON MOVETVR

1606		
1609		
1612		date between rosettes
1613		similar
1614	1614	similar
1615	1615	date between saltires
1616	1616	similar
1617	1617	similar
1618	1618	similar
	1619	similar
1623	1623	date between rosettes
1624		similar
1628	1628	similar

LIST OF DUTCH LION-DOLLARS

1629		
1633		
1634		
	1635	
1637?		
1638	1638	date between rosettes (except on half-dollar)
1640		date between rosettes
1644		
1645	1645	
1646		
1648		
1649		
1650		
1651		
1652	1652	

Utrecht

I *Obv.*: Warrior standing behind shield displaying quartered arms of Utrecht (1,4 lion, 2,3 cross), date at the bottom of the shield; MONETA NOV – ORDIN TRAI

Rev.: Lion rampant; escutcheon CONCORDIA RES PARVAE CRESCVNT

1585   known as piedfort only

II *Obv.*: Warrior standing behind shield displaying arms of Utrecht (lion bearing saltire on his shoulder), date at the bottom of the shield; legend (a) MO NO OR(D) TRA – AD VA ORD HOL or (b) MO NO ORDI – TRA(I) VA HOL

Rev.: Lion rampant; rose CONFIDENS DNO NON MOVETVR

1589		legend a; escutcheon on rev. instead of rose
1589		legend a
1597		legend b
1598		legend a or b
1599	1599	legend a or b
1600		legend b
1601		legend a
1602		legend b

III *Obv.*: Warrior standing behind shield displaying arms of Utrecht (lion bearing saltire on his shoulder); escutcheon MO ARG PRO CON – FOE BEL(G) TRA(I) (from 1647 onwards the escutcheon is placed at the end of the legend)
Rev.: Lion rampant; date CONFIDENS DNO NON MOVETVR (from 1674 onwards a mintmaster's mark is added, dividing the date)

1606	1606	
1607		
1608		
1609	1609	
1610	1610	
1613		
1614	1614	
1615		
1616	1616	
1617	1617	
1618	1618	
1623		
1626	1626	
1628		
1629	1629	escutcheon before MO or after TRA
1632		escutcheon after TRA
1634		escutcheon after TRA
1635		crowned lion in the shield on the obv.
1636	1636	crowned or uncrowned lion
1637		crowned lion
1638		crowned lion
1639		crowned lion
1640		crowned lion
1641		crowned lion
1642	1642	crowned lion
1643	1643	crowned lion
1644		crowned lion
1645	1645	crowned lion
1646		crowned lion
1647	1647	escutcheon before MO or after TRA

LIST OF DUTCH LION-DOLLARS

1648	1648	escutcheon after TRA		
1649	1649			
1650	1650			
1651				
1652				
1653				
1654	1654			
1655				
1656				
1657				
1658				
1660	1660			
1661				
1662				
1663	1663			
1664				
	1667			
1674	1674	mintmaster's mark: pascal lamb		
1676	1676		pascal lamb	
1679		mintmaster's mark: rose		
1680			rose	
1681			rose	
1682			rose	helmet with or without crest
1683			rose	helmet with or without crest
1685			rose	helmet without crest
1686			rose	similar
1687			rose	similar
1688			rose	similar
1689			rose	similar
1697			rose	similar

Gelderland

I *Obv.*: Warrior standing behind shield displaying arms of Holland (lion rampant); date at the bottom of the shield MO NO ORDI – GEL VA HOL

Rev.: Lion rampant; rose CONFIDENS DNO NON MOVET VR

1589		recrossed cross on rev. instead of rose
1589		
1593		
1597	1597	
1599	1599	
1600		
1602	1602	

II *Obv.*: Warrior standing behind shield displaying lion rampant; MO ARG PRO CON – FOE BEL(G) GEL (until 1638 inclusive followed by mintmark recrossed cross)
   Rev.: Lion rampant; date CONFIDENS DNO NON MOVETVR (from 1647 onwards a mintmaster's mark is added dividing the date)

1606	1606	crowned lion in shield on obv.	
1607		similar	
1608		similar	
1609		similar	
1610	1610	similar	uncrowned lion on half-dollar
1611		similar	
1613		similar	
1615		similar	
1616	1616	crowned or uncrowned lion	
1617	1617	crowned or uncrowned lion	
1618		crowned lion	
1619			
1622			
1628	1628		
1629			
1631			
1632		crowned or uncrowned lion	
1633	1633		
1634			
1635			
1636		without mint mark	

LIST OF DUTCH LION-DOLLARS 273

1637	1637	with mint mark	
1637		without mint mark	
1638		with mint mark	
1638	1638	without mint mark	
1639			
1640	1640		
1641	1641		
1642			
1643	1643		
1644			
1646	1646		
1647		no mintmaster's mark	
1647		no mintmaster's mark	warrior reversed (looking to the left)
1647		mark: fleur-de-lis	warrior reversed
	1647	fleur-de-lis	
1648		fleur-de-lis	warrior reversed
1648	1648	fleur-de-lis	
1649		fleur-de-lis	warrior reversed
1651		fleur-de-lis	
1652		fleur-de-lis	
1652		fleur-de-lis	warrior reversed
1653		fleur-de-lis	
1654		fleur-de-lis	
1655		mark: sitting dog	
1657		sitting dog	
1662		sitting dog	
1663		sitting dog	
1666		sitting dog	
1667		sitting dog	
1668		sitting dog	
1674		sitting dog	
1675		sitting dog	
1676		sitting dog	
1694		mark: mounted warrior	helmet without crest
1697		mounted warrior	helmet without crest
1699		mounted warrior	helmet without crest

Overijssel

I *Obv.*: Warrior standing behind shield displaying arms of Overijssel (lion rampant covering waved fess); date at the bottom of the shield; MO NO ORD TRS – ISL VALOR HOL
Rev.: Lion rampant; castle in roseate frame CONFIDENS DNO NON MOVETVR

1585
1589
1591
1593
1594
1597
1602

II *Obv.*: Warrior standing behind shield displaying lion rampant; MO ARG PRO CO(N) – FOE BEL(G) TRA or TRAN(S)
Rev.: Lion rampant; date CONFIDENS DNO NON MOVETVR

1606	1606	
1607		
1608		
1610		
1611		
1612	1612	
1613		
1614	1614	
1615	1615	on half-dollar sometimes reversed lion in shield on obv.
1616	1616	similar
1617		
1619?		
	1622	
1623		
1628		
1629	1629	
1633	1633	on obv. sometimes crowned lion in shield on rev. sometimes date repeated in field
1636		

LIST OF DUTCH LION-DOLLARS

    1637   1637
                  1638?
    1639   1639
    1640   1640
    1641   1641
    1643
    1644
    1647

III *Obv.*: as obv. of II, but helmet without crest
    Rev.: Lion rampant; date and mintmaster's mark before legend MO ARG CONFOE – BELG PRO TRANS (a) or MO NO ARG CONF(OE) (or CONE) – BELG PRO TRA(NS) (b)

1675	mark: flower	legend a	helmet with crest
1676	with or without mark	legend a	helmet with crest
1677	mark: flower	legend a	
1678?	flower	legend b	
1679	flower	legend a or b	
1680	flower	legend a or b	
1681	flower	legend b	
1682	flower	legend b	
1683	with or without mark	legend b	
1685	mark: flower	legend b	
1688	flower	legend b	
1689	flower	legend b beginning MON:ARG	
1692	flower	similar	
1697	flower	similar	
1700	flower	similar	
1701	flower	similar	

Friesland

I *Obv.*: Warrior standing behind shield displaying arms of Friesland (two lions passant); date at the bottom of the shield; MO NO ARG ORD – FRI VAL HOL
   Rev.: Lion rampant; lion CONFIDENS DNO NON MOVETVR
    1589   1589

II *Obv.*: Warrior standing behind shield displaying arms of Holland (lion rampant), date at the bottom of the shield; MO NO ORD – FRI(SI) VA HO(LL)
Rev.: Lion rampant; mintmark CONFIDENS DNO NON MO-VETVR

1591		mark: lion
1594		mark: escutcheon of Friesland
1594		mark: rectangle
1597		rectangle
1600		mark: escutcheon of Friesland
1601		escutcheon of Friesland
1602	1602	escutcheon of Friesland
1603		escutcheon of Friesland

III *Obv.*: As obv. of I, but legend MONE NOVA – ORDIN FRISIAE
Rev.: Lion rampant; NISI DOMINVS NOBISCVM

1603	only known as mule with rev. of type II
1604	
1605	

IV *Obv.*: Warrior standing behind shield displaying lion rampant; MO AR(G) PRO – CONFOE BEL(G) FR(IS) sometimes followed by mint mark lion
Rev.: Lion rampant; date CONFIDENS DNO NON MOVETVR; sometimes mint mark lion before or after date

1607		without mint mark
1608		without mint mark
1608		lion on rev.
1609		without mark
1610		without mark or lion on rev.
1611		lion on rev.
1612		without mark or lion on obv.
1613		lion on obv.
1614	1614	without mark
1615		lion either on obv. or on rev.
1616		without mark
	1616	lion on obv.

1617	1617	lion on obv. or on rev. or on both sides
	1619	lion on obv.
undated	undated	lion on obv. or on rev. or on both sides
undated	undated	without mark (struck ca. 1615–25)
	1626	date on obv. divided by head of warrior and lion on rev.
1628	1628	lion on obv. or date on obv. and lion on rev.
1629		lion on obv.
	1632	date on obv. divided by head of warrior
1650		lion on rev. dividing date
1653		without mark
	1663	lion on obv.

V Obv.: Warrior standing behind shield displaying lion rampant; MO NO(VA) ARG – ORDIN FRI(S) lion (or date)
   Rev.: Lion rampant; lion (or date) CONFIDENS DNO NON MOVETVR

undated	lion on both sides (struck ca. 1615–17)
1616	lion on obv. and date on rev. in legend
1617	lion on rev. and date on obv. at the bottom of the shield
1622	similar

Nijmegen

I Obv.: Warrior standing behind shield displaying lion rampant; MO ARG CIVI IMP – BELG NOVIOMAG
   Rev.: Lion rampant; date divided by mintmaster's mark CONFIDENS DNO NON MOVETVR

1692	mark: moor's head	helmet without crest

Zutphen

I Obv.: Warrior standing behind shield displaying lion rampant; MO ARG CIVI IMP – BEL ZVTPHANI
   Rev.: Lion rampant; date divided by mintmaster's mark CONFIDENS DNO NON MOVETVR

1691	mark: antlers	helmet without crest
1692	antlers	helmet without crest

Deventer

I *Obv.*: Warrior standing behind shield displaying arms of Deventer (eagle); IMP CIV CONF BE – LG PR SOCI date
   Rev.: Lion rampant; mintmaster's mark ME VIGILANTE FLORET DAVENT

    1640   1640   mark: fleur-de-lis

II *Obv.*: Warrior standing behind shield displaying lion rampant; legend MO ARG CIVIT – IMPER DAVENT (a)
    or MO ARG CIV IMP – BEL(G) DAVENTR(IAE) (b)
    or MO ARG PRO CON – FOE BELG CIV DAV (c)
   Rev.: Lion rampant; date divided by mintmaster's mark CONFIDENS DNO NON MOVETVR

1662	legend a	mark: moor's head	
1663	legend a	moor's head	
1664	legend a	mark: sitting dog	
1666	legend a	sitting dog	
1667	legend a	sitting dog	
1685	legend b	sitting dog	helmet without crest
1687	legend b	sitting dog	similar
1688	legend b	sitting dog	similar
1698	legend c	sitting dog	similar

III *Obv.*: Warrior standing behind shield displaying arms of Deventer (eagle); MO ARG CIV IMP – BELG DAVENTRIAE
   Rev.: as rev. of II

    1684   mark: sitting dog   helmet without crest

Kampen

I *Obv.*: Warrior standing behind shield displaying lion rampant dangling an escutcheon of Kampen (castle) on long strings; MO ARG R P IMP – CAMP VA HOL
   Rev.: Lion rampant; castle in roseate frame CONFIDENS DNO NON MOVETVR

    undated   undated (struck ca. 1593–95)
    1597   date on rev. divided by mint mark

LIST OF DUTCH LION-DOLLARS

II *Obv.*: Warrior standing behind shield displaying arms of Overijssel (lion rampant covering waved fess); MO ARG CIVI IMP – BELG CAMPEN
Rev.: Lion rampant; date CONFIDENS DNO NON MOVETVR
1639?

III *Obv.*: Warrior standing behind shield displaying lion rampant; MO AR(G) CIV(I) IMP – BEL(G) CAMPE(N)
Rev.: Lion rampant; date divided by (or preceding) mintmaster's mark CONFIDENS DNO NON MOVETVR

1646		without mark	warrior reversed (looking to the left)
	1646	mark: fleur-de-lis	
1646		fleur-de-lis	warrior reversed
	1647	fleur-de-lis	
1647		fleur-de-lis	warrior reversed
1648		fleur-de-lis	warrior reversed
1649		fleur-de-lis	warrior reversed
1650		fleur-de-lis	warrior reversed
1650		fleur-de-lis	
1651		fleur-de-lis	
1652		fleur-de-lis	
1653		fleur-de-lis	
1654		fleur-de-lis	
1655		fleur-de-lis	
1662		fleur-de-lis	
1664		mark: moor's head	
1667		moor's head	
1675		mark: mounted warrior	helmet without crest
1676		similar	similar
1677		similar	similar
1681		similar	similar
1682		similar	similar
1683		similar	similar
1684		similar	similar
1685		similar	similar
1686		similar	similar

1687	similar	similar
1688	similar	similar
1690	similar	similar
1691	similar	similar
1692	similar	similar
1693	similar	similar

IV *Obv.*: Warrior standing behind shield displaying arms of Kampen (castle); MO ARG CIVITA – IMP BELG CAM
   Rev.: as rev. of III
   1672   mark: moor's head

Zwolle

I *Obv.*: Warrior standing behind shield displaying lion rampant; MO ARG CIVI IMP – ZWOL A L IMP
  Rev.: Lion rampant charged with shield displaying arms of Zwolle (cross), date in the field divided by the lion; DA PACEM DOMINE IN DIEBVS NOST
  1633

II *Obv.*: Warrior standing behind shield displaying St. Michael bearing shield with arms of Zwolle (cross); MO ARG CIVIT(A) – ZWOL A L IM(P)
   Rev.: as rev. of I
   1637   1637
   1639

III *Obv.*: as obv. of II
    Rev.: Lion rampant standing on natural ground; rowel DA PACEM D(OMINE) IN DIEB(VS) NOST(R); date:
       (a) in the field divided by the lion, or
       (b) in the field behind the lion along the inner circle, or
       (c) at the end of the legend (from 1651 on followed by mintmaster's mark)

1639	1639	date a	obv. legend sometimes ending in ZWOL(L) IMP(ER)
1640		date a	
1641	1641	date a	

1641	1641	date c	sometimes one rowel in the field of the obv.
1642	1642	date a	sometimes one rowel in the field of the obv.
1642		date b	one rowel in the field
1644		date a	one or two rowels in the field
1644	1644	date b	one rowel in the field
1644		date c	
1646	1646	date c	sometimes one rowel in the field
1647		date c	
1648	1648	date c	
1649	1649	date c	
1650	1650	date c	
1651	1651	date c	
1651		date c	mark: flower
1652	1652	date c	flower
1653		date c	flower
1655		date c	flower

IV *Obv.*: Warrior standing behind shield displaying lion rampant
MO ARG CONFOE – BELG CIV(I) ZWOL

Rev.: Lion rampant; date and mintmaster's mark CONFIDENS DNO NON MOVETVR

1661	mark: flower
1663	flower
1664	flower
1665	flower
1666	flower
1677	flower
1685	flower
1688	flower

H. ENNO VAN GELDER

A PORTRAIT OF THE BUYID PRINCE RUKN AL-DAWLAH
(See Plates XLV–XLVII)

In the summer of 1960 M. R. Gurnet of Momignies, a small town in Belgium south of Charleroi, sent me a plaster-cast of a curious coin that he had acquired and requested my help in identifying it. The coin so aroused my curiosity that I seized the opportunity of a brief visit in Brussels to run down to Momignies with M. Gurnet so that I could examine it at first hand. The trip was well worth it, not only because of M. Gurnet's hospitality but also because the piece turned out to be unique and, I think, of uncommon interest.

The coin (Plate XLV, enlarged about 2½ diameters) is of silver, of unusually large dimensions and weight for a dirhem of its period (32 mm. in diameter and weighing 10.13 grams). The obverse presents in general the usual characteristics of a conventional Buyid coin; in the area, a six-line Kufic inscription reading:

لا اله الا الله

وحده لا شريك له

محمد رسول الله

المطيع لله

ركن الدولة

ابو علي بويه

—that is, the *shahadah*, or declaration of faith, in full, followed by the name of the Caliph al-Muṭīʿ liʾllāh, and the name of the Buyid prince Rukn al-Dawlah, abu-ʿAli Buyeh. The *ṭā* of *al-Muṭīʿ* is braided. The single marginal legend has some unusual features. It reads:

بسم الله عمل (؟) هذا الدينار بالمحمدية سنة احدى وخمسين وثلثمائة

صلى الله عليه. (about 8 letters) ...

The word following the *basmalah* appears to read *ʿumila*, "was made," rather than the usual formulary *ḍuriba*, "was struck." The coin, being of silver, should be called a dirhem, but the word after *hadha* seems to be *al-dīnār*. The words following the date (which usually concludes the marginal formula) are crowded and blurred and difficult to decipher, but I suspect they are *min hijrah nabī* (or *nabawīyah*), "of the *hijrah* of the Prophet," which would suit the concluding words, "may God bless him." I imagine that the die-engraver added these phrases after the date to fill the space provided by the unusually large size of the flan.

Thus the piece announces itself as a dinar, although in silver,[1] of Rukn al-Dawlah, struck in the year 351 H./962 A.D. at al-Muḥammadīyah, the ceremonial or beaurocratic name of Rayy, the great city of northern Jibāl, located a few miles south of present-day Teheran.

With the exceptions noted there is nothing particularly remarkable about this side of the coin, but it is when we turn it over that we meet with a real surprise. Instead of the usual epigraphical reverse we find a facing bust with two lines of Pahlevi inscription, one at either side of the head. Both the bust and the Pahlevi legend are strongly reminiscent of the Sasanian tradition. A ceremonial robe of honor is suggested by the oval compartments across the chest. The full face is bearded and moustached. On the head is a winged crown, which while it has no exact Sasanian prototype, is distinctly of Sasanian inspiration. The crescents in the margin are also a Sasanian survival. While most Sasanian numismatic heads are in profile, there are exceptions, such as the frontal portrait on a rare drachm of Khosrau II dated in the 36th year of his reign (PLATE XLVI, 1); and the goddess with the flaming nimbus, Khurāsān Khurrah, also appears frontally, as on the reverse of the same coin (PLATE XLVI, 2).[2]

The Pahlevi legend (Fig. 1) is, in the perverse way of most Pahlevi legends, difficult to decipher. It would be difficult enough, even if the

[1] The piece has been holed at some time, and later plugged. The plug has a brassy color, which suggests that at the time it was holed, or perhaps even immediately after it was struck, the whole piece may have been gilded. This might explain the anomalous "dinar" denomination.

[2] ANS (ex-E. T. Newell Collection), 33 mm., 3.98 gr. →. This specimen was mentioned by John Walker in "Some recent oriental coin acquisitions of the British Museum," *NC* 1935, p. 244, note 4. It is from the same dies as the British Museum specimen, loc.cit., pl. XVIII, 2. For the bibliography relating to Khurāsān Khurrah, see G. C. Miles, *Excavation Coins from the Persepolis Region* (*NNM* No. 143, New York, 1959), p. 30.

A PORTRAIT OF RUKN AL-DAWLAH

letters were not somewhat blurred through wear. I believe a possible reading is *GDH 'pzwt/MLKyn'n* (sic) *MLK'*, that is, *xvarreh afzūt/ shāhān shāh*, or "May the glory increase (of the) King of Kings," a reading which my friend Richard N. Frye agrees is probable. Further support for this probability is provided by another unique, almost contemporary piece, a gold medallion, published by Mehdi Bahrami in the Herzfeld Memorial Volume in 1952.[3]

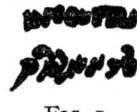

FIG. 1

This remarkable medallion (PLATE XLVI, 3) was struck at the mint of Fārs, that is, Shīrāz, in the year 359 H., just eight years after the coin of Rukn al-Dawlah under discussion. Both sides bear a similar portrait, but with different inscriptions, both in Kufic and in Pahlevi. The Pahlevi inscription on one side was read by Bahrami and Henning as *zīy dīr shā panā Kosraw*, that is, "May Shāh Fannā Khosraw live long," Fannā Khosraw being the name of the Buyid 'Aḍud al-Dawlah. The two Pahlevi lines on the other side of the medallion very closely resemble those on M. Gurnet's coin and were read *farrah afzud shāhān shāh*, in other words essentially the same legend as I propose to find on the coin of Rukn al-Dawlah. The robe bears quite a close resemblance to that on the Rukn al-Dawlah piece, and the head and crown are quite similar, although the execution in

---

[3] *Archaeologica Orientalia in Memoriam Ernst Herzfeld* (Locust Valley, N. Y., 1952), p. 18 and pl. I, figs. 2a and b. This medallion has subsequently been illustrated by Ernst Kühnel in "Die Kunst Persiens unter den Buyiden" (*ZDMG* 1956, pp. 78–92), Abb. 11, and by Gaston Wiet in "L'Islam et l'art musulman," in *L'Art et l'Homme* (ed. René Huyghe, fasc. 16, pp. 133 ff.), fig. 375. A drawing of the bust appears in Mehdi Bahrami's *Gurgan Faiences* (Cairo, 1949), p. 57, fig. 10. Some doubt has been expressed about the authenticity of this medallion, but its resemblance to the coin under discussion, about whose genuineness there can be no question, would be an argument in its favor. It might perhaps be a modern copy of an original, but I doubt very much that the busts and the legends are fabrications. I have not examined the piece at first hand, nor do I know where it is. In May 1963 during a brief visit to Teheran I endeavoured to determine its location. Evidently it is not in Teheran; it may be in Meshhed.

19 Notes XI

general is finer, the winged and jewelled crown more symmetrically and precisely defined.[4]

While we can scarcely call these two busts portraits in the ancient or the modern sense, I think there can be no doubt that they are intended as portraits of these two rulers, who were father and son. Rukn al-Dawlah abu-'Ali Ḥasan was ruler of Jibāl from 335[5] until his death in 366 H./946–976 A.D., and became overlord of the entire Buyid house from the time of his brother 'Imād al-Dawlah's death in 338.[6] He is believed to have been born in 284/897, so that at the time this portrait coin was struck he would have been about 65 years of age. We must search the chronicles for such biographical details as may enliven this face with more flesh and blood than the die-engraver has been able to achieve. While there is a very considerable body of information about the military and political events of Rukn al-Dawlah's reign, we learn relatively little about the man's character and personality. Ibn Khallikān's biography is lifeless.[7] Here and there scraps preserved in Miskawayh's *Tajārib al-umam* give us a few hints. Miskawayh says[8] that Rukn al-Dawlah, "though superior to the contemporary Dailemite princes, was still on the level of the predatory soldier, who is in a hurry for plunder, and saw no occasion to consider the effects of his conduct or the future of his subjects. By way of gratifying his troops he would permit them to commit acts from which no one else could restrain them and which were after-

---

[4] One wonders whether there may be some connection between this medallion and an allusion by Rūdhrāwari to a *dirham tāji* issued by 'Aḍud al-Dawlah. "One of 'Aḍud al-Dawlah's spies who returned from Cairo informed him among other things that he had gone to an old confectioner in Lamp Street, and handed him a dirhem of that prince's coinage (*Tāji*) to pay for something he was buying. The man returned the coin, and a dispute ensued wherein the confectioner abused the spy and the prince who had ordered the coin to be struck." (H. F. Amedroz and D. S. Margoliouth, *The Eclipse of the 'Abbasid Caliphate*, Oxford, 1920–1921, III, p. 60, transl. VI, p. 59). There follows a long and involved spy story, but no further light is shed on what kind of coin this was or why it was not acceptable. Was there perhaps a dirhem issue with a crowned (*tāji*) bust similar to this gold presentation piece, and were there objections to its portrayal of a human figure?

[5] Miskawayh (in *The Eclipse of the 'Abbasid Caliphate*), II, p. 108.

[6] Ibid., II, p. 120.

[7] Ibn Khallikān, transl. de Slane, I, p. 407.

[8] II, p. 279, transl. V, p. 298; cf. Gaston Wiet, *Soieries Persanes* (Mémoires de l'Institut d'Égypte, Vol. LII, Cairo, 1947), p. 117.

wards irreparable. He was compelled to do this because he was not himself of a royal house, and had not among the Dailemites the authority of an autocrat." This is an interesting remark, to which I will revert in a few moments. He goes on to say that Rukn al-Dawlah "was only their chieftain by virtue of the great liberality which formed a feature of his character, and his toleration of conduct which a prince does not ordinarily endure on the part of those whom he governs."

We know that he, like most of his contemporaries who were in a position to indulge their expensive tastes, amassed great wealth and practised extortion on a huge scale. We are told, for example, of one occasion before Rukn al-Dawlah succeeded to the rule when he was sent by his brother 'Imād al-Dawlah to Kāzirūn and other districts of Fārs and there not only extorted vast sums but also "unearthed great treasures that belonged to the Kisras, and had been inherited by certain families there; he raised more money than his brother had raised."[9] But if Rukn al-Dawlah was a robber baron of the first order, he also was not averse to dispensing great sums on occasion for the public weal. He spent 150,000 dinars on the repair of the great stone bridge known as the Qanṭarah Khurrah Zād over the Dujayl near Īdhāj;[10] and the irrigation and water-supply canal at Shīrāz known as Ruknābād was built at his order.[11] However avaricious and predatory he also could be personally generous. He had, as Ibn al-Athīr says, an "impulsive and emotional character."[12] Some idea of his munificence, at least when it was politic to be magnanimous, and of the splendor of his court, may be gained from the account of the gifts which Rukn al-Dawlah bestowed on Ibrāhīm b. al-Marzabān the Sallārid when the latter fled from Azerbaijān to Rayy in such dire straits that he arrived "with a horse and riding-whip only, none of his followers having escaped." The incident occurred in 355 H., just four years after the coin we are discussing was issued.[13] Miskawayh was an

[9] Miskawayh, I, p. 281, transl. IV, p. 319.
[10] Yāqūt I, p. 416, IV, p. 189; cf. G. Le Strange, *The Lands of the Eastern Caliphate* (Cambridge, 1930), p. 245; Wiet, *Soieries*, p. 191.
[11] Cf. Le Strange, *Lands*, p. 250.
[12] VIII, 493. Cf. H. F. Amedroz, "The Vizier Abu-l-Faḍl Ibn al 'Amîd, from the 'Tajârib al-Umam' of Abu 'Ali Miskawaih," in *Der Islam* III (1912), pp. 323–351, specifically p. 345.
[13] Miskawayh, II, pp. 218–219; transl. V, p. 232.

eye-witness. He stood with other sightseers close to Government House and watched the procession of gifts: "trays, bales and boxes of wearing apparel of all sorts ... borne on the heads of a hundred men ... gifts of perfume borne on silver dishes with the cases and other instruments that appertained thereto ... on the heads of thirty men ... sacks of coin ... on men's chests, with the purses of gold ... The bags of dirhems were upon fifty men, and the purses of dinars on twenty; the latter were of red silk, and the former of white, that they might be distinguished ... Stores of textiles on mules, which I did not count ... riding horses with saddles of gold and silver and horsecloths ... camels also beautifully equipped, laden with heavy articles of furniture, tents, pavilions, canvas sheets and marquees in great number and of fine quality. I never saw a gift of this size presented at a single time."

It was on just such occasions as this that special issues of dinars and dirhems were struck and distributed as presentation pieces or "pièces de circonstance." Perhaps the dinars and dirhems mentioned by Miskawayh were special issues. We know of several other Buyid examples. There is the gold medallion of ʿAḍud al-Dawlah discussed above. In 363 H./973–4 A.D. ʿIzz al-Dawlah struck a gold(?) piece in Madīnat al-Salām (Baghdād), with a lion devouring a gazelle or deer on one side, and a leopard (?) attacking an ibex or moufflon on the other (PLATE XLVI, 4).[14] And two years later, in 365, the same Buyid prince issued another gold presentation piece in Baghdād, portraying on the obverse a prince seated cross-legged, holding a cup and accompanied by two attendants (a familiar theme in Sasanian and Islamic art), and on the reverse a squatting lute-player (PLATE XLVII,

---

[14] So far as I know this piece has never been published. My photographs are of plaster casts presented to the American Numismatic Society by the British Museum in 1955. At that time Dr. John Walker did not know the provenance or location of the medallion. In my files are pencil rubbings, almost certainly of the same piece (in any case from the same dies), acquired from Mr. Edward Gans in 1941. Mr. Gans informed me that he had bought the piece from the estate of Dr. Hans Nussbaum of Zurich and that he had in turn sold it to Joseph Brummer in 1943. I have not been able to trace its subsequent history. Mr. Gans' (or Dr. Nussbaum's?) rubbings bear the notation "38 mm., 20.5 grms." As the mint/date formula gives no denomination (etc. .... ضرب بمدينة السلام), it is not certain that the metal is gold, but to judge by the weight I surmise that it is.

1).¹⁵ Comparable iconographically is an anonymous gold medal in the Freer Gallery of Art, the obverse of which is illustrated in PLATE XLVII, 2.¹⁶ Unfortunately no specimen of another Buyid "pièce de luxe" has survived, but in Ibn al-Athīr¹⁷ we are told of an enormous 1000-*mithqāl* (that would be 4250 grams) medallion of gold which the famous vizier al-Ṣāḥib Ibn ʿAbbād presented on the 1st of Muḥarram 378 H./988 A.D. to his master Fakhr al-Dawlah of Rayy.¹⁸

The Prime Minister Ibn ʿAbbād, or the Ṣāḥib, was the successor at Rayy of Ibn al-ʿAmīd II, Dhu'l-Kifāyatain, who in turn succeeded his father, Abu'l-Faḍl al-Kātib, Ibn al-ʿAmīd I, in this powerful position. The latter was Rukn al-Dawlah's vizier for many years and was in office in 351 when our portrait coin of Rukn al-Dawlah was struck. Ibn al-ʿAmīd was a man of many talents; a writer, poet, grammarian and philosopher, who among other intellectual gifts appears to have been endowed with an almost photographic memory. Not only was he a distinguished man of letters but he also enjoyed a

---

¹⁵ The photographs reproduced here were taken by me directly from the medallion in the Istanbul Archaeological Museum in May, 1963. This gold piece (36 mm., 18.30 grms.) was formerly in the Etnografya Müzesi in Ankara (Osman Ferit Sağlam, "Eşsiz bir madalya," in *Türk Tarih, Arkeologya ve Etnografya Dergisi*, 1935, figs. on pp. 3 and 4; cf. E. Kühnel, loc.cit., Abb. 10; Ibrahim Artuk, "Abbasiler devrine aid madalyalar," in *Tarih Dergisi*, VIII (1956), p. 152, and idem, "Abbasiler devrinde sikke," in *Belleten*, XXIV (1960), pl. II, no. 2). Almost identical is another specimen which has been illustrated and described several times: Sir Thomas W. Arnold, *Painting in Islam* (Oxford, 1928), p. 126, pl. LIX a; M. Bahrami, loc.cit. in footnote 3, above, pp. 18-19, pl. I, 3a and b; John Walker, "A unique medal of the Seljuk Ṭughrilbeg," in *Centennial Publication of the American Numismatic Society* (New York, 1958), p. 694, fig. 2. Walker's photographs are of plaster casts in the British Museum. I believe that this specimen is the same as one of which I have pencil rubbings from Edward Gans, a piece with the same history as that of the other medallion of 365 H., related in the preceding footnote. The rubbings bear the notation "36½ mm., 17.9 grms."

For the lute-player cf. E. Kühnel, "Der Lautenspieler in der islamischen Kunst des 8. bis 13. Jahrhunderts," in *Berliner Museen, Berichte aus den ehem. Preussischen Kunstsammlungen, Neue Folge*, I (1951), pp. 29–35.

¹⁶ Published by Bahrami in *AOiMEH* (see footnote 3), pp. 5-20, pl. I, 1a and 1b.

¹⁷ IX, 20; cf. M. Bahrami, *AOiMEH*, p. 6, and idem, *Gurgan Faiences*, p. 36.

¹⁸ Another luxury object of Fakhr al-Dawlah's is mentioned in the literature: a seal of *nadd* (a compound of amber, musc and aloes) of 1000 *mithqāls* in a Fāṭimid treasure (cf. P. Kahle, "Die Schätze der Fatimiden," in *ZDMG* 1935, p. 357).

reputation as a mathematician, physicist and mechanic. Among his inventions were remarkable weapons and siege machinery, and reflectors or mirrors which illuminated, or perhaps enkindled, objects a long way off. One detail in Miskawayh's encomium of Ibn al-ʿAmīd[19] has caught my eye: he had "knowledge of the refinements of the art of modelling and ingenuity in the application of it. I have seen him (says Miskawayh) in the room where he used to receive his intimate friends and associates take up an apple or something of the sort, play with it for a time, and then send it spinning having on it the form of a face scratched with his nail, more delicately than could have been executed by any one else with the appropriate instruments and in a number of days.[20] Is it too fanciful to suppose that Ibn al-ʿAmīd himself drew the round apple-like portrait which the die-engraver reproduced on the coin under discussion?

Whoever the portraitist was, there can be little doubt about his intention to produce a likeness of the Buyid prince in the Sasanian tradition. This was a period of vigorous nationalist revival in Persia when in literature and the arts there was a constant harking back to the great days of pre-Arab glory. The Buyids and their contemporary princelings took native Iranian names such as Bakhtiyār, Fannā-Khusraw, Shīrdīl, Fīrūz, etc. The title *shāhānshāh* is revived, and revived also is the use of Pahlevi on monuments such as Mil-i Radkān and Resget (both a little later), and on the Rukn al-Dawlah and ʿAḍud al-Dawlah presentation pieces. The Sasanian style portrait and the *shāhānshāh* title are reflections of Rukn al-Dawlah's and his Daylemite family's claim to royal descent, a claim which even in their own time was recognized to be spurious.[21] Rukn al-Dawlah's brother Muʿizz al-Dawlah himself is reported to have said that he had grown up carrying faggots on his head.[22]

[19] Miskawayh, II, pp. 275 ff., transl. V, pp. 293 ff.; cf. Amedroz, op.cit., pp. 339-345.
[20] In Amedroz's article in *Der Islam* the translation is "... toy with it for a time, and then twist it into the likeness of a face which he had moulded with his nails." The original Arabic is:

ولقد رأيته يتناول من مجلسه الذي يخلو فيه بثقاته واهل أنسته التفاحة وما يجري مجراها فيعبث بها ساعة ثم يدحرجها وعليه صورة وجه قد خطها بظفره ....

[21] Cf. Cl. Cahen, s.v. *Buwayhids* in *EI*[2]; E. G. Browne, *A Literary History of Persia* (Cambridge, 1928), I, p. 364.
[22] Fakhri, p. 376, transl. p. 480; cf. Wiet, *Soieries*, p. 117.

But regardless of whether we consider this coin as an attempt at a portrait, or whether we view it as a propaganda piece to bolster Rukn al-Dawlah's pretentions to royal lineage, it is certainly of interest to the art historian as a precisely dated and authentic piece of Buyid art. As such it is an object of rarity and value, because in other media we have very little Buyid material of unquestioned authenticity which can be exactly dated or even dated with any close approximation. There are a few Buyid inscriptions, including the well-known graffiti of Rukn al-Dawlah's son 'Aḍud al-Dawlah at Persepolis, but these of course are devoid of any figural representations.[23] Gold pitchers bearing the names of Bakhtiyār b. Mu'izz al-Dawlah, who died in 367 H./977 A.D., and of Ṣamṣām al-Dawlah abu-Kālīdjār Marzubān, who died in 440 H./1048 A.D., are fine examples of Buyid metal-work with characteristic bird ornament.[24] Ernst Kühnel in the article already cited has assembled all the known architectural remains and works of art in various media (metal-work, ceramics, woodwork, textiles, manuscripts, etc.) that can be assigned to the Buyid period. Some of these works have a certain relevance to our subject, but they cannot be discussed here. For example, certain of the controversial Buyid textiles offer comparative material: full-face representations, without however the characteristic pseudo-Sasanian headdress, and figures in profile wearing crowns of Sasanian derivation.[25] At the moment one can only hint at prototypes which furnished the inspiration for later representations, now lost, which in turn were, at least in some respects, the models for Rukn al-Dawlah's and 'Aḍud al-Dawlah's portraits. The figure of Bahram II at Naqsh-i Bahram[26] may be our ultimate Sasanian prototype; and the representation of Kavad I (?) on the famous rock-crystal cup in the Cabinet des Médailles in Paris[27]

---

[23] *Répertoire chronologique d'épigraphie arabe*, nos. 1475–6, 1830–2, 1901, 2087, 2118 (see also Vol. VI, p. 227); an unpublished tombstone from Iṣṭakhr may be of the Buyid period. G. Wiet published a chronological list of Buyid inscriptions in *L'Exposition persane de 1931* (Cairo, 1933), pp. 137–8.
[24] See Wiet, *Soieries*, pp. 91–98 and pl. XX; Kühnel, op.cit., p. 84 and pl. III, Abb. 5 and 6.
[25] Wiet, *Soieries*, pls. I and XXIV.
[26] Ernst E. Herzfeld, *Iran in the Ancient East* (London & New York, 1941), pl. CXX.
[27] Beautifully illustrated in detail in André Godard, *L'Art de l'Iran* (Paris, 1962), pl. 116. Godard assigns the work to the 6th century (p. 244).

offers suggestive points of comparison. Of closer relevance is a recently discovered small silver plate (PLATE XLVII, 3) now in the Ermitage Museum, published by Miss K. V. Trever in the Orbeli Festschrift,[28] which she describes as Hephthalite and ascribes to the 6th or the early 7th century. Whatever its precise date, we can, I think, recognize certain affinities between this facing figure with its winged headdress and our medallic portraits; as we can with probably earlier Sasanian and later post-Sasanian silver plates.

Finally I must touch briefly on the question of the possible specific occasion for the striking of Rukn al-Dawlah's coin. As I have intimated, it cannot have been a regular issue. Preserved dinars and dirhems of Rukn al-Dawlah's of conventional type struck at Rayy run in an almost unbroken series from 334 down to 365 H./945–976 A.D., and specifically there are regular dinars of the year 351.[29] Furthermore, Rukn al-Dawlah's conventional strikings are not, of course, limited to Rayy; my files show that coins were issued in his name from at least 35 different mints (of which no less than 16, incidentally, struck gold coins). In the chronicles I find no record of any extraordinary happening at Rayy in the year 351. During the course of the year Rukn al-Dawlah went off on one of his campaigns to Ṭabaristān and Jurjān.[30] However, there is a curious statement in Miskawayh which might just possibly have some relevance. Miskawayh says that in this year the Caliph bestowed the title ʽAḍud al-Dawlah on Rukn al-Dawlah's son Abu-Shujāʽ and that a rescript was issued to this effect.[31] Now the puzzling thing is that the *laqab* ʽAḍud al-Dawlah appears on Abu-Shujāʽ's coins at least as early as 341, and regularly thereafter.[32] Furthermore, we have his graffiti of 344 H. on the Tačara

---

[28] "Novoye Sasanidskoe blyudtse Ermitazha," in *Issledovaniya po istorii kultury narodov Vostoka* (Leningrad, 1960), pp. 257–270. I am indebted to Dr. Richard Ettinghausen and to Professor Richard N. Frye for bringing this article to my attention; and to Dr. Ettinghausen and Mrs. L. Fajans for providing me with a translation.

[29] G. C. Miles, *The Numismatic History of Rayy* (New York, 1938), nos. 173 ff. Some dates not appearing there have subsequently been published (dinars of 342, 345, 347, 348, 350, 352, 353, 354, 355 and 356, in *Sumer* X², and a dirhem of 356 in Østrup, no. 1251).

[30] Cf. *Numismatic History of Rayy*, p. 163.

[31] Miskawayh, II, p. 192, transl. V, p. 208.

[32] E.g., a dirhem of Shīrāz, 341 H. (Stanley Lane Poole, *Catalogue of Oriental Coins in the British Museum*, II, London, 1876, no. 658). The earliest numis-

at Persepolis, wherein he calls himself 'Aḍud al-Dawlah (PLATE XLVII, 4). Obviously there is something wrong with Miskawayh's statement. Did it take the Caliph al-Muṭīʿ eleven years to confirm Abu-Shujāʿ's *laqab*? Or did he confer some other honor on him in 351? And did Rukn al-Dawlah celebrate the honor done his son by striking this presentation piece? These and other questions remain to be answered.[33]

GEORGE C. MILES

matic use of the *laqab* may date from the previous year, 340 (J. Østrup, *Catalogue des Monnaies Arabes et Turques*, Copenhagen, 1938, no. 1262 = Jac.-Chr. Lindberg in *Revue des Séances de l'Année 1842, Royal Society of Northern Antiquaries*, Copenhagen, *1840–1844*, p. 229, no. 41, a dirhem with mint effaced).

[33] This paper was presented orally, in a somewhat different form, at the annual meeting of the American Oriental Society held in Washington, March 28, 1963.

DEUX TRÉSORS DE MONNAIES D'OR DES CROISÉS[1]

(See Plate XLVIII)

Lors de l'impression de notre précédent article nous avions pu signaler au dernier moment un trésor que le Musée de l'American Numismatic Society venait d'acquérir.[2] Un séjour à New-York de chacun d'entre nous a permis l'étude de celui-ci ainsi que d'un second.

Le premier, acheté en 1957, est composé de quarante-et-une pièces et a été découvert à Lattaquié (Syrie). Il a cette particularité intéressante d'être composé de trois séries de pièces: onze yéménites sulaïhides, cinq dinars fāṭimites d'al-Āmir bi aḥkām illāh et vingt-cinq pièces d'or à l'imitation des dinars du précédent frappés par les Croisés.

Le second, entré dans les collections en 1959 et provenant aussi du littoral oriental de la Méditerranée, sans plus de précision, est composé de quinze pièces à l'imitation des dinars d'al-Āmir.

Les pièces des Croisés de l'un et de l'autre trésor sont des imitations, les unes lisibles, les autres grossières et appartiennent toutes, avec quelques variantes intéressantes, aux deux seules classes 25 et 27 de notre article, sauf une, qui doit être attribuée à la classe 30. Monnaies des deux classes circulent donc ensemble. Mais elles sortent du même atelier: certaines, variantes de 25 ou de 27b, sont très proches les unes des autres; en outre, dans le second trésor, une pièce appartient par son droit à la classe 25 tandis que par son revers elle est de la classe 27b. La liaison est ainsi faite entre les pièces des deux classes.

Ces monnaies sont d'un or qui est d'une belle couleur jaune, habituelle à ces frappes. Leurs poids varient entre 3,57 et 3,96 g dans le premier trésor (une seule pièce à 3,19 g) avec un poids moyen de

---

[1] Nous voulons exprimer avant tout notre extrême gratitude au Dr. George C. Miles, conservateur en chef du Musée de l'American Numismatic Society, qui nous permet, avec son amabilité coutumière, de publier ces deux trésors.

[2] Paul Balog et Jacques Yvon, *Monnaies à légendes arabes de l'Orient Latin* dans RN, 6ᵉ série, t. I (1958), p. 150.

3,73 g; dans le second les poids oscillent entre 3,43 et 3,88 g avec un poids moyen de 3,78 g. Or il est à noter que les cinq pièces fāṭimites du premier trésor ont un poids moyen de 3,79 g et varient entre 3,62 et 3,91 g. Dinars des Croisés et dinars fāṭimites ne sont donc pas très éloignés les uns des autres par le poids.[3]

Le premier trésor est important en lui-même. Les monnaies d'or des Croisés sont mêlées à d'autres monnaies musulmanes, les unes yéménites, les autres fāṭimites. Les dinars yéménites, de la dynastie des Sulaïhides, sont venus là par le commerce très certainement. Elles portent toutes la date de 451 H.[4] Mais le fait le plus marquant est que dans ce trésor monnaies fāṭimites d'al-Āmir et monnaies des Croisés à ce type se côtoient. Ainsi prototypes et imitations circulent ensemble et ces dernières proviennent certainement du même atelier. Les dates, quand on peut les déchiffrer, dates simplement amorcées ou incomplètes, portent toujours le chiffre d'unité 6. La date imitée est donc soit l'année 506 soit l'année 516 H. En outre lorsque l'on peut lire un nom d'atelier celui-ci est toujours Miṣr, comme nous l'avions indiqué précédemment.[5] Les imitations sont en cela le fidèle reflet de la circulation monétaire. C'est l'or des ateliers égyptiens qui, à cette époque, circule en Syrie plus que l'or des ateliers syriens. Ceux-ci, que ce soit Ṣūr ou ʿAsqalān (Tyr ou Ascalon) paraissent avoir peu travaillé pour le khalife et sont, ensuite, tombés entre les mains des Croisés. Ni l'un ni l'autre ne sont d'ailleurs représentés parmi les pièces fāṭimites du trésor, car les cinq pièces appartiennent aux ateliers égyptiens d'Alexandrie, de Miṣr et d'al-Qāhirah.

Les dates de ces monnaies fāṭimites sont 508, 510, 514 et 518 H. Cette dernière donne un *terminus a quo* pour l'enfouissement du trésor, soit 1124 A.D. C'est une tâche ardue que vouloir préciser celui-ci. Les pièces d'imitation ont circulé longtemps: les deux trésors

---

[3] Rapport inférieur à celui qui est donné généralement, voy. notre article p. 136. Un tel trésor est précieux car il nous livre des pièces extraites de la circulation courante. Il paraîtrait donc qu'al-Āmir, ayant, du fait des Croisades, des difficultés monétaires, ait dû abaisser le poids de ses monnaies d'or et, selon Ehrenkreutz, "The Crisis of dinar in the Egypt of Saladin" dans *Journal of the American Oriental Society*, t. 76, 1956, p. 178 et suiv., également l'aloi.
[4] Par le commerce avec l'Egypte. C'est ce pays qui est en relations constantes avec le Yemen, voy. W. Heyd, *Histoire du commerce du Levant au moyen âge* (Leipzig, 1886), t. I, p. 378 et suiv.
[5] Notre article p. 139.

signalés par Mr. Grierson en sont une preuve.⁶ Cependant l'enfouissement n'est sans doute pas postérieur de beaucoup à la dernière en date des pièces fāṭimites. Il n'est peut-être pas téméraire non plus de le situer entre celle-ci et la prise de Lattaquié par Saladin en juillet 1188. La ville fut alors détruite et semble n'avoir repris toute son importance qu'une vingtaine d'années plus tard. Elle est alors étroitement unie à Alep et les Vénitiens obtiennent des positions avantageuses dans les deux villes. C'est entre elles deux que se fera tout le trafic de la Syrie du nord par la suite, Antioche et port Saint-Siméon étant tenus à l'écart.⁷

Le trésor présent permet donc de situer un peu mieux chronologiquement les imitations d'al-Āmir. La date exacte et le lieu précis de leur frappe n'en restent pas moins à résoudre, tout autant que pour les imitations d'al-Mustanṣir.⁸ Nous avons déjà dit combien il était malaisé de trancher le problème. Que l'on nous permette cependant de verser à ce débat quelques textes qui viennent l'éclairer. Parmi les actes concernant le commerce vénitien publiés par MM. Morozzo della Rocca et Lombardo⁹ il en est une dizaine, passés entre

⁶ Philip Grierson, "A rare crusader bezant with the Christus Vincit legend" dans *Museum Notes*, t. VI (1954), p. 174. Le premier trésor comprenait, en plus d'un *Agnus Dei*, des imitations des dinars d'al-Mustanṣir et d'al-Āmir ainsi que des pièces à dates et légendes chrétiennes. Le second était composé d'un *Agnus Dei*, d'une pièce à date et légendes chrétiennes et d'un dinar à l'imitation de al-Mustanṣir.

⁷ W. Heyd, op.cit., t. I, pp. 373–378; Claude Cahen, *La Syrie du Nord à l'époque des Croisades* (Paris, 1940), pp. 689–690. Sur l'importance de Lattaquié au cours des Croisades on verra René Grousset, *Histoire des Croisades et du royaume franc de Jérusalem*, t. I, pp. 75, 133, 136, 177–178, 191, 205, 240; Heyd, op.cit., t. I, pp. 168–169; Cahen, op.cit., p. 222, n. 46, 233. Sur la prise de la ville et la désolation qui suivit, Cahen, op.cit., pp. 429, 432; Grousset, op.cit., t. II, pp. 824–827; René Dussaud, *Topographie historique de la Syrie antique et médiévale* (Paris, 1927), (B. A. H. no. 4), pp. 414–5. A un moment indéterminé entre 1223 et 1260 Lattaquié redevint franque puis fut reprise par les mamelouks en 1287.

⁸ Il est intéressant de noter qu'il n'y a pas dans ce trésor ni de dinars d'al-Mustanṣir ni d'imitations de ceux-ci. Cela viendrait confirmer la thèse de Blancard selon qui ces imitations ont cessé d'être frappées au cours du XIIe s., voy. Blancard, *Le besant d'or sarrazinas pendant les Croisades* (Marseille, 1880), pp. 25–29 et 35. Mais il pensait que ces imitations avaient été reprises à Antioche et à Tripoli au XIIIe s. Il faudrait avoir en mains d'autres trésors pour vérifier cela.

⁹ R. Morozzo della Rocca et A. Lombardo, *Documenti del commercio veneziano nei secoli XI–XIII* (Rome, 1940), (*Regesta chartarum Italiae*). Des *Nuovi Docu-*

1161 et 1211, qui font mention de sommes exprimées en *bisancios aureos sarracenatos novos de moneta regis Hierusalem*, sommes payées ou à payer en Syrie, particulièrement à Acre et à Tyr (une fois à Antioche dans un acte de 1165). C'est là une preuve que ces besants sarracénats sortent bien de la Monnaie du roi de Jérusalem et ont cours en Syrie. Le droit de battre monnaie est un droit parfaitement régalien, proclamé d'ailleurs par Baudouin II.[10]

menti ont été publiés à Venise en 1953. La lecture d'autres textes de ce genre apportera sans doute de nouveaux témoignages de cette frappe de besants à la Monnaie du roi. Jean Richard, *Le royaume latin de Jérusalem* (Paris, 1953), p. 33, n. I avait déjà relevé dans ces textes-ci la différence faite entre les *bisantios perperos* et les *bisantios sarracenatos* par exemple.

[10] *Livre au roi*, chap. XVI dans RHC Lois, t. I, pp. 616–617. Sur ce point voy. Jean Richard, op.cit., p. 85 et J. Prawer, "Les premiers temps de la féodalité dans le royaume de Jérusalem. Une reconsidération" dans *Revue d'histoire du droit*, t. XXII, pp. 422–423.

CATALOGUE[11]

TRÉSOR DE LATTAQUIÉ (ANS Museum 57.114)

Fāṭimites authentiques

Toutes les pièces sont du khalife al-Āmir bi-aḥkām illāh (495–524 H./1101–1130 A.D.)
1. Alexandrie, 514 H. 23 mm. 3,84 g. Miles 422
2. Miṣr, 508 H. 22 mm. 3,62 g. Miles 460
3. Id., 510 H. 23 mm. 3,91 g. Miles 462
4. Id., id., id. 3,81 g. Miles 462
5. al-Muʿizzīyah al-Qāhirah, 518 H. 21 mm. 3,79 g. Miles 475

Yéménites. Dynastie des Sulaihides

Toutes les pièces sont au nom de ʿAli ibn Muḥammad et ont été frappées à Zebīd, l'an 451 H. Elles ont chacune le même diamètre: 22 mm. Références: Casanova, nos. 4, 5 et 6.

6. 2,46 g.	10. 2,46 g.	14. 2,48 g.
7. 2,44 g.	11. 2,48 g.	15. 2,45 g.
8. 2,46 g.	12. 2,47 g.	16. 2,46 g.
9. 2,45 g.	13. 2,46 g.	

Imitations des Croisés

17. Date avortée, 506 ou 516? سلەسد
    22 mm. 3,91 g.–BY 25 var.

*18. Au droit 3 annelets entre les légendes extérieure et intérieure.
    Date: [50]6 سەاسلە
    22 mm. 3,82 g.–BY 25 var.

---

[11] Miles ... = George C. Miles, *Fāṭimids coins in the collections of the University Museum, Philadelphia, and the American Numismatic Society* (New York, 1951), *NNM*, no. 121.
Casanova ... = P. Casanova, *Dinars inédits du Yémen* dans *RN*, 3ᵉ série, t. XII (1894), pp. 200–220, pl. V.
BY ... = Paul Balog et Jacques Yvon, *Monnaies à légendes arabes de l'Orient Latin*, dans *RN*, 6ᵉ série, t. I (1958), pp. 133–168.
Un astérisque devant le numéro du catalogue signifie que la pièce est illustrée.

19. Date avortée, 506 ou 516? ﺑﺴﻢ ﺍﻟﻠﻪ

22 mm. 3,80 g.–BY 25 var.

*20. Date incomplète mais certaine, 506 H.

21,5 mm. 3,75 g.–BY 25 var.

*21. Date: [50]6? ﺳﻠﻪ

23 mm. 3,73 g.–BY 25

22. Date: [50]6? Pointe sur les: ص =

23 mm. 3,69 g.–BY 25 var.

*23. Légende marginale se terminant ainsi:

Date: première lettre amorcée sans signification

22,5 mm. 3,70 g.–BY 25 var.

24. Légende marginale se terminant ainsi: Pas de date

22 mm. 3,93 g.–BY 25 var.

25. Légende marginale se terminant ainsi: Pas de date

22 mm. 3,84 g.–BY 25 var.

*26. Date manque. 22 mm. 3,69 g.–BY 25 var.

27. Id. Pointe sur les ص =

21,5 mm. 3,69 g.–BY 25 var.

28. Date manque. Sana (سنة) amorcée: Bism(illah):

22 mm. 3,67 g.–BY 25 var.

29. 21,5 mm. 3,81 g.–BY 27 a

30. 21,5 mm. 3,67 g–BY 27 a

*31. Deux globules sur les ص =

21 mm. 3,74 g.–BY 27 a var.

DEUX TRÉSORS DE MONNAIES D'OR

32. 22 mm. 3,85 g.–BY 27 b
33. 22 mm. 3,80 g.–BY 27 b
34. 23 mm. 3,75 g.–BY 27 b
*35. 22 mm. 3,71 g.–BY 27 b
36. 22 mm. 3,63 g.–BY 27 b
*37. 22 mm. 3,96 g.–BY 27 b var.
38. 22 mm. 3,91 g.–BY 27 b var.
39. 22 mm. 3,69 g.–BY 27 d
*40. 23 mm. 3,57 g.–BY 27 d
41. 22 mm. 3,19 g.–BY 30

TRÉSOR DE PROVENANCE INCERTAINE (ANS Museum 59.203)

1. Date manque: 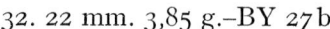 Sana amorcée
   22 mm. 3,74 g.–BY 25 var.

2. Date manque totalement. Légende marginale se terminant ainsi:
   21 mm. 3,88 g.–BY 25 var.

3. Légende marginale se terminant ainsi:
   21 mm. 3,65 g.–BY 25 var.

4. Légende marginale:
   22 mm. 3,60 g.–BY 25 var.

5. Légende marginale:
   22 mm. 3,43 g.–BY 25 var.

6. Légende marginale, assez rudimentaire:
   21 mm. 3,76 g.–BY 25 var.

7. Légende marginale, assez rudimentaire:
   21,5 mm. 3,80 g.–BY 25 var.

8. Date: 506 H.:

بسم الله الر حمن ا ـ حد ا المـ ـ سو ـ ـ له

س/ـ ـ د الله

Revers plus confus: 27 b ? 22 mm. 3,62 g.–BY 25 var. et 27 b ?

9. Légende marginale: ى ؟ ـحـا

22 mm. 3,72 g.–BY 25 var.

10. 22 mm. 3,78 g.–BY 27 a

11. 21 mm. 3,57 g.–BY 27 b, mais ressemble à 25

12. 21 mm. 3,54 g.–BY 27 b

13. 21,5 mm. 3,91 g.–BY 27 b

14. 22 mm. 3,49 g.–BY 27 b

15. 22 mm. 3,85 g.–BY 25 var. اا ـحـا pour le droit. Revers: BY 27 b

PAUL BALOG et JACQUES YVON

GOLD FORGERIES
OF TIGRANES THE GREAT OF ARMENIA*
(See Plate XLIX)

The coinage of the Artaxias dynasty of Armenia (190 b.c. to a.d. 6) has been subjected to a few cursory studies.[1] Because of the paucity of numismatic material and the uncertainty regarding historical events, however, it has been impossible to attribute the existing material with any degree of accuracy; consequently, the coinage of this period has generally been neglected.

Most of the extant coins of the Artaxias dynasty belong to Tigranes II (often called the Great), who established an empire by conquering Sophene, Syria, Cappadocia, and parts of neighboring countries. Most of these were struck in the mint of Antioch, which was under Armenian domination during the period 83–69 b.c.

In some instances,[2] the Tigranes coins struck at Antioch have been considered part of the Seleucid series, but this belief seems untenable in view of the fact that the obverse represents a type entirely different from the earlier Seleucid coins, and is typical of the coins struck by other Armenian rulers in Armenia proper.

As the Tigranes tetradrachm struck at Antioch was the most popular type of coin of the Artaxias dynasty, it is not surprising that all

---
* The writer wishes to thank His Holiness, Catholicos Vazken I, of the Armenian Church for the permission to take a plaster cast of the gold piece in the Etchmiadsin Museum, and Mr. Kh. Mousheghian of the Numismatic Department of the State Historical Museum in Erivan, Armenia, for a photograph of the cast. Thanks are also due to Mr. K. Jenkins of the British Museum for sending reproductions of the casts in their collection.

[1] V. Langlois, *Numismatique de l'Arménie de l'Antiquité* (Paris, 1859); E. Babelon, *Les Rois de Syrie, d'Arménie et de Commagene* (Paris, 1890); G. Macdonald, "The Coinage of Tigranes I," *NC*, 4th Ser., Vol. II (1902), pp. 193 to 202; E. T. Newell, *Late Seleucid Mints in Ake-Ptolemais and Damascus*, NNM 84 (1939), and *Some Unpublished Coins of Eastern Dynasts*, NNM 30 (1926); H. Seyrig, "Trésor Monétaire de Nisibe," *RN* (1955), pp. 85–128; G. Le Rider, "Monnaies grecques acquises par le Cabinet des Médailles en 1959," *RN* (1959–60), pp. 7–35.

[2] *BMC Seleucid Kings in Syria*, pp. 103–105.

of the gold forgeries of this period which have come to the writer's attention belong to this ruler. The fact that Tigranes the Great was one of the most illustrious kings of Armenia may also have been a deciding factor in the choice of this type for the gold forgeries.

It is interesting that these forgeries represent several varieties, both cast and struck, indicating that they were prepared by different forgers at different times.

The following are the six specimens described in this note:

1. Perhaps the earliest is the specimen which has long been in the museum of the Etchmiadsin Monastery in Armenia.

Obv.: Head of Tigranes right, wearing an ornate five-pointed tiara, decorated with an eight-rayed star flanked by two standing eagles facing outwards, their heads turned toward the star. The tiara is bordered with pearls. Diademed and the diadem ends hang down. A second diadem starting at the forehead joins the main one under the star. Part of the king's hair and earring (?) appear to the left of the eye.

Rev.: ΒΑΣΙΛΕΩΣ on right downward, ΤΙΓΡΑΝΟΥ on left downward. Tyche of Antioch, draped and wearing a turreted crown, seated on a rock facing right. In her right hand she holds a vase rather than the usual palm branch. At her feet, the river-god Orontes, swimming right, the left hand holding or touching the fillet border.

4.80 gr. ↑

Aderbed[3] gives the following romantic background to this coin. According to his account, it belonged to Muzzafar ed-Din, the Shah of Persia (1896–1906), who used it as an ornament on his watch chain. It then passed to his son, Mohammed Ali, who in turn presented it to Olferiev Sergei Petrovich, the Russian vice-consul in the city of Van. In 1910, Mr. Yervant Lalayan succeeded in acquiring this coin and presented it to the Catholicos Matthew II of the Armenian Church. His Holiness placed it in the Museum of Etchmiadsin in Armenia where it remains to this day. Aderbed does not consider this coin a forgery and gives an illustration and description of it. His contention that Tyche holding a vase represents a type different from all other

---

[3] Aderbed, *Azkakragan Hantes* (Tiflis), pp. 199–231 (1912); pp. 27–56, 200–223 (1913); pp. 57–67, 83–89 (1914) (Armenian).

tetradrachms is not valid, since a very similar type of tetradrachm is to be found in the Museum of the Mechitarist Monastery at St. Lazare, Venice. There is a six-pointed star on the Venice tetradrachm to the left of the ear, on the tiara. Because of the worn condition of the gold specimen, the star is not visible. There is a clasp attached to the lower part of this coin which partially obliterates the design. The coin appears to be struck rather than cast, on a thin flan, unlike the usual Tigranes silver tetradrachms which have the same diameter but are much thicker and weigh over 15 grams.

2, 3. Both are made with the same die, although the forgery from which the cast in the British Museum was made was struck on a much larger flan. The workmanship is very artistic.

Obv.: Smaller version of No. 1.

Rev.: As above, but Tyche wearing a three-pointed crown. In her right hand, she holds a palm branch under which there is the monogram ⚹. The river-god Orontes also holds a branch with her left hand. There is a branch to the left of ΤΙΓΡΑΝΟΥ. No trace of border.

BM forgery—4.36 gr. ↗

Author's specimen—1.55 gr. →

The British cast was obtained from Nussbaum, a Zurich dealer, in 1938. The author's specimen was acquired in 1950 from Mr. A. Poladian of Beirut.

4. This cast, again from the British Museum, is from a coin which was in the possession of Mr. Empedocles, a private collector in Athens. It is of very crude workmanship and lacks any resemblance to the coins of Tigranes.

Obv.: Very gross representation of the head of Tigranes, with a crown, unlike the characteristic Armenian tiara. Dotted border.

Rev.: ΒΑΣΙΛΕΩΣ on right downward, ΒΑΣΙΛΕΩΝ ΤΙΓΡΑΝΟΥ on left downward. As usual, Tyche seated on rock and facing right, holding palm branch in her right hand. River-god Orontes swimming right, below the figure of Tyche.

4.73 gr. ↓

5. In the ANS collection, acquired in 1946.

Obv.: Head of king, wearing tiara.

Rev.: Usual type with legend.

This coin appears to be struck. The king's features bear no resemblance to those of the Tigranes coins. On the reverse Tyche is portrayed very crudely.

7.25 gr. ↑

6. The author saw this specimen some years ago, and was able to get an impression of it through the kind permission of its owner, the late Dr. Khantamour of Hollywood, California. It appeared to be a tetradrachm, either gilded or covered with gold foil. The present whereabouts of this coin is unknown.

Obv.: Head of Tigranes right, wearing tiara.

Rev.: Usual type with legend.

Probably over 15 gr. ↑

Two other specimens have been mentioned in the literature. Aderbed discusses the existence of a Tigranes gold coin in the Vatican Museum, which he was unable to see because of the absence of the curator.

Recent inquiries made to Dr. L. M. Tocci of the Vatican Numismatic Museum disclosed the fact that no such gold coin was to be found in their collection. Apparently, Aderbed had been misinformed.

Another gold coin has been mentioned by Mr. Kurdian.[4] The present whereabouts of this coin is not known.

The author has recently been informed that a small gold Tigranes was acquired by the Mechitarist Monastery in Venice. No particulars of this coin are available.

The fact that all the Tigranes gold pieces have turned out to be forgeries is not surprising. No gold coins are known to have been struck by the rulers of the Artaxias dynasty.

PAUL BEDOUKIAN

---

[4] H. Kurdian, *Gotchnag, An Armenian Weekly*, XLVI, 5 (New York, Feb. 2, 1946), p. 113.

A MAMLŪK HOARD OF ḤAMĀH

(See Plate XLIX)

In January 1962 Mr. J. M. Eisenberg of New York was good enough to permit me to examine a lot of 305 Mamlūk silver coins which he had acquired.[1] All these coins, of which 297 were dirhems and eight apparently half-dirhems, were specimens of a single issue of the Baḥri Mamlūk sultan al-Manṣūr Sayf al-Dīn Qalā'ūn, struck at the Syrian mint of Ḥamāh in the last year of his reign 689 H./1290 A.D. As this particular issue is hitherto unpublished[2] and the lot appears to constitute a hoard, a short note on the subject would seem to be in order.

All the coins, both the dirhems and the fractions, appear to be from the same pair of dies. The dirhems range in diameter from 20 to 23 mm., the halves from 17 to 18 mm. The die positions are not fixed. All the coins are very weakly struck, not worn, as the specimens illustrated, [68]9, 68[9] and [689], Plate XLIX, 1–4, show. The following transcriptions of the legends are reconstructed from a comparison of several specimens:

Obv.:
ضرب بحماة
السلطان الملك
سيف
المنصور الدنيا
والدين قلاون
بحماة

Ornament above والدين.

---

[1] Five of these were subsequently presented by Mr. Eisenberg to the Museum of the American Numismatic Society (ANS 62.10).
[2] Cf. P. Balog, *The Coinage of the Mamlūk Sultans of Egypt* (ANS Numismatic Studies, No. 12, New York, 1964), no. 135, and Second Supplement, p. 394.

Rev.:

○ ودين الحق
○
لا اله الا الله
محمـد رسول الله
○ ارسله بالهـدى
○

Ornaments before على and after ذلك.

The mint name is preserved on 147 specimens. On no single specimen is the complete date preserved, but there are a sufficient number with either the digit or the decade or the century, or two of the three figures, preserved to leave no doubt whatever about the date, even where the digit is lacking, particularly as other details show the coins to be, as remarked, from identical dies. Five specimens are double-struck, reverse die on obverse, and obverse die on reverse. One specimen is a brockage with retrograde traces of the reverse die on the reverse and the obverse unaffected.

The eight specimens which I judge to be half dirhems because of their reduced diameters (PLATE XLIX, 5) range in weight from 1.08 grams to 2.06 grams (1.08, 1.46, 1.75, 1.93, 1.94, 1.97, 2.06, 2.06). The frequencies of the weights of the dirhems, scaled at intervals of .20 gr., are as follows:

Weight	No. of Specimens
1.61–1.80	1
1.81–2.00	1
2.01–2.20	6
2.21–2.40	14
2.41–2.60	15
2.61–2.80	22
2.81–3.00	64
3.01–3.20	76
3.21–3.40	51
3.41–3.60	28
3.61–3.80	10

Weight	No. of Specimens
3.81–4.00	5
4.01–4.20	2
4.35	1
4.77	1

The peak therefore is at 3.01–3.20 grams, somewhat above the figure given by Balog (op.cit., p. 41) for the period (2.80–2.90 grams). The large number of specimens in the groups on either side of the peak (64 from 2.81–3.00 grams, and 51 from 3.21–3.40 grams) would suggest that at this time the weight of individual dirhems was not controlled nearly as accurately as it was in Umayyad and early 'Abbāsid days.[3]

GEORGE C. MILES

[3] Cf. G. C. Miles, "Byzantine Miliaresion and Arab Dirhem: some Notes on their Relationship," *ANSMN*, IX, 1960, p. 213.

THE WILLIAM EWART GLADSTONE MEDALET

(See Plate L)

The American Numismatic Society has in its Collection a small gold medalet which seems not to have been previously published, having a distinct East Asian historical and numismatic connotation. The inscriptions on this small (16.5 mm.) medalet are as follows:

Obv.: Crown THIS GOLD/DISCOVERED IN/SYCEE SILVER/THE PRIZE OF BRITISH/ARMS IN CHINA/WAS EXTRACTED/AT H.M. MINT/ MARCH/1842
Rev.: THE RT HON/W.GLADSTONE/MASTER/BY A PROCESS FIRST/ APPLIED TO THE PUBLIC/SERVICE AND TO THE/BENEFIT OF BRITISH/COMMERCE UNDER/THE RT HON./J.C. HERRIES/1829

It was struck at the Royal Mint of England of gold extracted from silver which had been delivered to the British government in settlement of the "ransom" of the city of Canton amounting to 6 million Mexican dollars, as prescribed by the Convention of Chuenpi of January 30, 1841, negotiated by Captain Charles Elliot, England's "Chief Superintendent of Trade in China" and the Chinese Imperial Commissioner Ch'i-shan.

The payment, in sycee silver, was to compensate the British merchants for opium seized by the Chinese under orders of the Imperial Commissioner, Lin Tse-hsü, in 1839. The Convention ceded Hongkong to the British, reopened Canton to trade, allowed direct official intercourse between British and Chinese on equal terms, and agreed to the payment of the so-called "ransom" of 6 million dollars.

The agreement was shortly disavowed by both the British and the Chinese governments. The British Foreign Secretary, Lord Palmerston, considered that Elliot had exceeded his instructions as the amount agreed upon was insufficient to pay the merchants for the opium seized and the cost of the British operations incident to the affair, or to recompense the merchants for their losses incident to the bankrupcy of several of the Chinese Hong merchants. The subsequent

Treaty of Nanking superceded the Convention and cost the Chinese government an additional 15 million dollars.

Elliot estimated that the sycee silver obtained for the "ransom" of Canton had amounted to 150 tons,[1] and this medalet was struck to commemorate the increment in value which accrued to the British government from the unanticipated presence of the substantial amount of gold in the Chinese silver.

J. C. Herries (1778–1855) was Master of the Royal Mint from 1828 to 1830, and the date "1829" on this piece is that when the mint instituted a new process for the recovery of gold from silver. British Prime Minister William Ewart Gladstone (1809–1898) served as Master of the Mint from 1841 to 1845.

H. F. BOWKER

Selected Bibliography

Couling, Samuel. *Encyclopaedia Sinica* (Shanghai, 1917), pp. 114, 159f., 392.

Hummel, Arthur, Editor. *Eminent Chinese of the Ch'ing Period* (Washington, D.C., 1943), pp. 126–29, 511–14.

Morse, Ballou. *The International Relations of the Chinese Empire*, vol. I (London, 1910), pp. 270ff.

---

[1] As Chinese taxes were paid to the government in silver by weight, it was customary to melt down all the silver dollars into sycee before receiving it at the Treasury. The 150 tons of silver of Elliot's estimate is equivalent to the 6 million dollars demanded.

MANCHU INSCRIPTIONS ON CHINESE CASH COINS

(See PLATES L–LV)

European language publications contain very little in the way of reliable information concerning the Chinese coins having Manchu inscriptions. The purpose of this article, then, is to present an annotated distribution list of the mints operating during the various Manchu reigns including spans of operation and the distinguishing mint signs in Manchu. It is hoped that this list will provide the collector with a reliable guide and also serve as a contribution to the financial history of the Ch'ing period.[1]

The first Manchu ruler who issued coins was the famous Nurhachi, who proclaimed himself Khan in the year 1616 and chose T'ien-ming 天命 as the title of his reign. He ordered two different coins to be minted; one inscribed in Chinese for the newly conquered areas of what is now Liaoning and Kilin, and the other in Manchu for the original territory. The Chinese coin has on the obverse: T'ien-ming t'ung-pao 天命通寶 (Current coin of the T'ien-ming period) and reads in the usual Chinese order: top, bottom, right, left. The Manchu coin is inscribed: Abkai Fulingga han jiha (Money of Khan T'ien-ming) and is read: left, right, top, bottom (PLATE L, 1). This coin also exists without the top and bottom inscription (PLATE L, 2), both types having a plain reverse.

---

[1] The list by no means represents all coins cast in Chinese territory from 1657 through 1910. Coins omitted include the Taiping coins, which were inscribed entirely in Chinese and coins of Yakub Beg (d. 1877) which were in Arabic. Neither is it the intended purpose to go into the details of size, weight and mint statistics; nor the question of unofficial, i.e., rebel and private, mintings. Simple differences among the coins; dots, crescents, marks on the Chinese characters, etc., have been similarly disregarded. The numbers within the list refer to the illustrations on the plates.

His successor, Khan Abahai took two reign titles after he had pronounced himself Emperor: T'ien-ts'ung 天聰 (1627–1635) and Ch'ung-te 崇德 (1636–1643). He issued one large coin during the first years of his reign, written totally in Manchu. It reads: Sure han ni jiha ᡧᡠᡵᡝ ᡥᠠᠨ ᠨᡳ ᠵᡳᡥᠠ (Money of Khan [T'ien-] Ts'ung). On the reverse: reading left, right: juwan ᠵᡠᠸᠠᠨ (ten) indicating that this coin is worth ten common coins, emuyan ᡝᠮᡠ ᠶᠠᠨ (one liang = one ounce of silver; Plate L, 3, 4). The coins are inscribed in ancient Manchu without the more modern diacritical marks. The style of these coins is obviously copied from the late Ming T'ien-ch'i 天啓 coins (1621–1627).

In 1644, Emperor Fu-lin 福臨 conquered Peking and immediately established two mints there. The first mint belonged to the Hu-pu 戶部 (Board of Revenue), the second to the Kung-pu 工部 (Board of Works). The coins of these mints had on the obverse the standard inscription Shun-chih t'ung-pao 順治通寶 (Shun-chih being the title of his reign; Plate L, 5); the reverse was plain as in the preceeding Ming dynasty.

In 1645, concurrent with the production of the first coins by the mints in the provinces, an imperial order dictated that the coins would show the place of minting by means of a single Chinese character on the reverse. This was a revival of the practice used during the K'ai-yüan period 開元 (713–741) of the T'ang dynasty. The characters were, in general, the same as were later used, transcribed into Manchu, to indicate mints. The only exceptions were: hu 戶 used by the Board of Revenue and kung 工 used by the Board of Works. The characters were placed top, left or right without any apparent systematic positioning.

In 1653, imperial order dictated that the coins show on the reverse: left, the two Chinese characters i-li 一厘 = one thousandth of one tael, i.e., an ounce of silver); right, the Chinese character for the mint. This coin type, one of the few cases where a relation to another form of money is indicated on Chinese cash coins, was minted for only five years.

The types discussed thus far have not been included in the distribution list since they do not display any Manchu mint characters and also because the mint changes that occured during this brief period would necessitate a description beyond the scale of this article.

The descriptive list begins with 1657, since in that year a law was passed requiring each mint to put on the reverse of its coins: right, the mint character in Chinese; left, the Manchu transcription of the character. the only exceptions to this were the two government mints at Peking, the Board of Revenue and the Board of Works.

The coins of these mints were inscribed on the reverse: left, boo for the Chinese character pao 寶 (coin); right, the Manchu transcription of the names of the two mints (PLATE L, 6, 7). Official Chinese sources of the period indicate that two additional mints existed at the time: Miyün 密雲 in Chihli (Hopei) using the character mi 密 and Yünnan 雲南 (Kunming) in Yünnan province using the character yün 雲. It would appear that neither mint exercised its privilege for one reason or another as coins of this description are unknown.

In 1662, Hsüan-yeh 玄燁 ascended the throne and chose the name K'ang-hsi 康熙, his coins being inscribed K'ang-hsi t'ung-pao 康熙通寶 (PLATE LI, 22). There is also another type issued during the reign of Hsüan-yeh with a different style character hsi 熙 (PLATE LI, 23). These accurate, carefully made coins are quite rare, their origin being generally ascribed to a special issue prepared by the Board of Revenue from the metal accumulated from melting down eighteen Buddhist statues.

During the period 1662–1721, Hsüan-yeh opened new mints, but during his last years, he closed seven. According to the Chinese sources the mints of Szechuan and Kweichow bearing the identifying characters chuan 川 and kuei 貴 should have been operating during his reign, but no coins with these inscriptions have been found. The assumption that these two mints did not open until later is strengthened by the fact that the character 貴 is not used in the next period for the Kweichow province.

The two government mints retained the same reverses as in the previous period except that there is a difference in the Manchu style of writing for the characters chang 昌, shan 陝, and ning 寧 (cf. nos. 17 and 24, 20 and 25, 21 and 26). In addition to the coins listed there was one very common forgery in circulation at that time (PLATE LII, 36). Its reverse reads: left, boo ᠪᠣᠣ and right, the corrupt character 萴 which might be chi 薊 (cf. PLATE LI, 9) or might even be ching 荆 (Chingchow 荆州, presently Hupei), a mint that had ceased operations as early as 1653.

In 1723, the throne passed to Yin-chen 胤禛 who chose the reign title Yung-cheng 雍正 (PLATE LII, 37). In addition to continuing the operation of all the mints inherited from his father, Yun-chen instituted a policy whereby all the mints in the provinces copied the system employed by the two Peking mints. All coins produced had boo on the left and the name of the mint in Manchu on the right. In general the style of writing remained the same with slight changes in the characters of the two Board mints.[2]

The next ruler, Emperor Hung-li 弘歷 took the reign title Ch'ien-lung 乾隆 (PLATE LIII, 58). Hung-li greatly expanded China's territory, conquering Sinkiang and the Ili-area, where he opened several mints; and he even ordered coins to be struck for use in Annam, however these were inscribed only in Chinese. The coins produced during this period for Chinese Turkestan are a numismatic curiosity in that they have an obverse written in Chinese and on the reverse, the left character is Manchu and the right is Arabic for the Islamic population of that area. For the mint at Aksu the Arabic reads اقصو (PLATE LIV, 64). In 1761, Yerkim (PLATE LIV, 65) became Yarkand (PLATE LIV, 66) but the Arabic remained the same ياركند. The Arabic for Wushih appears اوشى, for Kuche كوجا, for Kashgar كاشقار, and for Khoten هوتين. Frequently the coins of Chinese Turkestan have several Chinese characters on the reverse which are primarily indications of date and value. During this time also, many small coins were privately minted (PLATE LIV, 71, 72).[3]

---

[2] Cf. nos. 6 and 38, 7 and 39.
[3] No. 71 (PLATE LIV) is the smallest coin in the author's collection. The period is identifiable, the mint is not. No. 72 (PLATE LIV) is a small coin from Kweichow.

The following rulers Yung-yen 顒琰 and Min-ning 旻寧 with the reign titles Chia-ch'ing 嘉慶 (PLATE LIV, 73) and Tao-kuang 道光 (PLATE LIV, 77) effected very few changes. No. 80 (PLATE LV) depicts a forgery produced during this time in imitation of a mint at Wuchang.

The next period of great change came during the reign of I-chu 奕詝 (Hsien-feng 咸豐; PLATE LV, 81). In order to finance the war against the Taiping rebels, he re-opened every previously shut-down mint that was not located in territory held by the enemy. Paper money and iron and lead coins were issued, together with an abundance of very heavy, large coins.[4] Instead of the usual obverse inscription 通寶 (current coin), these large pieces usually read chung-pao 重寶 (heavy coin) or yüan-pao 元寶 (large coin). The reverse reads: top, t'ang 當 and bottom, a number (equal to ... coins). They were issued with face values of 10, 20, 50, 100 and even 1000 normal coins, whereas the intrinsic value never exceeded 60 normal coins. There are also heavy coins of this period with Chinese inscriptions on the broad brim.

Yung-yen was succeeded by the young Tsai-ch'un 載淳 who originally chose as his reign title Ch'i-hsiang 祺祥 (PLATE LV, 84), but was forced by his mother, the Dowager Empress Tz'u-hsi 慈禧 to chose the title T'ung-chih 同治 (PLATE LV, 85). Some of the coins already produced were retained as souvenirs but the majority were melted down. In 1864 the suppression of the Taiping rebellion was concluded successfully and the country enjoyed a small "economic miracle."

In 1874, Emperor Tsai-t'ien 載湉 ascended the throne, taking as his reign title Kuang-hsü 光緒 (PLATE LV, 87). Very few mints operated normally during his reign, and an unusual number of forgeries are reported; none of which, however, shows any new Manchu writing. No. 88 (PLATE LV) is uncertain. The Manchu clearly reads "ku" which is not listed as a mint in either the official or private sources. P'eng Hsin-wei 彭信威 reads it as 沽 with a question mark.[5]

---

[4] These coins ranged up to 7 cm. in diameter and 185 gms. in weight.
[5] *Chung-kuo huo-pi shih* 中國貨幣史, p. 529. The interpretation, though unproven, appears correct.

This, if accepted, would place the mint at Taku 大沽, the harbor city of Tientsin.

During the last years of the Manchu rule, minting machines were introduced in the coastal towns. Also the mint at Canton innovated a small specimen with a round hole (PLATE LV, 94) which was not accepted by the older Chinese because of its size and more importantly, according to some accounts, because of the long-held idea that the roundness of the coin symbolized the round sky and the square hole the square earth and more specifically, China.

With the death of Tsai-t'ien, the little child P'u-i 溥儀 became the new "Son of Heaven" under the title Hsüan-t'ung 宣統. The mints producing cash coins dwindled to two. The new coins being produced were in the European style without the hole in the center (e.g., PLATE LV, 90).[6]

WERNER BURGER

[6] The new coins, not described here due to the fact that no new mint names in Manchu appear on them, are very well described by Eduard Kann in his *Illustrated Catalogue of Chinese Coins*, Los Angeles, 1954.

Manchu Inscription	=	Chinese character		Mint Location		Province	Shun-chih 順治 1657–61	← K'ang-hsi → 康熙 1662–66	1667– 1721	1721– 1722	Yung-cheng 雍正 1723–35	Ch'ien-lung 乾隆 1736–95	Chia-ch'ing 嘉慶 1796–1820	Tao-kuang 道光 1821–1850	Hsien-feng 咸豐 1851–61	Ch'i-hsiang 祺祥 1862	T'ung-chih 同治 1862–73	Kuang-hsü 光緒 1874–1907	1882– 1907	Hsüan-t'un 宣統 1908–10
ciowan		泉	ch'üan	戶部	Hu-pu Board of Revenue	Peking	6	6	6	6	38	59	59	59	59	59	59	59	59	with Machine 59
yuwan		源	yüan	工部	Kung-pu Board of Works	Peking	7	7	7	7	39	60	60	60	60	60	60	60	60	—
siowan		宣	hsüan	宣府	Hsüanfu	眞隸 Chihli (Hopei)	8	8	8	—	—	—	—	—	—	—	—	—	—	—
gi		薊	chi	薊州	Chichow	眞隸 Chihli (Hopei)	9	9	9	9	—	—	—	—	96	—	—	—	—	—
j'i		眞	chih	保定	Paoting	眞隸 Chihli (Hopei)	—	—	—	—	—	61	61	61	61	—	61	61	—	—
de		德	te	承德	Chengte	眞隸 Chihli (Hopei)	—	—	—	—	—	—	—	—	82	—	—	—	—	—
ku		沽	ku (?)	大沽 (?)	Taku (?)	眞隸 Chihli (Hopei)	—	—	—	—	—	—	—	—	—	—	—	88	—	—
jiyen		津	chin	天津	Tientsin	眞隸 Chihli (Hopei)	—	—	—	—	—	—	—	—	—	—	—	—	89	—
lin		臨	lin	臨清	Linching	山東 Shantung	10	10	10	—	—	—	—	—	—	—	—	—	—	—
dong		東	tung	濟南	Chinan	山東 Shantung	11	11	11	11	—	—	—	—	—	—	—	—	—	—
ji		濟	ch'i	濟南	Chinan	山東 Shantung	—	—	—	—	41	41	—	—	41	—	—	—	—	—
yuwan		原	yüan	太原	Taiyüan	山西 Shansi	12	12	12	12	—	—	—	—	—	—	—	—	—	—
si		西	hsi	太原	Taiyüan	山西 Shansi	13	13	13	—	—	—	—	—	—	—	—	—	—	—
tong		同	t'ung	大同	Tatung	山西 Shansi	14	14	14	—	—	—	—	—	—	—	—	—	—	—
jin		晉	chin	太原	Taiyüan	山西 Shansi	—	—	—	—	40	40	40	40	40	—	40	40	—	—

								1	2	3	4	5	6	7	8	9	10	11	12	13	14
ho	河	ho	開封	Kaifeng	河南	Honan		15	15	15	15	42	—	—	—	42	—	—	42	—	—
giyang	江	chiang	江寧	Chiangning (Nanking)	江蘇	Kiangsu		16	16	16	—	—	—	—	—	—	—	—	—	—	—
su	蘇	su	蘇州	Soochow	江蘇	Kiangsu		—	—	27	27	43	43	43	43	43	—	43	43	43	—
ning	寧	ning	江寧	Chiangning (Nanking)	江蘇	Kiangsu		—	—	—	—	—	—	—	—	—	—	—	92	—	—
an	安	an	江寧	Chiangning (Nanking)	安徽	Anhwei		—	—	—	—	44	44	—	—	—	—	—	—	—	—
cang	昌	chang	南昌	Nanchang	江西	Kiangsi		17	24	24	24	45	45	45	45	45	—	45	45	—	—
je	浙	che	抗州	Hangchow	浙江	Chekiang		18	18	18	18	46	46	46	46	46	—	46	46	46	—
fu	福	fu	福州	Foochow	福建	Fukien		19	19	28	28	47	47	47	47	47	—	86	47	—	—
jang	漳	chang	漳州	Changchow	福建	Fukien		—	—	29	—	—	—	—	—	—	—	—	—	91	—
tai	臺	t'ai	臺灣	Taiwan (Tainan)	福建	Fukien		—	—	30	30	48	48	48	—	48	—	—	—	—	—
nan	南	nan	長沙	Changsha	湖南	Hunan		—	—	31	31	49	62	62	62	62	—	62	62	—	—
u	武	wu	武昌	Wuchang	湖北	Hupeh		—	—	—	—	50	50	74	78	50	—	50	50	50	—
guwang	廣	kuang	廣州	Canton	廣東	Kwangtung		—	—	32	32	51	51	51	51	51	—	51	51	93, 94, 95	94, 99
gui	桂	kuei	桂林	Kweilin	廣西	Kwanghsi		—	—	33	33	52	52	52	52	52	—	52	52	—	—
yôn	雲	yün	雲南	Yünnan	雲南	Yünnan		Chin. Lit. only		34	34	53	53	53	53	53	—	53	53	—	—
dong	東	tung	東川	Tungchwan	雲南	Yünnan		—	—	—	—	—	—	75	79	79	—	79	79	79	—
kiyan	黔	chien	貴陽	Kweiyang	貴州	Kweichow		—	—	Chin. Lit. only		54	54	54	54	54	—	54	54	—	—
cuwan	川	chuan	成都	Chengtu	四川	Szechuan		—	—	Chin. Lit. only		55	55	55	55	55	—	55	55	—	—
san	陝	shan	西安	Sian	陝西	Shensi		20	25	25	25	56	56	76	76	76	—	76	76	—	—

Manchu	Chinese	Wade-Giles	Chinese	Romanization	Chinese	Province															
ning	寧	ning	寧夏	Ninghsia	甘肅	Kansu	21	26	26	—	—	—	—	—	—	—	—	—	—	—	—
gung	鞏	kung	鞏昌	Kungchang	甘肅	Kansu	—	—	35	35	57	—	—	—	57	—	57	—	—	—	—
di	迪	ti	迪代	Tihua (Urumtsi)	甘肅	Kansu (Sinkiang)	—	—	—	—	—	—	—	—	83	—	—	—	—	—	—
i	伊	i	伊犁	Ili (Kuldja)	伊犁	Ili (Sinkiang)	—	—	—	—	63	63	63	63	—	63	63	—	—	—	—
aksu	阿克蘇	a-k'o-su	阿克蘇	Aksu (also Wensuh)	新疆	Sinkiang	—	—	—	—	64	64	64	64	—	64	64	—	—	—	—
yerkim	葉爾奇木	yeh-erh-ch'i-mu	葉爾奇木	Yerkim	新疆	Sinkiang	—	—	—	—	65	—	—	—	—	—	—	—	—	—	—
yerki-yang	葉爾羌	yeh-erh-ch'iang	葉爾羌	Yarkand (also Sochefu)	新疆	Sinkiang	—	—	—	—	66	—	—	66	—	66	—	—	—	—	—
uśi	烏什	wu-shih	烏什	Wushih	新疆	Sinkiang	—	—	—	—	67	—	—	—	—	67	—	—	—	—	—
kuce	庫車	k'u-che	庫車	Kuche	新疆	Sinkiang	—	—	—	—	68	—	68	68	—	68	—	—	—	—	—
kaśigar	喀什噶爾	k'o-shih-ko-erh	喀什噶爾	Kashgar (also Shufu)	新疆	Sinkiang	—	—	—	—	69	—	—	69	—	In Arabic only	—	—	—	—	—
hotiyan	和闐	ho-t'ien	和闐	Khoten (also Hotien)	新疆	Sinkiang	—	—	—	—	70	—	—	—	—	—	—	—	—	—	—
gi	吉	chi	吉林	Kirin (Kilin)	滿洲	Manchuria (Kilin)	—	—	—	—	—	—	—	—	—	—	—	96	—	—	—
fung	奉	feng	奉天	Fengtien (also Mukden Shenyang)	滿洲	Manchuria (Liaoning)	—	—	—	—	—	—	—	—	—	—	—	—	97	—	—

THE JAMES II 1/24TH REAL FOR THE AMERICAN PLANTATIONS*

(See Plate LVI)

The identification of a new major variety of the James II 1/24th real struck in 1688 for the British Dominions in America has created an opportunity to restudy this unusual series and to revise and amend the author's previous article on the subject.[1] The series is referred to as unusual because: (1) the coins are the first duly authorized mintage specifically for the British colonies in America; (2) the coins are the only issue in pure tin for American use; and (3) the coins constitute the only British mintage using a Spanish denomination.

It is well known that by the latter part of the seventeenth century sterling exchange had already become a foreign exchange in transactions in the British colonies in America. Both in North America and the West Indies silver and gold coins struck in Spanish colonial mints were valued in the local money of account of each British colony. Although each such money of account system was calculated in pounds, shillings, and pence, each fluctuated independently, unrelated to English sterling and unrelated to each other. Efforts by England to place a maximum value in local American money of account on Spanish and other specie were unsuccessful and finally culminated in the 1704 Proclamation of Queen Anne followed by the 1707 Act of Parliament (effective May 1, 1709), both of which regulatory measures were virtually unheeded in the colonies.

The American colonies, from their establishment, continually requested circulating coin with a reasonable intrinsic value. They were particularly short of small change, and, as evidenced by the Mas-

---

* For cooperation and helpfulness, an expression of appreciation is due to the British Public Records Office, Department of Coins and Medals of the British Museum, Ashmolean Museum, Fitzwilliam Museum, American Numismatic Society, C. Wilson Peck, Leonard Forrer, Curtis P. Nettels, A. H. Baldwin and Sons, Ltd., B. A. Seaby Ltd., R. H. M. Dolley, Edward F. Schweich, Walter Breen, and Ivor Noel Hume.

[1] Eric P. Newman, "First Documentary Evidence on the American Colonial Pewter 1/24th Real," *The Numismatist*, Vol. 68, No. 7 (July, 1955), p. 713.

sachusetts Bay silver threepence issues beginning in 1652 and the twopence issue dated 1662, small change had to have some realistic and acceptable value.

Before being able to give consideration to small change for its colonies, England had to solve its domestic small change problems. After royal copper coin had secured an acceptance in England the use of tin instead of copper for English minor coins was proposed in 1679 and materialized when English halfpence and farthings were authorized to be struck in tin on May 28, 1684. The purpose was threefold: (1) To satisfy the tin farmers (holders of the mineral rights) whose political power was used to force the Crown to help the tin industry; (2) To produce revenue for the Crown from franchise payments, coinage profits, and coinage duties; and (3) To prevent the extensive counterfeiting of current copper coin. The price of tin had fallen from 12 pence per pound weight in 1676 to 8 pence by 1684 and coinage as a means of price support by the Crown was a solution. The cost of minting and distributing tin coin was approximately 4 pence per pound weight which, added to the cost of the tin, totaled 12 pence per pound weight. The private patents issued for standard minor coinage of tin under Charles II, James II and William and Mary provided for tin coins with a copper plug, the circulating value of which was 20 pence (finally 21 pence) per pound weight, so that the coin passed for about two and one-half times its intrinsic value as metal. This discrepancy in due course caused the cessation of the use of tin for English minor coinage by 1692 and a reversion to copper.[2]

The tin coinage under Charles II, 1660–1684(5), consisted only of farthings dated 1684 and 1685 which averaged close to their legal weight of 87.5 grains. The coinage was authorized by warrant on the basis of 40% of the profit payable to the Crown and was terminable at the Crown's discretion. James II, 1684(5)–1688, continued this procedure by granting a patent to Thomas Neale, James Hoare and Charles Duncombe on the same basis and tin halfpence were produced dated from 1685 to 1687 and farthings dated from 1684 to 1687.[3]

---

[2] John Craig, *The Mint* (Cambridge, England, 1953), p. 178.
[3] Thomas Snelling, *A View of the Copper Coin and Coinage of England* (London, 1766), p. 38; C. Wilson Peck, *English Copper, Tin and Bronze Coins in the British Museum 1558–1958* (London, 1960), p. 147.

There are no farthings or halfpence dated 1688 so that tin coinage appears to have been discontinued in 1687. New problems as to tin mining and coinage had arisen. The price of tin in 1686 had fallen so low as to cause "the great decay of our stannaries" and because of urgent pleas of the tin mining interests the Crown by an order of August 16, 1687 "out of compassion of their ill circumstances" agreed that it would undertake to arrange to buy all tin produced in Cornwall and Devon at a price of £ 3/10 per hundred weight (7 pence per lb.) which was above the then current price. Devon tin farmers accepted the suggested price on December 14 and the Cornwall tin farmers agreed on December 19, 1687.[4] Long and tedious negotiations then ensued as to other details. A draft of the proposed Articles of Agreement was prepared in May, 1688 between the Commissioners of the Treasury and John Earle of Bathe, who was Lord Warden of the Stannaries and a cousin of James II. The proposed contract provides an eleven year commitment to buy all tin mined after June 24, 1688 at the agreed price of 7 pence per pound from approved tin farmers. The contract included the sole privilege of coining "pence, halfe pence and farthings of Intrinsic value of Tynn throughout all his Majesty's Dominions (free of all Customes & other Dutys whatsoever for such pence, 1/2 pence & farthings as shall be bonafide coyned to pass (f)or may be exported only for ye purpose". The Commissioners were to receive an annual rent of £ 16,000.[5]

The franchise to mint a distinct coinage for use in the colonies was therefore quite specific and was about to be granted for the first time.[6] Marginal notations on the draft raised two critical questions: (1) was there a limit on the amount to be coined annually, and (2) what was meant by intrinsic value?

Petitions of May 31 and June 2, 1688 proposed a limit of £ 10,000 per year for three years, after which either the matter would be

---

[4] British Public Records Office, S. O. 8/20; T. 52/13, p. 62.
[5] Ibid., T. 1/2, No. 49.
[6] The right granted Lord Maltravers on February 16, 1639 to circulate copper farthing tokens in the British plantations, excluding Maryland, referred to farthing tokens made for England, Ireland or Wales. See *The Calendar of State Papers* (*Colonial Series 1574–1660*), pp. 285, 290; C. Wilson Peck, *English Copper, Tin and Bronze Coins in the British Museum, 1558–1958* (London, 1960), p. 47n.

reconsidered for a renewal by the Crown or the tin interests could withdraw from their commitment to sell at the agreed price and be free to sell on the open market.[7] A personal appointment with James II was arranged for June 19, 1688 so that the King might accept particular tin farmers as the proposed contract provided.[8] Apparently some contract was signed about that time although the text of the final form cannot be found in the British Public Records Office. The reason that some similar contract must have been completed is that there is a reference to it in a petition by the Earle of Bathe dated June 26, 1688 beginning with the statement, "The Farmers of his Majesties Preemption and Coynage duty of Tyn with the sole Privilege of making Tyn-farthings, Pence and Halfpence of Intrinsick value for all his Majesties Dominions ..." The June 26, 1688 petition was a request that the Commissioners of the Treasury permit "the Engines, Presses, tools and Utensils belonging to his Majesty in Skinners Hall" which equipment was used "in making or vending the late Tyn farthings" (the royal farthings of James II) to be made available to Richard Holt who had been approved as one of the tin farmers to make tin coins for the dominions.[9] Since rent on Skinner's Hall had been paid by the Crown up to the lease expiration on August 8, 1688, the tin farmers asked for the free privilege of using that site for coining for the balance of the term. They also agreed to return the equipment to the Crown after using it.[10]

The petition asked for the use of the equipment forthwith to make patterns to be submitted to the King for his approval. No patterns or coinage of any minor coinage under James II are known and thus it appears that the only patterns prepared under the contract were the 1/24th real pieces for the plantations. These patterns were submitted

---

[7] British Public Records Office, T. 1/2, Nos. 48 and 50.
[8] Ibid., T. 27/11, p. 393.
[9] Ibid., T. 1/2, No. 51; Curtis P. Nettels, "British Policy and Colonial Money Supply," *The Economic History Review*, Vol. III, No. 2 (Oct., 1931), p. 10; Curtis P. Nettels, "The Money Supply of the American Colonies before 1720," *University of Wisconsin Studies in Social Sciences and History*, No. 20, (Madison, 1934), p. 177.
[10] The lease on Skinner's Hall was extended by the Crown until December, 1869 when the premises were vacated. John Craig, *The Mint* (Cambridge, England, 1953), p. 179.

for approval as to design as well as to intrinsic value in the following letter:[11]

Officers of the Mint
  Gentlemen
    By order of the Lord's Commissioners of his Majesty's Treasury I send you the enclosed letter from Mr. Holt on behalf of the Tynn ffarmers with a Modell of the New ffarthings intended to be Coyned. Their Lordships direct you to Certify them if you have any objection to what is therein desired. I am etc H. Guy 13th August 1688.

London 27th July 1688
My Lord
    The ffarthings which Wee intreat your Lordship to present for his Majesty's approbacon is made after the rate of 10 d p l (10 pence per lb.) and 2 d p l (2 pence per lb.) for the Coynage of them. The Inscription on the Revers, Vis: vall 24. part Riall Hispan. is because the said Coynes are intended to pass in his Majesty's Plantacons & such parts of his Dominions where they only take Spanish money & value all coynes by that Measure, Soe that without that Inscription those people will not take them.
    And a Ryall being 6d Sterling in value it's alsoe convenient for his Majesty's Europian Dominions. And we entreat your Lordship to obtain his Majesty's approbacon soe as Wee may proceed on the Coynage of them pursuant to the Groat charge we have been at to procure the Modell. Your Lordship's most humble servant, Richard Holt, for self and company.

To introduce a tin coin into circulation in the American Dominions required substantial intrinsic value and for that reason the July 27, 1688 letter indicates that the tin coins for the dominions would have a circulating value of 10 pence per pound weight which was twice the amount of tin as was contained in the English royal tin coinage having an equal circulating value. The "groat charge" of 4 pence per pound weight for coining was therefore twice the cost of making the same circulating value in tin coin of the earlier issues under James II. The fear of the rejection of tin coinage in the dominions was a matter of concern to the coiners as they stated in the July 27, 1688 letter that the coins would be rejected if a Spanish denomination was not designated on the coin. The value of 1/24th of a real in Spanish exchange

[11] British Public Records Office, Treasury Out Letter Book, Tome 27/11, p. 424.

was about equal to one farthing in sterling exchange. Thus forty pieces of the 1/24th real would circulate for 10 pence sterling and would have only 7 pence in intrinsic value of tin because they would weigh one pound. With normal coinage and distribution costs the planned intrinsic value was reasonable. Unfortunately, none of the 1/24th real pieces weighed 40 to the pound weight or 175 grains each as stated. They only weighed 135 grains each on the average making them have an actual tin value of less than $5\frac{1}{2}$ pence per pound weight and were intended to circulate for 1–2/3 reales (10 pence sterling) per pound weight.

The word "plantacons" could only mean American dominions because no other plantations used Spanish money. Plantations in America meant Newfoundland, the colonies on the North American continent, and the West Indies. If the "plantacons" were only the colonies of the West Indies then it would have been pointed out that coins bearing a Spanish denomination could be conveniently used on the North American continent in the same manner as their possible use in the English dominions in Europe was mentioned.

The diameter as well as the weight of these plantation 1/24th real (one farthing) pieces were equivalent to the Royal tin halfpence which were in circulation in England. The plantation issue would therefore have been very disruptive of tin circulation in England by virtue of having twice the tin weight of the farthing in England and being of the same diameter as the halfpence. Even if sent to America some were bound to come back to England. It is therefore somewhat doubtful whether the circulation of the Plantation farthings was formally approved as no record to that effect has been found. It is also possible that even if approval had been obtained the few remaining months of the reign of James II had elapsed before distribution in America had been planned or carried out. Even though many pieces were struck in anticipation of formal approval and actual distribution it is unsound to conclude that any reached America until evidence of their circulation in the American plantations is found.

The tin interests did not seem satisfied with their contract and on July 30, 1688 James II authorized the Earle of Bathe to work out further agreements with the tin farmers to buy all of the tin which they could produce at 7 pence per pound weight, to pay 6 days after delivery, to waive the Crown's coinage duty of 4 shillings per hundred weight, to permit four free coinages yearly at coinage towns and to lend money on a short term basis for the mining operations.[12] These coinages never took place so we can reasonably assume that the political troubles of James II, culminating in his flight from England on December 23, 1688, ended all further negotiations relating to tin coinage during his reign. Thereafter the control of coinage and the Mint passed from the Crown to the ministers and Parliament.[13] Those 1/24th real pieces which had been minted were left without anyone to support their circulation after the change in government. Noel Ivor Hume, prior to becoming the present archaeologist at Colonial Williamsburg, found three Plantation 1/24th real pieces in London in the mud on the bank of the Thames river, but no other archaeological evidence of finding coins of this issue has been reported.

THE AMERICAN ATTITUDE TOWARD TIN COINS

In 1690 a shipment of royal tin farthings and halfpence and some copper halfpence was sent to the Leeward Islands for payment of salaries of an English regiment. The governor, on July 13, 1691 pointed out that the coins could not be used for trade at English values and would, contrary to English policy, have to be deflated by one-third in order to circulate.[14] This indicates that the 1/24th real would have circulated well in those islands.

Thomas Neale who was master of the Mint and a promoter of speculative enterprises suggested on January 19, 1691 that New England might "be supplied with Pence, Halfe Pence, & farthing of Tinn, from England, to their Majesties Advantage,"[15] but nothing came of it.

In 1698 the reaction of the American colonists to a threat of lead and pewter coinage being circulated in quantity was demonstrated by a protest of fifty-three merchants in Philadelphia in the following manner:[16]

---

[12] British Public Records Office, S. O. 8/20.
[13] John Craig, *The Mint* (Cambridge, England, 1953), p. 180.
[14] Codrington to Lords of Trade, C. O. 152/38, No. 33.
[15] Robert Chalmers, *A History of the Currency in the British Colonies* (London, 1893), p. 10.
[16] Harrold Gillingham, *Counterfeiting in Colonial Pennsylvania*, NNM 86, p. 6.

To the Generall Assembly now Sitting the petition of Sundry the Inhabitants of this province most humbly Sheweth.

WHEREAS your petition's being Inhabitants of this province and being given to understand that there is great Quantities of Leaden and pewter farthings & half pence whereby your petition's are likely to be mutch Damaged by Reason such great Quantity's are Liable to be Crowded upon us.

Now these are to Protest & humbly Interest that you would be pleased to make an act of Assembly That all such farthings & half pence that are made of Lead & pewter may be wholly suppressed & Cryed Down and only those of Copper which are the Kings Coyn may pass the farthings for two a penny & the half pence for a penny ... Philadelphia the twenty first of the third month 1698.

In Massachusetts Bay Colony on February 21, 1700 an act was passed prohibiting the coining or passing of base or counterfeit money due to the fact that "some persons for private gain have of late presumed to stamp and emit peices of brass and tin at the rate of one penny each, not regarding what loss they thereby bring on others, ..." The tin pieces referred to have not been identified, although Crosby suggests the remote possibility that the reference might have been to the "New Yorke" token. The Act, however, does not reflect a specific attitude toward the circulation of tin coinage, but indicates a general opposition to the issuance of private token money coined in any metal.

CHEMICAL COMPOSITION

In order to verify why the plantation 1/24th real is often found so deteriorated a modern chemical analysis has been made. Its composition showed 97.46% of tin and .015% of antimony with the balance being non-metallic.[17] The non-metallic elements are natural impurities such as clay and ash from mining and smelting. Since no other metal was mixed with the tin and the amount of antimony is insignificant the pieces are not properly referred to as pewter which the writer and others have done in the past. The deterioration which sometimes takes place on the surface of the coins is therefore a natural change in the allotropic form of tin, caused by a breakdown in its crystalline struc-

---

[17] Chemical data were supplied through the courtesy of the Lewin-Mathes Division of the Cerro Corporation, St. Louis, Missouri.

JAMES II 1/24TH REAL

ture. This change is stimulated by exposure to winter temperatures and the surfaces of many specimens of the 1/24th real are defaced in isolated areas by this deterioration. The effect of such deterioration is illustrated in obverses 6 and 7 (PLATE LVI).

The specific gravity of the coins ranges from 6.4 to 7.3. In some cases the changes in the crystalline structure of the tin has increased the volume of the coin and thus lowered its specific gravity.

A NEW MAJOR DIE VARIETY

A newly identified major variety (Reverse G) of the 1/24th real has the unusual distinction of having the Irish harp and the Scottish lion transposed. The four coats of arms on the reverse of all other varieties maintain the following order in a clockwise direction: England, Scotland, France and Ireland. This normal order is in accordance with the title of James II in the obverse legend. To find Ireland in second position on the new variety, displacing Scotland, might humorously be construed as an Irish revolt from being placed in last position, but it is merely a diemaker's error. The punch for each coat of arms was separately used in cutting the die and thus the transposition of the coats of arms is a similar mistake to the "sidewise 4" on reverse C. The HB for HIB on Obverse 1 was not an unintentional error as the diemaker, when punching in the legend, did not have enough space remaining.[18]

The new reverse G was first located in the British Museum cabinet and has since been located only in a very few collections.

A comprehensive revision of data on all known die varieties has been prepared now that collectors have had the opportunity of checking their pieces against the 1955 listing. Seven obverses and seven reverses are now noted in nine combinations. The obverses are generally similar, the only major variation being the spelling of the legend with HB instead of HIB. The reverses show 5, 6, 7, 8 and 11 strings in the harp; and either large or small fleurs-de-lis are found in the French coat of arms. The die cutting errors in Reverse C and G have been noted. The edge of all pieces contains a band of about 90

---

[18] See comments by Walter Breen in "Blundered Dies of Colonial and U. S. Mints," *Empire Topics* (July, 1958), p. 16.

raised dots milled onto the planchet with a Castaing machine before striking. Since illustrations of the die varieties have not heretofore been published a plate has been included showing such varieties and their combinations. The following descriptive table of die varieties showing their combinations has been revised to accompany the plate:

TABLE OF DIE VARIETIES

Obverse descriptions

Obv. No.		With Rev.
1	Head directly under G. HB instead of HIB. Hoof ends under center of right base of X.	A
2	Head directly under G. Top leaf touches G. No period after X. Hoof ends under right end of base of E.	B G
3	Head centered under space between G and B favoring G. O in JACOBUS high. Hoof ends under right side of right base of X.	C
4	Head centered under space between G and B favoring B. F in FRAN higher than preceding I. Hoof ends under space slightly right of base of X.	D E
5	Head centered under space between G and B favoring B. D G widely separated. Hoof ends under right side of right base of X. Die break connecting AN and HI.	D
6	Head centered under space between G and B favoring G. Right side of base of second I of II higher than base of adjacent D. Hoof ends under left base of X.	F
7	Head under space between G and B favoring G. Leaf touches B. First I in II much too high. Hoof ends under center of X.	F

Reverse Descriptions

Rev. Letter		With Obv.
A	6 strings in harp. Large fleurs-de-lis and lions. Head of lowest lion left of heads of other two.	1
B	7 strings in harp. Large fleurs-de-lis and lions. Line of lions' heads rises to left. Right fleur higher than left fleur.	2

JAMES II 1/24TH REAL

Rev. Letter		With Obv.
C	8 strings in harp with diagonal string between third and fifth. Sidewise 4 in 24. Large fleurs-de-lis and lions. Right fleur is higher than left fleur.	3
D	11 strings in harp. Small fleurs-de-lis and lions. Right fleur slightly lower than left fleur. Lions' heads in vertical line.	4 5
E	7 strings in harp with top three close. Small fleurs-de-lis. Highest lion distant from and left of other two.	4
F	6 strings in harp. Large fleurs-de-lis and lions. Lowest lion's head right of heads of other two.	6 7
G	5 strings in harp. Large fleurs-de-lis and lions. Irish and Scottish coats of arms transposed so that Irish follows English coat of arms in clockwise direction.	2

RESTRIKES

The dies for the 1/24th real were apparently cut by John Roettier, who with other members of his family, although originally from Flanders, devoted most of their lives to engraving for the Royal English Mint.[19] Customarily, coinage dies were the property and responsibility of the die sinker. In the course of political difficulties all of the Roettier dies and punches were seized by the Crown on March 27, 1697, but soon thereafter returned.[20] Over a century later the Roettier descendants decided to sell the dies and Matthew Young, an English coin dealer, acquired them in 1828. Young thereupon sold many of the coin dies to the British Museum in that year[21] and the dies for medals in the following year. He retained the 1/24th real dies and the edging dies and undertook to make restrikes from these dies shortly thereafter.[22]

[19] Philip Nelson, "The Early Coinage of America (1558–1774)," *The Connoisseur*, Vol. 31 (Sept., 1911), p. 18.
[20] John Craig, *The Mint* (Cambridge, England, 1953), pp. 195, 196.
[21] H. Farquhar, "Concerning Some Roettier Dies," *Numismatic Chronicle* (1917), p. 126; Corroborative correspondence from the British Museum.
[22] Henry Christmas, "The Anglo-American Coinage," *AJN*, Vol. 7, No. 2 (Oct., 1872), p. 39, and in *Numismatic Chronicle* (London, 1862), Vol. 2, New Series, p. 20; Phillip Nelson, "The Early Coinage of America (1558–1774)," *The Connoisseur*, Vol. 31 (Sept., 1911), p. 18.

Although Philip Nelson stated that the restrikes could be easily distinguished from the originals by the "suspicious quality of the metal" the passage of time has made it much more difficult. Apparently Young only used two obverse dies (4 and 5) and two reverse dies (D and E). Quantities of combination 5–D were restruck in tin, along with a few 4–D and 4–E. All of these restrikes have a properly dotted edge. In copper one restrike is known struck in combination 4–E and with a plain edge.

The surface of the field of the tin restrikes is very smooth whereas the originals have a granulated surface and often show signs of tin pest. The restrikes retain a uniform bright appearance (possibly because of the tin being purer) whereas the originals have turned grey in some parts or throughout. American sales catalogues were distinguishing restrikes from originals by 1864.[23] At least three-fourths of all 1/24th real pieces in collections are restrikes of combination 5–E.

PRIOR NUMISMATIC COMMENT

Because of the complexity in the determination of the background of the 1/24th real a brief review of previous articles seems desirable.[24]

[23] W. Elliot Woodward, Sale of the McCoy Collection, May 17, 1864, Lots 199 and 1645.

[24] Stephen Martin Leake, *An Historical Account of English Money* (London, 1726), p. 127; *English and Scottish Coins with other Numismatic Material Collected by Thomas Earl of Pembroke and Montgomery* (1746), Part 4, pl. 21; Thomas Snelling, *A View of the Coins Struck in the West India Colonies* (London, 1769), p. 38; Noel Humphreys, *The Gold, Silver and Copper Coins of England* (London, 1849), p. 96, and *The Coinage of the British Empire* (London, 1854), p. 125; Montroville W. Dickeson, *The American Numismatical Manual* (Philadelphia, 1859), p. 69, 70; William C. Prime, *Coins, Medals, and Seals* (New York, 1861), p. 70; Sylvester S. Crosby, *Early Coins of America* (Boston, 1875), p. 348; Edouard Frossard, *Monograph of the United States Cents and Half Cents* (Irvington, 1879), p. 48; James Atkins, *The Coins and Tokens of the British Possessions and Colonies of the British Empire* (London, 1889), p. 257; Robert Chalmers, *A History of Currency in the British Colonies* (London, 1893), p. 10n; Gertrude B. Rawlings, *Coins and How to Know Them* (New York, 1908), p. 319; Fred W. Burgess, *Chats on Old Coins* (London, 1913), p. 314; Wayte Raymond, *Standard Catalogue of United States Coins and Tokens* (New York, 1934–57); Richard S. Yeoman, *A Guide Book of United States Coins* (Racine, 1947 to date); Phares O. Sigler, "James II Plantation Half Penny," *The Numismatist*, Vol. 57, No. 5 (May, 1944), p. 393, and in *Coin Collector's Journal*, Vol. 11, No. 4 (July, 1944), p. 86; Eric P. Newman, "First Documentary Evidence on the American Colonial Pewter 1/24th Real," *The Numismatist*, Vol. 68, No. 7 (July, 1955), p. 713.

The Plantation 1/24th real, designated as a farthing by its coiners, was first described numismatically in 1726 as "the Plantation Half-Penny" by Stephen Martin Leake. This error in the denominational value is logical because the coin was the size of a royal English tin halfpence. The error was continued by Burgess in 1913 and Sigler in 1944. The coin was first illustrated as "K. James's Small Money for the Plantations" in 1746 in the Pembroke Plates and described as "pewter with a copper cross inserted." The small copper cross embellishment on each side of the coin was one of the many frauds perpetrated upon the Earl of Pembroke in his eagerness to acquire unusual items for his collection.[25] No copper plug of any kind is found on any 1/24th real piece, such plugs being confined to the royal English tin coinage. The reference to pewter composition was a mistake which Burgess, Sigler, and this author followed.

Snelling in 1769 properly described the pieces as "coins of the plantations" and Humphreys in 1854, Dickeson in 1859, and Atkins in 1889, justifiably enlarged this to "American plantations." Prime in 1861 and Crosby in 1875 eliminated the coin as an early American piece, but that opinion was based upon lack of evidence rather than negative evidence. Burgess in 1913 said that the coin was minted specially for Virginia and Henry Chapman went along with that thought.[26] The fact that a Spanish denomination was used did not deter numismatists from assigning the piece to Florida, even though Florida was not even English at the time. While Crosby, Chalmers, and others refute the Florida allocation Raymond and Yeomans in all of their editions list it under Florida, but Raymond after 1945 points out that a better view is to assign it to American Plantations in general. J. J. Mickley was alleged to have "thought it was coined for William Penn."[27] Walter Breen, in graciously mentioning the author's 1955 article on the coins, indicated that they were known as "Black Doggs."[28]

[25] In 1848 when the Pembroke Collection was auctioned Lot 231 contained the Plantation 1/24th real and there was no trace of any copper cross on the coin. See also Eric P. Newman, *The Secret of the Good Samaritan Shilling*, NNM 142, p. 15.
[26] *The Numismatist*, Vol. 29, No. 3 (March, 1916), p. 105.
[27] Stan V. Henkels, Sale of the Collection of Edward Maris on June 21, 1886, Lot 306.
[28] Walter Breen, "The Collector's Necessary Equipment," *Numismatic Scrapbook Magazine*, Vol. 29, No. 3 (Mar., 1963), p. 656.

While the royal English tin coinage or the 1/24th real or a host of other coins might have been known as such in America there is as yet no evidence to support the 1/24th real being so referred to.

The various expressions of opinion as to the 1/24th real, right or wrong, demonstrated the need for securing valid numismatic proof. With the documentary and other evidence presented in the 1955 article and herein it seems clear that the James II 1/24 real was struck in 1688 for general use in the British Plantations in America as a whole and because Spanish money circulated there, its denomination was in Spanish money which had a sterling equivalent of one farthing.

ERIC P. NEWMAN

ALUMINUM FOIL IMPRESSIONS FOR NUMISMATIC STUDIES

(See Plates LVII–LIX)

In this age of fast travel and communication, it seems appropriate to discuss the availability of a more rapid means of communication between numismatists.

The time-honored custom of preparing plaster casts of coins for numismatists who wish to study them is still the most satisfactory method when the specimen itself is not available.

Unfortunately, it is not always practical to prepare a large number of casts, especially when the number reaches into the hundreds or thousands; in such cases, a quicker and more convenient method of securing images of coins becomes imperative.

In the preparation of the Corpus of his book *Coinage of Cilician Armenia*, the author was faced with the problem of preparing several thousand images of coins within a two-week period. Paper impressions could not be used because of the time factor—each one takes at least fifteen minutes—and also because paper impressions do not show sufficient detail of the coin.

After some experimentation, it was found that aluminum foil gave excellent impressions of coins when pressed with rubber sheets. Eventually, this led to the use of a blank corporation seal with a circular rubber sheet glued permanently to the upper jaw. A rectangular piece of aluminum foil was folded over the coin, placed on a small sheet of rubber, and pressed between the jaws of the seal. The result was an excellent reproduction of the coin, and it was possible to prepare about one hundred impressions an hour.

It was considered more satisfactory to use thin sheets of aluminum foil for worn specimens as this reproduced the maximum detail. Somewhat thicker foil and softer rubber sheets were preferable when the coin possessed greater relief. It was also found advisable to fold the aluminum with the bright side to the coin so that the image appeared on the dull side. This made its study and photography easier.

In the case of coins with high relief and especially thick coins with high relief such as Ancient Greek, this technique proved inapplicable as the limited tensility of the aluminum foil causes it to tear.

The method described above is in no sense a discovery, but is perhaps an improvement over older techniques. Excellent impressions of coins have been made in the past on thick tin foil. The use of both tin foil and aluminum foil using screw presses has also been reported. But the employment of a corporation seal does make possible a more rapid and practical method of preparing a large number of impressions. These impressions must, of course, be shipped in boxes to prevent flattening.

Although aluminum impressions are fragile, they may, nevertheless, be catalogued and mounted, provided they are not subjected to pressure. Pertinent notations can be made on the unused portion of the foil.

Photographing aluminum foil impressions proved to be rather difficult and the results not as good as photographs of casts. Photographing slightly dented impressions was particularly difficult because of light reflections from the shiny surface.

In order to achieve the best results, the student takes aluminum impressions of a collection, studies them at his leisure and chooses the specimens to be photographed for publication. A plaster cast is then prepared from each aluminum impression in the same manner as from a wax impression of a coin, and photographed.

For purposes of comparison, three different coins possessing varying degrees of relief and wear were chosen to demonstrate this technique: a large Munster Taler, Sede Vacante 1683 (PLATE LVII, 1, 2; PLATE LVIII, 1, 2), a worn English Testoon of Henry VIII (1509–1547) (PLATE LVII, 3, 4; PLATE LVIII, 3, 4), and a Teston of Francis I (1515 to 1547) (PLATE LIX, 1–4).

Shown are photographs obtained from the coin, its aluminum impression, the cast prepared from the aluminum impression, and the cast prepared from a wax impression. It will be seen that while the photographs obtained from the latter are slightly better then those obtained from the cast prepared from aluminum foil, both are satisfactory for publication purposes. The photographs obtained directly from the foil or from the coins themselves show less contrast and are not as satisfactory.

It is hoped that the above-mentioned technique will help the student to secure a large number of impressions of specimens from many sources with the least delay and effort, and make it possible for him to pursue his studies with greater ease. The writer's fifteen thousand aluminum impressions of the coins of Cilician Armenia certainly proved a boon in the preparation of his book.

PAUL BEDOUKIAN

PLATES

I

DAMARETE'S LION

DAMARETE'S LION

III

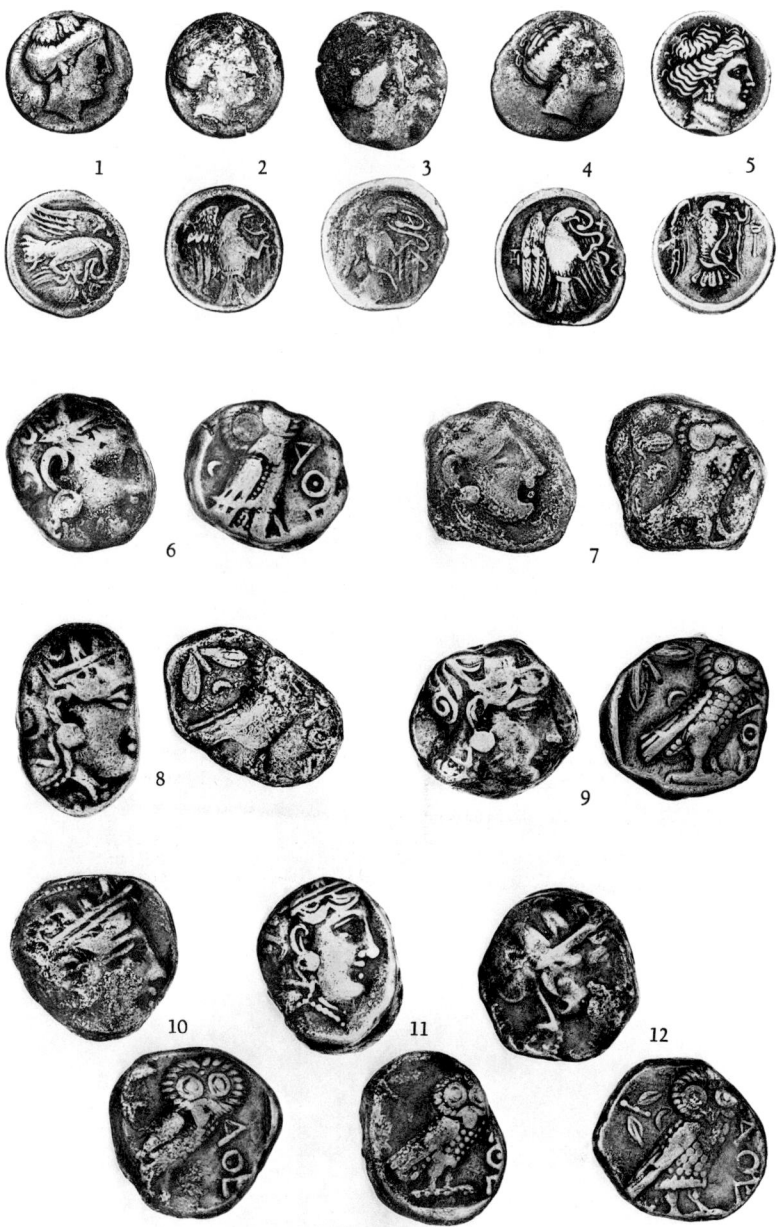

KOZANI HOARD OF 1955

IV

KOZANI HOARD OF 1955

V

KOZANI HOARD OF 1955

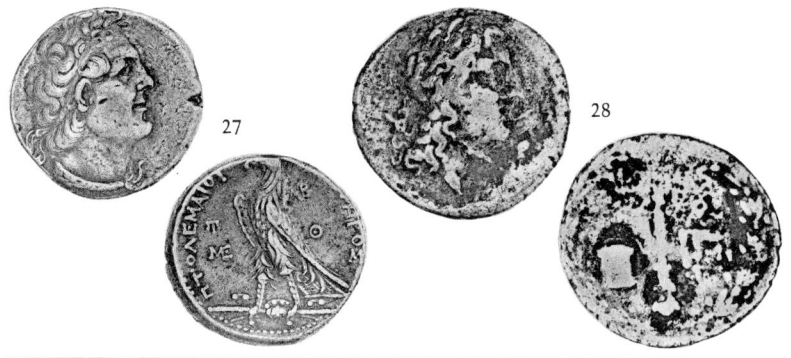

KOZANI HOARD OF 1955

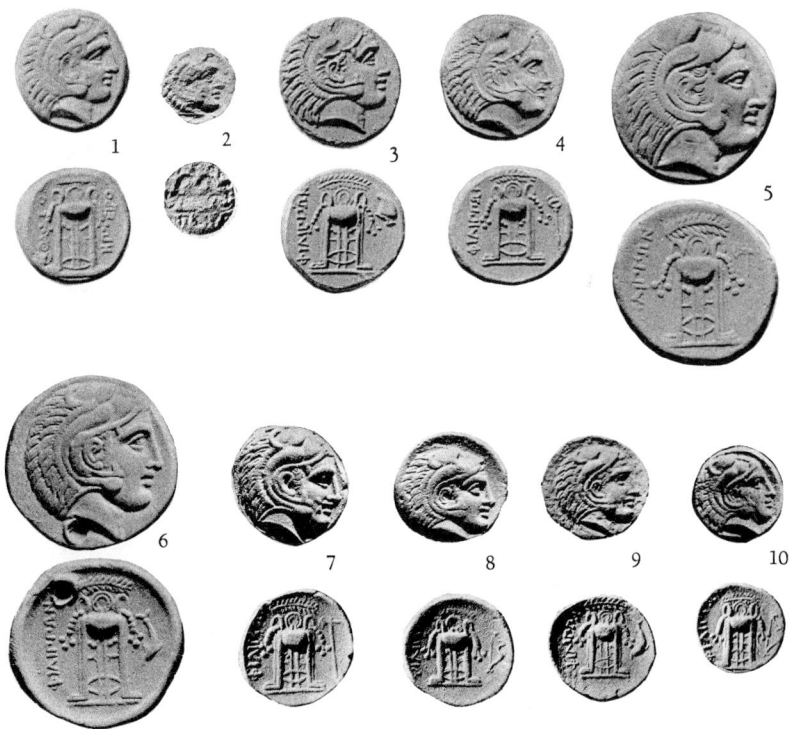

PHILIPPI — GOLD AND SILVER

VII

PHILIPPI — GOLD AND SILVER

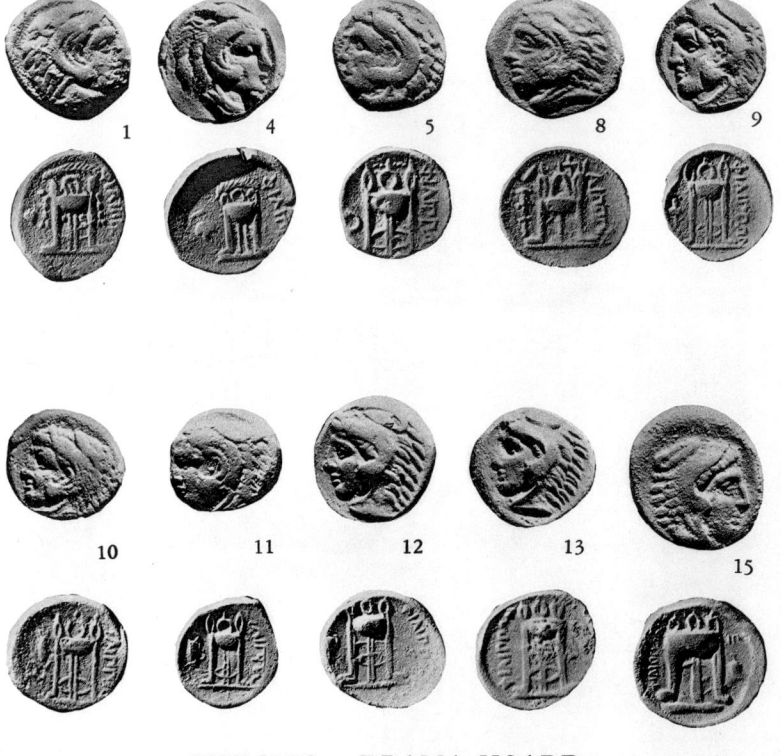

PHILIPPI — DRAMA HOARD

PHILIPPI — DRAMA HOARD

IX

PHILIPPI — DRAMA HOARD

PHILIPPI — DRAMA HOARD

XI

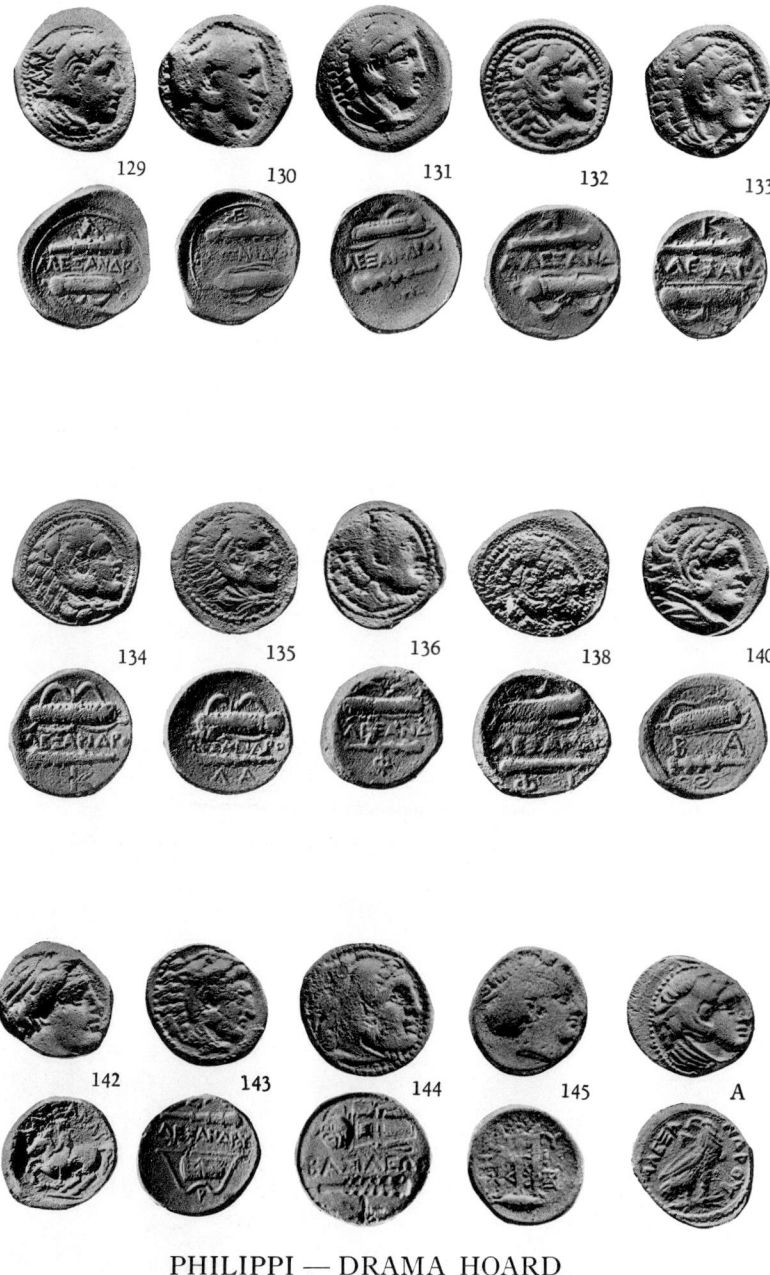

PHILIPPI — DRAMA HOARD

XII

SELEUCID COINS FROM CILICIA

XIII

SELEUCID COINS FROM CILICIA

XIV

ANTIOCHUS IV OF SYRIA

XV

ANTIOCHUS IV OF SYRIA

XVI

ANTIOCHUS IV OF SYRIA

XVII

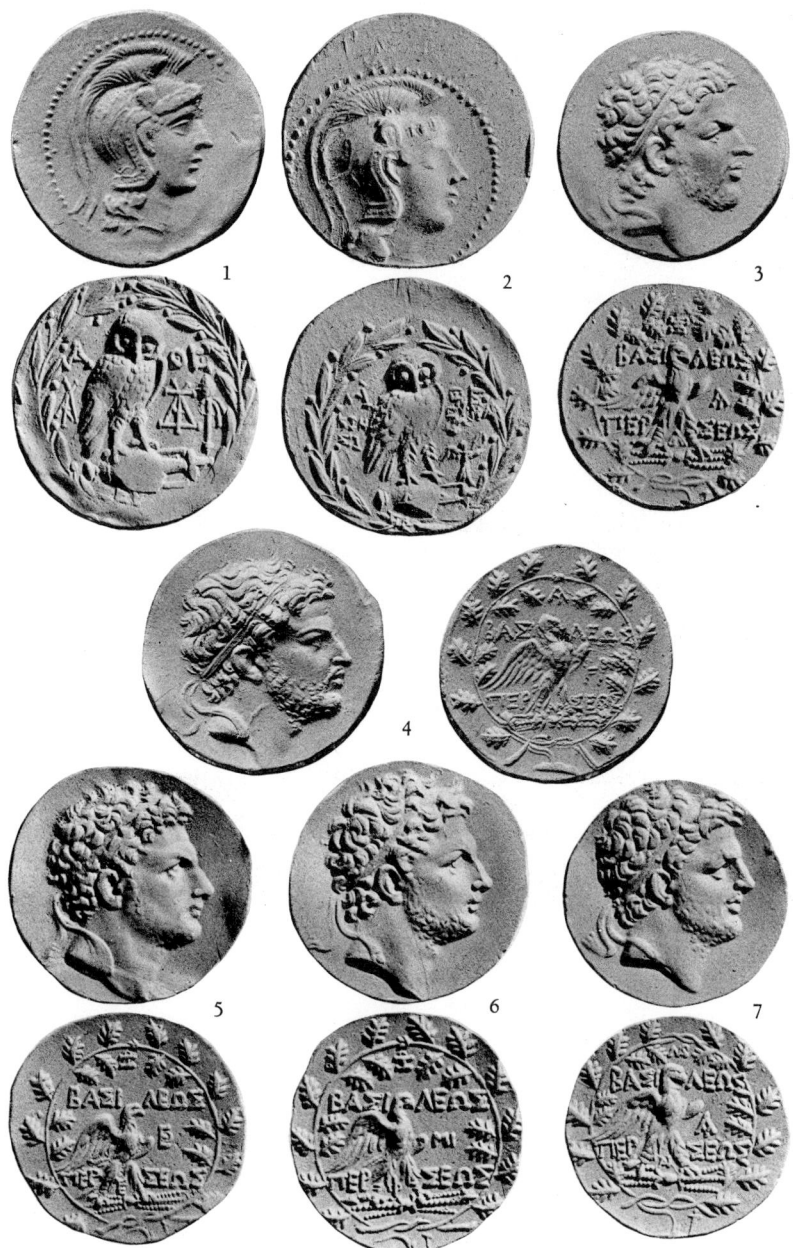

HOARD FROM THESSALY

ΗΡΑΚΛΕΟΥΣ
ΣΩΤΗΡΟΣ
ΘΑΣΙΩΝ

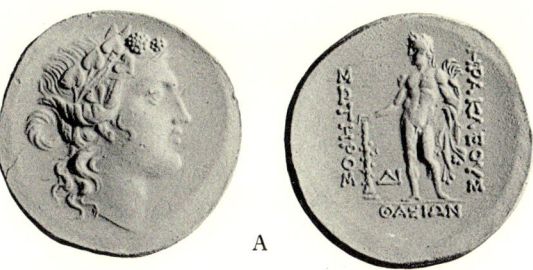

A

HOARD FROM THESSALY

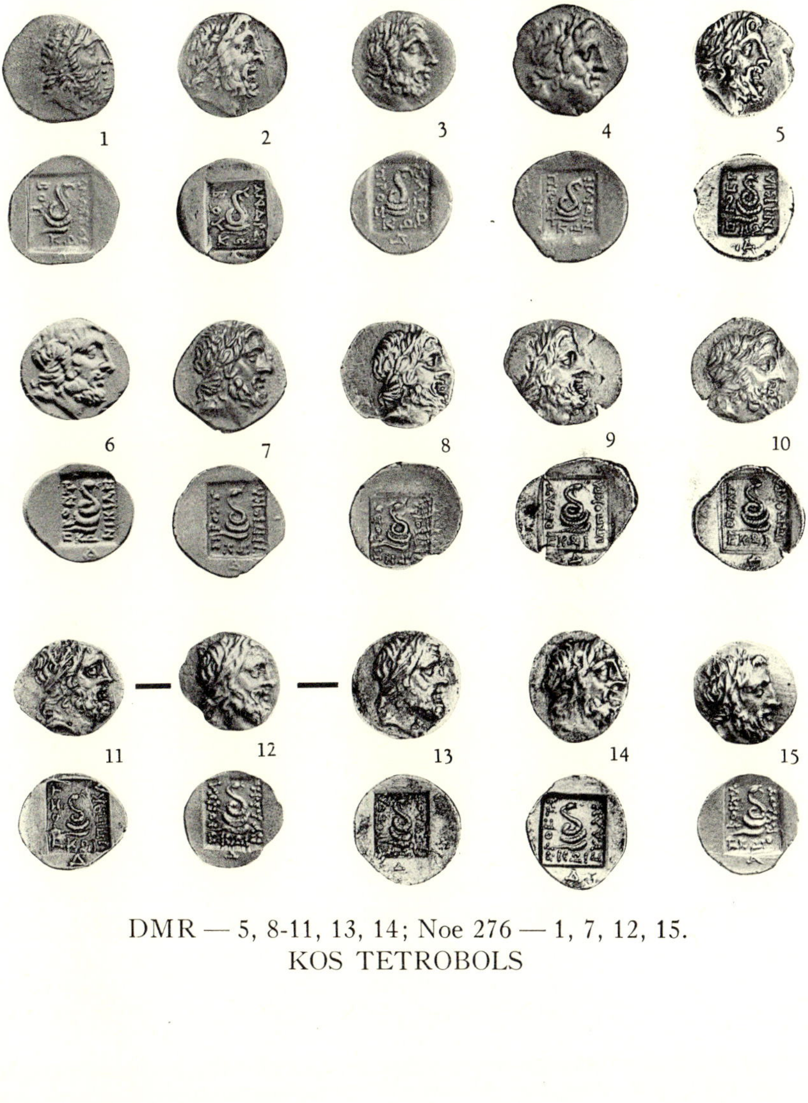
1
2
3
4
5
6
7
8
9
10
11
12
13
14
15

DMR — 5, 8-11, 13, 14; Noe 276 — 1, 7, 12, 15.
KOS TETROBOLS

XIX

DMR — 1, 3, 4, 6, 8-14, 17, 18; Noe 276 — 2, 5, 7, 19.
KOS TETROBOLS

XX

DMR — 1, 6-11, 14-17, 19, 20; Noe 276 — 2, 5, 12, 18.
KOS TETROBOLS

XXI

DMR — 4, 5, 8-13, 15-18, 20; Noe 276 — 3, 6, 7, 14, 19.
KOS TETROBOLS

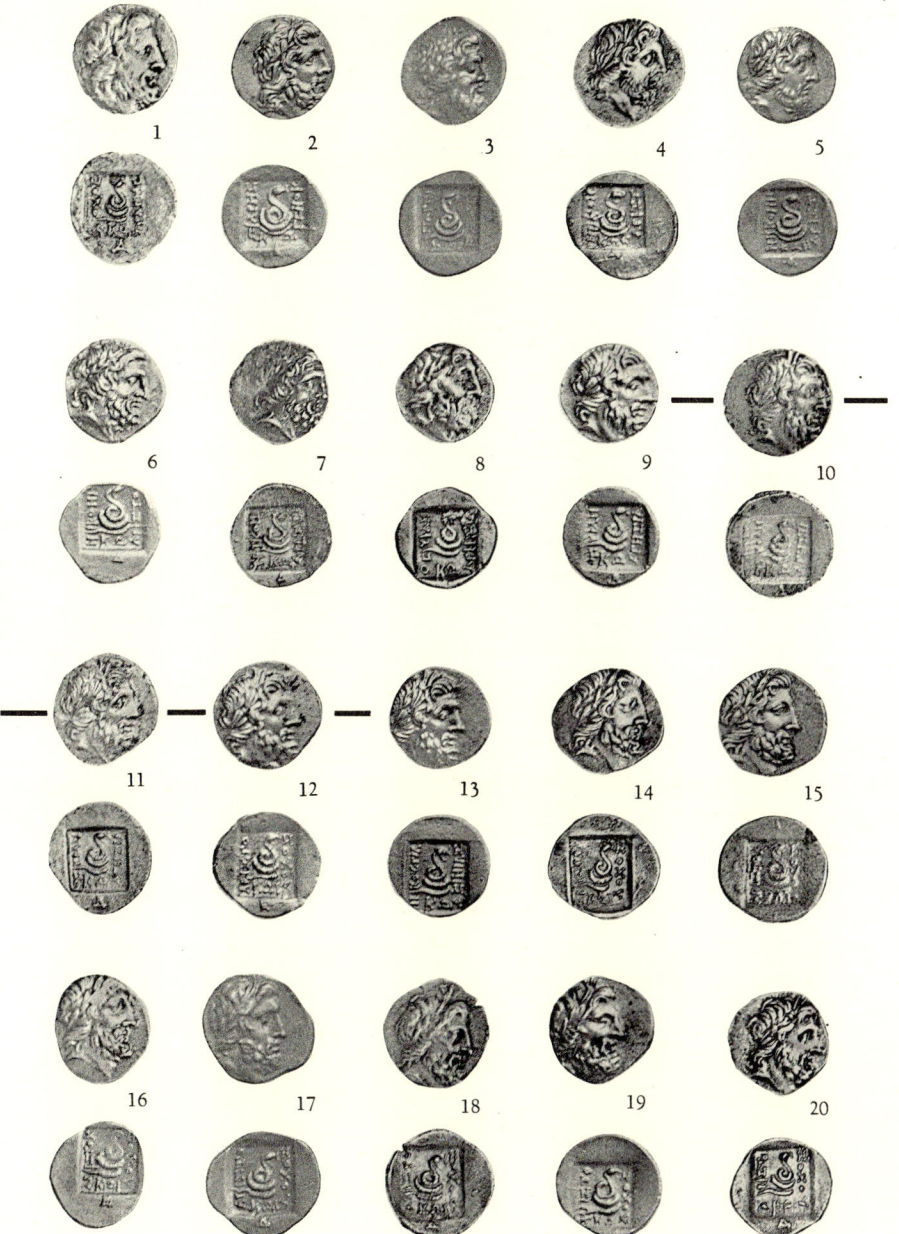

DMR — 1, 4, 7, 8, 10, 11, 14-16, 18, 20; Noe 276 — 2, 5, 6, 9, 12, 13, 17, 19.
KOS TETROBOLS

XXIII

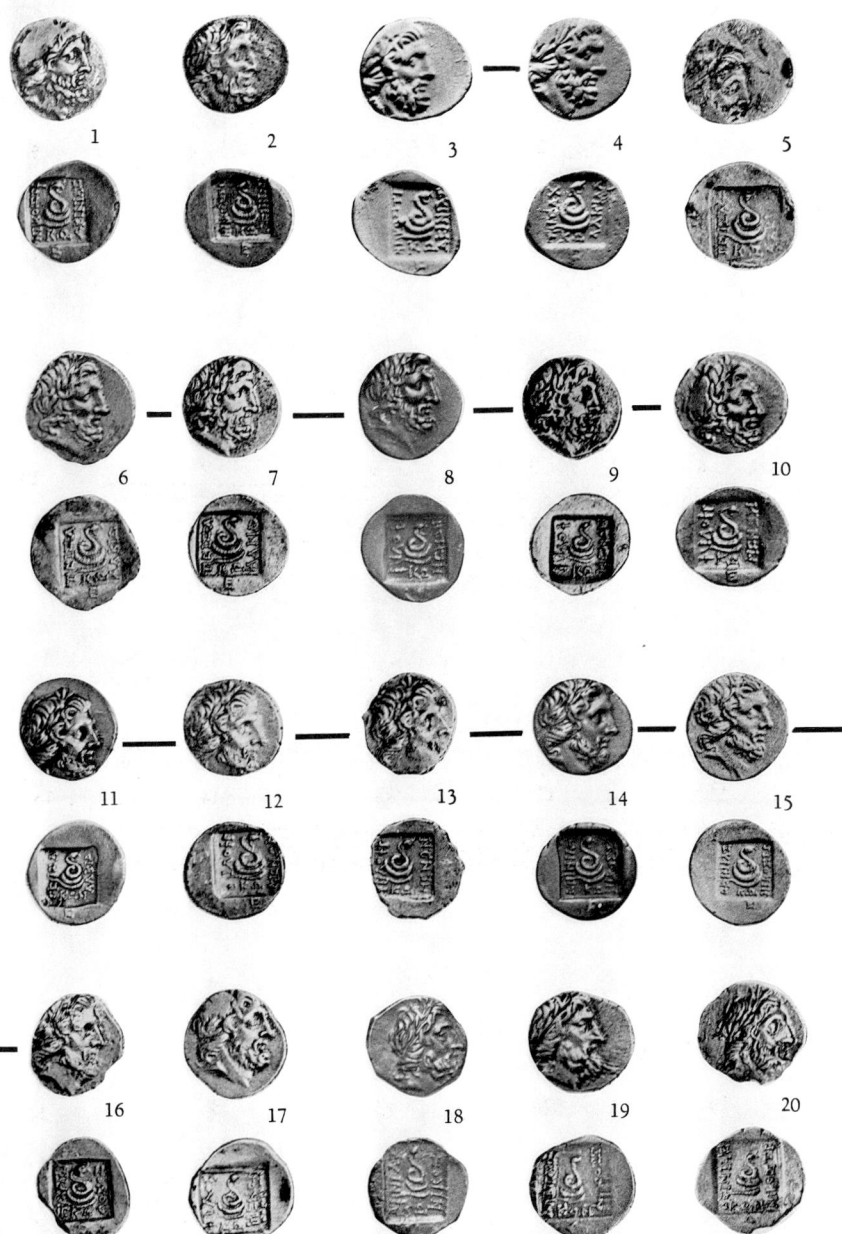

DMR — 1, 2, 5-7, 9, 12, 13, 16, 17, 19, 20; Noe 276 — 10, 18.
KOS TETROBOLS

XXIV

DMR — 1, 2.
KOS TETROBOLS

XXV

Fig. A

Fig. B

PTOLEMY AND ATHENS

PTOLEMY AND ATHENS

Fig. C

XXVII

PTOLEMY AND ATHENS

XXVIII

HERCULES — MELQART

XXIX

TETRICUS II

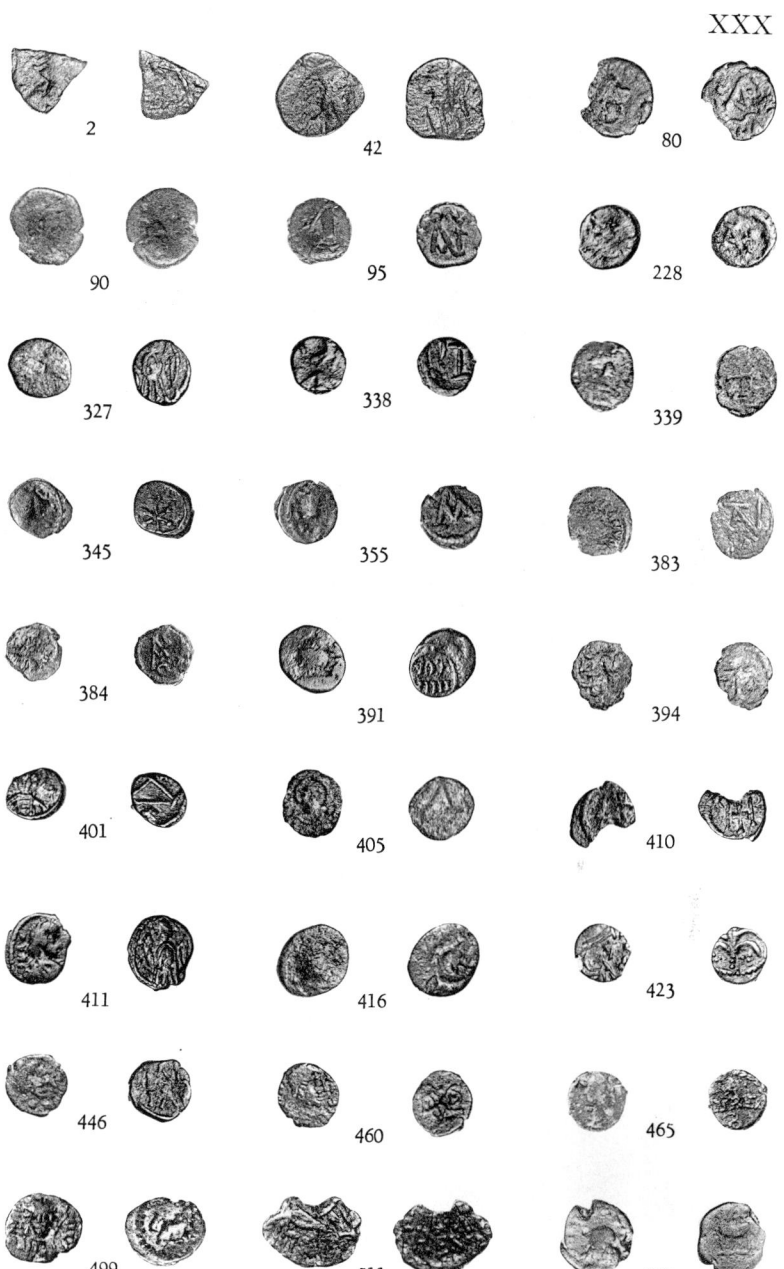

SIXTH CENTURY HOARD OF MINIMI

XXXI

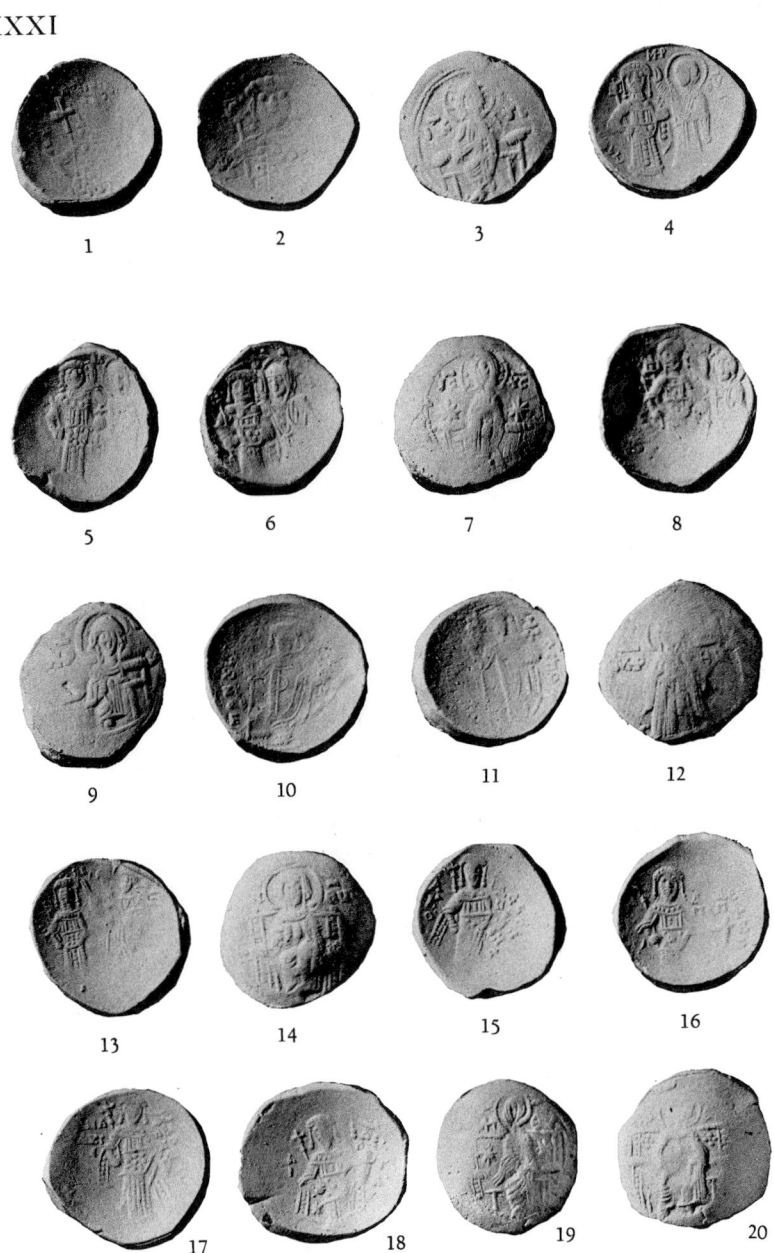

ISTANBUL HOARD OF 1946–A

XXXII

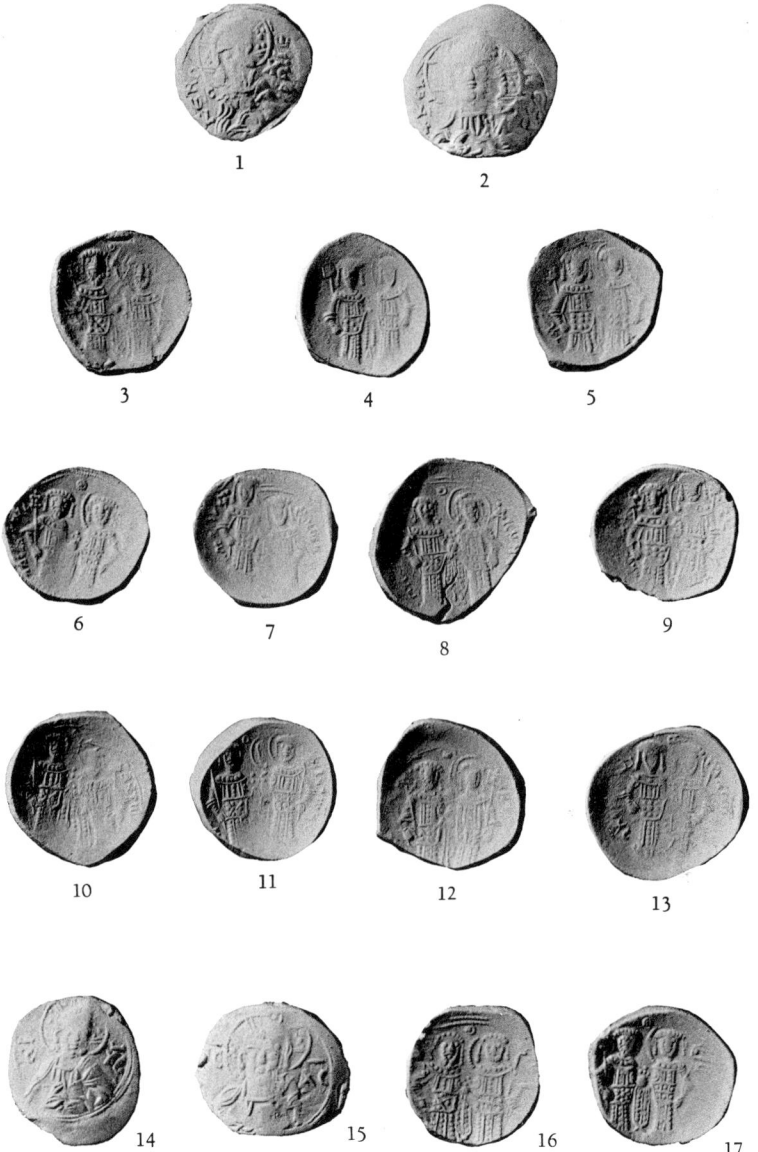

ISTANBUL HOARD OF 1946—A

XXXIII

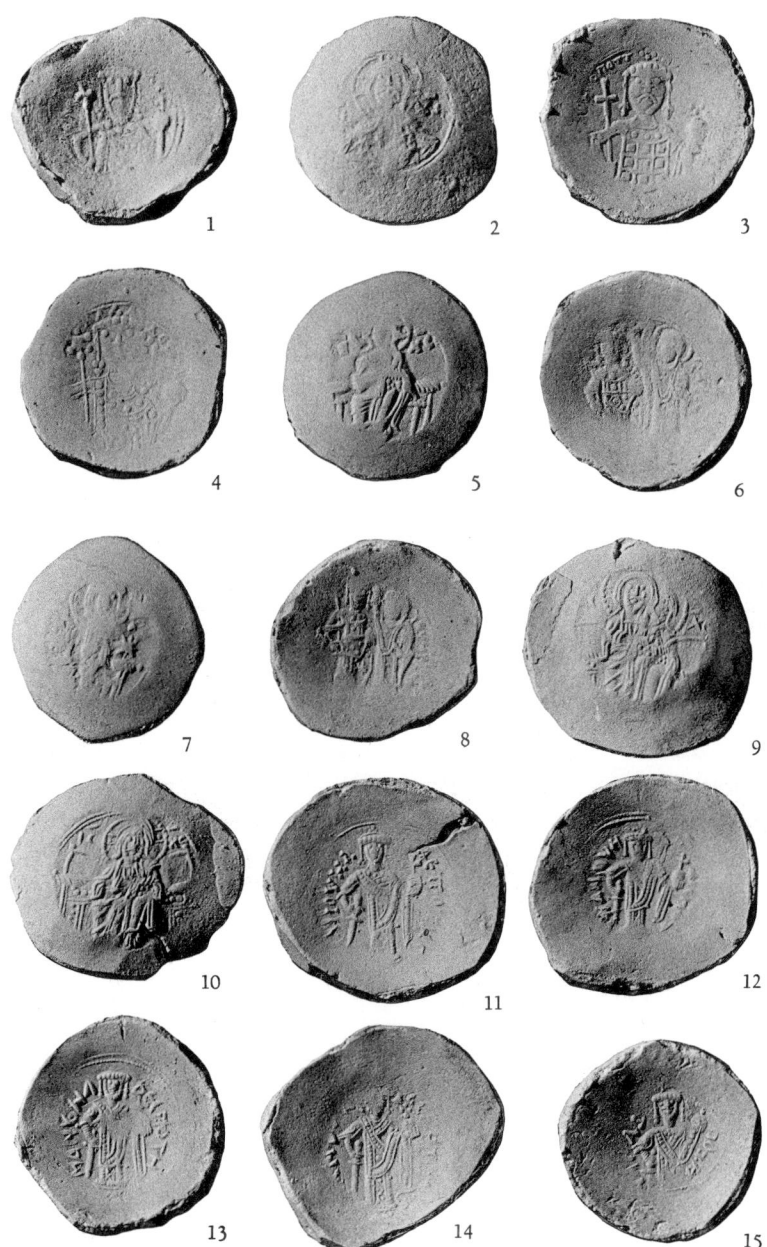

ISTANBUL HOARD OF 1946−B

XXXIV

ISTANBUL HOARD OF 1946–B

XXXV

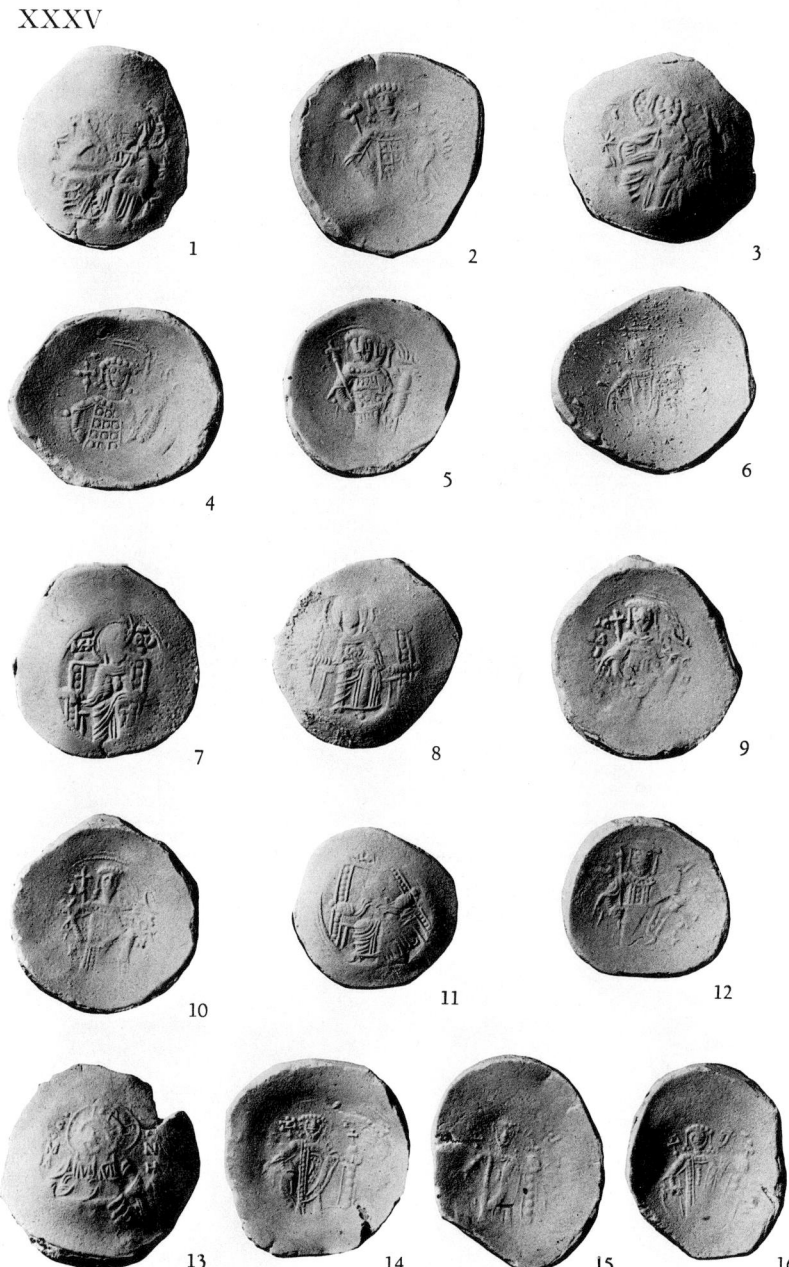

ISTANBUL HOARD OF 1946—B

XXXVI

ISTANBUL HOARD OF 1946–B

XXXVII

ISTANBUL HOARD OF 1946–B

XXXVIII

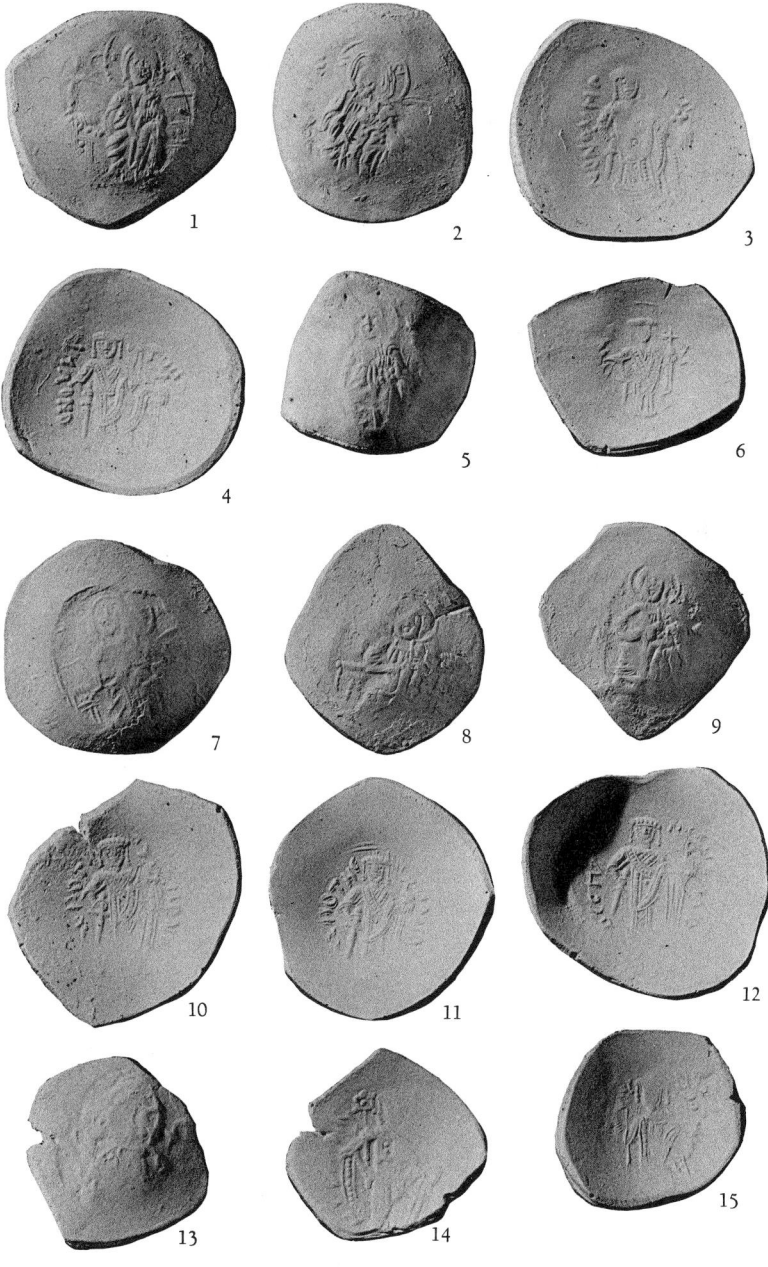

TROAD HOARD

XXXIX

TROAD HOARD

ICON OF THE VIRGIN (PERIBLEPTOS)

XLI

ROMANUS III — MICHAEL IV

THE STAVRATON

THE STAVRATON

XLIII

A HOARD OF LEEUWENDAALDERS

XLIV

110

112

113

A HOARD OF LEEUWENDAALDERS

XLV

PORTRAIT OF RUKN AL-DAWLAH

PORTRAIT OF RUKN AL-DAWLAH

XLVII

PORTRAIT OF RUKN AL-DAWLAH

XLVIII

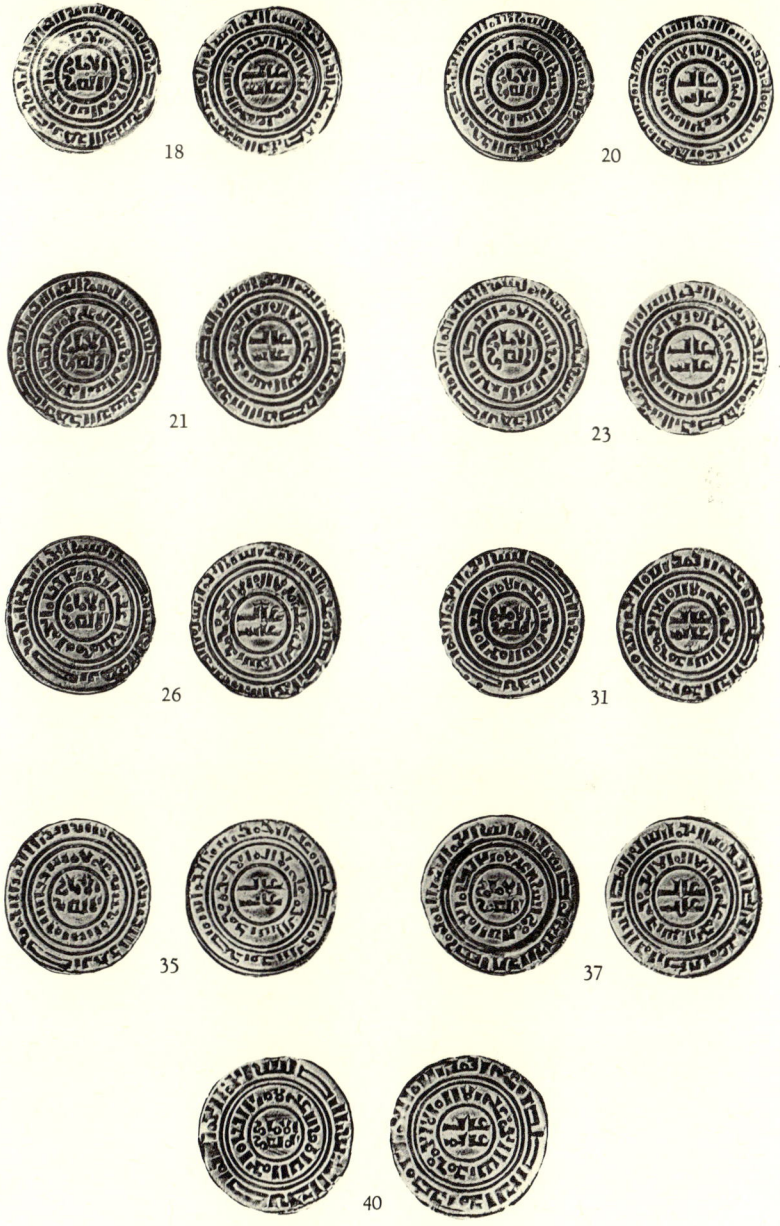

DEUX TRÉSORS DE MONNAIES D'OR

XLIX

GOLD FORGERIES OF TIGRANES

A MAMLŪK HOARD OF ḤAMĀH

L

Enlarged 2×.

GLADSTONE MEDALET

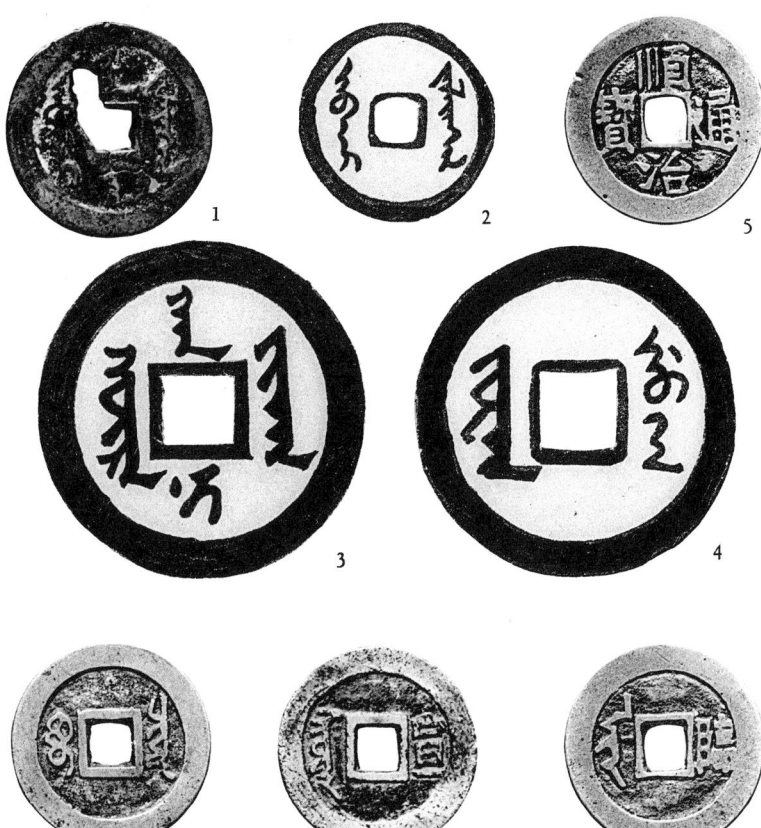

MANCHU INSCRIPTIONS

LI

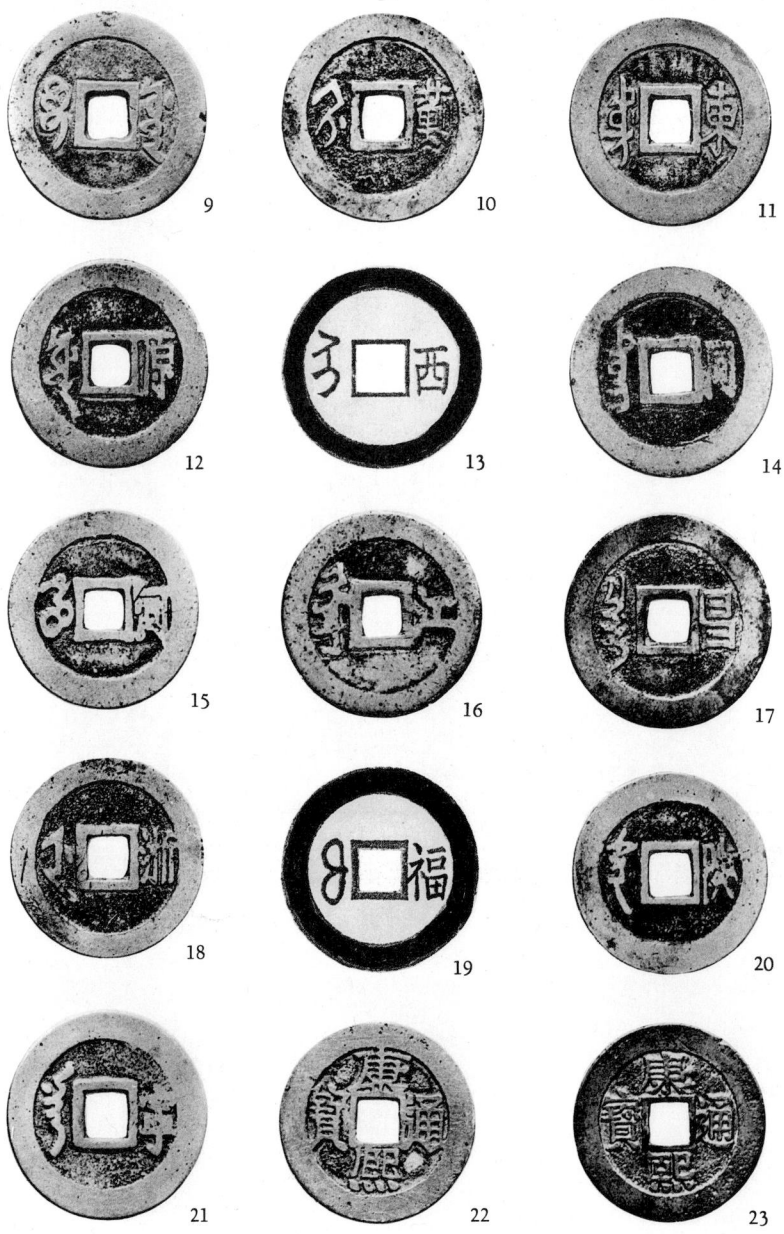

MANCHU INSCRIPTIONS

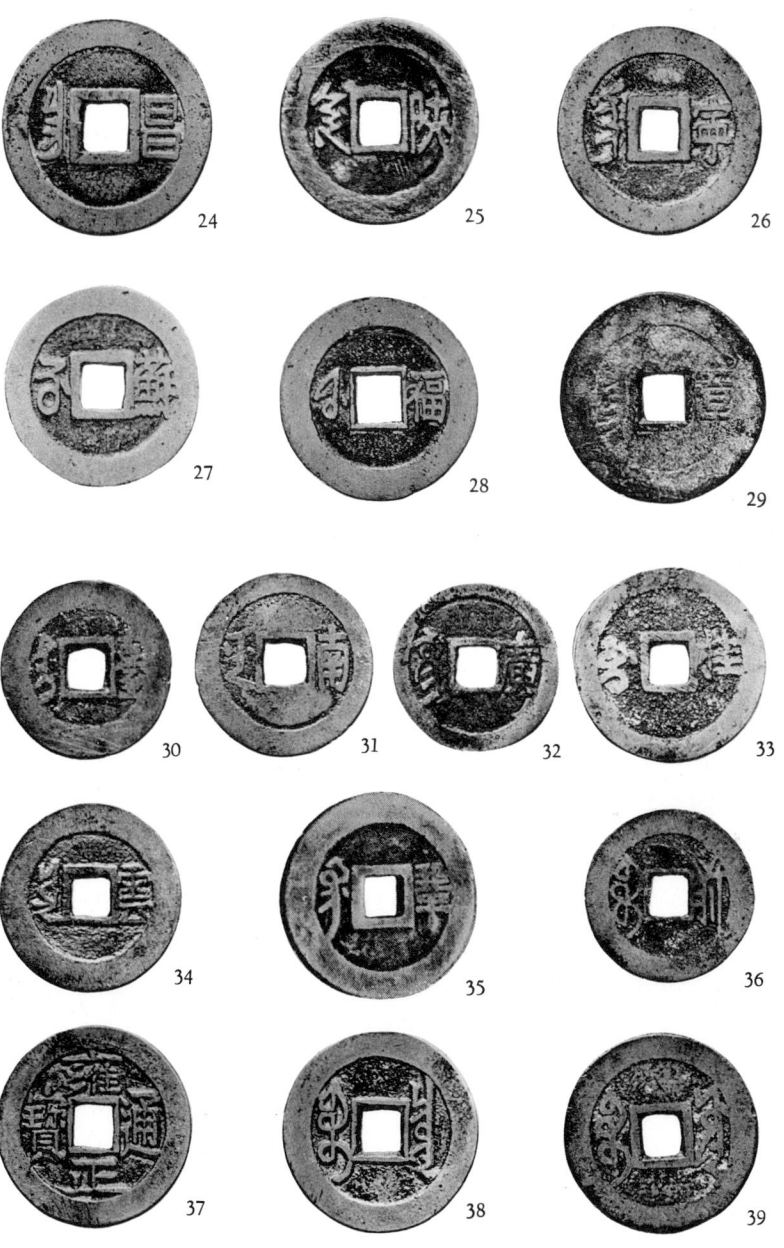

MANCHU INSCRIPTIONS

LIII

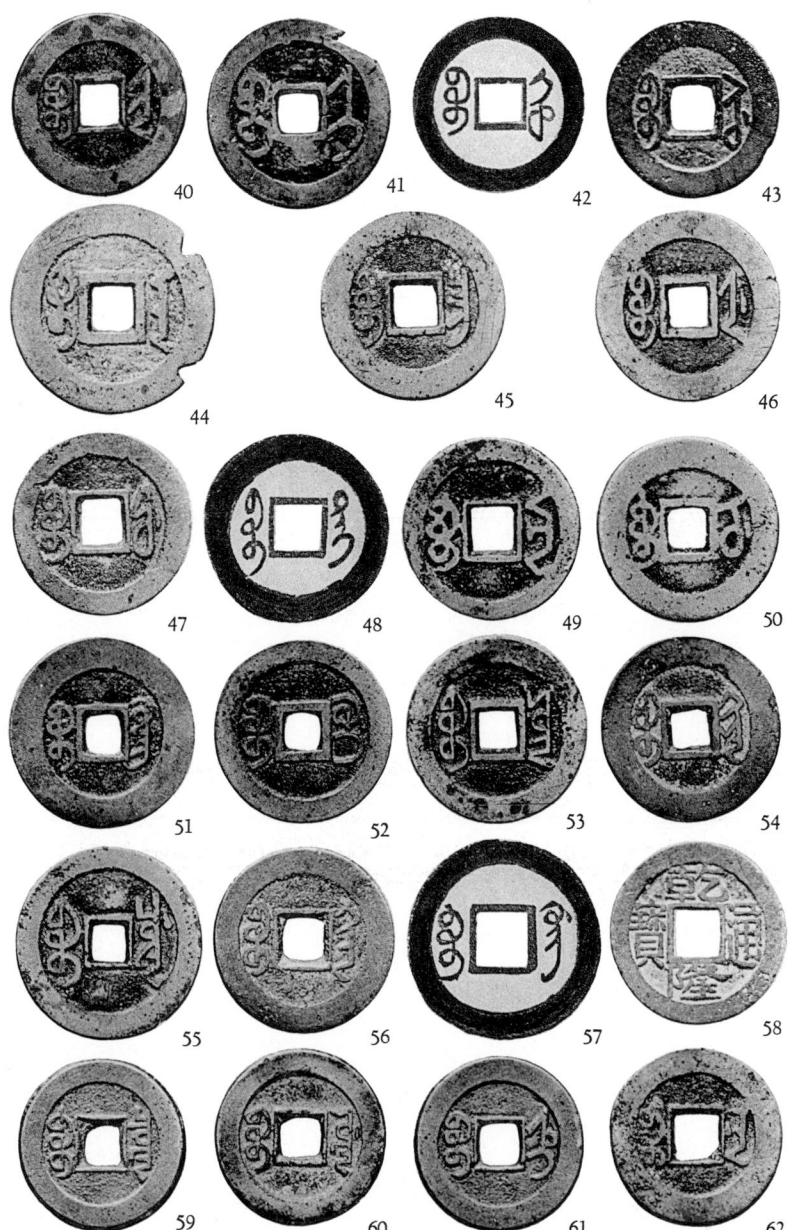

MANCHU INSCRIPTIONS

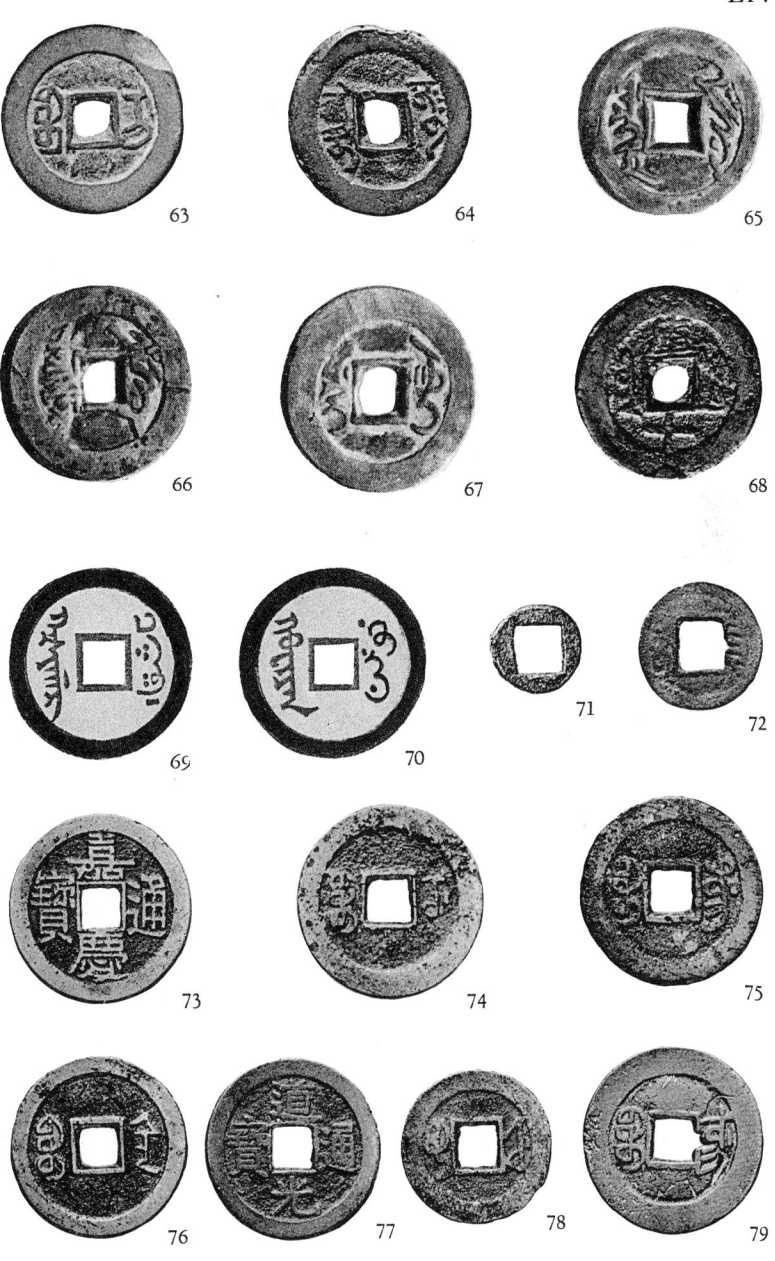

MANCHU INSCRIPTIONS

LV

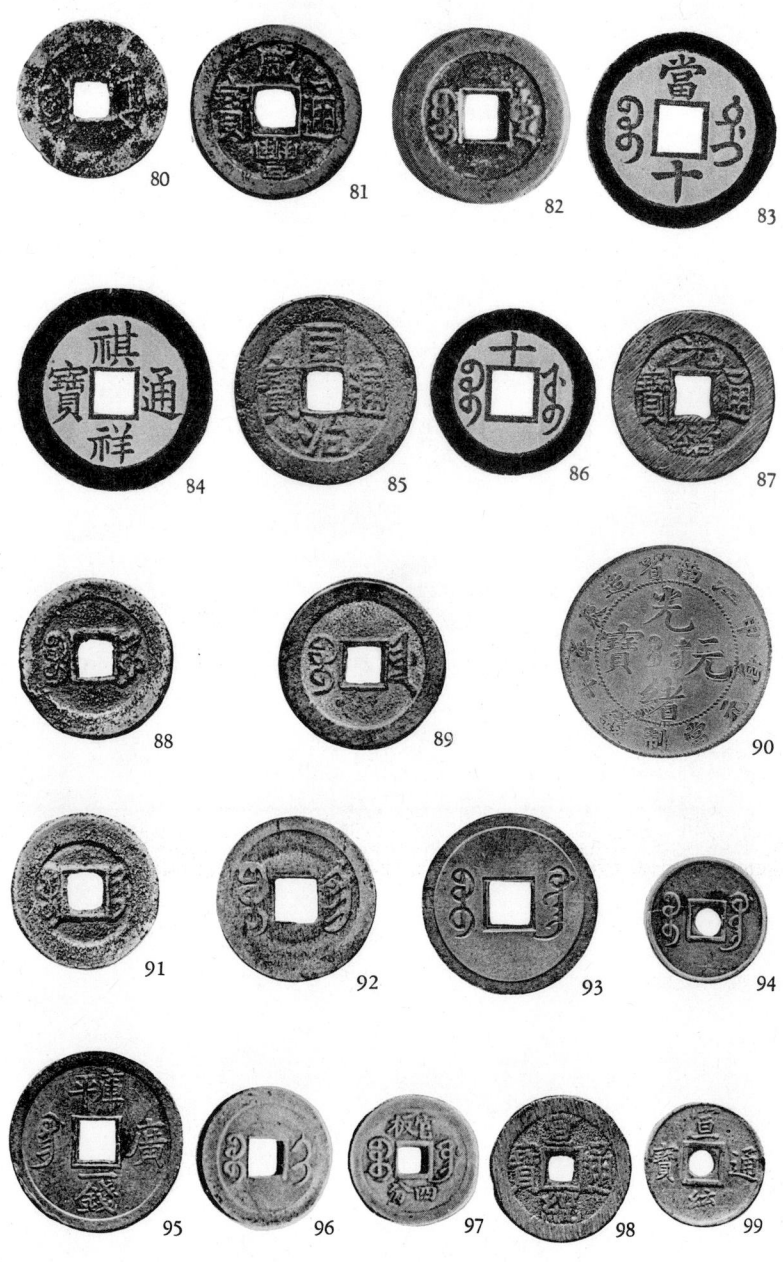

MANCHU INSCRIPTIONS

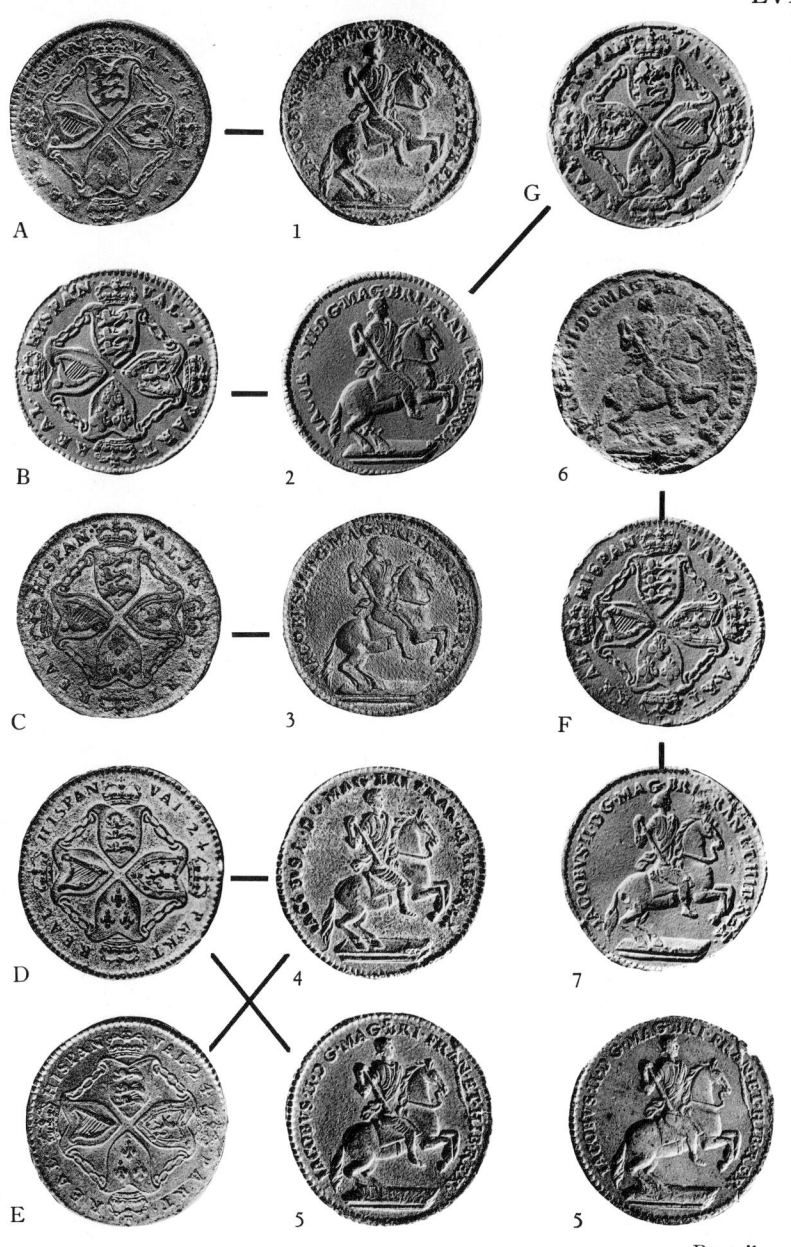

JAMES II — 1/24TH REAL

LVII

1   Silver Coin   2   Aluminum Coin

3   Silver Coin   4   Aluminum Coin

ALUMINUM FOIL IMPRESSIONS

ALUMINUM FOIL IMPRESSIONS

LIX

1
Silver Coin

2
Aluminum Foil

3
Aluminum Cast

4
Plaster Cast

ALUMINUM FOIL IMPRESSIONS